Getting $tarted

In Real Estate Investing

Getting $tarted

In Real Estate Investing

Robert G. Allen

and

Richard J. Allen

The Allen Group, Inc.

ISBN: 0-943402-05-0

10 9 8 7 6 5 4 3 2 1

© 1984 The Allen Group, Inc.

Published by:
The Allen Group, Inc.
145 East Center Street
P.O. Box 8000
Provo, Utah 84603-8000
(800) 453-1364

Table of Contents

Introduction

You've probably heard the one about the little boy who asked Farmer Brown how much he wanted for one of his ripe, juicy tomatoes growing on the vine. "Five cents," says Farmer Brown. "Well," says the little boy (who has only two cents to his name), "how much for one of those small, green ones?" "Two cents," says the farmer. "Good," says the little boy, "I'll take one." The farmer smiles and opens the gate so his customer can make the selection. The boy smiles back innocently and says, "Oh, not today. I'll come back in four weeks and get it."

The boy understands creative finance — at least part of it. He has solved his own financial problem in an ingenious way. And if Farmer Brown is happy to part with one of his red tomatoes "on option" while it is still green, then the boy understands the *full* meaning of creative finance, for he will have solved his older colleague's problem as well. That will mean that both he and Farmer Brown will win, and if both parties to a creative finance transaction don't win, it isn't worth it.

Creative finance means solving money problems in innovative, win/win ways. If the business at hand is real estate investing — as opposed to tomatoes — then we have put our finger on the gist of this book.

Getting Started in Real Estate Investing is designed to help the private investor become familiar with the concepts of creative finance as it applies to buying real property — and then to go out into the marketplace and put these powerful ideas to work.

The end-purpose of this book is to show you, the reader, how to solve problems for people, specifically the sellers who need to divest themselves of property, and to create wealth for yourself through real estate acquisition and prudent property and portfolio management while you are doing it.

There are four things about *Getting Started in Real Estate Investing* that are unique. *First* is the logical, step-by-step organization based on over seven years of careful research with more than 100,000 students who have learned the process embodied in this material. *Second* is the principle of bringing to the reader a consistent philosophy of real estate investment but from multiple points of view — not only the wisdom and experience of Robert G. Allen, whose "Nothing Down" approach to real estate has caught the attention of millions of people, but also the supporting experience and know-how of some seventeen other practitioners of note. *Third* is the accent on win/win principles of professional practice in which people are as important as profits. *Finally,* the book is unique in that it is not only a reflection of, but also provides access to, the concept of an existing, viable educational network of like-minded investors known as ACRE/RAND to which interested readers may turn for continuing education and motivation. (ACRE stands for The American Congress on Real Estate; RAND stands for "Robert Allen Nothing Down.") More information on this network, its products and services, is available from the publishers.

The material is arranged to flow logically with the process of real estate investing. All the steps are fully explained: understanding the principles of creating wealth, applying the correct strategies, locating don't wanter (bargain) properties, analyzing and choosing properties wisely, dealing with cash flows (avoiding negatives and balloons), understanding how to negotiate so that everyone wins, putting creative finance to work, making offers without risk, team building (using professionals where needed), principles of follow through (tax planning, management, selling), and the steps to follow in launching yourself dynamically on your own program of real estate investing.

How should you use the material in this book? The beginning investor will want to read it systematically from beginning to end, with special emphasis on understanding the principles of creating wealth (Part I), the initial articles dealing with strategies in real estate investing (Part II), and the fundamentals of the Robert Allen Nothing Down System (outlined in the opening article of Part VII). The more seasoned investor will be drawn to those sections and articles that may serve to update his or her knowledge and skills where there seems to be a need. All readers should keep *Getting Started* at hand as a resource book of rich insights and practical ideas that will be invaluable during the long-term process of acquiring, managing, and re-investing real-property resources.

Just a word about real estate in general. Several years ago an acquaintance of mine in Los Angeles — a Russian engineer who had emigrated to this country — made a statement to me that opened up some new perspectives on the value of American real estate. He said, "Why do you suppose people from foreign countries are buying so much property here? Because they know that American real estate is pure gold! Why are

Americans so slow to realize this?"

Pure gold! He is right. There is no more valuable commodity to acquire and use for investment purposes than American real estate. Its dependability and performance over the years have made it the foundation of prudent investment strategies everywhere.

Getting Started in Real Estate Investing is your passport to the most exciting personal investment program possible. By applying these principles with prudence and diligence, you can open up to yourself the world of "pure gold," the world of American real estate.

These introductory remarks would not be complete without a word of acknowledgment for the many people who have contributed to the development of this book. Foremost, an expression of thanks to my two partners, Robert G. Allen, whose unique stamp of authority in real estate education is evident as the guiding force throughout this book, and David A. McDougal, who has had a substantive role to play in shaping the forces that made the publication of the book possible. Special thanks to contributors Don Berman, Richard Powelson, and David Read, who have distinguished themselves as instructors of the Robert Allen Nothing Down Seminar nationwide. We acknowledge the wise advice in these pages of our colleagues William Nickerson, Jack Miller, John Schaub, and Wade Cook, all of whom have had a major impact on bringing creative real estate methods to the American public. William Nickerson, in particular, has been instrumental as the pioneering crusader for many of these ideas over the years. To our additional contributing colleagues, Bill Broadbent, Bob Bruss, Sam Hall, Dick Lee, Clint Murdock, Wayne Phillips, and Don Tauscher, we express our grateful thanks. And, finally, we thank Jeff Horvitz for his contributed article; as representative of the nearly 100,000 graduates of the Nothing Down Seminar, Jeff stands as persuasive evidence that the student can match, if not surpass, his teachers.

Grateful expression of thanks go to all who have participated in the production of this book: Stanley E. Miller as managing editor, Grant S. White as production manager, Eric Melander and Stephanie Rodriguez as layout artists, Jonathan Skousen and his associates at the Allen Typesetting Center, Jim Knight as cover designer, and as editorial assistants, Linda Prussey, Susan Mumford, and Duane Woodward. Once again, it all goes to show that the important factor in making things happen is people!

Richard J. Allen, Ph.D.
Provo, Utah

PART I

Understanding the Principles of Creating Wealth

The Problem with Conventional Wisdom: Eight Things That Most People Know About Money That Just Ain't So!

Robert G. Allen

What would you do if I told you that most of what you "know" about money and wealth was absolutely false... even harmful to you financially? Would you listen? Would you open up your mind for a few minutes... to try to be teachable?

I know. It might be hard to admit that your assumptions about wealth could be wrong. These assumptions have been precious. You have forged them over long hard years of almost stubborn adherence to the general consensus. There are lessons that you feel you learned from the Great Depression or the Great Recession. There are the proverbs of so-called wisemen which have been adopted into the conventional wisdom that are hard to ignore. And, most powerful of all, there are the admonitions of parents and loved-ones. All of this lifetime training (programming) has left indelible impressions.

Nonetheless, most of what you have learned from these well-intentioned teachers is false.... at least when taken in the context of today's investment climate. And still these false assumptions prevail, are nourished and passed on...a literal case of the blind leading the blind, transferring this knowledge from generation to generation like a communicable disease.

I'll never forget a radio interview I did in Pittsburgh. While I was talking with the host/interviewer, his assistant, a young woman, listened intently to our conversation as we discussed the dimensions of the road to wealth. After the interview, she came up to me and questioned, "Mr. Allen, all of what you say sounds interesting, even feasible. But it goes against everything my parents have always taught me!" I asked, "How are your parents doing financially?" She replied, "They are really strapped for money." I thought to myself, "By their fruits ye shall know them," but I didn't say anything because I saw the light of understanding come on in her eyes . . . if only for a moment. But when we began to discuss it further, I saw the doubts start to creep back in and I lost her.

I lost her because she couldn't let go of her programming. These assumptions which we all carry with us are deeply rooted into the fabric of the conventional money wisdom. And since they are so deeply embedded, they are equally difficult to dislodge.

It reminds me of a story I heard recently about monkey traps. It seems that in Africa the natives use an ingenious method for catching monkeys. They hollow out a coconut shell by cutting a fairly small hole at one end . . . small enough to barely allow a monkey's hand. Inside the hollowed shell they place a few peanuts. They connect the coconut shell to a thin, strong cord and wait in hiding for the monkeys to smell the peanuts. When a monkey discovers the nuts inside the shell he reaches in and grasps them in his fist . . . but the hole is too small to allow the tightly-clenched fist to escape. At this precise moment the natives pull on the cord and the monkey, who won't let go of the peanuts *to save his life,* is caught.

Many of us are like those monkeys. We hold tightly to our own peanut ideas for fear that we may lose them . . . when all the while, it is these very ideas that hold us captive and prevent the very freedom we long for. When approached with new and better ideas, the majority of us recoil and in essence say, "My mind is made up. Don't confuse me with the facts!" And thus the blind remain dumb because they will not hear.

Well, what are these false assumptions which most of us cling so desperately to? And how can we rid ourselves of them? The answers follow. I have tried to research these ideas by doing a broad cross-section survey of the rich and poor. I have chosen several millionaires recently and have begun interviewing them about their attitudes on money. To seek another opinion, I have tried to choose a representative sampling of middle- and low-income workers. Although my research is not yet complete, I think I can draw some conclusions which offer some insight. Here are the assumptions and some comments on each:

False Assumption No. 1. Having a job is good and leads ultimately to wealth.

One young telephone receptionist I interviewed recently in Columbus, Ohio, replied that the most important factor in wealth acquisition was, "a good job, a great job, a fantastic job." You would be surprised how often this answer is given by those whose income is average or below. Of course, it is rarely given by those who have reached millionaire status.

We have been programmed since childhood to believe that if we find a good job, work hard, move up the ladder to more and more responsibility that eventually, in 20 to 40 years, we will find success, wealth, happiness . . . after which we will retire in glory to a place in the sun. The fact is that a job merely provides monthly income to support the habits we have (like eating) . . . but it rarely leads to wealth.

"Wealth is when small efforts produce large results. Poverty is when large efforts produce small results." (quote from George David, M.D.)

Working at something you don't really enjoy with the hope that eventually your ship of wealth will come in is folly. If your large efforts are only producing small results you had better check the roadmap. You may, be on the road to poverty. Here are two good questions to ask yourself if you still wonder which road you are on:

1. Are you developing an automatic pilot? In other words, if you quit working tomorrow, could you hire someone in your place who would generate a surplus income to support you? Or do you have investments that would provide this surplus living income? If not, are you planning and working toward this goal?

Many people assume that just because they make a large income, they are wealthy. Take the case of a medical doctor. Although he makes lots of money, he is still a virtual slave to his practice, the I.R.S., and his patients . . . and often he is so busy that he doesn't have the time to generate adequate outside investment "automatic pilots" to fall back on if he should wish to retire. The goal of a wealth seeker is not to make a lot of monthly income from a job. It is to transfer the burden of the generation of monthly income from his own back to the back of his "automatic pilot."

2. Have you set a definite goal for your own Declaration of Independence? In other words, if you sold all of your assets tomorrow, could you place the after-tax proceeds in a bank account drawing the highest interest and live off the interest alone? If not, how long could you live before your capital would be depleted? Charles Considine has stated that the sign of true wealth is when you can spend as much as you want to each year and still have your net worth go up.

In summary: Don't work harder. Work smarter!

False Assumption No. 2. Saving your money is a good investment.

I asked a group of investors at the Investment Expo in San Francisco last spring how many millionaires they knew personally who had become wealthy by investing in savings accounts. The whole room broke out in laughter. If we all know that inflation makes our savings accounts look like a joke, why are there literally hundreds of billions of dollars invested in savings accounts, insurance policies, C.D.'s and money market certificates? Almost everyone I interview about wealth mentions the importance of saving money . . . but few of them understand the real reason for saving. Saving money as an investment is just the slow liquidation of your wealth. With inflation running over 6% a year, it doesn't take a master's degree in finance to realize that any dollar that earns less than about 15% per year after tax is a losing venture. "But," you say, "savings accounts are safe and the money comes easy." And I reply, "Does it make you feel safe and secure to know that every day you are getting poorer and poorer?" You are like the merchant who was losing 50¢ a widget but wasn't worried because he figured he could make up the loss by increasing his volume. One of my grandfathers' favorite sayings was:

> Early to Bed
> Early to Rise
> Work like Hell
> And economize!

This is only partly right. Governor Brown of California once told his people: "You've got to learn how to think smaller. You've got to learn how to be satisfied with less." This is only partly right.

The only wealth-producing answer is this: If you plan to save, economize, "be satisfied with less" and invest these funds in savings accounts for the long run, you are on the road to poverty. Even if you break even, it is tantamount to treading water in the swimming pool on the deck of the Titanic. However, if you want to become wealthy you must learn how to save smart. The money you save is only parked temporarily in a savings account waiting for a better place to invest. This smart money is then shifted into long range investments that produce rates of return closer to 50 or 100% per year—such as real estate. Obviously, it is much harder to invest in real estate, but the wealth it produces is worth the effort.

False Assumption No. 3. Debt is bad. Avoid it like the plague.

Our parents and leaders advise us to avoid debt but, once again, they are only partially right. Of course, we must and should avoid *consumer* debt like the plague. Paying high interest rates on loans for consumer items that are, more often than not, worthless by the time we make the final payment on the loan is not the way to wealth. *But self-made wealth never comes without going into debt.* Let me repeat for emphasis. You can never become wealthy in a financial sense without going into some form of *investment* debt.

I have been reading a book entitled *The Gospel of Wealth* by Andrew

Carnegie. It is interesting to note that this most famous of multimillion-aires, who had donated to worthwhile causes over $311 million before his death in 1919, began his road to wealth by putting a $500 mortgage on *his parents'* home, worth at that time about $800. I do not question the fact that debt is terrifying to most people. Even the word *mortgage* in French is translated as "a pledge until death." Nevertheless, the key to wealth is the wise use of investment debt. For every dollar you owe on long-term mortgages secured by prime real estate today . . . you will reap a dollar of equity seven years from today. If you want to become a millionaire in less than seven years you must learn how to live with a million dollars worth of mortgage debt as soon as possible. There is no other way short of theft or inheritance. If you can't handle debt, then set aside your dreams of wealth and stop worrying about something that will never happen. At the very least, you should be buying at least one single family home each and every year for the next ten years.

And that brings us to our next false assumption which is the reason most of us fear debt in the first place.

False Assumption No. 4. Security is good. Get as much of it as you can, whatever the cost.

Our entire society is obsessed with security. We want pension plans, social security, seniority, federal deposit insurance. Golden handcuffs all. You can hear the sound of people running scared. But we settle for "the illusion of safety," writes Marilyn Ferguson in her book, *The Aquarian Conspiracy.* Let me explain.

One of our friends is a fireman. A few months ago he was called out to fight a large brush fire. He and his cohorts rushed to the closest fire hydrant, connected their water hoses and ran the line to the flames . . . and then they turned the water on at the hydrant. And nothing happened! The water lines had not been properly connected by the developer. All they could do was to stand there and watch the blaze, helpless.

Most of us have fire hydrants that we psychologically rely on in times of trouble. But what we don't realize is that these fire hydrants are only the illusions of safety. In reality, *there is no such thing as ultimate security and there never was.* Think about it. How many stories have you heard of people losing their "excellent" jobs due to either recession, competition, automation, change, sickness or simply office politics (or any number of other reasons)? That would never happen to you, right? Just last week a man sat in my office and told me how he had to declare bankruptcy because the new home he had just bought had been liened up to the hilt by a dishonest builder. He lost everything and was starting over from scratch at age 47.

In the final analysis, death is only a heartbeat away for any of us. You cannot amass enough wealth to make you feel secure. In fact, it seems the more you amass, the less secure you become because you have more assets to protect (from the I.R.S., thieves who break in and steal, moths who doth corrupt, and freeloaders). Once you can face the reality that any material safety in this life is at best illusory and transitory, the better able you will be to cope with the changes and the "curves" that get pitched at you in this day of financial turmoil. And you will be more able to assume risk.

Remember, when you buy security, you pay an awful price . . . because not only do you not get what you bargain for, but you lose any hope of attaining wealth in the process.

False Assumption No. 5. Risk is bad. Avoid it at all costs.

Our pioneer forefathers should have taught us something about risk. Weighing the risks of a hostile frontier against the boredom of security in the thirteen colonies, they loaded their families into covered wagons and trecked out into the unknown. Aren't you proud that they did? Nothing ventured, nothing gained. We are the pioneers of the twentieth century. If we don't act, upon what foundation will our generations build? Risk is not something to fear. It is a necessary part of progress. To quote Marilyn Ferguson again, "Eventually, we know deeply that the other side of every fear is a freedom."

False Assumption No. 6. Failure is bad.

I used to be ashamed of my many failures and mistakes. Now I talk about them openly because I am proud of them. I no longer fear finding a crew from *60 Minutes* waiting to interview me at my office because I have finally learned that failure is a part of success. A very important part. When you temporarily fail to obtain something you really want, you join the ranks of some pretty important people . . . like Abraham Lincoln and Thomas A. Edison. Do you know of any successful person who has risen to the top of his field without some failure? Even Dan Rather and Mike Wallace have made their share of blunders. That is the nature of life. Herb True once said, "What people don't realize is that successful people often have more failures than failures do. But they keep going." You don't drown by falling in water. You drown by staying there. Failure is not bad. Failure can be the best thing that ever happened to you.

False Assumption No. 7. Wealth is measured in material possessions.

Zig Ziglar teaches that "it's not what you get by reaching your goal that counts. It's what you become by trying." I have known the wealthiest families in the city who couldn't afford enough money out of their family budget to buy a half-gallon of ice cream. I have known families with money to burn who were below the poverty level when it came to real wealth. And so have you.

In reality, wealth is an attitude. Hollis Norton says it well: "Broke is a temporary condition, poor is a state of mind." Wealth is a way of life . . . regardless of your financial position."

False Assumption No. 8. The government is responsible for my financial well-being.

The birth of this idea can be traced back to the New Deal—Roosevelt's brain child to get the country out of the depression of the 1930's. It had its pluses, but its minuses are still with us. This was the beginning of such ideas as social security, unemployment insurance, and our present welfare system. From this time began the almost imperceptible shift in public thinking away from personal responsibility for financial well-being to government responsibility. Now we look to government for almost everything. We expect government to "redistribute the wealth" so that the underprivileged can be part of the American dream. Instead of protecting the equality of opportunity, the government is expected to legislate the equality of income. And "Big Brother" can guarantee anything. The government loan guarantees to New York City and Chrysler Corporation did much more harm than good. They perpetuated the falsehood that failure is bad and that "sugar daddy" government can solve all of our financial woes.

A whole generation of depression-trained retirees are reaping the rewards of having trusted government to take care of their social security. Rather than rely on government's inept approach, we must learn that *we alone are responsible for our ultimate financial welfare.* The sooner we realize this, the quicker we can start on our road to wealth. And this applies not only in wealth acquisition, but in all other areas of life as well.

Let's review the eight false assumptions again and compare them with their opposite wealth-building truths. (See box below.)

In my opinion, these eight basic false assumptions have been the major cause of the shackling of generations of Americans. Look into your own situation and see if some of these shackles are not found on *your* feet.

The Falsehood	The Reality
1. Having a job leads to wealth.	A job is a temporary situation while you create an "automatic pilot."
2. Savings accounts are good investments.	Savings accounts are temporary parking places for money waiting to be invested at higher rates.
3. Debt is bad. Avoid it.	Consumer debt is bad. Investment debt is *essential* to wealth building.
4. Security is good. Get it.	There is no such thing as security.
5. Risk is bad. Avoid it.	Wealth cannot come without risk.
6. Failure is bad.	Failure is a fact of life. Be proud of your failures and learn from them.
7. Wealth is measured in material possessions.	Wealth is an attitude.
8. The government is responsible for my financial well-being.	I, alone, am responsible.

Launching Yourself Into Financial Self-Reliance

Robert G. Allen

The journey from financial bondage to financial freedom is much like launching a satellite into space. In launching a telecommunications satellite like Telestar or Satcom, the objective is to transport an expensive piece of machinery from the earth's surface into a stationary space orbit, high above the earth, outside the earth's enormous gravitational pull. To call this a complicated task would be an understatement. It takes precision planning and careful coordination. Anyone hoping to launch his or her financial satellite into permanent orbit high above the monetary troubles of normal life and beyond the gravitational pull of inflation and taxes should be prepared for an equally complicated task. Although, as they say, the end result is worth the effort.

As of September, 1980, the U.S. has 574,342 millionares. In other words, less than 3 persons in 1,000 had reached the magic million mark. Of the remaining 997, I am sure there are hundreds who have tried and failed or who have made it and lost it. Why do so few ever make it through? I believe that very few Americans understand what it takes to become financially independent. In fact, there is an enormous misunderstanding about the four specific stages in the wealth building process. Let me share them with you.

STAGE ONE. The Pre-Launch Stage

The pre-launch stage is the preparation stage. Just like launching a satellite takes enormous preparation, so does the launching of your financial spaceship. So few wealth seekers ever get past this stage of the game.

I read a thought on a locker room wall: "The will to prepare to win is more important than the will to win." Preparing to win usually means doing those kinds of things that failures don't like to do. It means studying and learning. It means going to seminars. (I have been to over twenty of them in the past few years . . . and that wasn't cheap.) It means reading books. It means not being afraid to corner experts and ask questions which may make you look foolish. *It means extra effort. It means doing something rather than thinking about it all the time.*

This is the time when you set your goals and make commitments to follow through on them. It is a time of budget planning . . . rearranging your butter purchases to leave some room for saving. It means clearing up your installment debts and vowing not to add anymore for a while. Now is the time for checking out your credit rating . . . and trying to clear up those inevitable "slow pays" on your record. It is also a time of visiting with your banker and arranging for loans which you may not need now but will come in handy in the future. It is a busy time.

As one wise man put it, "One small good deed is better than a grand intention." This pre-launch stage is a time of many small, practical, mundane, seemingly insignificant actions which compound our grand intentions into the realities of grand deeds.

All of this takes sacrifice. And so few of us are willing to pay the price . . . and paying the price is what the next stage is all about.

STAGE TWO. The Struggling Years Stage

How many trillions have been lost by those traveling down (gambling on) the wrong road of wealth. The wreckage is incalculable. Why is so much money lost and so much time wasted? Because most people choose the wrong investment vehicle. *You don't launch space ships with firecrackers. You launch them with Titan booster rockets that are proven and tested.* The most important attributes of your boosters are *power and stability.* You need an investment vehicle which has enough power to propel your portfolio to escape velocity . . . to escape the earth's gravity. You also need an investment which you can count on to maintain that velocity for a certain period of time. At what speed and for how long do you have to travel to reach escape velocity? That depends on your goals.

Let's say ten years is our target date. And $1 million dollars is our goal. The following chart shows some interesting information:

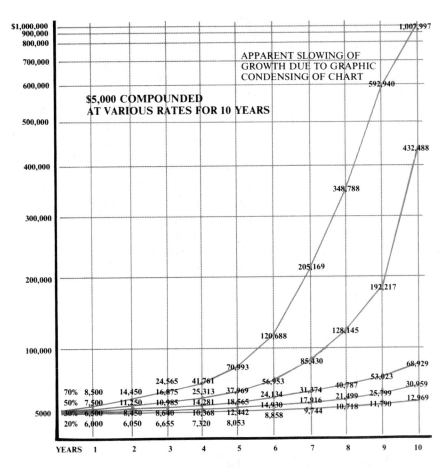

APPARENT SLOWING OF GROWTH DUE TO GRAPHIC CONDENSING OF CHART

$5,000 COMPOUNDED AT VARIOUS RATES FOR 10 YEARS

YEARS	1	2	3	4	5	6	7	8	9	10
70%	8,500	14,450	24,565	41,761	70,993	120,688	205,169	348,788	592,940	1,007,997
50%	7,500	11,250	16,875	25,313	37,969	56,953	85,430	128,145	192,217	432,488
30%	6,500	8,450	10,985	14,281	18,565	24,134	31,374	40,787	53,023	68,929
20%	6,000	7,200	8,640	10,368	12,442	14,930	17,916	21,499	25,799	30,959
	5,500	6,050	6,655	7,320	8,053	8,858	9,744	10,718	11,790	12,969

What we learn is that in order to reach a million-dollar goal in ten years or less we have to choose an investment which has average annual growth rates of at least 70%! And this investment must have a track record that shows it is stable enough to sustain these high rates of growth over a ten-year period of time. There aren't many investments which qualify. Those investments which can be powerful enough such as stocks or commodities are not stable enough (meaning that because of their volatility they can produce not only great gains but also great losses.) Those investments which are stable enough such as money market certificates and bonds are not powerful enough to compound at the rates of return necessary to produce great wealth in less than ten years. That leaves us with real estate. I didn't have to convince you of that, but it helps to understand the logic behind the philosophy. When one learns how to buy real estate with little or no money down it is simple to see how a small nest egg could grow to $1 million dollars in ten years or less. Any serious real estate investor knows that a well-selected property can earn well in excess of 100% per year ROI (Return on Investment) with the proper leverage. That is why real estate has produced more wealth than all other investments combined. Real estate is powerful. Real estate is stable. Real estate is the perfect booster rocket.

With that in mind, let's design a sample investment program. We'll assume that you can invest $5,000 per year into real estate and that you have the time to find two little-or-no-money-down single-family homes each year for the next ten years. At the end of the period you will own 20 houses. Lets assume that properties appreciate at 10% (this will vary widely from area to area.) per year on the average... although we may not be seeing across-the-board increases in that range until this nasty housing recession is over. Since most of our graduates live in areas where it is still possible to buy $50,000 homes, we'll use this as our base price. If your area has higher prices, don't fear. It will just make the numbers I am going to project that much better for you. Your main concern will be overcoming the problem of negative cash flows.

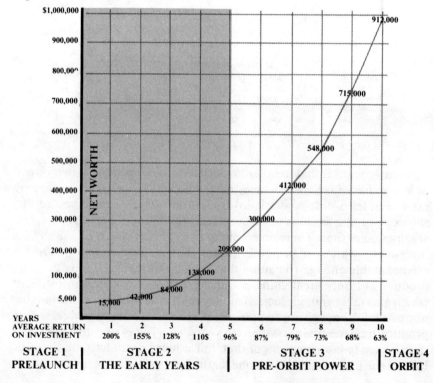

YEARS										
AVERAGE RETURN ON INVESTMENT	1	2	3	4	5	6	7	8	9	10
	200%	155%	128%	110$	96%	87%	79%	73%	68%	63%

| STAGE 1 PRELAUNCH | STAGE 2 THE EARLY YEARS | STAGE 3 PRE-ORBIT POWER | STAGE 4 ORBIT |

As you can see from this chart, the early years don't seem to produce much wealth gain. After three years of sacrifices your net worth is still $100,000. And it is just over $200,000 in five years. To say this another way, after having used up *half* of the time alloted to reaching your goal you are *only one-fifth* of the way there. That can be discouraging; after all, the get-rich-quick myth starts to wither and die along about the third year when we realize that becoming financially independent is not *fun* anymore. This is where we lose most of the crowd. The price demanded has exceeded our ability to pay . . . and many drop out, content to tell stories about "the big one that got away" rather than continue.

These first few years are fraught with another kind of temptation. The impatient are quick to abandon ship for the first fool's gold opportunity that comes along. For every solid booster rocket investment there are 10,000 imitations being bantered about. This is not the time to change horses in mid-stream. This is the time for persistence. As the chart shows, it is only in the fifth year and beyond that your wealth starts to gather momentum.

The reason your rocketship is able to grow at such a rate is because you have made the commitment to concentrate all of your investment energies into one and only one investment vehicle. I know this advice goes against conventional money wisdom which preaches the doctrine of diversification. But listen to what one of the wealthiest men of the century said about the secret to wealth:

"Put all of your eggs in one basket and then watch that basket." — Andrew Carnegie

During the second stage of wealth building you need to follow Carnegie's advice. Don't be tempted with diversification. At least 90% of your available assets should be invested in real estate. Put all of your eggs there . . . *and don't forget to watch over your basket!*

And don't be swayed by those who say that real estate is illiquid. It is the illiquidity of real estate which is its greatest asset. Liquidity is achieved by either giving up *power* or *stability.* At this stage you can't afford to sacrifice either.

What do you do with the other 10% of your available investment assets? You buy insurance with it. Not the kind of insurance you might think. You need to buy *staying power* insurance. Remember Murphy's Law. If you are maintaining a buying program of two single family homes every year for the entire ten-year period, you are bound to encounter problems along the road. You may invest in a property in the wrong location and be forced to sell at a small loss. You may miscalculate the negative cash flow from one of your properties. You may have trouble with one of your tenants for a period of time. You need to be prepared to solve some of these problems with cash.

Therefore, I suggest that you maintain an emergency fund equal to at least three monthly mortgages payments for every property you own. For example, if you own four properties whose combined monthly payments equal $2,500, you should have at least $7,500 in a bank account earning the highest possible rate . . . to be used only in the event of emergency. I think that this is only wise (although I must confess that I personally have never maintained such accounts until recently). Before you buy a property you should plan to add to your emergency account the necessary funds.

In our example, if we average mortgage payments of $600 per month, we would expect to carry the following amounts in liquid cash:

1st year	$ 3,600
2nd year	7,200
3rd year	10,800
4th year	14,400
5th year	18,000

If you are well into a program of buying and don't have amounts close to what I have recommended, don't panic. These are recommended amounts only. You should plan to add to your emergency fund as soon as it is feasible.

All of this is done to insure you against the probability that a string of bad luck might wipe you out. You need staying power and that comes only in the form of liquid cash.

To recap then, the second stage consists of the following:

1. Concentration of 90% of assets in real estate.
2. Avoid diverting attention from prime goal.
3. Accumulate an emergency fund equal to at least three monthly payments for every property you own.
4. Minimum buying program of one property per year for ten years.

STAGE THREE. The Powerful Pre-Orbit Stage

It is during the last five or six years of our sample investment trajectory that things start happening . . . and fast! We start to notice some significant changes in the way our wealth grows. First of all, for the first time our net worth exceeds $200,000. Although it took five years, we can now see some tangible results from all of our efforts. We start to feel wealthy.

Then, every year after the fifth year, our net worth increases by at least $100,000. In the last two years, our net worth increases by more than $200,000 per year.

Our space ship is gathering momentum. Although we are still very much involved in buying real estate, at least two properties per year, we have some other things to worry about. What about the economy? Can real estate prices continue to escalate at an average clip of 10% per year. Will there be a real estate crash? What about a depression?

You might ask, "Bob, why haven't you concerned yourself with these questions before now? After all, we have been concentrating all of our investment efforts in real estate for the last five years." The answer is simple. Up until the fifth year you don't have enough to lose to bother with such questions. Once you cross over the *quarter of a million* line you slowly begin to change from a liberal stance to a more conservative one. You begin to ask questions like, "Where would I be if I lost everything?" Although the probability that a calamity like a *deflationary depression* will happen is small — certainly, at this writing, the probability is less than 20% — we need to hedge against this probability.

Don't get me wrong here! I am not a doomsayer. I am a probabilist. I play the probabilities. I view my investment portfolio as a vehicle which I am trying to guide safely to my goal of financial independence. I feel fairly comfortable about my ability to guide my vehicle down the road, but in case of accident I maintain an adequate insurance policy. No prudent driver would be caught without one. So now, in the fifth through tenth years, I am going to buy some more insurance.

If our economy goes off track for a while . . . and real estate values plummet like a rock. . . I want to be able to salvage at least enough of my net worth to prime the pump with . . . so that I can start all over again if necessary.

Up until now we have maintained a cash reserve system to hedge against unexpected emergencies in our buying program. This amounted to three monthly payments for every property we owned. This insurance fund was in the form of liquid cash invested in areas such as money market funds and Merrill Lynch Cash Management Accounts. In the fifth year we would have as much as $18,000 socked away. This would not be quite 10% of our net worth.

From the fifth year onward we will attempt to maintain 10% of our assets in liquid form. Rather than maintaining these funds in savings and loan associations and with more risky money market funds (which invest in corporate notes), we will carefully select those liquid funds which invest solely in *government* offerings such as *treasury bills.* In this way, we insulate

our liquid assets even further from the small probability of an economic collapse. If we have a deflationary depression, like the last Great Depression, we will want to have lots of cash on hand. Cash will be king and bargains will abound. Even if we lose 90% of our net worth, the remaining 10% cash will give a great head start on everyone else.

In the event of an inflationary collapse, the dollar becomes worthless and our hard assets increase greatly in value. We will be in good shape with our real estate assets but it wouldn't hurt to also be prepared with some other liquid assets. In the opinion of most hard money experts, this should be kept in silver and gold. Initially, you may want to start off small. You may want to get into the habit of buying one ounce of gold (one Krugerrand) for every additional real estate property you add to your portfolio . . . as suggested by Bob Steele. Or, you may decide to own the equivalent value of silver . . . which would be between 40 and 50 ounces of silver. As extra funds come into your hands, you may want to increase your holding of precious metals to as much as three ounces of gold for every property you own (or the equivalent value in silver). By the end of the tenth year it would be ideal to have as much as 10% of your net worth tied up in these kinds of "bad news" hedges. Rather than gold coins, you may venture into numismatics — or rare coins — with proven silver and gold content.

Once you are covered with extra cash reserves and precious metals, you can forget about them. *These are not investments any more than you could call term life insurance an investment!* In other words, once you are insured, you can forget about what will happen and get on with making some money! (The best defense is a good offense.) If these assets increase in value, so much the better. If not, we chalk it up to buying our insurance policy.

Where does this prime the pump insurance money come from? If you have been careful, it may come from the positive cash flows that you experience from some of your older properties. You may even decide to mortgage one of the older properties and put the borrowed money into your insurance fund. (Your mortgage costs could be mostly offset by the return on your money market fund.) It may also come from your prudent savings. Any extra cash you receive from wind-fall should be distributed according to the guidelines of the Stage Three:

1. 80% real estate.
2. 10% liquid paper assets such as treasury bills.
3. 10% precious metals.

In the ninth and tenth years, or as you approach your investment goal, you will begin to prepare for the next stage.

STAGE FOUR. The permanent orbit stage (automatic pilot)

We now arrive at the end of the tenth year of your investment program. Our real estate net worth has grown to approximately $920,000. Hopefully, if all has gone well, we could have as much as $90,000 in liquid cash plus an equal amount in precious metals. We must now decide what to do with all of this wealth. The problem with our real estate net worth is the fact that it doesn't generate enough cash flow to retire on. It has been a wealth generator, not a cash flow generator.

Up to this point we have been concerned with creating great wealth. We have therefore used the greatest tool ever invented for this purpose — *leverage.* We have not been concerned about beating inflation. And luckily, real estate, our power booster, has been a perfect tax shelter in addition to being a great wealth builder.

In stage four, in order to retire (go into permanent orbit), we are going to break all of our rules up to now. We are going to jettison our power boosters and get rid of our leverage. They have served our purposes well.

For the next 12 to 24 months we start the careful process of redistributing our wealth to suit our goal of retiring with cash flow without debt.

In getting rid of our leverage, we also get rid of its great power to produce high rates of return. Our two main concerns as we get ready to go into orbit are *inflation* and *taxes.* our new goals is to have our net growth grow fast enough to outpace these two wealth destroyers.

Retirement

I hate the word "retirement." It sounds so *final.* To many it connotes a declining standard of living and social insecurity. I would rather use a more positive term.

Since I am a private pilot, I have adopted the term "automatic pilot." If you're familiar with flying at all, you know that an automatic pilot is an instrument the pilot uses to make flying a lot easier. It is not used during take-off when the pilot must concentrate on every detail. However, once at cruising altitude, the pilot can set his course, speed, and altitude, turn on the automatic pilot, and presto... the plane takes over! The pilot is now free to do other things. This does not mean he can forget his job. He must occasionally check his guages and instruments. But the pressure of flying has been significantly reduced.

Your goal, as a creative investor, is to launch your ship into financial orbit... and then put it on automatic pilot. You then have the cash flow and the time to devote to the pursuits you think are most important. This is the domain of the Fourth Stage of Wealth.

In our sample investing program, you have been buying two single-family homes each and every year for a ten-year period. In the tenth year you should be the proud owner of twenty single-family homes with equities totaling around $900,000 and an aggregate value in excess of $2,000,000. (See the chart to the right.)

In addition to the $912,000 in real estate equities, you should have as much as $90,000 in liquid cash plus an equal amount in precious metals. Now, what are you going to do with all of this wealth? My bet is that you probably aren't going to feel all that wealthy. Real estate is a wonderful wealth-generator but a terrible cash flow-generator. As they say, "It's all on paper." And "paper" won't put groceries on the table. You need cash flow. It will be necessary to make some changes.

Wealth-Perpetuation

In order to make these changes you're going to change the way you have been doing things. The principles which guide an investor during the first three stages of wealth are going to be completely different from those in the fourth stage. The first three stages are wealth-*building* stages. The fourth stage of wealth is the wealth-*perpetuating* stage. Let's review these principles:

Wealth-Building Principles During The First Three Stages of Wealth

1. Invest only in guns and rarely in butter.
2. Always think in terms of profit after taxes and inflation.
3. Don't diversify; concentrate your eggs into the right basket.
4. Be on the offensive, not the defensive.
5. Have your assets growing steadily at wealth-producing rates.
6. Get heavily into debt to benefit from the power of leverage.
7. Maintain maximum control over your investments.

During the fourth stage, or wealth-perpetuating stage, the above principles will be reversed for a time. Here are the new principles:

Wealth-Perpetuating Principles During The Fourth Stage of Wealth

1. Jettison the debt! You heard me right. Get rid of your booster rockets. They have served their purpose well. More on this in a minute.
2. Lower your compound rates of return from the wealth-producing rates (above 50%) to wealth-perpetuating rates (below 30%).
3. With lower rates of growth you will need to do more careful tax and inflation planning.
4. For a time, you will think defensively rather than offensively.
5. You will be more prone to diversify rather than concentrate.

6. Once you are on automatic pilot, you will pay less attention to the need for guns-and-butter discipline. If you want something nice, buy it. You earned it. You can afford it. Who cares if it goes down in value.?

7. You will maintain less control over your investments. You will choose different investments which either require less personal involvement or you will hire your own in-house management team as I have done. You will never relinquish complete control . . . just day-to-day supervision.

8. During the three wealth-building stages, you will probably want to keep your present job and do your investing on the side. Once you put your investments on automatic pilot, all of this may change. If you don't enjoy your job, quit. Your investments can now carry you.

The emphasis during the first three stages is equity growth and wealth-building. In the last stage, it will shift to cash flow and wealth-perpetuation. Let's have another look at our investment choices:

Hard Asset Investments	Passive Capital Growth Investments
Gold, Silver	Stock market
Precious gems	Bonds
Collectibles (antiques, stamps,	Commodities
art, etc.)	Mutual Funds

Liquid Money Investments	Active Investments
Bank Savings	Buy own home
Treasury Bills	Real estate investments
Money Market Funds	Businesses
	Discounted Mortgages

It would still be wise to maintain your insurance funds; 10% in liquid money investments yielding the highest short-term interest as well as another 10% in precious metals. The remaining 80% of your assets should be shifted into investments which, in the words of Howard Ruff, "beat inflation and taxes plus a little bit more." Although this figure will change, you probably should aim for a target yearly growth rate between 10 and 30% for the major portion of your assets. The higher the better.

Using 10% as a minimum guideline, you can diversify your wealth into many areas. There are several excellent "when-to" investments, such as the stock market and the bond market . . . if you know what they are doing. I personally would stay away from commodities. Some collectibles such as fine art, numismatics or rare stamps have excellent supply and demand features which insure steady price increases to the prudent expert, and are

Home #1

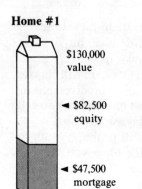

$130,000
value

◄ $82,500
equity

◄ $47,500
mortgage

Home #2

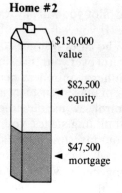

$130,000
value

◄ $82,500
equity

◄ $47,500
mortgage

Home #3

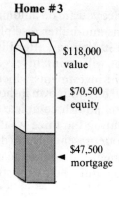

$118,000
value

◄ $70,500
equity

◄ $47,500
mortgage

Home #4

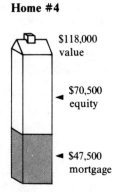

$118,000
value

$70,500
equity

◄ $47,500
mortgage

Home #5

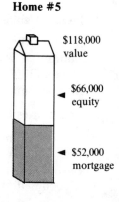

$118,000
value

◄ $66,000
equity

◄ $52,000
mortgage

Home #6

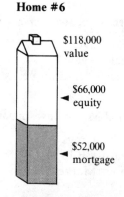

$118,000
value

◄ $66,000
equity

◄ $52,000
mortgage

Home #7

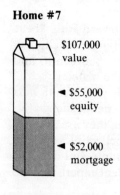

$107,000
value

◄ $55,000
equity

◄ $52,000
mortgage

Home #8

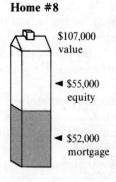

$107,000
value

◄ $55,000
equity

◄ $52,000
mortgage

Home #9

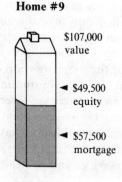

$107,000
value

◄ $49,500
equity

◄ $57,500
mortgage

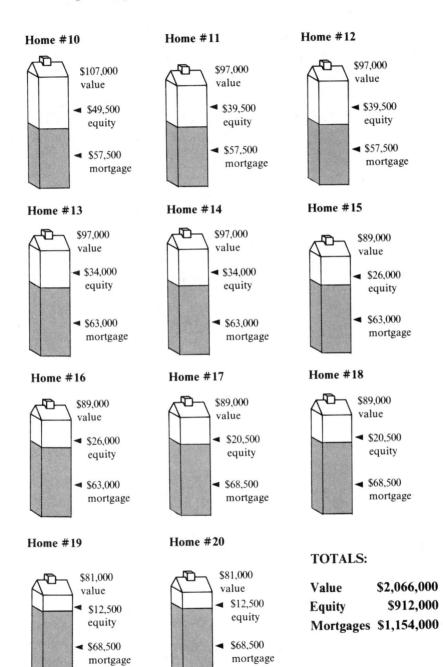

Home #10

$107,000 value

$49,500 equity

$57,500 mortgage

Home #11

$97,000 value

$39,500 equity

$57,500 mortgage

Home #12

$97,000 value

$39,500 equity

$57,500 mortgage

Home #13

$97,000 value

$34,000 equity

$63,000 mortgage

Home #14

$97,000 value

$34,000 equity

$63,000 mortgage

Home #15

$89,000 value

$26,000 equity

$63,000 mortgage

Home #16

$89,000 value

$26,000 equity

$63,000 mortgage

Home #17

$89,000 value

$20,500 equity

$68,500 mortgage

Home #18

$89,000 value

$20,500 equity

$68,500 mortgage

Home #19

$81,000 value

$12,500 equity

$68,500 mortgage

Home #20

$81,000 value

$12,500 equity

$68,500 mortgage

TOTALS:

Value   **$2,066,000**
Equity   **$912,000**
Mortgages **$1,154,000**

fun hobbies as well. In the active investment area, discounted mortgages
have marvelous potential. You may want to do as I have done. You may
stick with real estate and its related businesses only, without relying heavily
on debt or leverage as much as before.

The main thrust of your investing will be to preserve your wealth while
generating a cash flow sufficient for you to retire on. To better illustrate the
"automatic pilot" aspects of the fourth wealth stage, let me share three
alternative investment plans.

Plan One. Free and Clear Real Estate

During the first ten years we have become used to being highly leveraged
... being deeply in debt for our real estate. Let's see what happens when you
completely reverse this philosophy. Let's sell off houses #1 through #10...
your oldest properties with combined gross equities of around $765,000.
Your goal is to sell for cash. This may take as long as a year. The maximum
tax bill would be 20% of the profit. With proper planning, this bill could
feasibly be reduced to $115,000 leaving you with $650,000 in cash. Use this
cash to pay off the remaining $641,000 in mortgages on houses #11
through #20. You are now the proud owner of ten free and clear single-
family homes worth $900,000.

What about retirement? Each home will rent for between $750 and $1,000
per month after expenses. That equals as much as $10,000 cash flow per
month or $120,000 per year. In today's dollars this is almost $5,000 per
month or $60,000 per year. It is not a king's ransom, but I'm sure you can
manage.

What about inflation? The homes will continue to keep pace with
inflation so your net worth will rise steadily. Your rents should also rise
over the years although perhaps not quite as fast as inflation.

Now, what about income taxes? Your homes will generate some tax
shelter. With the next tax laws in effect, your properties can be depreciated
over 15 years. With accelerated depreciation, you would be able to shelter
as much as $60,000 of your rental income from income taxes... leaving you
with only the other $60,000 to worry about. You can either take your lumps
and pay about $20,000 to the Feds... or you can start into a heavy tax
shelter program.

In order for you to pay *zero taxes* you would have to buy more real estate.
"But, wait a minute," you say, "I just sold ten houses. Why do I want to buy
some more?" You sold the homes to get completely out of debt. Doesn't that
feel good? And you created a marvelous cash flow for yourself. You solved
one problem and created another... a tax problem. If you want to eliminate
the tax problem you will re-enter the real estate market and buy approxi-

mately $500,000 worth of property in the next two to five years. You have become accustomed to buying two homes per year . . . why not just keep it up . . . until you own enough real estate to shelter the income from your free and clear properties?

But this time when you buy your yearly quota of properties things will be quite different. You will no longer be in a "strung-out" position, in debt up to the eyeballs and taking what some may call inordinate risks. You will own ten free and clear properties which, through wise estate planning, have been socked away into insulated family trusts far from the greedy reaches of malicious litigation. Your other properties, purchased only for tax shelter, will be kept outside your family trusts. If the world collapses around your ears and you lose your tax shelter properties to default (heaven forbid), you can retreat to your free and clear haven and wait for the storm to blow over.

Let me show you a chart of what this might look like.

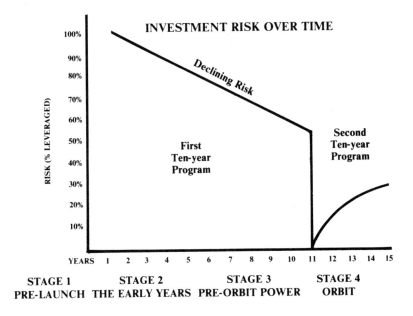

You notice that your leverage line (debt-to-equity ratio) is very high in the beginning of stage two and decreases steadily throughout the holding period. In stage four, since the goal is to eliminate debt, you sell ten properties and pay off the remaining ten. That puts you in a zero-leveraged position as shown on the chart in the eleventh year. Then, to avoid taxes, you continue your investment program for several years until you reach a zero tax position where your leverage line holds steady.

You are now in permanent orbit with steady cash flow sheltered from taxes. Your net worth is shielded from inflation with appreciation assets and increasing rents.

At this point, you may decide to quit your job to devote more time to other interests. If you don't want to manage your properties personally, you can put them on "automatic pilot" by hiring, as I have done, a full-time manager on your own payroll. I have found that I retain much better control over my situation by hiring and training my own employee versus hiring an outside management company. With your own employee overseeing your "crops," your time is now free. You are what they call "financially independent."

Plan One, as described here, still relies heavily on real estate as not only wealth-perpetuator, inflation-protector, and tax shelter but also main cash-flow generator. Essentially, you are now in a defensive posture. You may not be significantly diversified into other investments, but you can always fall back on your insurance funds in time of trouble, if any. Your mortgageless assets are insulated in trusts. And you maintain a great degree of control over your investments.

Now, if you should want to venture into other risky areas such as commodities, penny stocks or selected business ventures, you are free to do so. It's fun to take some play money and see how far you can run with it. However, you would be wise to make a vow to never dip into your orbiting capital. If you should fail, you take the risk of dropping out of orbit. Whenever you see someone lose great wealth, you can be sure that they made this fatal mistake. They gambled it all on one more roll of the dice... and they rolled a seven.

Plan Two. Selling Real Estate With Nothing Down

Rather than selling your oldest properties for *cash,* you may wish to sell them instead for *terms...* nothing down, even. You won't have any trouble selling them. Your only problem will be qualifying your buyers. You probably will be able to ask higher pricers than in Plan One and you definitely will be able to spread out the tax consequences over a longer period of time, saving you tens of thousands of dollars. If you carry back your entire equity of $765,000 in the form of contracts or mortgages at, let's say, 15% for 25 years... you could earn as much as $10,000 per month. The same as in Plan One.

However, there is one major difference. In Plan One, the major portion of your estate —80% — is in inflation-proofed real estate. In Plan Two, 60%

of your estate is in depreciating notes and mortgages. The other 20% is in the form of ten highly-leveraged single-family homes. And the rest is in insurance funds. You take a risk that your monthly cash flow will be slowly eroded by the power of inflation. If you retain your mortgages through the twenty-fifth year, the last mortgage payments totaling $10,000 will be worth only $1,460 in today's dollars... if you factor in an inflation rate of 8%. At an inflation rate of 15%, your $10,000 will be worth about $304. Terrible, isn't it?

Of course, you will have some inflation protection from your real estate holdings. Your income tax problems are only slightly different from Plan One. You still will need to shelter the $120,000 yearly interest income from your mortgages. In order to pay no taxes, you will need to buy more real estate as in Plan One.

If you are worried about the effect of inflation on your wealth, you may also decide to buy an extra property or two per year. You can still hire a full-time manager not only to manage but to find new properties for you to invest in. In essence, you reach a different kind of financial independence. Perhaps the only major disadvantage of Plan Two over Plan One is the level of your overall leverage line. You will still own at least ten homes which are heavily mortgaged.

The reason I have included this alternative plan is to hedge against the probability that you will not be able to find ten cash buyers for your properties. The market may be soft. Mortgage money may be tight. If so, you can move your properties another way... and still retire handsomely.

Plan Three. Discounted Second Trust Deeds

You can proceed along the lines of Plan One by cashing out your oldest properties, but instead of paying off mortgages you may opt for a more lucrative route. With $650,000 in cash you may decide to invest in discounted second and first trust deeds or mortgages. You would search for private "don't-wanter" mortgage holders who are willing, for a number of reasons, to accept deep discounts in the face value of their mortgages in exchange for your cash. We will cover the mechanics of this in a future chapter. Your $650,000 cash could easily move into $1 million in mortgages ... making you an immediate profit. Your yield on your invested dollars would be at least 20% and could go much higher. Suppose you found mortgages bearing an interest rate of 12% for 25 years? This would generate a monthly payment of $10,500.

As in both previous plans, the tax problems could be solved by buying more real estate. Your inflation protection would be in your ten remaining homes plus any additional purchases.

As I have tried to illustrate in these three plans, there are a number of viable routes for you to take. Instead of the alternatives I have outlined, you could be equally as successful in many other investments. The goal is to perpetuate your wealth while generating a monthly cash flow.

PART II:

Strategies in Real Estate Investing

You Can't Teach a Man the Truth. You Can Only Help Him Discover It Himself

Robert G. Allen

Recently my brother Richard and I were having a meeting when the telephone rang. On the other end was a graduate of the Nothing Down Seminar reporting a success story. He had graduated about six months before with no prior in-depth knowledge of real estate investing and had just completed a large purchase which brought him up to $8.3 million worth of property. *$8.3 million!* I looked over at Richard (who was as stunned as I was) and thought to myself, "What happened to that man?" I spend a lot of time wondering about what happens to our graduates during the Nothing Down Seminars, wondering what gives them the courage to go out and do what they have never before dared to try. Almost daily we receive letters from graduates who have equally impressive stories to tell. I read every story and get *almost* as much joy from the success stories of my grads as I do from my own investment successes. But still the question nags at me:

Why is it that two people equal in every way can take the same seminar on the same day with such unequal results? One person catches the vision and runs with it, never again the same, full of confidence and motivation, assured of a bright financial future. And the other leaves the seminar enlightened in the same way but without the same drive and not having the courage to put the program into action. (If you have been attending our RAND meetings you will recognize the two types of people easily.)

I'm not naive enough to think that we can change everyone, but I keep searching for a magic serum that I could patent and administer to all of our graduates to ensure success and financial freedom. Then, I remembered the famous quote of Voltaire:

"If all of the Christians in the world were to simultaneously blow the dust off their Bibles... it would create a dust cloud which would blot out the sun for thirty days!"

In other words, going to a Nothing Down Seminar doesn't make you any more of a successful investor than going to a garage makes you an automobile. There is no magic serum! Only dogged determination can help you cross the formidable barrier that separates those who *know* what to do from those who *do* what they know!

May I make a few suggestions to those of you "lost sheep" who seem to be having trouble crossing the Action Barrier (realizing with humility that all of us, including myself, find ourselves each day facing this barrier sometimes without the slightest desire to climb it):

A. *The snowball principle: have a small success.*

B. *Concentrate on something you are interested in and proceed with your own system.*

C. *Jump off a small cliff.*

D. *Return to the fountain of knowledge often for rejuvenation.*

A. The Snowball Principle.

I graduated Magna Cum Laude from Brigham Young University in 1972. It wasn't because I was smart or worked harder than the others but simply because I got off to a good start. I can pinpoint for you the exact experience that gave me the motivation to shoot for the honors. I took a zoology class in my first semester in college and because I had an excellent teacher in high school the college material was a repetition. I knew all of the answers and had no trouble scoring the highest on every test. It was like a long distance runner competing in a March of Dimes parade. On the first test of my college career I got an A. I remember saying to myself, "Why spoil a perfect record? If I can get A's in zoology maybe I can get A's in English." And for the next four years, I kept saying to myself, "Why spoil a perfect record?"

With investing I had the same experience. I located a duplex by calling the first ad in the newspaper. I bought it with $1,500 down and to my great surprise was offered $3,000 more than I paid for it only 4 days later. I remember saying to myself, "If I can make $3,000 a week in real estate, why work for a living?" Of course, it never was that simple ever again but at least I got off to a good start. I had tasted one small success.

As I have often said in the seminar, "Sometimes it just takes one small success to get your snowball rolling down the mountain until it gathers full momentum." If you're having trouble finding that "one small success" to get you started, then remember that we all go through feast and famine periods or cycles. If you haven't had your feast yet, it's just around the corner—if you persevere.

B. Concentrate on something you are interested in and develop your own style.

In almost all of the great success stories from Nothing Down grads I seem to notice a common denominator. They all seem to become experts by concentrating in one area of real estate. Some examples that stand out:

—One young man of San Diego has bought over $1 million of property by concentrating in the use of partners. After all, if you are 19, with no credit or steady job, and no cash to speak of, you need partners to get going. He has his own style and works with Realtors tirelessly to uncover the best deals. He makes lots of offers and doesn't expect every offer to go through. He spends full time at it . . . and loves it because he has developed a system that fits into his lifestyle, something he is comfortable with. It's no longer a chore; it's a lot of fun.

—A marketing executive in Philadelphia had over $8.3 million worth of property in escrow shortly after he finished the seminar. He concentrated in an area that I have never even thought of, or would have had the courage to tackle. He bids on HUD repossessed properties. One project was appraised for $1 million dollars more than his purchase price. He has become an expert in a very small, concentrated area of real estate and in doing so has become very successful.

—An engineer in Salt Lake City has concentrated in foreclosures of single family homes. In doing so he has become one of the West's foremost experts in this highly complicated area, and bought over $1 million worth of property in the space of two years, with a net worth increase of several hundred thousand dollars. Here again, the pattern is familiar. The student gets turned on by creative financing, decides to concentrate in an area that he can like, becomes an expert and uses his knowledge to give him the courage and confidence to make profit.

—A graduate in Phoenix has been concentrating on the fix-up of run-down homes for future trade or resale. He completed over 30 homes even before he took the Nothing Down Seminar. He has found his area of expertise and is pursuing it with passion.

Of course, I could go on and on. There is a tendency for the beginning investor with his first exposure to creative financing to throw up his or her hands in despair and complain, "It's all so new. It's all so complicated. It's so much information that I can never hope to assimilate it all." If this is your feeling, please learn to pick just *one idea or technique* from the course. Concentrate on it. Perfect your own system by trial and error. Become an expert in it. Then when you really know what you are doing, share your information with the rest of us so that we can benefit from your experience.

C. Jump off a small cliff.

When Cortez came to the New World to conquer it, he landed all of his troops on the shore. That night he sent a secret party to the harbor to burn his own ships. As they watched the ships burning there in the darkness, I suppose those soldiers were saying to themselves, "There's no turning back now! We either conquer these natives or we'll have to die here on the shore trying." Guess who won? I find this kind of determination in the stories of many of our successful graduates. I know that I felt this way in the beginning. I am not suggesting here that you go and burn all of your ships, but it may help to burn a few of them. (Please do not follow the example of one of my graduates from San Francisco who, after finishing the course, quit his job and moved to another city to "make his fortune" ... no job, no cash, cold turkey. I'm sure he'll make it, but I'll be worrying about him until he does.)

Here are a few examples of what I call "jumping off a small cliff" or "burning some of your ships":

—Making a public commitment to your family, friends or enemies that you plan to buy a property within a certain time frame.

—Pulling your money out of your other "pet" investments such as the stock market and letting it sit in your checking account until you get up enough starch to go out and invest it (knowing the longer you wait the more money you will lose to inflation).

—Looking for partners even before you are ready to use them.

—Borrowing some money from your banker to be used in real estate investments knowing that unless you get the cash invested the interest will eat you alive.

Do you get the idea? Make a decision that is costly but not deadly if you don't act, but which may give you the incentive to get off dead center. All self starters devise cunning little systems like these to keep themselves motivated. If you are stuck, pick a small cliff, take a deep breath and jump.

D. Return to the Fountain of Knowledge Often.

Long before I was a teacher of seminars, I was an investor ... and I still am an investor. I'll tell you what has worked the best to motivate me in the past and what will continue to work for me in the future: *seminars.* I took 14 seminars during an 18-month period a few years ago. When I started I had a net worth of less than $20,000 and when I finished I had gleaned enough knowledge and motivation to give me a 2,000% return on my original $5,000-6,000 cost of attending these seminars. They literally changed my life. One of the first was taught by Bob Steele. It was my first introduction to creative financing. He turned the lights on for me.

Something happens at a seminar that could never happen during the reading of a book. There is an active changing process. It is an opportunity to leave the real world and enter into a concentrated period of recommitment. Besides the Nothing Down Seminars, there are many excellent seminars available on real estate investing. Make it a practice of attending as many as you can to keep your batteries charged and your strategies up to date. Contact the Allen Group, Inc. for information on the latest conferences and seminars. Return to the fountain of knowledge often. Education is an endless process. All successful people take the opportunity to learn and grow as often as possible.

The Best of Times or the Worst of Times?

Robert G. Allen

"It was the best of times, it was the worst of times, it was the age of wisdom, it was the age of foolishness, it was the epoch of belief, it was the epoch of incredulity, it was the season of light, it was the season of darkness, it was the spring of hope, it was the winter of despair, we had everything before us, we had nothing before us, we were all going direct to Heaven, we were all going direct the other way . . ." (Opening paragraph of *A Tale of Two Cities* by Charles Dickens.)

Sound familiar? As we march into the Eighties, I think that there is no better paragraph to describe out times than the above quote from Dickens. Are these the best of times or are these the worst of times as far as you are concerned? How you answer this question may well determine your financial future over the next ten years.

Even though we have just come through a gut-wrenching recession, I must admit that I find it difficult not to side with those who feel that these are the worst of times.

The gloom has been tangible . . . you could taste it!

And, it seems, many are spreading pessimism as if there was a reward for it. If there was ever a time for following the advice of conventional thinkers, you would think that this would be it. Conventional thinkers counsel us to draw our knowledge from out of the vast storehouse of conventional wisdom. And conventional wisdom is blaring its message loud and clear:

- Pull in your horns!
- Be careful!
- Preserve your capital!
- Wait on the sidelines until this blows over!
- Another recession is just around the corner!

You would think that this was the end of the world. Remember, this was just *another* recession! They are no strangers to the United States and its business cycle. There have been ten slowdowns periods in our economy since the end of World War II. Several of these slowdowns resulted in actual recessions — 1948, 1953, 1960, 1969, and 1973. This latest recession was just another in a series of normal economic ups and downs. In a few years, we'll have another one. So don't be surprized. Just plan your investment strategy around it. Turn lemons into lemonade.

After all, what is so bad about a recession? A conventional thinker hears nothing but the bad news. A creative thinker, on the other hand, is motivated by the philosophy that, "Every adversity has the seed of an equivalent or greater benefit." (W. Clement Stone.)

Then, what could be good about a recession? How could bad economic news have any positive benefits? Let's take a look at what recessions cause:

- High interest rates
- Tight money
- Sluggish real estate markets
- A buyer's market in most areas of the country
- Pessimism

Did you catch that? Recessions cause an *increase* in the number of *pessimists.*

Many an optimist has become rich simply by buying out a pessimist!

Many of these pessimists are real estate owners. This slowdown in our economy causes an increase in the number of *don't wanters.* Since creative financing is built on the assumption that there must be flexibility on the part of both the buyer and the seller, then a recession can be the best of all times for real estate investors!

In other words, while all the conventional thinkers are thrashing around waiting for the sky to fall, all of the creative thinkers need to be going against the stream. They need to be out there in the marketplace buying real estate. It's a buyer's market, and we get altogether too few of them. This is no time to pull in your horns and wait to see what spring brings. For those of us who can see the vision, we must declare that, although these recession are the worst of times for many people, they can be the best of times for real estate buyers. Don't let these opportunities slip by you.

Let me be more specific. This current period is the best of times for real estate investors. We will not have another opportunity like this for years to come. Don't let this opportunity slip by you!

Do you remember what happened in Seattle in 1969-1970? Boeing laid off thousands of its employees and engineers in the Seattle area in response to the recession at that time and the general overall slump in aircraft business. I have talked with the survivors of that serious slump (and it's reassuring to note that there *were* survivors), and they all report that apartment vacancies in Seattle were astronomical. Many of the local banks and savings and loan associations were repossessing properties and immediately selling these same properties *for Nothing Down* to any investor who could make the negative monthly payments. Some pessimist with a sense of humor paid for a billboard which appeared throughout the city which read, "Will the last person to leave Seattle please turn out the lights." You would not think that this would be a good time to buy real estate in Seattle. It was what you could call the ultimate buyer's market. Well, some creative thinkers did not listen to the doomsayers. They had vision enough to know that Seattle would not sink into the sea and go away. They pooled together a syndication of outside investors and bought up everything in sight...and are probably sitting on a $20 or 30 million profit today. They took the less-traveled road, and that made all the differnce.

There are some doomsayers who are figuratively saying, "Will the last person to leave the United States please turn out the lights." They are falling back on the conventional wisdom which always prevails in times of turmoil and pessimism. But they do so without vision. They sell us short. The decade which spreads before us will bring with it the seeds of great expansion and continued growth in real estate prices.

Why There Will Not Be A Crash In Real Estate Prices in the 1980's

Not only will real estate prices not crash, they will continue to rise. There are four major reasons for this, all of which relate to the supply and demand forces which are facing off in the coming decade.

1. The Apartment Housing Shortage

The vacancy rate on a national basis has been hanging around 5%, which is the lowest it has been for 35 years since the Department of Commerce has kept statistics. We are facing a severe housing shortage in many cities in our country. On a national basis, the United States needs anywhere from 400,000 to 520,000 additional rental units per year to keep up with the demand. Every year the net increase over and above the amount of units which are being abandoned, demolished, or converted to condominiums is only 50,000 to 100,000 units. That leaves a shortfall of at least 300,000 units (according to Lawrence Simons, Assistant Secretary for Housing at HUD). There is not adequate incentive for private investors to make up the supply shortage. The high mortgage rates of recent months, coupled with the understanding that rental rates have not been increasing at a fast enough pace to keep up with operating costs (and in some cities rental rates are frozen with rent controls) have slowed construction considerably. During the recession in the early 80's vacancy rates remained constant or increased due to doubling up. As the recession ended this trend toward doubling up declined and the vacancy problem renewed. In only a few cities, especially in the sun belt, was there a temporary problem with over building of apartment units. In general, vacancy rates will continue to drop. Rental rates will be forced upwards. Apartments owners will reap the benefits. If these figures haven't convinced you, take a look at what is happening in the single family home market.

2. Single Family Homes and The Baby Boom

The government tinkers with the economy to cool things down. The most visible impact of tight money policy is a slowdown in the building industry. Home buyers either refuse to pay the higher interest rates or cannot afford to pay them. And housing starts, which were 2 million in 1978, can scarcely top 1 million per year these days. What the government does not take into consideration is that by discouraging demand, it just creates a worse problem when the credit becomes loose again. The demand for housing does not stop because of high interest rates and tight money. It just lies dormant. It is like a high lake of demand which backs up behind the dam of artificially high interest rates. When the dam is lowered, the demand floods over the market, which does not have enough housing to supply the need. And this extra demand forces the prices up even further. According to the *Wall Street Journal* article entitled, "Homes Wanted: Shortage, High Prices Loom in Housing Field After Slump of 1979-1980," the baby boom during the 1980's will force a demand for at least 2 million housing units to be built each year for the next decade. We started out the decade almost 1 million housing units short.

"Given such a shortfall, economists say, the stage is set for a stunning round of housing cost increases after the current housing slump passes.... But unless inflation is wrung out of the economy — and consumer attitudes—many economists see unbridled increases in home prices when mushrooming demand starts to chase lagging supply. The primary effect of a tight-money period is to postpone demand, Mr. Jaffe of Princeton says it's like squeezing a balloon. The demand is going to pop out somewhere or maybe even burst." (ibid.) WSJ, October 30, 1979.

According to Jay Janis, until recently head of the Federal Home Loan

Bank Board, the long-range outlook for housing is strong and will stay strong through the 1980's. "At the present rate of housing starts, we won't be able to meet the need in the decade ahead," Janis said. The decade will mean something like 43 million Americans reaching the age of thirty— the age of family formation— as contrasted with about 32 million people in the decade of the 1970's (*San Diego Evening Tribune.* November 30, 1979.)

3. Inflation

I don't think it is necessary to dwell excessively on the statistics or the remarks of the experts about inflation. We all know that it is with us for a long time. As long as there is inflaton we will have housing price increases. They may vary according to geographical location and the current economic climate—but over the long haul prices will tend to increase. With the cost of fuel increasing over time it is inevitable that the cost of every item in the average American new home must go up... lumber will be more expensive because of fuel costs necessary to harvest the timber! Plastics will be more expensive; carpets, electrical items, and plumbing fixtures will increase also. And, of course, wages will rise to offset the increased cost of living experienced by workers who manufacture the items needed for homes.

4. The American Dream of Owning a Home

No matter what the economic outlook, there is one dream that is held dear to the American people: The hope of one day owning their own homes. This dream is firmly entrenched. It will continue to cause young home buyers to stretch and sacrifice to obtain a home. This is why I have always advocated that most of an investor's portfolio of homes should be in the lower-priced category. This is the area in which the greatest demand will occur in the near future. This area will experience the greatest price increases. Demand will remain constant or increase. Prices here will not drop; they will be forced upward.

When is the Best Time to Buy Real Estate?

The answer to that question is: *Yesterday!* And tomorrow the answer will be the same. Don't wait to buy real estate; buy real estate and wait. That is my message. I don't intend to change that basic message for many years to come. Let me make you a challenge which I hope you will accept.

Set your goals for the decade of the eighties. Plan to reach your financial independence on or before January 1, 1990. You have the better part of a decade ahead of you. I doubt that you will find better years when the supply and demand factors will work more in the favor of the real estate investor.

Plan to buy at least one home a year for the rest of the decade... if that is not enough, then buy two or three. Start now. If you have already started your program, recommit. Within the past two weeks, I have heard from seminar graduates in Tampa, Florida; St. Louis, Missouri; Philadelphia, Pennsylvania; Los Angeles and San Francisco, California, and Phoenix, Arizona. All have bought properties with little or nothing down. They are on their way and are excited. I didn't say it would be easy, but it will be well worth it. Some of you have tried and failed. Don't despair! Go back out and try again.

And may God bless you.

The Key to Success: Pick the Investment Approach That Works Best for You.

Robert G. Allen

"A chacun son gout." So goes the French expression which roughly translated means "to each his own," or "different strokes for different folks." You get the idea.

The question arises from this: Is the Nothing Down system for everyone? We teach our students to be flexible and creative and yet we teach a very rigid investment method. This very specific system is designed to provide a secure investment foundation for the average investor. The goal is maximum return on investment with minimum risk and beginning capital. The elements of the system are as follows:

1. Find a don't wanter.

2. Make sure that his property fits narrow investment parameters such as residential income property (nothing else) in good condition (avoid fix up) in a good location (stay away from low-priced property in poor locations no matter what the terms).

3. Buy property using creative techniques with nothing down.

4. Hold for the long term. Never sell the goose that lays the golden eggs.

5. Repeat this process at least once a year for the next ten years. If you want to be more wealthy, buy more properties each year.

I have no doubt that this is the best approach for the average American. It is logical. It is simple. It is easy.

But, it is not the only way to make money in real estate. There are thousands of our graduates who are unaverage... to say the least. For them, this approach takes too much time. And granted, there are faster ways of making money in real estate . . . but they require more effort. For those of you who want the faster approach, let me share with you some of the alternative investment styles that we have been hearing about lately.

I have recently reviewed a new book by Wade Cook entitled *How to Build*

A Real Estate Money Machine. In it he describes his system of reaching financial independence. In a nutshell, here it is:

1. Find a don't wanter... he doesn't use this word, but in essence it is the same.

2. Concentrate in low-priced housing which has low interest rate assumable financing or arrange for long-term contract financing with the seller. (The key here is long-term, low-interest rates.)

3. Buy the property with little or no money down.

4. Fix up the property using as little money as possible to create a favorable impression on a new buyer.

5. Immediately turn around and *sell the property within 30 to 60 days.* Arrange the terms of the sale to be small down payments... just enough to reimburse you for your down payment plus fix-up and closing costs. Therefore, you have recouped your initial investment and can repeat the process with your seed capital. To cut costs and save time, always sell the property on contract (also referred to in other states as agreement for deed, contract of sale, land sales contract, wrap around mortgage, etc.). Structure the monthly payments so that the underlying mortgage is at a lower interest rate than the new mortgage... and thereby creates a positive cash flow to the investor for the next 20-30 years. Of course, always check with competent legal and accounting professionals in structuring the paperwork.

To test his idea out, Wade started by buying small properties and immediately selling them as described above. In less than six months, he had accumulated $151,000 in contract equities with a monthly cash flow of $1,290 per month. At the end of two years he had bought and sold 45 properties... with a monthly income between three and four thousand dollars a month ... *for the next twenty five years.*

What are the benefits of this approach? Obviously, there are many.

1. *No management hassles.* He didn't deal with tenants because he never rented out a property. He just bought and immediately resold. This involved time for looking and selling... but no more collecting of rents.

2. *Immediate profit.* Rather than waiting for inflation to work, he created his profit and recognized it immediately. No more wondering or worrying about the economy.

3. *Cash flow.* Rather than worrying about negative cash flows, he turned his properties into positive cash flows, immediately.

4. *Equity build-up.* Wade structured the notes so that the underlying, original mortgage was being paid off faster than the note (or mortgage) that he accepted from his buyer. In this manner, he had equity building up in each mortgage.

Although these benefits are great, there are disadvantages:

1. *No appreciation.* He was not building lasting wealth in the form of ownership of an appreciating asset.

2. *Tax problems.* Rather than generating a tax deduction in the form of depreciation, he was actually creating a taxable event with short-term capital gains. His solution to this was to sell on contract with an installment sale, which, as he explains in his book, significantly minir 'zed the taxable consequences and spread the tax burden over the length of the loan.

3. *Time.* Rather than take the slower route, Wade chose to speed up the process and generate a retirement income in a short two-year period of time. This is really not a detriment, if you are so inclined. But there was an enormous expenditure of time and effort on his part. How would you like to buy and sell 45 homes in 24 months?

4. *Inflation.* When you sell hard assets and accept paper for them you open yourself up to the ravages of inflation. In 25 years the monthly payments which may seem adequate now will not be enough to buy a package of gum. One solution to this is the fact that many of the contracts will be paid off through property sales and refinances over the years.

The reason that I have gone into detail on this approach is to give you some idea of the alternatives that are available to you. A good example of this approach is found on page 213 of my bestselling book, *Nothing Down.* I call it Plan #1: Buy low, sell for nothing down with high price. The details are as follows:

Four-unit apartment building

Purchase Information
Cost: $120,000
Down Payment: $10,000
Mortgage: $110,000
Terms: $849/month; 8% interest
Fix-up expenses: $2,000
Total cash invested: $12,000

Sales Information
Sales price: $142,000
Down payment: $12,000
Mortgage: 130,000
Terms: $1,181/month; 10% interest
Net to you: $12,000
You also receive the difference between the old and new loans: $332 a month.

In this example we buy a property for a good price and great terms. (It doesn't matter if the rates are higher than this in today's market. We simply buy our properties with 11% rates and sell them at 13%.) We put up a small down payment plus fix-up costs and we immediately sell it to recoup our investment cash plus our profit in the form of paper with a steady monthly cash flow of several hundred dollars per month.

How could this example be of use to you in your own investment activities? You may consider using this approach in conjunction with your regular buying program. You buy two and sell one of them to help with the negative cash flows on the one you do keep. I will always be of the opinion that real estate should be in your investment portfolio as a long-term holding. But there are times, as I have shown here, when the selling does have advantages that are too good to overlook.

While you mull these thoughts over, you might want to get a copy of Wade's book to instruct you on the ins and outs of a different approach. Wade gave me a copy of his book for my birthday last May and I was impressed enough by it that I have purchased one for my own property purchasing department. It is available through our bookstore under the title *How to Build a Real Estate Money Machine* by Wade Cook.

Whatever you decide, remember our motto: Don't wait to buy real estate, buy real estate and wait. Good luck and God bless.

There Isn't a Property on the Market Today that I Can't Buy with Nothing Down

Robert G. Allen

Now, that's a pretty bold statement. As you know, I have been known to make bold statements from time to time. But I generally have a fairly good reason for sticking my neck out and have a good track record of making good on my claims (as the *Los Angeles Times* found out). Let's analyze this statement to see why I am so confident.

First of all, let's determine what this statement doesn't say. I did not say that I could buy any property on the market without using cash. "Nothing Down" does not mean that there will be no cash involved in the transaction ... it just means that none of the cash will be mine. This point has been largely misunderstood by most of the public—including most Realtors, lending institutions, and real estate sellers.

Secondly, although I did say that I *could* buy any property that is on the market today, I did not say that I *would* buy any property. In other words, as a Nothing Down investor with the ability to buy virtually any property I choose, I also realize that some properties have greater profit potential than others, Thus, if I am wise, I will target only certain properties . . . leaving the rest for others. To me, this target property is described as follows:

> Low-to moderately-priced (bread and butter) residential real estate (single-family homes, condominiums, townhouses, or small apartment buildings) located in stable neighborhoods within 50 miles of my own home that I can buy using creative financing with little or no money down . . . and preferably with little or no negative cash flow and no balloon payments.

That narrows the market down considerably. Still, there are plenty of properties which fit this description. And, of course, there isn't a single one of these which can't be bought with nothing down using the Nothing Down system.

Do you remember the story of the Emperor's new clothes? The gullible king was convinced by some sharp but crooked salesmen that his gold was being woven into a beautiful garment which all the people in his kingdom would admire. In reality, the gold was being woven into nothing but thin air. In a similar but opposite way, a Nothing Down investor takes nothing and weaves it into gold. He combines all of the elements except his own cash and invests the results into real estate.

There are four ingredients that are important to the real estate investor: Cash. Credit. Financial statement. Cash flow. One if not all of these financial ingredients are usually necessary in every real estate purchase. It is the rare real estate investor who is strong in all four of these areas. The magic of the Nothing Down system is in learning how to assemble each of these strengths from whatever source necessary to put a deal together. There is a motto that I think all real estate investors should become familiar with:

"If I don't have it, someone else does."

In other words, if I don't have the cash necessary to buy property, I can, depending on the property and the circumstances, use a technique or a combination of techniques to bring the cash together. The same goes for credit. If you don't have the credit necessary to qualify for loans, you can always borrow someone else's credit. If you can't afford to pay negative cash flows, you can always find an equity-sharing partner who can be motivated to help you out. If I don't have what is necessary, I have to go and get it. This takes time and effort, but it works.

The reason I am successful at buying properties using the Nothing Down system is because I wear a special pair of magic glasses. I call them "Flexibility Glasses." I am an expert at spotting flexibility and relating that flexibility to the 50 Nothing Down techniques. Basically, there are nine areas of flexibility:

The seller	The renters	The private-money lenders
The buyer	The Realtors	Investors
The property	The hard-money lenders	Partners

As I examine each property, no matter what it is, I am mulling over these nine areas of flexibility in my mind. I try to sense out the needs and not the wants. I try to get to the bottom dollar and not the top dollar. I try to solve problems. Let me go through this process with you so you can get a feeling for what happens.

Let's go to a normal mutiple listing book with your personal Realtor.

We'll open it to any page. It doesn't matter. And we'll point our finger at any property at random. Suppose you have pinpointed a $75,000 house. It has a loan of $23,000. Payments of $310 PITI at 10% interest. The seller's equity is $52,000. The commission is 6%. There is no indication of flexibility. How in the world is it possible to buy this property with nothing down?

Lets go through our list of flexibile areas. Buying real estate using leverage means you will be doing a lot of borrowing of money. It is always wise to borrow the cheapest dollars possible... both in interest rate and in terms of time and hassle to acquire. The cheapest source of borrowed dollars is from the seller. The interest rates are normally lower than market and there is usually little paperwork or red tape to qualify. If he is willing to be flexible to carry part or all of his equity, so much the better. This should be our first question.

"Is the seller willing to carry any paper? If so, how much?"

Suppose the listing Realtor indicates that the seller has indicated to him that he needs about $20,000 down and would be flexible with the rest (the slow real estate market has been the best thing for motivating sellers to be flexible). Therefore, of the $52,000 equity, we have determined that the seller needs $20,000 and will carry $32,000. We have just reduced our problem from a $52,000 problem to a $20,000 cash problem.

Let's ask the next most important question:

"What are you going to do with the $20,000?" In other words, is this $20,000 a need or a want? Does he have to have it? I now examine my area of flexibility. How can I help solve the seller's problem without using my own cash? Is he going to spend the $20,000 on items that can be bought with my credit (or if I don't have it, someone else's credit) and delivered to him in lieu of cash? Can I trade him items I have but don't want? Could I use my time and not my cash to solve some of the problem?

Suppose we determine that the seller has a $10,000 loan at a bank which he wants to get off his back. Could we assume it? That would take the debt off his shoulders and place it squarely on mine...but I would not have to come up with cash. I have therefore reduced my problem from a $20,000 cash problem to a $10,000 cash problem.

What about the remaining $10,000 cash needs? What about the Realtor's $4,500 commission? Is the Realtor flexible? Let's ask. Perhaps the Realtor would be amenable to a $5,000 commission in the form of a note... or even an ownership of the property. This is all negotiable. Many Realtors will want all of the commission in cash, but it never hurts to ask. Suppose our Realtor friend says that half of the commission could be paid in the form of a note. That cuts our $10,000 cash problem by $2,250. Now we only have to worry about coming up with $7,750. That's a far cry from $52,000.

A Slight Change of Strategy

Robert G. Allen

"Toto, I've a feeling we're not in Kansas anymore."

So said Dorothy to her dog after the tornado had carried them to the Land of Oz. By the same token, we can say that as far as real estate investing is concerned, things don't feel the same anymore. The landscape has changed in just a few short years. We are on new ground. The whirlwind that brought us from the fast-paced appreciation of the 1970's has left us in a different world.

We have always been led to believe that when the Fed caused a tight money crunch which raised interest rates to choke off inflation, the ensuing recession would bring with it a lowering of long-term interest rates followed by renewed demand for housing . . . and upward pressure on prices. This has been the case in the seven previous recessions since World War II. But we can't blithely assume that this housing recession that we find ourselves in will be like the ones that preceded it. In fact I'm becoming more and more convinced that it is a fatal mistake to believe so. The changes that are taking place during *this* recession are much more monumental. They are similar in nature to the enormous consequences of the Arab oil embargo of 1973-74. America came to the rude awakening that our government's policy of keeping a ceiling on domestic oil prices caused us to enjoy artificially low gasoline costs. this increased our consumption of oil, discouraged conservation, and made us dependent on foreign suppliers to feed our habit. When foreign suppliers decided to turn off the spigots, we went cold turkey. We are still feeling the shock waves. We all learned that the prosperity we enjoyed during this period of price controls was a false one. Price controls always cause this sort of distortion. Sooner or later, the piper has to be paid.

Today, we are paying the piper for another kind of price control. It has

What about the rents and deposits from the renters? Suppose this property would rent for $500 per month and we can ask first and last month's rent and a deposit of $250. That totals $1,250 ... and if we can find a renter to move in on the day of closing, we can expect to use this money toward the down payment. Thus, we have reduced our down payment by another $1,250 to only $6,500.

We have gone through the first four areas of flexibility. We also inspect the property to see if there isn't some personal property which could be sold off or mortgages to raise some cash. Or perhaps the lot could be split. Turning an apartment building into condominiums is just a splitting technique . . . and many an apartment building has thus generated the funds for its own down payment. If this doesn't yield results, we can also look at hard money sources for the remaining $6,500 cash requirement. Can you use a credit card? Do you have a line of credit at your bank? Would the seller let you put a small $6,500 second on the property and carry his $32,000 note in the form of a third? If we have no luck here, we may ask about the underlying mortgages ($23,000). Is this a private loan? Could we discount it and thereby refinance and generate some cash? What about creating a second mortgage and discounting it to get enough cash to give as a down payment . . . using investors?

And if all of this rigamarole hasn't produced a feasible solution, what about finding a partner who could come up with the remaining $6,500 in cash? He puts up the cash, you manage the property, and you split benefits 50/50. This last resort of using a partner is probably the most expensive source of capital. It costs lots to borrow it and it takes the most time and effort to put the details together. But as a last resort, I could always go out into the market place and find a partner to put up the cash to buy my properties for me. And it would thus be nothing down to me ... although there would be cash involved.

You see, when you understand how to smell out the flexibilities in every transaction, you learn quickly that there isn't a property for sale which can't be bought using the Nothing Down System. It's just a matter of putting the right ingredients together.

But just finding and putting together a nothing down deal is not enough. Anybody can do that. What is tough is putting together the right property, with the right financing, in the right location, with the right partners, at the right time. The analysis part is the key to success. You have to look at the information on 20 or 30 properties before you find one that shows promise. And you may buy only one in a hundred. But when you find a good one, there is not greater feeling in the world.

Good luck and happy hunting!

been with us so long, we hardly even recognize it as a sort of artificial ceiling on prices. What I am referring to is the ceiling on interest rates placed on savings accounts at your neighborhood Savings and Loan association and commercial bank. Haven't you ever wondered why you could never earn more than about 6% on passbook savings? The government, in an effort to be able to provide plentiful mortgage funds (plus a host of other reasons), limited the amount of interest Savings and Loan associations had to pay for your deposits. The lending institutions took in your money at artificially low rates and lent it out at higher rates on long-term mortgages. In essence, you were subsidizing the mortgage business. Mortgage rates would have been a lot higher ten years ago if it weren't for the fact that much of the money was being obtained at bargain-basement rates through artificial interest-rate ceilings.

Until ten years ago, with low inflation, the problem wasn't particularly noticeable. But with the explosion of inflation in this past decade, people began looking for higher and higher returns. The gap was filled by the Money Market Funds. More than $150,000,000,000 (that's *billion*) of short-term money flowed into these money market funds much of it from artifically-regulated, low-interest-bearing accounts. The technical term for this is "disintermediation." The little saver has decided that he will no longer subsidize consumption. He has started his own kind of embargo. Tired of earning less than the market will bear, he has cut off the flow of funds to low-paying interest-bearing accounts. And the ensuing disintermediation has left dead and dying dinosaur Savings and Loan strewn all over the country.

And this is only the beginning. The enormous shudderings going through the lending business may take years to subside. Just as it has taken us almost ten years to get used to higher energy prices and smaller cars, we will now have to get used to higher mortgage interest rates, shorter terms, and smaller homes. Just as the energy crisis caused General Motors, Chrysler, and Ford to lose billions of dollars trying to adjust to a new attitude about transportation, the Savings and Loan associations are struggling for their very existence due to the changes brought about by the mortgage money crisis.

And they can't hope for much help from government. The current Administration has already made its position clear concerning the priority it places on money for housing by proposing cuts in government-backed FHA lending limits. As economists have argued for years, too much money has been allocated towards housing at the expense of available funds for the expansion of private industry. In March of 1980, the Depository Institutions Deregulation Committee was formed to phase out, over a six-year period of time, all interest-rate ceilings. Clearly, we are moving in the direction of a free money market. And that means higher prices for interest rates. The piper will have to be paid. And we will be feeling the effects for years to come. It's a whole new ballgame.

I don't know where this is going to lead. I only know that these enormous convulsions bear with them enormous opportunities for those who are flexible... and enormous risks for those who refuse to see the writing on the wall and adapt to the new ways of doing things.

How do you cope in these times of change?

I think that it is healthy to have a balanced philosophy. I try, in my own dealings, to expect the *best* but prepare for the *worst*. What is there in the present situation from which we can expect the best? There are two things I am encouraged about:

1. First of all, I believe in this country. We have our problems, but sometimes we wallow in them without comparing notes with others. What looks like a disaster area to us is enormous opportunity to people who live in other countries. And while we sit and moan, foreign investors buy up our bargains with both hands. Billions are pouring into this country every month.

What do they see here that we don't see? How would you like to have your wealth invested in Lebanon, France, or Greece right now? How about Poland? Or South Africa? When you look at what is happening around the world, you will come to the conclusion that our foreign friends have long since come to. This is a great nation. It is stable. It is going through great problems and will come out on the other side in great shape... although enormous pockets of wealth will change hands in the process.

If an American can't buy American real estate safely, where can he go?

2. Secondly, housing is a basic commodity that we need. It isn't a frivolous item or a consumer good. And it is in extreme demand. Because of the shortage of reasonably-priced funds, people haven't been buying. That doesn't mean they don't want to buy... or that they don't need to buy.. just that they can't afford to buy at the moment. Since we live in a profit-oriented society, I am encouraged that someone will come up with an idea that meets this enormous demand for housing... at a rate that more and more people will be able to afford. In a sense, the recent interest in the shared-appreciation mortgage (SAM) is filling this void.

On the other hand, it is important to sprinkle this optimism with a healthy dose of caution. If you know that you have planned for the worst, you can proceed ahead full steam. What is the worst that could happen?

What happens if interest rates *never* come down?

What happens if we go through five years of stagnant or declining prices while we sort out the mortgage market problems.

I'm not saying that these things *will* happen. But at least in my own personal investing, I am *pretending* that these things will happen. In this way, I wring out of myself the last bit of speculation and greed that linger in the corners of my mind. If I pretend that the property I buy today may not appreciate for three to five years—if ever—it changes the way I look at balloon mortgages. It makes me a better negotiator. I become a don't wanter for any property which doesn't meet my strict standards.

If I pretend that there will be no appreciation, I start looking for the other benefits that real estate has: tax shelter, equity build-up, and cash flow. And I am less likely to sacrifice cash flow for the hope of future appreciation profits.

Let me illustrate:

I recently bought a property. It was a duplex appraised at $59,500 with a 10% assumable VA mortgage of $38,000 and a $10,000 second at 18%. No balloons. There is less than $100 in negative cash flow per month. This could be eliminated within a year. The seller called in on our newspaper ad which we run regularly to attract don't wanters. He was three payments behind and was willing to walk away from the property if we could just bring the payments current.

He told us that he was moving away and didn't want to be saddled with the duplex anymore. "I'm sick of it! Take it off my hands! I realize that I am walking away from some equity, but if you will just make up the back payments and relieve me of the property, I will be thrilled." Of course, we were willing to meet his needs! The appraisal confirmed the value of the property. We would have given him more consideration for his equity if he had wanted it. But, he responded to our ad of his own accord, laid down his own conditions, and we bought the property accordingly. It cost us about $1,500 to pick up the $11,500 in equity.

Since I bought this property right, I could sell it tomorrow for at least a quick $2,000 cash profit. Or, I could sell it for nothing down and take a $5,000 note back with payments spread out over the next twenty years. Or, I could keep it forever. Now, what will happen to me if this property never appreciates? First of all, my first-year depreciation for tax purposes is over $5,000 and I also get to write-off the negative cash flow. Then, I have no balloons to worry about. The rents will increase slowly over the years, and when the second mortgage is paid off in nine years, I will have a handsome positive monthly cash flow. When the first mortgage is paid off in 25 years, I will own the property free-and-clear and my family will enjoy a positive cash flow for many years.

I recently heard of one investor who got so excited after attending a popular seminar (not mine), that he immediately went out and bought twenty single-family homes. Unfortunately, all of them were saddled with heavy negative cash flows and short-term balloons. He lost all of them a year later. How much more prudent it would have been to have looked for an entire year and bought only one property... but to have bought this one right... either with fabulous terms, or a fabulous price, or both.

When you buy a property right, you never have to worry about the future of real estate. You can sleep at night knowing that even if it *never* appreciates, you can hold on to it forever... and it will eventually be a money machine which will crank out monthly cash to you and your heirs for as long as they hold it. And if it *does* appreciate (as I'm sure it will... although I *pretend* it won't), you are that much better off.

It is easy to buy property with nothing down. But it is much more difficult to buy a nothing down property right... and well worth the effort.

Remember when you buy in this market: what used to look like a bargain may not prove to be so in the future. With so many flexible sellers out there to choose from, be careful not to buy for appreciation only. John Schaub and Jack Miller have been counseling for years that a wise investor should always try to make money "on the way in," and therefore be able to sell the property the next day for an immediate profit. In our confused real estate markets, this advice sounds even prophetic.

The ultimate advice has changed only slightly since I began saying it five years ago:

Don't wait to buy real estate. Buy real estate (right) and wait.

The Successful Real Estate Investor: A Schizophrenic Phenomenon

Robert G. Allen

May I take this opportunity to salute those of you who have been successful in your real estate investments. I have enormous respect for you ... I think we all do. In order to be successful, you have to wear so many hats in the process of a profitable real estate transaction that I sometimes wonder how you come through it intact. Just think of it. You had to have the vision of an economist. The independence of a pioneer. The courage of an entrepreneur. The judgment of a businessman. The sensitivity of a psychiatrist. The patience of an accountant. And the determination of Rocky Balboa. That's enough to give anybody a split personality. Let's look at each of these faces of the successful investor to see if the rest of us can learn something from you.

The Vision of an Economist.

An economist is one who specializes in seeing the big picture and how all of the parts interrelate and fit together. You, as a real estate economist, have to digest information from a number of sources to make projections about interest rates, vacancy rates, inflation rates, rental rates, unemployment rates, and appreciation rates. From this, you distill your investment strategy. In doing this you are already miles ahead of the ordinary investor who simply calls up his stock broker and asks advice of what to buy and when. A successful real estate investor not only needs to know what and when to buy ... but also how to buy and why. In essence, you become the stock broker, the stock exchange and *The Wall Street Journal* all rolled into one. And that is why I respect you.

The Independence of a Pioneer.

What motivates you to do all of this? Is it the money? Are you more greedy than most? I don't think so. You are just accutely jealous of your freedom. And money can buy freedom. While most Americans belong to the "Give Me Security At Any Cost" Club you are a charter member of the Patrick Henry Club . . . whose motto is: "Give me freedom or give me death." Sometimes it takes that kind of commitment to go against the current.

The Courage of an Entrepreneur.

An entrepreneur is a lonely, brave soul who has a need to take risks, to surmount obstacles and to win. But you shouldn't mistake him or her for being foolhardy. Because, although an entrepreneur loves to take risks and tackle obstacles, he doesn't like to lose. He only likes to take chances when the circumstances dictate that he has a better than average chance of winning. That is one reason that entrepreneurs rarely get serious about Las Vegas. The odds don't favor the gambler. A famous researcher devised a game to study the characteristics of entrepreneurs. The object of the game was to toss a bean bag into a bowl from across the room. The participants could choose any spot in the room from which to toss the bean bag. They could stand 30 feet away or they could choose to stand right over the bowl and drop the bean bag in. It was discovered that the entrepreneurs specifically chose to toss their bean bags from neither too far or too near. They didn't stand back too far because the probability of scoring would be too slim (like gambling). But they didn't stand too close because there would be no challenge. So what does this have to do with the successful real estate investor? He doesn't like long shots. Each real estate investment is chosen specifically to have a better than average chance of success . . . anything less than this is speculation. He likes to hit singles, not home runs. He likes to make ten yards a carry instead of the long bomb. He would rather have a short jump shot over a three-point attempt. In his investments he likes circumstances where if he loses he loses small but if he wins he wins big... he doesn't like to live his life so that every play is third down and thirty, but rather first down and goal. Most successful real estate investors are entrepreneurs when they buy. But that is where the similarity ends.

The Judgment of a Businessman.

Entrepreneurs are great starters but lousy finishers. They love the challenge of the hunt but they hate the details of following through. And for this reason they make lousy real estate investors because real estate is exciting to buy but a pain in the neck to take care of. So a successful real estate investor has to be a little entrepreneur and a lot of businessperson. A businessperson must buy something at wholesale to sell at retail or he goes out of business. He has to have wholesale prices, wholesale terms, or both. Preferably both. If he can't get this, he has to pass onto the next property. He doesn't speculate. He doesn't take undue risks. His judgments are made with the cold precision of a diamond cutter. But that doesn't mean he has to be cold-hearted. Because he is part psychiatrist, too.

The Sensitivity of a Psychiatrist.

Real estate is not a property business. It is a people business... although only the truly successful real estate investors understand this. You can't run rough shod over peoples' fears, hopes, and expectations and expect to be successful. That is why the win/win philosophy is so powerful. When, you negotiate with the understanding of the other person's needs and wants in mind... when you speak the seller's language... you significantly increase the probability of success. This takes sensitivity, empathy, and love. Now, that is the dilemma. How can you be a cold, ruthless businessperson when at the same time you are sensitive and loving? Doesn't this destroy your negotiating edge? Aren't these competing emotions? In other words, will you need to go to a psychiatrist sorting out these various conflicts?

The answer is no. But it is not an easy answer either. It helps if one takes the posture of a problem-solver... willing to give advice, help, counsel, a shoulder to cry on if necessary, without worrying about whether or not you are going to be a buyer for the property. You can explain options and the hard realities of the marketplace to the seller without any conflict of interest because you maintain the attitude of a don't wanter yourself. Once the seller is aware that you are on his side, things will go much smoother and both parties can feel a true kinship as opposed to animosity. But where does that leave you? Well, you don't ever have to buy anything until it meets with your criterion. You simply analyze the facts and see if there is room for you to win also. If not, you're onto the next property. If so, you just bought yourself a property. I have many people tell me that this win/win concept is just about the most insane, crazy, ridiculous, unworkable idea I have ever come up with. I have two answers for that. First of all, I didn't come up with the idea. It's two thousand years old... known more commonly as "The Golden Rule." And secondly, I love the quote by Einstein: "For an idea which does not at first seem insane there is no hope."

The Patience of an Accountant.

I hate minute details. And for years, I wondered why I couldn't really turn the corner of profitability in my real estate investing. My wife understood the problem fully, but I had to learn the hard way: several hundred thousands of dollars worth of education from the school of hard knocks. I think I am slowly learning the lesson that the taking care of the small numbers is where the big money is at. Joel Weldon, a national speaker, has a speech which he entitles "Elephants don't bite" and he starts his speech by asking the question, "How many of you have ever been bitten by a mosquito?." Of course, everyone raises his hand. Then he asks, "How many of you have ever been bitten by an elephant?" and no hands are raised. He then is quick to point out that it's the little things in life that get us . . . not the big ones. Enough said.

The Determination of Rocky Balboa

How do you last 15 rounds with a world heavy-weight champion if you are just a light-weight yourself? It is done all of the time in the business world . . . especially the Nothing Down kind. We have stories of our Nothing Down Seminar graduates that make the fight scenes in Rocky I, II and III look like "The Sound of Music." People who have all the strikes against them hang in there long enough to slay the dragon, kill Goliath. The least we can do for them is to honor them for their courage. I hope I have done an adequate job of it. And for those of you who are still hanging on, I offer encouragement. Good luck and God bless.

Two Predictions and Three Challenges: Taking Stock of the Investment Trends

Robert G. Allen

The recent period has been a bit confusing to real estate investors. Interest rates have been high (although the trend is downward as I write). Appreciation has been dismal in most areas; declining prices have been in some areas the rule rather than the exception for the first time in decades. All of this has been enough to drive a novice investor back to the stock market. As professional real estate investors, however, we look upon the events of the recent past as positive signs. "How can high interest rates be a positive thing?" you ask. I had one successful woman investor tell me that she was terribly upset when the long-term mortgage rates dropped from their high perch above 18%. The lower the rates, she argued, the harder it will be to convince a seller to carry financing. The lower the rates, the more speculators there will be to compete with. The lower the rates, the fewer don't wanters there will be. She has a point. At the very least, this is a positive way of viewing the situation.

The same argument holds true for the new due-on-sale clause controversy. Is it good or is it bad to have due-on-sale clauses? Well, I suppose it matters little whether we are "afor or agin' 'em," since the Supreme Court laid down the law and it is now up to us to see some good in the decision. And there is some good. It will mean more don't wanters ... folks who are adversely affected by the decision and will want to bail out of their property, which may now be worth less because of unassumable financing. Then, we also have to be thankful for the bad news that flooded through the entire real estate investing world when the decision was handed down. It made real estate a little less attractive to the rest of the world and therefore, by definition, it became all the more attractive to serious investors who know that the due-on-sale decision only affected a minority of the total outstanding loans in the market. We generally spend more time in the area of assumable FHA and VA loans anyway, so having the Supreme Court make many loans due-on-sale was like having your doctor cut out your appendix: it hurts for a little while after the operation but the pain goes away soon enough and leaves you in no worse a position than when you started.

Now, where is the silver lining with respect to the lack of appreciation in the past three years? Put pure and simple, we got rid of the speculators. In fact, the bargains most of us investors are picking up today are those which are being dumped at a loss by the quick-buck artists. Many an optimist has become wealthy by simply buying out a pessimist. So although we may not be experiencing much appreciation, we are building in our profits on the front end rather than waiting for a dubious appreciation. I suppose these past few years have also taught many of us to be more careful, to look before we leap, to invest rather than speculate. There are many other benefits... including the increased numbers of bargains... but the education is by far the most important one.

So where does this leave us for the future? Well, the nice thing about being a professional real estate advice giver is that real estate is so powerful, and there are so many ways of making money in real estate that my main counsel has been and will always be, "Don't wait to buy real estate, buy real estate and wait." I don't have to guess how high the Dow will go or what commodities to buy or when the peak in gold or silver will be reached. But just in case you want my prognostications, I have included them for you here so that you can plan your next year accordingly.

1. I am pretending that real estate will not increase in value significantly during the next period of time. That doesn't mean that it won't... but just that my investment strategy does not rely on appreciation. I will concentrate on buying wholesale properties and I suggest that you do the same. Therefore, if we don't have appreciation, we won't get hurt, and if we do, we will be wonderfully surprised.

2. I am pretending that interest rates for long-term mortgages will dip for a few more months and then begin to increase again. I think that this is a window in time just like the one we experienced in August, 1980, where rates decreased before the election and then skyrocketed. I have decided to refinance some of the properties which have balloons I don't want to worry about. I am also refinancing other properties to pay off high-interest second mortgages which contribute to negative cash flows. The new FHA rate, which has gotten as low as 12% in recent days, is good enough to entice me to jump. I doubt it will go much lower. If it does I will be surprised and thrilled because it will open up the use of the Second Mortgage Crank

technique described in *Nothing Down* and in the Seminar Workbook as Technique #32. But I am betting that the rates won't stay down for long. Like I said, I would love to be wrong, but I'm assuming that I will be right.

One final opportunity that refinancing makes possible at this time is discounting existing private financing. For instance, on one property we bought about 18 months ago, the seller carried back a $12,000 second at 13% with no monthly payments for six years. With the accrued interest the note has a balance of $15,000. But the hard times have caused this seller to reconsider and he now wants to discount the note for $7,000 cash. I have to decide whether or not this discount will be worth giving up the existing 10.5% first mortgage and a $15,000 second at 13% with no payments. It turns out that the new financing will cause approximately $100 extra per month in mortgage payments.

So the decision is cut and dried... am I willing to invest $100 per month now in order to pick up an immediate $8,000 profit? I decided that if I kept this property for three years and sold it, my increased expense from the refinance in negative cash flow would amount to $3,600 and my profit would be at least $8,000 assuming no appreciation... so that would be over 200% on my money. So I decided to refinance. Opportunities like this should be explored. Send a letter to all of the people who are holding your private paper and tell them that you could be enticed to refinance... even at the exhorbitantly high rates... if they would consider a healthy discount in their paper for cash. I have so far batted a thousand. Cash talks... even though it is a lesser amount than hoped for.

Technically, these predictions of mine are not predictions. They are just plain common sense. But that is what is nice about real estate. If you just use your common sense, you will be OK. Let me finish this section with a few challenges for you for the near future. You notice I don't call them resolutions. I am challenging you to do at least one of the following:

1. Buy one property at a discount this year which can be sold (although you may decide not to sell) for enough profit to equal your yearly salary.

2. Buy one property next year which has a real positive monthly cash flow of at least $200 per month.

3. Buy one property from a bank or financial institution which is trying to unload one of their foreclosure properties and negotiate for the bank to carry back a mortgage which is at least two points under current market rate. (You'll love being in the driver's seat for once with a bank.)

If you choose to accept my challenge, drop me a line. I'd love to hear from you.

How Real Estate Can Change Your Life

William Nickerson

Most of you are familiar with my formula, and many other writers have referred to it. I will review it, slightly updated, to refresh your memory. As it came to me, it used to take an average of 20 years to make a million, but now it is common to make it in 5 or 6 years. Although prices have gone up, that is only relative, and the formula still works and will always be a true guide. This we know from the many thousands who have followed it and already become millionaires. You could start today with $1,000, as my wife and I did, and buy income property. Many have told me recently that they have bought a rental house or duplex with little or nothing down. One of our apartment managers bought a brand new duplex with nothing down. They arranged to do the painting in place of a cash down payment.

There are many ways to work out 100% financing. Another of our experienced apartment-manager couples bought over $2 million worth of apartments with nothing down but their notes! They fixed up the property and in just a few years sold for a million dollars profit. But for a sound start on today's market, I figure the average investor should have a minimum nest egg of about $5,000. This is the average savings on a nationwide basis for a typical family where the breadwinner is between 25 and 34. Most older investors (especially professional people,) have bigger nest eggs.

In this average example, $5,000 would be the result of two years savings at $100 a month, including some interest. I want to emphasize that my million-dollar formula is not based on unusual expectations, but on average savings, average ability, and average luck for anyone who follows my guidance. Here is the way it works out:

You take your $5,000 savings and pay 10% down to buy a rundown but basically sound rental house. You thus borrow nine times your down payment, $45,000, making a total price of $50,000. As you know, there are many ways to arrange the financing. The $45,000 loan might be borrowed from the seller or a lending institution as a first mortgage. Where the first loan falls short of required financing, a common practice is for the seller to grant a secondary mortgage to make up the difference. And when necessary to complete financing, Realtors may grant a third mortgage, covering their commission, and so on into many, many combinations.

While getting started with a small nest egg this would usually be a spare time investment, of course, like mine while I worked for the phone company. You fix up the property, painting and renovating and modernizing fixtures. You pay operating expenses and loan payments from the rents, and plow back into improvements the net income, plus, in this example, your $100 a month in savings. It is important to continue saving in the initial stages. It helps a great deal to speed your progress, especially if you start with a small nest egg. Many slow down after buying their first rental property because they expect to immediately start living like millionaires!

After the property is fixed up it is worth more to a tenant, so you raise the rents, sometimes in an overall boost, and sometimes in several steps. For example, you might put in a wall heater or room air conditioner and immediately raise the rent $50 a month. You increase the overall income an average of 25%. This increases the sales value 25%, as income property values are, of course, based mainly on income.

When you are fixing up your home, what you do is a matter of personal preference. But on rental or resale property, don't get carried away with personal preferences. Always remember my 2-for-1 formula. Every dollar you spend on improvements should increase value at least $2. Otherwise don't do it! This gives you an ample safety margin in case you miscalculate. I know of many improvements that have increased value five and even ten-fold.

In 12 months you sell or trade for the increased value at a gross capital profit of 25%. This is a nominal return for your imagination and effort. You pay sales costs, which average about 5%. I advocate buying and selling thru Realtors and paying their regular fees. They usually start at 6% on smaller properties and are less on larger properties. Realtors will help you go faster and farther than on your own. At the end of 12 months, after paying sales costs, you would have a net worth of $15,160. Then you turn around and trade this equity for a larger income property, perhaps four to eight apartments or houses, again with average financing at nine times your down payment.

Maximum Financing The Very Heart

Most new investors are afraid to borrow, because they believe they should not go into debt. In school Shakespeare taught us, "Neither a borrower or a lender be." It is wise not to borrow heavily for personal pleasure, for then you are only a money consumer. But it is sound to borrow for investment to make money. Maximum financing is the very heart of making money, because you thereby earn a profit on the savings of others. This is the way that banks and other lending institutions make money, normally charging a reasonable fee in exchange for their essential services. When they take your savings, they are money wholesalers, and you become a money retailer when you borrow from them for investment. Then your tenants who pay rent are the ultimate consumers.

Many make the mistake of borrowing too little when they invest. For faster progress you want to borrow the most that you can safely handle on each new long-term mortgage. The only safeguard you need is that you can repay loan payments plus expenses from your income. It's absolutely impossible to make a fortune today without the power of O.P.M. As you know, that's "Other People's Money!"

You Might Turnover Faster

I am often asked, "Must I follow your formula exactly in order to succeed?" Of course not! It is a guide to show you the potential. You might turnover faster, as I know of many profitable resales within a few months of purchase. You might make a bigger profit, as I know of many recent deals with profits between 50 and 100%. Such investment profits have been made throughout history. Remember the Parable of the Talents way back in Bible times? Jesus cited a profit of 1,000% to encourage investment enterprise: A master gave his three servants talents, — we call them nest eggs today, — to invest while the master was gone on a journey. One buried his talent, and nothing happened except that it got moldy. Two of the servants invested their money. The master returned to find that one made a profit of 500% and the other 1,000%. Thus Jesus emphasized that your money will lose value if you just bury it, and should be put to work by investment.

Here's an example of how the $1 Million Formula works: A white-haired fellow got up after one of my lectures and said he had read my book when he had only $400 in the bank. He was over 65, drawing Social Security, and he couldn't wait to save more. He bought a dilapidated looking house and painted it inside and out. In one month he sold his equity for a $4,000 profit. This made a 1,000% monthly profit, or 12,000% a year!

We'll get back to my fairly conservative formula of an average 25% per year gross capital profit in an average turnover time of every 12 months. In 2 more years 3 years after your start with $5,000, you would be worth a net of $119,935. Note that in this average example your progress with a small start is gratifying, but usually much slower than later on. That is why many people get discouraged. Even though they start off fairly well, they don't keep at it. My proven formula is not a get-rich-quick scheme, but a get-rich-stick-to-it process based on a sound plan for maximum success. After all, it does take time to build a solid pyramid!

You can start your pyramid at any stage you are able to. With $100,000 for your first real estate investment, you would be at our 3-year level. One investor told me of putting $30,000 into an apartment house after reading my book, and turning it into a net worth of $¼ million in 14 months. After two or three years of plugging along and laying a sound base of experience, you do start moving much faster. At the end of five years you would be worth close to $1 million. And, if you keep at it, in six years you have a net worth of over $2 million.

Ambition, Imagination, Courage Persistence, & Judgment

Does this seem a little fantastic? I invite you to calculate it yourself, and you will see that it actually works out. In fact, many of my students have actually made their million in five years, and many more have made it in ten years. Anyone who really wants to can make a real estate pyramid work for him. And you need only average intelligence, average savings, and average luck. Then why doesn't everybody do it? I figure you do need five special attributes for maximum success. They are *ambition, imagination, courage, persistence,* and *judgment.*

First, you need the *ambition* to get ahead financially. Some people just don't give a damn. One sad example was a young hippie who stayed for years on welfare. I asked him if he had any amibition to change. "You bet I do," he said, "I want to move to a Commune out in the country where we can grow our own marijuana!"

Second, you need the *imagination* to see the tremendous opportunities awaiting you in real estate. Third, you need the *courage* to make up your mind, — to get off the fence and do something. Have you noticed that some procastinators always find an excuse to do nothing?

All of you who attend this Congress possess some degree of these first three attributes of *ambition, imagination,* and *courage.* You have proved this by committing yourself to spend the time and money to add to your investment education. Then what else is needed for maximum success? Fourth, you need the *persistence* to keep at it. Some get off to a fine start, then slacken off. How far you want to go is a matter of your personal choice. If you want to make a million or so, you have to keep going. As Calvin Coolidge said, "Nothing in the world can take the place of *persistence.*"

Finally, you need Number five, the *judgment* to continue following our proven principles that give you such a big advantage. Some get so enthused about making money in real estate, they think they can do well in any field. Then they may wander off on a wild, speculative tangent, and lose their shirt!

Speculation — Investment

This brings up the question, What is the basic difference between speculation and investment? Investment property pays an income to help carry itself right from the beginning, while you are making improvements to increase its value. Buying anything with no income is pure speculation. This applies to vacant land, to gold and silver, and to diamonds, for example, one way to make money is to buy wholesale and sell retail. With diamonds, it's often the other way around. A friend bought a diamond from a dealer at a "big discount." Soon after, with no income from his purchase, he needed to raise money, and the same dealer would only pay half the cost of the diamond.

Some buyers make a killing on speculative property, like buying vacant land by the acre, and holding until they can sell it as subdivision lots. But many guess wrong, or wait too long. Taxes, interest and inflation can eat up all profits, as they cost at least 20% a year nationally on vacant land. Speculation might profit those with sufficient income to carry a no-income alligator, but is not sound for total use of funds. Of course, if you build new, competitive income property on vacant land, as many are successfully doing, that is another way of improving property that can be a good investment. So is improving rundown farm land. But your first investment should be a property already built, with proven rents. After you gain experience operating property with proven income, then you might consider new construction.

I'm often asked, "What are the odds against me on property investment?" As pointed out in my books, the odds are not against you, but strongly for you. Both government and insurance company studies show that if you take out a mortgage to buy property, the odds are 400-to-1 in your favor that it will be paid off. This is 20 times surer than taking out a life insurance policy, where 1-in-20 is cancelled for failure to keep up payments.

By contrast, if you start a new business (according to the U.S. Dept. of Commerce) the odds are 4-to-1 that you will go broke. Thus your chances as a property investor are 1600-to-1 better than if you start a new business. A typical new business prone to failure is opening a restaurant. There are many ways to make a fortune, but investment in rental dwellings is the surest road, meeting a vital necessity of life.

Win/Win

It makes me angry when people who don't know any better say, "You can't make money without cheating somebody." Doesn't it make you angry, too? That's the beauty of real estate if handled properly, as we all agree, — all real estate deals should mean *win/win*, — that the buyer and the seller should both be happy and well satisfied. But, let's face it, not everybody conducts business as we would like to have it, and some need a little education. My wife and I want to show we mean what we say by putting our money on the line. We have committed $1 million to found a new Chair, — which means pay a full-time Professor and expenses, at Harvard Divinity School in perpetuity. The Chair will be in Economic Ethics, preaching the gospel of win/win ethics in business and investment. And Harvard says this example is bound to be copied by other schools throughout the country.

Opportunity Always Knocking

In just about every audience for several years now some tell us they have already made their million or close to it, and many have made a find start towards being wealthy. Yet, every day, as mentioned earlier, some pessimists say there is no opportunity anymore. Back during the depression, many experts, like our Economics teacher, said, "The days of opportunity are over." Now they say, like our Economics Professor when we went back to Fresno State for a visit, "I wish I had started investing back there when you did. But now that we have better times, it's *too late* for opportunity!"

Just think, you can find it, but that poor Professor, like a lot of other prophets of doom, will never find opportunity! Opportunity in real estate is always there, waiting for you. Let it change your life so you may become wealthy. All you have to do is recognize opportunity and take advantage of it.

I can tell you of thousands of opportunities that have been won, and some that have been lost. Often opportunity is there and we don't see it. Or we may see it and pass it by. Some sceptics never recognize an opportunity until after they have missed it!

I have come to the conclusion that, to a great extent, opportunity is in your state of mind. Opportunity does depend on your personal attitude — whether you really want to recognize it and make progress. Opportunity is always there for you, yesterday, today and every day, in good times or bad. Opportunity in this free enterprise land of America knocks not just for the favored few, but for all who aspire to better themselves. And opportunity knocks not just once, but many times. All you have to do is open the door that is offered to you.

If you will embrace these fundamental investment truths of free enterprise we present to you, they will set you free to make a million dollars, or whatever you earnestly aspire to, as your share of the Great American Dream.

Back to Basics: You Need Tenets Before Tenants!

Richard J. Allen

What are the basic tenets of the Robert Allen Nothing Down Program?

At the heart of the Nothing Down Program is a unified set of principles leading to defined outcomes. The ACRE/RAND leaders' discussion at a recent conference returned again and again to the importance of following the basic, fundamental plan strictly and faithfully. The central mission of ACRE/RAND goes back to these principles, for ACRE/RAND was founded in August 1979 as an educational and motivational organization designed to follow through with the teaching of the principles of win/win creative finance as articulated in the Nothing Down Seminar and its support materials. That was and still is the mission of the ACRE/RAND network: to teach correct principles of good practice in creative real estate investing so that enterprising people can take charge of their financial futures.

What are the underlying tenets of the RAND program? The seven RAND chairpersons in consultation with officers of the Allen Group looked back over the history of the program came up with the following set of "basics" that seem timeless. We print them here for two reasons: so that readers can test their own investment approach by way of comparison, and so that readers can offer opinions, suggestions, and comments. Let's make this an ongoing discussion in the first step toward tightening up the RAND organization and letting our friends outside the network know what we stand for.

The Basic ACRE/RAND Tenets

1. People Come First.

Real estate investing is big business. Even in the smallest deals there is a great deal of money at stake. According to an independent study conducted on the ACRE/RAND Network by Brigham Young University, ACRE/ RAND followers are buying over $1 billion dollars worth of real estate annually. That is a significant amount.

However, in all of this activity, there is one cardinal rule that takes precedence over any tendency to overemphasize buying more, making more, having more, and accumulating more wealth for its own sake — and that is the ACRE/RAND conviction that people come first. *People* are important, *not* real estate.

That is why there is so much emphasis in the Nothing Down program and in the ACRE/RAND follow-up on the principle of "win/win." In all of our flurry of real estate activity, we must preserve the central tenet that *all* parties to a transaction must win in order for satisfaction to ensue.

The seller must win. The buyer must win. Tenants, Realtors, lenders, partners, investors — all parties involved in a transaction must emerge winners. Not that everyone should expect to have very smallest aspect of their fondest hopes realized in a deal. Win/win negotiations — like any negotiations — leave room for compromise, for give and take. But win/win negotiations leave no room for deception, misrepresentation, going behind anyone's back, or taking advantage of anyone involved in a transaction.

Win/win is not the cosmetic frosting on the cake, a veneer of respectibility on an otherwise dog-eat-dog enterprise. Win/win *is* the cake. The success of ACRE/RAND graduates is in large measures due to their commitment to the idea of putting people first. The strongest thing they have going for them — apart from the powerful tool of creative finance — is a fresh attitude of being upfront with the world (80% of the Nothing Down graduates are beginners to real estate investing) and a sincere desire to win and others win, too.

On occasion, critics of the Nothing Down program have disparaged the fact that we emphasize "win/win" principles. They claim that the world of business does not operate in this way, that cleverness and manipulation — not win/win — lead to success and a place at the top of the heap. Really? Is it not possible to be astute and honest at the same time? To have a good business head and still have your heart in the right place?

What do Mr. and Mrs. America have to say on the subject? The graduates of the Nothing Down Seminar are a cross-section of America. If there is one underlying reaction that seems to crop up invariably in the evaluation forms submitted by the 50,000 graduates of the program to date, it goes something like this: "We appreciate the win/win approach to investing that you teach. It is refreshing to know that we can uphold our values and still make it!"

Astute planning? Sure. Careful analysis? Always. Tough negotiating? Absolutely. Prudent management? Naturally. But still "people first." That is the win/win way.

2. Getting Places Depends on Following Correct Principles.

The second ARCE/RAND tenet places central emphasis on following an accurate roadmap. There has to be a program—a comprehensive plan for achieving desirable outcomes—and the program has to proceed from basic, fundamental ideas that work and have lasting validity.

The Nothing Down Program is designed to carry a person step-by-step to targeted goals. There are 17 fundamental levels of progress involving such essentials as establishing the correct philosophical frame-work for creating wealth, locating flexible sellers, analyzing properties, negotiating effectively, solving financing problems creatively, and effective management. And each of the 17 levels is broken down into smaller units that contribute their part to the whole.

The mission of ACRE/RAND is to teach these principles in effective ways. ACRE/RAND is an educational organization. It's central purpose is not to buy and sell real estate, not to offer syndications, not to deal in the secondary paper market—but rather to teach correct investment principles so that individuals can take charge of their program for financial betterment.

3. Action is Paramount.

The ACRE/RAND program is designed to promote action, to give people the tools and motivation essential for implementing change. Gaining an understanding of investment principles is fundamentally important, but success depends on translating theory into practice.

The main reason for organizing mutual support groups (ACRE/ RAND investor groups) in most American cities is to make it easier for people to put the ACRE/RAND program into action. People are strengthened in their convictions if they can learn from others, share ideas, brainstorm creative solutions, and update their knowledge through the ACRE/RAND Tape-of-the-Month Program and other educational opportunities. The ACRE/RAND groups are designed: first to place people in situations where they can help one another in the spirit of win/win; second, to help them continue the process of learning correct investment principles; and— above all—third, to give them the stimulus, motivation, and courage they need in order to act.

To this end, all continuing educational materials developed by the Allen

Group for use by practitioners of the Nothing Down system are designed to foster action. For example, *The Real Estate Advisor*, a national monthly newsletter, has as its subtitle, "The Action Newsletter of Creative Real Estate Investing." Its features, case studies, statistical reviews, and commentaries are all structured to impart information and techniques that people must know in order to take action. Similarly, the book by Richard Allen, *How To Write A Nothing Down Offer*, gives full details on fifty actual cases of nothing down buying, with full coverage and commentary on how to reduce risk when making offers.

4. Quality is the Pervasive Goal.

From the beginning, a major tenet of the ACRE/RAND operation was the importance of making quality a central and pervasive goal. If it is worth doing, then it is worth doing well. How does quality manifest itself in the organization of the Nothing Down program? In the instructional process. In the support materials. In the continuning education program of tapes, newsletters, books, seminars, and conferences. In customer services. In research carried out to keep the system current and viable.

For the individual, quality is paramount in the way transactions are analyzed and structured, in the way a team of support professionals is put together, in the way properties are managed, in the way goals are set and monitored, in the way competence is updated and improved.

For the ACRE/RAND groups, quality is often a greater challenge because of the voluntary nature of ACRE/RAND service at the local level. But the record of service is more often than not quite exemplary. Quality in the local ACRE/RAND groups is manifested in the excellence of the programming effort, in support and encouragement given to ACRE/RAND investors (particularly where they are new to creative finance), in the way in which local members are kept informed through new bulletins and telephone calls, in helping people to identify dependable professionals, and in planning and holding help sessions to get people started.

There is always room for improvement — but improvement is slow unless quality becomes an express goal. For ACRE/RAND, quality has always been such a goal.

5. Affirmation is the Soul of ACRE/RAND

Finally, we subscribe to an affirmative approach to investing. What is meant by affirmation? Not just positive mental attitude, which could be naive unless coupled with comprehensive planning and effective tools.

Not just optimism, which could be the spirit of Pollyanna unless coupled with careful analysis and creative problem-solving. Affirmation is an underlying conviction that well-informed and self-reliant individuals can take control of their own financial destiny and achieve success if given the proper training and support.

It is a fundamental policy of ACRE/RAND not to structure our efforts as a "survival program," not to place emphasis on "holding the line." Rather, ACRE/RAND is an affirmative program form meeting positive, realistic goals that will greatly advance the financial well being of its practitioners.

The very first national edition of the *Nothing Down Seminar Manual*, published in August of 1979, contained a chart that underscored this principle of affirmation. Every edition since then has carried the same chart. It is well to review these words now and frequently in the future:

SIX STAGES OF INVESTMENT SUCCESS

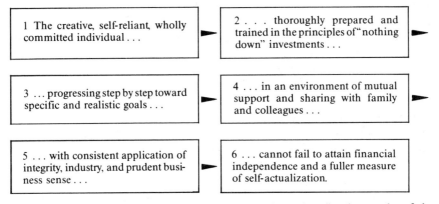

1 The creative, self-reliant, wholly committed individual . . . ▶ 2 . . . thoroughly prepared and trained in the principles of "nothing down" investments . . . ▶

3 . . . progressing step by step toward specific and realistic goals . . . ▶ 4 . . . in an environment of mutual support and sharing with family and colleagues . . . ▶

5 . . . with consistent application of integrity, industry, and prudent business sense . . . ▶ 6 . . . cannot fail to attain financial independence and a fuller measure of self-actualization.

By way of summary, here are the five main points in the credo of the Nothing Down system:

1. People Come First
2. Getting Places Depends on Following Correct Principles
3. Action is Paramount
4. Quality is the Pervasive Goal
5. Affirmation is the Soul of ACRE/RAND

We invite readers to ponder whether their own investment program is a reflection of these tenets. We also encourage comment and suggestions on these ideas and how they might be expanded for the betterment of the ACRE/RAND network generally, and for any established or emerging investor who may be attracted to its ranks.

Seventeen Reasons Why Housing Values Will Continue to Rise

Proponents of the "Gloom and Doom" theory in housing currently point to four basic reasons why they believe real estate is about to collapse. *First,* when the post-World War II baby boom crests in a few years, demand for housing is supposed to shrivel. *Second,* land is so plentiful in the United States that the appreciation of real-property values cannot forever persist. *Third,* inflation, one of the principal ingredients of real estate appreciation, will, it is claimed, soon be bridled. (including owning your own home) could well be modified in the future, causing ownership incentive to abate.

I like to remember these factors in terms of what I call the "BLITZ" theory, i.e.: **B**abies + **L**and + **I**nflation + **T**axes = **Z**ap! The problem with the BLITZ theory is that it is in part misleading, in part oblivious to other significant and equally potent forces *sustaining* real property values, and in part just false.

No one can predict anything with certainty, of course. But the forces acting to sustain the value of real estate in this country are so enormously powerful that the chances of the housing world collapsing under its own weight are, on balance, slight. In our readings and discussions around the country, we have noted 17 such supportive forces and tendencies. For the sake of clarity we have organized them into four categories around the key word **MIND,** i.e.:

A. Market Factors
B. Image Factors
C. Nature of the Product
D. Demographic Factors

Let's review them.

A. Market Factors

1. Protective Profit Margin. In the building industry the profit margin tends to be narrow, putting a protective lower limit on prices. The prices *cannot* fall below actual cost or the supply will dry up. Builders have been sorely tested in recent times with the credit and mortgage crunch. Many have been forced out of business, and prices in some areas have fallen somewhat. However, the temporary decline will quickly be reversed as credit is eased in the coming months. Moreover, much of the decline is due to the fact that in a recessionary period a greater percentage of the houses sold are *smaller,* hence less expensive, causing the median prices to drop accordingly.

The situation with stocks is far less tangible. David Read likes to ask these two questions at the Nothing Down seminars: "How many of you have real estate you would like to sell today for what you paid for it?" and "How many of you have stocks that you would like to sell today for the price you originally paid?" In the case of stocks, he always gets many willing takers. In the case of real estate—hardly any. Real estate has a very tangible built-in lower price barrier.

2. Local Nature of the Market. Unlike stocks, which are subject to national scrutiny and hence snowballing effects, real estate is more localized. There is no "Big Board" for housing. Each real estate market is unique. Each is determined to a great extent by local conditions. A leveling (or dramatic rise) in prices in one market does not necessarily spill over into the situation in other markets.

3. Emphasis on Monthly Payments. The banks are not so much concerned with price shifts as they are with monthly payments. If the value of your property should fall below the original price, would the bank call your loan? Certainly not. They just want you to keep up with the monthly payments. Houses are not called on margin. With stocks, however, the sale of marginal stock is a principal factor contributing to a sluggish market.

4. Government Influences. Mortgage guarantees, subsidies, and tax breaks (such as interest deductions for home owners and depreciation allowance for income properties) have sustained the market success of housing over the years. With the value of home ownership in the United States amounting to around $2.3 trillion (to say nothing of income property!), the incentive to influence continuing government support of housing is and will remain enormous. Moreover, government regulation itself contributes to the rising cost of housing. There is not much chance that regulation will go away. If anything, it will continue to increase.

5. Earnings. Over the long haul, earnings have tended to keep pace with price increases, especially as a result of the increasing numbers of families with *two* bread earners. Fully 45% of all home purchases today are double-income purchases. The debt factor is therefore not as dangerous as some claim.

6. Supply and Demand. This is no doubt the most potent factor working to sustain real property values. The fact is, there is an acute shortage of housing today. Vacancy rates are the lowest they have been in the quarter-century since occupancy statistics have been kept. Housing starts are down. But demand stays high. Demand is enormous and growing. The recession is affecting *volume* drastically, but not so much *price*. And when credit becomes more readily available, prices will shoot upward. This has been the pattern following each crunch over the last half-century. Supply and demand in housing does not adjust itself through a collapse, but rather through a leveling of prices from time to time, followed by a continuation of the rise in prices.

To summarize these six market factors:

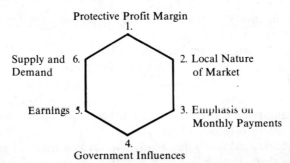

Protective Profit Margin
1.

Supply and 6.   2. Local Nature
Demand   of Market

Earnings 5.   3. Emphasis on
                      Monthly Payments

4.
Government Influences

B. Image Factors

1. The American Dream. The dream of owning one's home is one of the core objectives of the American experience. It is a potent and lasting force in sustaining sales, hence prices.

2. Luxury Factor. Related to this is the desire to own a larger and more luxurious home. Call it greed or whatever—it is still a very real force in housing. Only 8% of the houses built in 1950 had *more* that one bathroom; now only 15% are built with *just one* bathroom. Moreover, today houses tend to be larger than before.

3. Community Reputation. Who wants to buy in a community where word is out that prices are falling? The local fathers will tend to apply pressure to counteract any such tendency.

4. Expectation. People *expect* homes to appreciate. People *believe* in the principle of appreciation. It has become an axiom, and such axioms tend to become self-fulfilling prophecies. This factor is not insignificant in the growth of home values.

To summarize this set of factors:

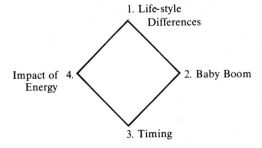

C. Nature of the Product.

1. Necessity of Life. People *must* live somewhere. When it comes to your home, you will go to any length to preserve it. The *last* payment you'll neglect is the mortgage payment. That is why the "Nothing Down" system focuses on "bread and butter" properties, the kind that are in the greatest demand by the greatest number of people.

2. Intrinsic Value. Unlike other assets (stocks and bonds, for example), housing has intrinsic value. Land, materials, and labor are tangibles. They go *up* in value, and that translates into sustained and rising prices.

3. Preservation Factor. Unlike consumer items, houses can be maintained, remodeled, expanded, and kept in good condition over decades. This also sustains their value.

To summarize this set of factors:

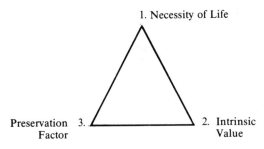

D. Demograpic Factors

1. Life-style Differences. Today there are more singles buying homes, more homes per capita, longer life expectancy— all contributing to greater demand for housing, hence higher prices. In a recent broadcast of the *David Susskind Show,* a representative of the National Association of

Realtors pointed out that one-third of all condo purchases are being made by single women, and one-fifth of all purchases generally by singles. Only 16% of home purchases now are "traditional." Fully 84% are "non-traditional"—by singles, double-income purchases, etc.

2. Baby Boom. The post-World War II baby boom will not crest until the end of the decade and the beginning of the 1990s. In the 1970s some 30 million people turned 30 (the prime house-buying age); in the 1980s the number will be 41 million! Think of the impact on demand. Even after the crest, the life-style differences pointed out in the previous item will help offset the moderate decrease in the numbers of buyers coming up through the ranks.

3. Timing. Couples are now buying houses earlier in life than their parents. This is another factor that influences demand, hence real property values.

4. Impact of Energy. Because of the dramatic rise in the cost of fuel in recent years, the tendency to move further out into the suburbs is being reversed. There is plenty of land in America, but less and less land within acceptable commuting distances. What does this do to land values? It increases demand for housing within acceptable areas and causes prices to rise. This factor will become more and more crucial with each rise in fuel costs. According to Marvin Levin, President of Consolidated Capital Corp. (a California-based real estate syndication firm): "I believe that the fuel shortage will cause the suburban home to become as economically obsolete as the gas-guzzling automobile. By comparison, the close-in home or apartment unit will, I believe, hold its value." (*New York Times*, April 1, 1980).

To summarize this last set of factors:

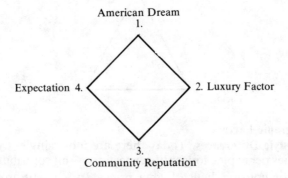

American Dream
1.

Expectation 4.   2. Luxury Factor

3.
Community Reputation

In contrast to the BLITZ theory, therefore, the four sets of factors constituting the MIND theory (17 items in all) predict a long-range growth in real estate values according to the formula:

Market + Image + Nature of Product + Demography = Growth.

Once more, no one can predict the future of housing with complete certainty. In fact, no one can predict *anything* with utter certainty. Remember the last line of Sophocles' play *Oedipus?* "We must call no one happy who is of mortal race, until he hath crossed life's border, free from pain." Still, when it comes to choosing between the BLITZ theory and the MIND theory in housing, we'll cast our lot with MIND any day. Only the future will tell.

Supreme Court Upholds Due-On-Sale: What Now? Strategies for Creative Investors

Richard J. Allen

Now that the Supreme Court has upheld the lenders in the due-on-sale controversy, what are the implications for the real estate investor?

Our perspective on the matter is this:

Don't panic! Canada has had exclusively short-term renewable mortgages for a number of years without going under. There are always creative solutions to the challenges that face us. Often it is a matter of shifting gears and following different paths to success. Only 26.2% of the home mortgage loans are immediately affected by the recent court ruling, i.e., those held by federally-chartered financial institutions. Of course, the ruling will no doubt eventually have important consequences for regulations governing state-chartered lenders as well. Many state-chartered institutions will no doubt soon apply for federal charters. Some states already have "parity" laws whereby changes in regulations affecting federally-chartered institutions automatically apply to the state-chartered institutions. The impact of the decision remains to be seen. Meanwhile, here are nine strategies for Nothing Down investors to consider:

1. Discriminating Purchases

Be more discriminating about your property buying. Look for properties with fully-assumable FHA loans, VA loans, or conventional loans that have been sold by the lender in such a way that assumptions are now possible. Recently a colleague of one of the Allen Group staff was negotiating for a California home having what the seller described as a non-assumable loan. Wisely, the buyer probed more deeply into the matter at the bank. Sure enough, the loan was of the non-assumable variety; however, the bank disclosed that they had sold the loan to a group of private investors and would therefore permit the new buyer to assume it formally without any change in the terms! Another Nothing Downer in our staff circle recently bought a home with what appeared to be a non-assumable loan. Once more, a little probing turned up the good news that the lender had sold the loan to an insurance company, and would therefore permit assumption under very favorable terms.

The moral of the story is — ask more questions, look around, probe more deeply, be more discriminating, select more carefully.

2. Free and Clear Properties

More than ever before, buyers should be on the lookout for free and clear properties. Seller financing continues to be an important tool for creative finance. Naturally, the recent Supreme Court decision has nothing to do with free and clear properties, which are the seedbed for some of the most exciting opportunities available.

3. FNMA

Buyers should continue to look for FNMA resale/refinance opportunities. While only 5% of the loans currently are held by FNMA, creative refinance using their program (or any number of other similar local programs cropping up around the country) completely disarms due-on-sale problems and generates capital as well.

4. Wrapping Assumable Loans

In effect, the contract sale that wraps a non-assumable loan is now virtually dead as a viable technique. Of course, it is still important to note the usefulness of wrapping a wrap that has a "safe" (assumable) underlying loan. The contract of sale involving a free and clear property is also still useful, although the seller may instead insist on a purchase money mortgage or purchase money trust deed. The contract of sale involving a free and clear property is also still useful, although the seller may instead insist on a purchase money mortgage or purchase money trust deed.

5. Flexibility of Price

We believe the new court decision has important implications for the negotiating process. Sellers with non-assumable loans will now have to take into account the fact that their buyers must now very likely face assumption fees and higher interest rates (since contract sales in such cases are no longer viable). The decrease in the flexibility of the terms will have to be made up with an increase in the flexibility of the price, i.e., it will have to go down! Buyers will have to sharpen their pencils and determine the limits of tolerability in their bottom line cash flow situation. Sellers will have to be more flexible if a deal is to be struck. Carry-back situations will have to be structured to favor the buyer just a little more, since he will take it on the chin with the formal assumption.

6. Watch For Deals

Watch for creative lenders to step in with competitive "deals" after the dust settles. No doubt the hike in interest rates for assumptions will rise around the country. But there will always be a few lenders who will start to sing the song, "Come to us, we only bump one point, etc., etc." Moreover, as seller financing is curtailed by the court decision, sales will be further restricted and the number of REO's (Real Estate Owned) at the banks will increase. Therefore, look for opportunities to strike good deals with lenders who don't particularly want to be property holders. There is always a good side to every set-back!

7. Equity Sharing

Equity-sharing will no doubt become more and more important. In theory, a property owner who sells part-interest in his property has not relinquished "title." The due-on-sale clause should theoretically not be triggered. However, this theory has not been fully tested in the courts, and good legal advice is essential for anyone who wants to set up an equity-share arrangement. Still, equity-sharing, (with tax benefits accruing in the same ratios as ownership) may be one important answer to the challenges arising as a result of the Supreme Court decision on acceleration.

8. Options and Lease-Options

Where it is to the advantage of the buyer, options and lease-options are still highly effective creative finance tools. Where can it be advantageous? Wherever you can lock the price in at a low level while putting together the necessary financing, or wherever the current rent is so low that you could turn around and have a "sandwich" lease at a higher level and generate monthly income. An option may have the effect of only putting off the problem of due-on-sale, but sometimes it is important to buy time.

9. Be Informed

What about the buyer who has bought on contract and now fears proceeding according to his own policies. There will not be a wholesale movement to raise every relevant loan to market levels. Still, the investor should be informed about the nature of the underlying loan (he should have found out all the details before buying!). The seller may need to pin down the details, especially the current policy of the lender, and whether the loan is still held by the lender. It would be well for the investor to play "best case/worst case" and test his own ability to meet the lender's qualification standards if it came to that. If he can qualify — no need to panic. If he cannot — it might be time to see how to get those rents up and look around for partners with a strong financial statement and the ability to help with a bit higher negative cash flow. Note also, that the matter of retroactivity has not been firmly established with regard to the new bank policies. We'll have to wait and see! In summary — don't panic, but rather get your creative juices flowing.

What Kind of a "Bird" Are You in Setting Goals?

Richard J. Allen

There's one thing to be said about goals: if you don't *set* them, you don't *reach* them. It's that simple. Someone once said: "An *aim* is even more important than a *name.*" And there is a lot of truth to that. Without a specific destination in mind, there's not much point in making the trip in the first place. Goal setting is essential to success.

The Nothing Down program recommends that you express your goals in terms of the desired amount of annual cash flow that will accrue to you without working following an investment period of a specific number of years. To achieve that cash flow, you need to build towards the appropriate net worth through a consistent program of acquiring income property year by year. Refer to "Gross Equity Accumulation Schedule" in *Nothing Down* and in the goal-setting chapter of the seminar manual. The schedule tells you how much real estate you need to buy *each* year in order to achieve your net worth target in the time span of your choice. The process of setting up your goals in this way is indispensible.

What kind of a "bird" are you when it comes to goal setting? Maybe we can have a little fun with a very serious matter. There are two questions involved: How *realistic* is your goal? and how *visible* is your goal? Depending on the answers, you might be characterized as an Eagle, a Peacock, an Ostrich, or (heaven help you) a Turkey. Let me explain:

One young man I learned of recently (he happens to be the son of Bob Steele, the "grandfather" of creative financing in this country) has a goal that requires him to have bought 100 "nothing down" houses by the time he finishes his business degree in college. That is a mighty steep goal! And yet he has already acquired 25 houses with nothing down and continues to climb steadily. In his case, the goal is realistic. Not only that, it is highly *visible* — he shares it with others regularly and displays it prominently to himself on posters throughout his apartment. His goal is constantly before his mind. And there is a high probability that he will reach it.

For most of us, a goal of one, two, or at most three houses each year would be steep enough and very adequate to attain our end result over a period of five to ten years. For young Steele, however, the "slope" of his goal (25 houses a year for four years) is uniquely appropriate to his circumstances. This fact, together with the way he makes his goal highly visible, qualifies him for the Eagle Award to be explained below. Maybe you qualify, too.

The "slope" of your goal is an index of how *far* and how *fast* you intend to climb. An appropriate and steady pace toward financial independence might be illustrated like this:

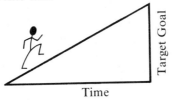

If the slope is too steep, either because the target goal is unrealistically high or because the time span is too short (or a combination of the two), we get this situation:

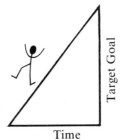

It is nice to envision having $48 million after 1½ years, for example, but not many of us can realistically hope to achieve this.

And of course, there is the other possibility, equally counter-productive, that you won't challenge yourself adequately ("By George, I'm going to double my net worth in the next 75 years!"):

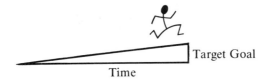

The key is that the slope must be uniquely appropriate for your situation. And the goal must also be highly *visible.* According to William James, the best way to form a good habit or achieve a worthwhile goal is to make a *public pledge.* Commit yourself publically—to your family, friends, ACRE/RAND colleagues. Let them be a part of your success. Display your goals prominently where you can see them often—on your mirror, in the refrigerator, in the bathroom, on the dashboard of the car. Invisible goals will barely even stay present in your consciousness, let alone get translated into action. Visible goals, on the other hand, will propel you to success.

Now for the fun. The following matrix relates slope and visibility in goal setting. Assuming that we can discount the shallow-goal problem (not steep enough), the four cells of the matrix show the possible combinations of four factors: appropriate slope, too steep a slope, low visibility, and high visibility. What kind of "bird" are *you?* Unless you come out as an Eagle, you might need to change your approach. If so, *do it now!* When it comes to your own financial independence, the stakes are too high to procrastinate. Happy flight!

SLOPE / Appropriate	Appropriate Slope but Low Visibility **OSTRICH** (The goal is fine, but this bird loses sight of it by keeping his head in the sand.)	Appropriate Slope, High Visibility **EAGLE** (Soars in magnificent, ever-climbing spiral.)
Too Steep	Too Steep a Slope, Low Visibility **TURKEY** (This bird loses out all the way around; good only for getting plucked.)	Too Steep a Slope, But High Visibility **PEACOCK** (All show, no go!)

VISIBILITY

The Con Artist Verses the Nothing Down Investor

Richard J. Allen

The remarkable popularity of the Nothing Down Creative Financing System is the best evidence that the program is filling a crucial need in the United States at this time. Nothing Down is becoming a watch word in investment circles everywhere. The graduates of the program are buying real estate at a rate of over $1 billion worth per year. The system really works!

But every good system has its detractors and scam imitators. As creative financing comes more and more into public view, the stories of abuse and win/lose practices on the part of scheming con artists multiply. We are concerned to note in the press occasional reports about abuses on the part of investors who—in the name of creative financing—take unsuspecting sellers to the cleaners.

A recent situation in California is a good case in point. As reported in the *Sacramento Bee* of January 18, 1981, one seller got stung by turning over his property to an unscrupulous "creative investor" who pulled money out of the deal and then walked away: "The home, priced at $50,000, had a VA loan balance of $13,000. The buyer asked the seller to obtain a $15,000 second under the guise it was to be used for remodeling the home. Out of the $15,000, however, the seller was to pay the agent's commission and closing costs, give $6,000 to the buyer for the remodeling work, and keep the rest—about $4,000—himself. At the same time, the buyer requested that the seller—for the balance of his equity—carry back a third note in the amount of $27,000, with both principal and interest due in three years.

"What happened in this case is that the buyer declined to make payment on either the VA loan or the second mortgage, and both lenders have instituted foreclosure proceedings. The buyer, of course, still has the $6,000, while the seller is now stuck with $28,000 in loans on his property—the original $13,000 mortgage plus the $15,000 second. He did come out with about $4,000 on the deal, but this 'profit' will be more than canceled out by expenses that will be incurred in the resale of his home."

The real estate industry is alarmed by such reports—and rightly so. Real estate professionals are concerned about deals where buyers pull cash out of the transaction with the intent of leaving sellers with no recourse in case of default (as in the illustration above). They also warn against transactions where properties are left over-encumbered (with mortgages totaling more than the fair market value of the property).

In another deal reported widely in the California press recently, a buyer offered $154,000 for a free and clear home in exchange for the right to put a new $108,000 first on the property ($45,000 to the seller; the rest—less commissions and closing costs—to the buyer). In addition, the seller would carry back a $100,000 second (total encumberances, therefore, of $208,000). The seller refused, fearing that the buyer would pick up nearly $60,000 cash and then walk away from the deal.

Here is our perspective on this important issue. There are now well over 50,000 graduates of the Nothing Down program—the largest and best-informed single group of people engaged in the creative acquisition of real estate in the United States. Creative finance techniques have been around long before "Nothing Down," of course, but the Robert Allen program is the only comprehensive creative acquisition program that is consciously and openly placed within the context of the win/win philosophy. In other words: the Nothing Down system itself is the best deterrent to the kind of investment practice being singled out as dangerous by the real estate industry. The best defense against abuse is a good education.

Just a few points to illustrate why:

1. No adherent of the Nothing Down program could willfully enter into a transaction with the intent of taking unfair advantage of a seller and still remain in harmony with the win/win philosophy. What we teach is this: every party to a transaction must feel satisfied that he or she has won—the seller, the buyer, the agent, the banker—everyone. While it is true that "Nothing Down" targets the flexible seller—the don't wanter—the accent is on *problem solving* and not *high pressure.* If everyone is to win, then everyone has to be clear about the risks and benefits. It must all be conservatively analyzed and carefully documented.

2. The Nothing Down system is based on trust building, and trust building is based on security. Nothing Down transactions do not mean transactions in which the seller's security is jeopardized; quite to the contrary: the Nothing Down buyer puts plenty on the line—partnership funds, equities, notes, talents, credit reputation, proceeds from second

mortgages put on other properties, etc. A Nothing Down purchase, under our definition, means 5% or less of one's *own cash* put into a deal (if this were a questionable practice, all the VA and FHA mortgages ever written are scam rip-offs).

3. A crucial point in the Nothing Down system is this: "Don't wait to buy real estate, buy real estate and wait." We are into real estate for the long haul, not the fast buck turnover. There is, of course, nothing wrong with a legitimate and responsible "turnover" transaction to generate cash. But the accent in the Nothing Down system is not on *selling* but creative acquisition and *holding* of real estate. The Nothing Down investor is a long-term investor. There is no more secure buyer for a seller to deal with.

4. The Nothing Down system *discourages* the over-encumbrance of properties. Frequently properties are offered at a price well below market. In such cases the seller would in no way jeopardize his security by carrying back paper up to the fair market value of the property. Even then, the Nothing Down system recommends in such cases a blanket mortgage arrangement (involving not only the subject property, but also equity in other properties held by the buyer). The Nothing Down buyer says, "Here is *more* collateral than the note calls for. Here's double security; give me a chance to prove myself."

5. The Nothing Down system encourages the involvement of competent professionals at all levels—Realtors, title company officers, appraisers, attorneys, accountants, exchangors, tax experts, etc. The Nothing Down system is creative and innovative, but the heart of it is conservative analysis and professional competence in documentation and follow-through. The con artist shuns professional scrutiny and moves in and out before the seller has a chance to evaluate and assess. The Nothing Down buyer says, "Here's a creative way for us both to win. Let's analyze everything carefully and make sure the documentation is perfect. Then let's proceed."

6. Finally, the Nothing Down system is designed to help the investor achieve a satisfying level of financial independence where liberating values and activities can be practiced—whether that be involvement with family, community affairs, higher education, philanthropy, creative a-chievement, etc. The con artist, on the other hand, has no such goals; he may achieve a measure of freedom in shorter order (unless he's caught) but he deceives himself if he thinks inner satisfaction will be the result.

These points can be summarized in the following chart:

The Con Artist	The Nothing Down Practitioner
1. Win/Lose Orientation	Win/Win Orientation
2. Slick Promises	Trust-Building Based on Security and Performance
3. Fast Buck Getaway	Long Range Holding of Property
4. Over-encumbered Property	Over-secured Property
5. Invisible Transactions (avoiding professional scrutiny)	Highly Visible Transactions (encouraging professional scrutiny)
6. Short-range and Self-serving Goals	Long-range and Values-oriented Goals

We urge all graduates of the Nothing Down system and their like-minded colleagues to help counteract the occasional reports of con-artist abuse of creative financing tecniques. How do you do this? Follow the win/win system. Educate your professional colleague about our Nothing Down philosophy. Go out of your way to build trust with all of your associates and potential sellers. Submit instructive letters to the editors where bad press occurs. Review your commitment to long-range goals and values. The Nothing Down graduates constitutes the greatest body of practicing experts in creative finance in the country. The greatest defense against ignorance and abuse is good education.

"Win/Win" or "Dog-Eat-Dog"?

A final word about values: In evaluation sheets submitted each week by participants in Nothing Down Seminars around the country, the two most frequently mentioned factors are (1) the excitement and confidence instilled in the students through exposure to powerful and effective creative financing techniques, and (2) the very positive reaction to the win/win framework of the Nothing Down program. These reactions are most gratifying. We are particularly pleased that so many graduates respond with favor to the idea that creative real estate investments *can* and indeed *must* be based on attitudes, values, and techniques that permit everyone to emerge from a transaction a winner and feel good about it.

Unfortunately, not all real estate spokesmen around the country agree. In a recent conversation, a well-known real estate writer from another publication disparaged the idea of win/win in real estate investments; he felt "dog-eat-dog" would be closer to the current *modus operandi.*

We don't agree. It does not *have* to be "dog-eat-dog." Marvin Stone's editorial, "Ethics—Making a Comeback?" in the *U.S. News & World Report* (December 8, 1980) is a case in point. He referred to the many thoughtful educators and policy-makers across the U.S. who are currently facilitating programs that reemphasize the development of character and concern for others.

We are convinced that the idea of win/win must underly all endeavor. The Nothing Down program will continue to do its part in contributing to the upholding of high values in business enterprise. From our perspective, it is the only way to go.

The RAND Family – Our Greatest Investment Resource

David A. McDougal

Nearly one hundred years ago, a humble Scotsman strolling near his home in Darvel rescued a boy who was dangerously mired in a bog. The lad turned out to be the son of a nobleman who wished to reward the rescuer. The Scotsman refused gratitude for himself but agreed that the nobleman might help him to educate his own son. This the nobleman did. The Scotsman's son was graduated from St. Mary's Hospital Medical School. His name was Sir Alexander Fleming, the discoverer of penicillin.

There is a sequel to this story. During World War II, when Britain faced its darkest hour, the nobleman's son was stricken with pneumonia. His life was saved because of penicillin. His name was Winston Churchill.

I like this story because it shows how dependent we are on one another and points out how unselfish service to others is often a greater blessing to us. The Scotsman had no idea there would be any reward for helping a young boy in trouble, and the nobleman had no way of knowing that the young man he would help educate would later discover the medicine that would save his own son's life. Both men did the right thing for the right reason.

Contrast this example with the following illustration.

A famous surgeon received a phone call one night from a doctor friend who said that he had a young child on the operating table and needed the surgeon's help at once in order to save the child's life. It was a long drive across town to the hospital and the surgeon drove as quickly as he could with safety. As he pulled up to a stop sign, a man wearing a brown leather jacket opened the door and slid in beside him with his hand in his pocket as though he had a gun. The man was excited, demanded the surgeon's car, and was obviously in no mood to discuss it. The surgeon stood helpless on the highway as the man in the brown leather jacket sped away with his car.

By the time the surgeon finally arrived at the hospital, it was too late. The child had died only minutes before. The other doctor asked the surgeon to come with him to meet the child's father in the hope that together they might give him words of comfort. As they entered the waiting room, the father came forward—he was the man in the brown leather jacket.

The surgeon and the father had the same goal, to see the child live. The father, unwilling to ask for help, but choosing rather to take advantage of the surgeon and steal his car, denied his child the only hope he had for life.

Our RAND groups across the country are made up of a wide variety of investors ranging from the professional who has purchased many properties over several years, to the novice investor who has yet to purchase his first real estate property. Both groups of investors have much to gain from the RAND family.

The experienced investor has the opportunity to sharpen his skills, review the basics, learn new techniques and to be exposed to many more investment opportunities and partners. He may have substantial financial resources, but not the time and energy to find properties, nor to manage them.

On the other hand, our newest and youngest investors in the RAND family may not have the experience or financial capability, but they are loaded with energy and anxious to spend the time to find good properties and become excellent property managers. It is this new group of investors that keep up the enthusiasm in the RAND group and consistently make lemonade purchases out of lemon interest rates and a lemon economy.

What a great opportuity to learn, invest, and grow exists in the mutual support groups we call RAND. The RAND group is our greatest investment resource. For every area of weakness in your own investment strategy, someone in the RAND group has the corresponding strength. For every one of your strengths, you will find a corresponding need in the RAND group that you can fulfill. The Scotsman and the nobleman both gave freely of their talents and both benefited in ways they never imagined. The man in the brown leather jacket refused to ask for help and the surgeon who was ready, willing and able to help was denied the opportunity. Which group do you fit into?

A short while ago I learned of a RAND chairman who rented a bus to take his RAND group to buy a piece of property. He was a very capable and experienced real estate investor and many in his group had never written an earnest money agreement, nor presented an offer. What a great RAND activity. All involved benefited and learned from a great RAND chairman.

A lady representing the women's group of a major religion was asked by the leader of her church to attend a certain national conference. She had attended for several consecutive years and responded that she felt it was a waste of time and she gained nothing by going. The leader smiled kindly and responded, "But don't you have anything to contribute to help their organization?" She got the message. After returning from the national meeting, she reported that she had gained much and it was the most outstanding convention they had ever held.

It is the same with our RAND group. We can only get as much out as we are willing to put in. As the popular song says, "No man is an island, no man stands alone." It takes the cooperation and support of all our members to make RAND meetings great.

I can't leave the subject of mutual help and support from one another without this final example which may indeed be the most important relationship in our investment activities.

Several months ago I received a phone call from a recent graduate. He was extremely excited about the "Nothing Down" concept and he described to me several properties he had just purchased, and two others he was anxious to acquire. It was obvious he had been very successful in his investing, had learned the techniques of creative financing, and had a bright future.

After describing all of these activities, he paused and said, "I've got one problem. What do you do if your wife won't support you in your investment pursuits?" I said that it's not uncommon for this situation to exist. Sometimes it's the wife, and sometimes it's the husband who is slow to catch on. My suggestion would be to take her to the RAND meetings, and show her what you are involved in so she understands the philosophy and how it works. Then, enroll her in the basic course the next time it's in town, so she will become a creative investor and gain the same enthusiasm for real estate that you have. He said, "It didn't work. I've tried all of that and she thinks that we can't afford the money for her to take the class." He then paused, and with a smile in his voice said, "I guess the only thing I can do is take her out in back and shoot her." I responded that we didn't recommend that solution, and that I had one more idea to try first. The phone line was silent and I knew I had his undivided attention. "The first chance you get, take your wife out for a lovely dinner and when the time is right, put your arms around her and tell her how much you love her. Then explain to her that you are investing in real estate because you know it's the best thing you can do to assure her financial security and to provide for all the wonderful things in life that you want her and your children to have and enjoy. Tell her how much you need her help and support and that you will do your very best to make good, sound, profitable investments which will protect and secure your needs and financial well-being."

Just as I finished, a woman's voice said, "That sounds great to me." The husband then apologized and explained that when he told his wife he was going to call us, she asked if she could listen in. He hoped that I didn't mind. I said it was all right, and wished them the best of success, reminding them that some of our most successful investors were husband and wife teams.

First we need the help and support of our families, then we get the enthusiasm, direction, and expertise from the RAND group, then we seek out the professionals we need—and then there is nothing we can't accomplish with the help of these people.

Questions Most Often Asked by the Public

Hollis Norton

As a real estate investor, what's going to happen to me in a recession?

You can easily protect yourself against recession by investing in real estate. The *kind* of real estate you buy is most important. The safest investment is what I call "bread and butter" real estate. This type of investment is based on what the average working man would pay for rent in any given neighborhood... or around 25-30% of the average working man's take home pay. The number of living units you buy isn't important. The rent structure is! If you own "bread and butter" rentals and times get very good, the person in the low rent building will upgrade his standard of living and move into your building. If times get very bad, the people living in the big "white elephants" (the high rent district) will feel the pinch and move down to your rental units.

This works very much like the tide coming in and out at the seashore! There is some movement in your "bread and butter" building as times change, but your occupancy rate will stay much higher than if you owned in the low-rent or high-rent districts. The tide goes in and out but you pick up the economic surge in both directions. When you buy "bread and butter" housing units you have invested in one of the two basic essentials of living—food and shelter. Since everyone has to live somewhere, no matter what happens to the economy, your investment will still be making money. People may be forced to move in hard times, but nobody is going to give up a place to live.

What kind of real estate should I buy?

Don't pay as much attention to the kind of property you buy, as to the attitude of the seller. You can make far more money buying a single-family house *right . . .* than a ten-unit apartment complex *wrong!* Whether you're calling ads in the newspaper or driving neighborhoods, look for a flexible seller. The key to making abnormally high profits in real estate is to control a piece of property with very little of your own money.

Every dollar in real estate mortgages today is a dollar in net worth in just a few short years. The day you control a million dollars in mortgage you make $100,000 a year (assuming a 10% per year increase in value) *without getting out of bed!* Real estate is an infinite source of wealth. Learn what you need to know and then *go out and get your share!*

For Sale: DuPont, for Nothing Down: The Basic Investment Strategies Are Timeless

Richard J. Allen

From time to time it would do us all some good to set aside our involvement with big and little deals and take a lesson from the pros of an earlier year. Consider the following account of the greatest nothing down deal of the century. We think it will give you some perspective on how creative finance is based on the same principles no matter how big the deal—a multi-million dollar corporation or that single family home you are thinking about acquiring.

With the death of Eugene DuPont on January 28, 1902, the great DuPont gunpowder and explosives combine, at that moment in its history in the throes of a decline, was thrust into a leadership crisis that now threatened its very existence. When the DuPont partners despaired of finding a suitable successor among their ranks, they decided to sell out to their chief competitor, Laflin and Rand Powder Company. That would have brought an end to the DuPont operation after a century of glorious development.

Then Alfred I. DuPont stepped forward, a great grandson of the founder, with the assertion that he, rather than Laflin, would buy the business. Having jumped off that little cliff, Alfred set up an alliance with two DuPont cousins, Coleman and Pierre, whose savvy and ability he needed in order to pull off the deal. Coleman was a brilliant financier and salesman who functioned at his best in a nothing down situation ("You always run out of cash before you run out of good deals.") The third cousin was a proven management expert. Together, the three cousins were to pull off the creative-finance coup of the century.

The old regime put a $12 million price tag on the DuPont holdings and gave the cousins one week to raise the money. Problem: the three could muster only $1 million among themselves. While they were mulling the solution, Alfred quickly and secretly made a determination that the $12 million evaluation was far too low, that DuPont was worth at least twice or three times that amount. That lent a sense of urgency to the project since the three now stood to make an enormous amount of money up front. They lost no time in taking action.

Coleman put his financing genius to work. He asked the DuPont partners the magical questions: (1) Did they really want the $12 million? (2) Wouldn't it be an embarrassment for them to sell out this way? (3) Wouldn't they have difficulty finding a suitable way to reinvest their funds? (4) Wouldn't they prefer to consider an alternative plan that would solve all of their problems and give them the benefits they wanted?

Coleman's plan was this: He would give them 25% interest in the new company that was to be formed, plus 4% on their $12 million over the next 30 years (minus any interest they would receive from the profits of the new company). This offer—much to Alfred's amazement and delight—was accepted. ("You never know until you ask.") Except for $2,100 in closing costs, the three cousins had acquired DuPont *for nothing down!*

But they didn't stop there. An audit of the books showed that DuPont had valuable investments in rival powder companies, even controlling interest in one, Hazard Powder, and at least a minority position in the chief DuPont rival, Laflin and Rand. Coleman once again put on his creative thinking cap and turned on his unfailing charm and salesmanship. He knew that the Laflin directors were aging and probably concerned about the formation of a new DuPont rival. Feelers were put out to Laflin, whose directors came up with the exhorbitant figure of $700 per share (a total of $6 million) to buy them out.

The deal seemed doomed. But much to Alfred's astonishment, Coleman accepted—not because he was reckless, but because he had already worked out a nothing down deal in his head. The Laflin directors could have their price if they would give him his terms. Instead of paying cash for each $700 dollar share of Laflin, Coleman gave the shareholders $400 in 5% bonds of Delaware Security Co. and $300 in 5% bonds of Delaware Investment Co. (two holding companies that he had set up overnight—backed up by the DuPont collateral—just for this very purpose.) Then Coleman added the frosting on the cake that pushed the Laflin directors over the edge—a bonus of 20% of the par value of their bonds in the stock of the two holding companies.

That did it! Laflin accepted and Alfred immediately conducted a verifying audit of their books. To his delight, he discovered that the Laflin old guard had valued their company far too conservatively. It was worth millions more than expected.

The three cousins were now masters of the U.S. powder industry, soon had 54 corporations under their control, and were in a position in May, 1903, to form the E.I. DuPont de Nemours Powder Company with an authorized capital of $50 million. By 1905 (just three years after they took over DuPont and Hazard, then bought out Laflin), the three cousins had increased DuPont's share of the U.S. powder industry from 36% to 75%. The combined DuPont assets were conservatively put at $60 million. This feat had been accomplished with a total cash outlay of $8,500, shared among three very creative cousins—the biggest nothing down deal of the century.

What can we learn from their experience? Their strategy can be summarized in a dozen creative rules that will sound a bit familiar to graduates of the Nothing Down seminar:

1. Find the right cliff and jump off.
2. Bring in partners to add the strength you need.
3. Look for deals where you can get value up front.
4. Determine the needs and disposition of the sellers.
5. Have the courage to ask the sellers the right questions.
6. Come up with alternatives and solutions that meet the needs of the sellers so that everyone wins.
7. Make the sellers an offer they cannot refuse (add bonuses if necessary in order to build trust).
8. Give the sellers their price (even more) if you get your terms, especially where there is value up front.
9. Always use leverage (The Nothing Down principle).
10. Be creative in finding alternative sources of capital (the seller, the property itself, etc.).
11. Act swiftly to close hot deals before the sellers cool off.
12. Don't stop there—move quickly to seize the next creative opportunity books used with Realtors, and 4. Realtors' referrals.

These principles are universal. They work with multi-million dollar corporations or 12-plexes or duplexes or single family houses. The important point is to put things in the right perspective—a perspective of creativity, courage, confidence, and action. Your next nothing down deal is waiting for you—right under your nose. Go get it!

[Source of information on the DuPont history: *Forbes Magazine,* March 17, 1980; based on the book by Leonard Mosley, *Blood Relations: the Rise and Fall of the duPonts of Delaware* (Atheneum)].

Questions and Answers on Real Estate Investment Strategy

Richard J. Allen

Question:

"I have $17,000 to invest in real estate. What's the best approach or techniques to use in maximizing the use of this cash in building a real estate portfolio?"

Y.T., Oklahoma City, OK

Answer:

The best approach, in our opinion, is to start with a careful examination of your goals and objectives. Read carefully the sections on goal-setting in *Nothing Down* or the *Nothing Down Seminar Manual.* Study the techniques and strategies in the article "Launching Yourself into Financial Self-Reliance" (included in this volume). Be clear on your objectives before spending a penny. Review carefully the material in the article "Specific Ways of Making Money in a Sluggish or Declining Real Estate Market" (included in this volume).

The way you invest your $17,000 will depend entirely on the personalized roadmap you chart for yourself. The person who sets out to buy one and only one single-family home a year will respond differently than the person who wants to buy ten single-family homes or many multi-units. Perhaps the only universal rule is to invest as little of your own money as possible and still come out with a tolerable cash-flow situation (no unmanageable negatives... if any... and no balloons). Is it still possible to buy this way in today's market? Absolutely! But it takes careful searching and analysis.

Question:

"If property values don't go up, how can I win by investing in real estate?"

J.P., Santa Maria, CA

Answer:

Yields on real estate investments are calculated on the basis of four factors: income (cash flow), tax benefits (because of the depreciation), equity buildup, and appreciation. For an example of how this is calculated, see the article "Your Best Partner: Uncle Sam" (included in this volume). In that illustration, the following yields (on a typical deal) were realized:

> Income . . . . 6.90% return
> Tax savings . . . . . 23.72% return
> Equity buildup . . 10.04% return
> Appreciation . . . 100.00% return
> Total . . . . 140.66% return

Even without the appreciation factor, the property used as an illustration in the article achieved a return of 40.66% based on a down payment of $10,000 for a $100,000 purchase. Of course, the smaller the down payment, the greater the yield. The yield on a nothing down deal would be infinite. (Try that next time you buy gold or silver!)

To offset the reduction in the rate of appreciation, the investor would need to look for situations where the other three factors were even more attractive. It would be critically important to have as large a positive cash flow as possible (negatives would be out of the question). The purchases would need to be made to maximize the tax advantages. Equity buildup would need to be attractive as well. For techniques designed to achieve just these kinds of accents, see "Specific Ways of Making Money in A Sluggish or Declining Real Estate Market" (included in this volume).

The oversupply of apartment units appears to be ebbing. Supply and demand will very likely produce tensions that will force rents up in general. This is good news to every investor, and particularly the investor who is concerned that appreciation may not be as dramatic in the future as in the past.

Question:

"I am 56 years old. What special investment strategies should I be using for my real estate program?"

C.G., Chicago

Answer:

At any age the strategy depends centrally on what your goal is. If you are following a 5- to 10-year retirement program involving one or two single-family homes per year, you should be able to succeed admirably and still have plenty of time to "harvest" your money crop. If you are looking for tax shelter, you may wish to increase the amount you acquire proportionate to your needs. If you are more interested in generating a cash flow from your real estate at an earlier date, you may want to be more cautious about property selection, avoid fully-leveraged deals, look for discounted opportunities, shun short-term balloons and high negatives. This advice, of course, is good for any of us, young or old! One factor that might be a function of age is the tolerance of management hassles. If management is a concern to you, then you will want to select properties in locations that will minimize the required effort and take the pressure off your heart. The alternative is to make generous use of partners—the "automatic pilot" principle that Bob Allen talks about. Look at it in a positive way: your age probably puts you in a more favorable credit situation and might give you an edge in building trust. If anyone ever raises the issue of fulfilling a contractual obligation, you could always offer to buy a life insurance policy in the name of the seller for the amount he is carrying back on the deal. It is amazing how quickly that will build trust.

PART III:

Locating Don't Wanter Properties

Putting Powerful Ideas Into Action

Robert G. Allen

"Fly me to any city in the United States. Take away my wallet. Give me a $100 dollar bill for living expenses. And I'll buy an excellent piece of real estate within 72 hours using none of my own money."

Come with me!

The airplane is about to take off. In a few hours we'll be landing in Cleveland.

Why Cleveland?

The name of the city was chosen by drawing from a list of well-known American cities . . . out of a hat at random. And we have been given a challenge:

"Buy an excellent piece of real estate (either a single family home or an apartment building) within 72 hours. The closing itself doesn't have to take place within 72 hours but the seller must agree to our terms in writing. And the terms are simple: nothing down."

But that is not all. We won't be able to use any of our own cash for down payment. And to make things interesting we won't be allowed to use any identification. No wallet. No credit cards. No Social Security number. No drivers license. No financial statement. No nothing. just you and $100 bill between us.

That leaves us with about as much as we came into this world with . . . or to be more exact, with about as much as we will leave this world with . . . the clothes on our back. But we have one great advantage. We will have the use of ideas. Very powerful ones. Creative financing techniques that work if we know what to do and say.

Are you still up for it?

The trip in the airplane will give us time to organize our thinking. As soon as we land, we will have to be off and running... with no time to waste. It helps to know exactly what our plan of attack will be. My plan of attack consists of five parts:

1. Determine what kind of seller would be willing to sell on our terms.
2. Determine which sources of information we will use to locate such an individual.
3. Determine which questions to ask the seller to determine if a nothing down offer is realistic.
4. Determine which techniques to use to close the deal.
5. Write an offer and have the seller accept it.

Before I launch into a discussion of the plan of attack, I'd better prepare you mentally for our three-day challenge. It is important to have the right attitude. I love challenges. They motivate me. Deadlines create courage. That is why the three-day deadline is important. I am no longer afraid to ask unconventional questions... or to do unconventional things. I have a goal, and I have a very short time in which to accomplish it. Therefore, I leave no stone unturned. I am more direct and to the point in dealing with sellers, Realtors and bankers. I want them to know all of the bad news up front. If a deal really is impossible, then I want to find out about it immediately. I need to talk to flexible sellers who have problems that I can solve. And there aren't too many of them. So I can't waste time with an inflexible seller.

Back to our plan of attack. Let's review the first two points.

1. **Determine what kind of seller would be willing to sell on our terms.**

The question in our minds is: "Why in the world would anyone sell his property to us if we don't have any cash or credit?" The answer to this question lies with the individual motivations of sellers. Most sellers are inflexible in the sale of their real estate. They want their price and their terms and they are willing to wait until they get it. But this is not true of all sellers. There is a small percentage of sellers who are flexible in their price and terms. They have different motivations. There are four classifications of flexible sellers (or "don't wanters", as I like to call them):

When it comes to cash down payments:

A. Some sellers don't care about cash or credit. They are too concerned about their problems at hand to worry about our strengths and weaknesses. They want out at all costs.

B. Some sellers don't *need* cash down payments.

C. Some sellers don't *want* cash.

D. Some sellers need some cash but not *all* of their equity needs to be

FINDING AND DEALING WITH DON'T WANTER SELLERS

> Use this chart to identify don't wanters, analyze their needs, and plan your negotiation strategy.

TYPES OF DON'T WANTERS	PROBLEMS OR CIRCUMSTANCES	Newspapers	MLS Book	Realtors	Courthouse	Property rental cos.	Exchangors	Drive around looking at properties	Successful investors	CLUES AND KEY WORDS TO LOOK FOR	KEY MOTIVATORS: PLACE EMPHASIS IN NEGOTIATIONS
DON'T CARE ABOUT CASH	1. Management problems.	●		●				●		mgt. problems, negative cash flow. high loan/ low equity	1. Stress quick closings so that seller can rid himself of quickly. "We could arrange to have this problem out of your hair in 24 hours."
	2. Transfer/out of state.	●		●	●	●				transfer, out of state, moving date for move is very close	2. Stress quick closings plus saving commissions if property does not sell fast. Seller won't have to leave wife and list with Realtor. He can use your note as down to buy house in new city. "You don't need any more stress at a time like this!"
	3. Behind in payments.			●	●					behind in payments, motivated seller	3. Stress credit rating and how important it is to save it. Stress ability to pay back payment shut that is all. (You can get the money from a partner later, if you're worried about the money)
	4. Fixer-upper.	●		●			●	●	●	fixer-upper. handy-man special. needs work. property not rented out because it needs work	4. Stress his problem property and how nice it will be when he has the headache out of his hair. "Life is too short to worry about this."
	5. Time problems, too busy.	●		●		●		●	●	other interests — going on long vacation, promotion to new job	5. Stress quick closings. Stress importance of time and how precious it is... how it's not worth wasting on something you can't stand.
	6. Sickness/health.	●		●						Too much for me to handle, seller in hospital, other family members handling investment	6. Stress quick closing. Stress cash flow to help with medical bills.
DON'T NEED CASH	7. Divorce.	●			●					Single owner, divorce	7. Stress starting a new life... how important it is to cut your losses and run with your winners. Stress psychological freedom that will come when this "curse" is removed from your neck.
	8. Retirees.	●		●			●			Time to relax, retirement near, needs cash flow to supplement pension	8. Stress cash flow to aid retirement and tax savings for no down payment sales. "Why pay all that money to the government when you could use it for a better retirement."
	9. Already bought new property.	●		●		●				Option to buy, buy or rent, rent to own, vacant	9. Stress how he doesn't need any cash. Your payments will coincide with his so that he is not at a disadvantage. Offer to pay the same interest rate he has on his new loan... or higher.
	10. Investor, builder.	●	●	●			●		●	Interest in % return, will consider trade. need to sell out subdivision to clear bank loans. slow moving projects	10. Stress the amount Uncle Sam will take of his profits if he gets cash. Offer to pay him more than he would earn at the highest local "paper" certificate return. Stress security. Remember "greed."
DON'T WANT CASH	11. Wealthy owners.			●			●		●	Don't need cash	11. Stress no necessity of cash. Stress profit. Stress that you are an honest, hard working individual who is trustworthy but cash poor. "How did you get your first break?" Act like a beginner, let him "counsel you." Try sympathy.
	12. Tax problems.		●	●			●			Installment sale, exchange only	12. Stress tax consequences — the best way to avoid this is to sell with little or no money down. Offer to bend over backwards to help him with his tax planning
NEED SOME CASH BUT NOT ALL	13. Flexible seller.	●	●	●						Will carry second, paper, OWC, wrap around mortgage, owner will finance, consider second, contract sale, no qualifying, low loan/high equity. seller doesn't need to have money for several months, even longer but wants to sell now, needs cash for small consumer items that could be obtained with a credit card (not ours). Debts to be paid off.	13. Stress the ability to get him the cash he needs for his minor problems but that it will be necessary to carry some paper. Stress honesty and ability to close. Credibility is all important

PROBABLE SOURCES THIS KIND DON'T WANTER

cashed out.

The chart accompanying this article describes thirteen types of don't wanters and their special circumstances, indicates clues and key words to look for in identifying them, and outlines what to emphasize in the negotiation.

2. Determine which sources of information we will use to locate such an individual.

Sources of information about flexible sellers fall into 8 categories:
1. Newspapers
2. MLS books
3. Realtors
4. Courthouse
5. Property rental companies
6. Exchangors
7. Driving around and looking at FSBO signs and run-down properties
8. Talking to successful investors

Of the above eight sources we will probably only have time to use about four—newspapers, MLS books, Realtors and exchangors. The chart indicates some of the key words and clues we should be looking for as we search through the newspaper.

That's enough theory. Let's get back to reality.

As our plane lands, we will immediately begin looking for a copy of the local newspaper. The morning copy is called the *Cleveland Plain Dealer.* It will be the most current. The evening paper is called the *Cleveland Press.* We'll also want a copy of it. There are also smaller newspapers circulated throughout the city but these are usually only available at supermarkets and drug stores. We'll make a note to pick up copies of these also.

As we wait for our luggage, we will also be looking for the airport information booth. We will need a map of the city and answers to the following quesitons:

1. Can you tell me the busiest street in town? I am looking for a major thoroughfare where the most real estate offices in the city are located. I don't want a freeway. I want a busy street.

2. Can you tell me of a modest motel along this busy street close to a large real estate office? It may take some looking in the yellow pages. Hopefully, this motel has airport pick-up. If not, either try another motel or arrange for an airport limousine service. Remember, we don't have much cash.

3. Where can I find a middle-class neighborhood of single family homes?

4. What about centers of demand, shopping centers, universities, etc?

While we are waiting for the motel pick-up we will study the city map and become familiar with the major streets. While we are driving to the motel we will pump the driver for information about the city. An experienced driver can be a goldmine of information. Where can I find a modest three-bedroom home? How much would I expect to pay for it? Do you own a home? Where? How much is it worth? If you were to buy a home today, where would you start to look? Do you happen to know of anyone who wants to sell some real estate? Do you know if they are flexible? (It doesn't hurt to start asking questions of everyone! Remember, if you want to percolate, you've got to circulate!) Do you know of a good Realtor in town who might be flexible with his or her commission? (Who knows, maybe his brother is a Realtor!) What is the real estate market like here? Have things slowed down a bit? Do you know of any subdivisions of new homes where the builder may be having trouble selling? It is amazing what you can often learn from an experienced taxi driver. Our main goal is to pinpoint don't wanters. If we find the driver's answers are leading us in the direction of don't wanters, we dig further. If not, we steer him in another direction and try to gain more information about the city. Anything we find out now will give us help later on. No chit-chat. Facts.

We will also try to notice several things as we are driving. We may even ask the driver to point out all banks, savings and loan institutions, finance companies, and real estate offices along our route. We will also impose on him to stop for a quick five-minute trip to get a copy of the "black market" newspapers that were mentioned earlier and are found in most super-markets and even in some motels. He should know the name of the local consumer "Dime" sheets. While we run into the super-market, we will get a copy of the paper and also look at the bulletin board. Someone may be advertising a house for sale that looks interesting.

Upon arriving at the motel we check in, pay in advance for two nights, and head straight for the room. Most motels will let you make unlimited local calls at no charge. Since this is important for the budget, it may pay to choose a motel that has this service. It should now be early evening (we have timed our flight to get us to Cleveland around 3 p.m. . . . most sellers won't be home from work until evening). We will set up our base of operations by taping a copy of the Cleveland map on the wall near the phone. On it we will mark the banks, real estate offices and other businesses we noticed on our way to the motel. It pays to be organized.

Now starts the search for the right don't wanters. Our sources, in descending order of priority, are: 1. Newspapers, 2. Exchangors, 3. MLS books used with Realtors, and 4. Realtors' referrals.

We'll start by looking in the most likely source—the local newspaper.

Our task will be to check the paper for the clues that most don't wanters display. (See the chart for the clues.) I have two alternatives in searching through the paper. I can circle only those ads that include the clues I am looking for, or I can call all ads without regard for the ad copy. Sooner or later I am bound to run into a flexible seller. Personally, I like to circle ads that seem flexible and eliminate the wholesale calling technique, although both are effective. By only searching through the paper for clues, I am able to tell by the volume of flexible seller ads just what kind of market I will have to be working in. If Cleveland is experiencing a seller's market, the flexible ads will be hard to find. If a buyer's market is in full swing, I won't have trouble finding a don't wanter.

To start with, I will disregard all ads paid for by real estate companies. The first 24 hours of the challenge will be spent entirely with the FSBO... the For Sale by Owner. I would rather deal directly with the seller at this point because my time is so short. Realtors and all third-party unconventional thinkers may slow down the process of negotiation. Until I am certain that a Realtor is necessary, I will try to go it alone.

Dealing with the FSBO also has other advantages. The FSBO is usually avoiding the Realtor's listing because he doesn't want to pay the commission. (FSBO should be really FSBG—For Sale by Greedy). This means he may be more amenable to profit techniques such as raise the price, lower the terms. Also, the seller will be able to tell me immediately if an offer is feasible, whereas a Realtor go-between often is a learning experience and tends to prepare us for the marketplace. It should take about one to two hours to completely scour the papers for don't wanters. We will search houses for sale, houses for lease or rent, and investment or income property. We can begin our calling around 6 p.m. when we can be assured that most folks are home.

A scouring of a representative real estate section reveals 61 don't wanter ads. There are not very many FSBO ads, which is bad in a way, but it also indicates a slow market (more people list when the selling job is very difficult). A few representative ads follow (locations and conditions have not yet been determined):

1. Builder's close-out. Lease option and land contract available. Why pay rent when you have a chance to own a brand new split or ranch? Prices starting mid 50's and up. Builder will cooperate on financing. Better hurry.

2. $2600 down. Owner wants action. Lowest 50's.

3. Lease with option to buy. Grovewood area, single—potential double. Rent goes toward down payment. May call collect.

4. 1-2 bedroom, 3-3 bedroom units, gross rent $600 mo. Needs work. Owner willing to finance. Low terms. Will carry 1st and 2nd mtg. or pledge,

in the heart of Ohio City. Owner relocating and is anxious to sell.

5. Rent-buy. Model home—builder's closeout. $4000 down/$498/mo.

6. Harbor light Condos. 3 bdrm from $58,500, builder will help finance 9½% with 2,300 down. Immediate occupancy.

7. Bay village new home 3-bedroom, 1½ baths, 2-car detached garage, basement, wooded lot, fireplace $500/mo. or option to purchase, owner financing available.

8. Harvard-Warrensville area. 3-bedroom ranch with family room, $36,900, 1½ garage, FHA appraised $1,900 down. By owner.

9. Maple Hts. Split 3 bedrooms. Owner can finance. Flexible terms.

All in all we locate:

—7 don't wanters asking for a small down payment (less than 10%)
—22 rent with option to buy
—4 will trade
—2 must sell
—7 moving, out of state or transfer
—16 sellers willing to help finance, 2nd mortgage, land contracts, etc.
—2 fixer uppers
—1 mentioned financial commitments are pressing
for a total of 61.

My only task when calling is to determine: 1. what kind of don't wanter this is (don't care, don't need, don't want, don't need all cash); 2. if he is flexible; 3. what his problem is, and 4. will one of the 50 techniques work to solve the problem without the use of cash. I will start out with the following questions.

1. "I saw your ad in the newspaper this evening. May I ask you a few questions?" (If the ad answers any of these questions below I may skip to other questions.)

2. "Why are you selling?"

3. "When do you have to close?"

4. "What are you going to do with the money from the sale?" (I may preface this question with the following statement: "I know that this may be none of my business, but it may help me to buy your property if you would be kind enough to tell me what you are planning to do with the money from the closing."

5. "If the seller doesn't mention any problems with management in the conversation, I may come right out and ask, "Are you selling because the management is too much hassle for you?"

6. "What are the current rents and deposits for each unit?" (If it is a rental unit).

7. "What is the mortgage balance?" (A high or low balance is a clue for a nothing down technique.)

8. "Are there any private lenders?" (This may help to know, but we may not have enough time to follow through with the techniques that would make a nothing down deal possible).

9. "Do you have to have all of your equity in cash? "(A nice way of asking if he or she will be flexible).

These questions are asked in a persistent and determined manner but at no time do I have to be inconsiderate. I am trying to find out which kind of don't wanter the seller is . . . but if I am too pushy I will destroy the credibility and trust which are so important to creative financing. Laugh with them. Empathize about their problems. At the right moment you could let them in on your problem. Be sensitive. Listen, but as soon as you can see that you will not be able to help them in their problem, you must move on. Perhaps as a last question you can explain the challenge to them. (Sure, why not. We have a challenge, but that does not mean that it must be kept secret. The challenge in itself could bring the seller onto your side. "Mr. Seller, I came to Cleveland with a challenge to meet . . . to buy a piece of real estate within 72 hours with nothing down. That's why I called you. Is there any way you might consider selling on such flexible terms, or do you know of anyone who might be amenable to such an offer?").

It will probably take all evening to make the calls. If a property is found that falls into the Nothing Down category we will probably prequalify the seller by asking some tougher questions to make sure that he or she is not just fishing for a buyer. If we feel that a trip to the property is warranted, we just have to call a taxi.

Here is a list of the ten most probable techniques which I have in my mind as I talk with the seller:

4. **Knowing which techniques to use. Ten most likely, quick purchase/no cash/no credit techniques** (from seminar manual).

1. The Ultimate Paper Out
5. Balloon Down
6. Raise the Price, Lower the Terms
11. Assume the Seller's Debts
19. Borrow the Realtor's Commission
20. Rents
21. Deposits
32. Second Mortgage Crank
41. Borrowed Financial Statement
42. Borrowed Cash for Down Payments

Sometimes in our calling we run into a seller who has a particular don't wanter situation but we are not certain how to proceed. It helps to talk with a seller always in terms of the benefits he is seeking through the sale of his real estate. For example, a person with management problems will probably like to hear us talk about a quick closing so he can rid himself of his problems. See the chart for key motivating factors.

If, after one full evening of calling, we are unable to locate a good don't wanter (which is unlikely judging from the ads we are finding) then we will shift into second gear. But first let's have a good night's rest.

Up early the next morning, we search the new morning paper for fresh ads and continue our calling. As soon as 9 a.m. arrives, we call up the local Board of Realtors and ask for the name and number of the president of the local exchange group. Exchange groups are found in almost every major city in the country and consist of Realtors and investment councelors who specialize in flexible sellers (even the word don't-wanter comes from exchangor vocabulary). If possible, I will obtain a current member roster, which I may have even obtained before arriving in Cleveland. My calls today will be concentrated on exchangors and other investors who may be flexible. My questions will be specific and to the point:

"Mr. Exchangor, my name is Robert G. Allen. I'm trying to find a don't wanter seller (he'll understand this) who doesn't need a cash down payment but who wants out of his property. Do you have a client who might be that flexible? Do you know of any exchangors who represent such clients? Were there any similar properties mentioned at your last exchange meeting? (If possible, I might even try to arrange my trip to Cleveland to coincide with the exchange meeting... usually once a month... so I could ask the president to let me attend as his guest. This, of course, would be the best situation of all!) Do you or your colleagues have any properties or know of any that would be willing to sell for a high price and flexible terms?"

Exchangors are very good sources of nothing down deals because they understand "benefits" and try to counsel their clients that cash is not always important or necessary. Their pre-counseled clients are usually more flexible than normal conventional thinkers.

If I have no luck with the exchange route, I will begin to concentrate on the MLS book. We can walk to the closest large real estate office and ask any Realtor to let us examine a copy of the MLS book under his or her guidance. The clues we are looking for are simple and easy to spot:

1. Free and clear properties or ones with low mortgages
2. Seller indicates in listing that he will carry a 2nd mortgage or contract.

I can usually find 3-5 properties in any MLS book which have both of these clues together on the same listing. This obviously means Nothing Down to a creative thinker. (See technique #32 in the Seminar Manual or the technique entitled "Second Mortgage Crank", p. 148 of RGA's book *Nothing Down.*) To help with obtaining a new loan I could have a Realtor help qualify for me or have the seller refinance his own property. I don't need credit or cash with this technique . . . just guts.

As a last resort, although I'm sure I wouldn't need it, I would call all real estate offices in town and ask to talk to all agents and ask them if they have don't wanter clients or if they own property themselves that they would sell with nothing down. Someone has to know at least one desperate seller. And of course, I will also have to ask the Realtor to carry the commission instead of cash . . . some will, some won't.

5. Getting the seller's name on the dotted line.

Once a serious flexible seller is located, either through the paper, an exchange group, the MLS book, or Realtors, I will proceed immediately to get the seller's name on the dotted line. This whole process, in one case, took me less than 20 hours.

The most important asset any investor can bring to a nothing down/no credit situation is the knowledge that it can be done . . . and it is being done hundreds of times each day all over this great country by fearless investors who refuse to be bogged down by conventional thinking. Try the 72-hour challenge some time! It'll be a lot of fun and a great learning experience.

Plugging Into the Sources for Wealth: New Ways to Find Don't Wanters

Robert G. Allen

Our surveys of recent graduates shows that, on the average, a real estate investor has to make about six offers before buying a property... and about eleven offers in order to buy a "nothing down" property. When I examine this information as related to my own investment experience of last month, I have come up with the following conclusion:

"I didn't buy any property last month because I didn't make any offers."

If you had similar results, maybe it is caused by the same problem. The basic problem that the real estate investor has is to manage the "interface" between himself and the real estate marketplace. Hollis Norton, our incomparable preview lecturer, puts it in more simple terms. "Becoming wealthy," he states, "is just learning how to plug into the source of all wealth. How much do you think the real estate within a ten- mile radius of where you are standing will go up in value in the next five years? $5 billion? Ten, Twenty? If you don't own any of it, it won't be my fault!"

Your problem is to figure out a way to *plug into that source!* Each of us has different methods for plugging in. Basically, there are two ways to interface, or plug into the market. We can go directly to the source, which is talking directly to sellers about selling their property... or we can go indirectly to this marketplace which is normally represented by real estate agents. In this article, I would like to spend some time exploring a new and direct way of finding those don't wanters . . . the source of the best real estate deals.

Once again, the basic problem is to find sellers willing to sell on good terms, hopefully nothing down. We are constantly reminded by those more conventional thinkers in our midst that *don't wanters do not exist.* I think the problem is slightly different. Don't wanters don't exist in the minds of many people because they never bothered to look. Or they did not have the stamina to continue looking, and making at least 11 offers, in order to find one.

Recently, my own buying program, in order to keep up with my need for tax shelter, I decided to try a new approach to finding don't wanters. In the Nothing Down Seminar manual, I explain that the newspaper is not only the cheapest tool in finding don't wanter ads but it is also used effectively in attracting don't wanters through *your own form* of advertising. Most major newspapers have a *Real Estate Wanted* column which dispalys ads from local investors. The typical ads reads something like this:

Have cash. Will buy property fast. Call United Investors Exchange.

Normally, there are many such ads competing for the same don't wanters. And what is it they are looking for? They are trying to attract the desperate seller who is willing to take a 20-30% discount in his equity for the luxury of immediate cash. This is a very successful investment strategy for the cash-logged investor (as is evidenced by the number of this type of ads running constantly . . . if only one deal is closed every six months under *such terms it can more than pay for the ad costs). But this strategy only reaches what I call the Wholesale Don't Wanter* . . . a seller willing to discount equity for cash. In reality, this type of don't wanter represents only a small segment of the flexible seller universe. There are far more sellers who will sacrifice the luxury of cash for the promise of a *Full Price Offer.* This is what I call the *Retail Don't Wanter* . . . who is interested in getting out from under a tight negative cash flow problem or management situation but who doesn't necessarily want to lose money doing it. How do you advertise to attract such individuals?

I originally ran an ad several years ago which read something like this:

I buy real estate from distressed sellers. Will give you a high price if you are willing to sell on easy terms. Can close in 48 hours. No closing costs. Bob 555-1234.

I received several good calls but did not continue my program because I was having so much success with other methods. Then, this spring I heard about one of our RAND chairmen who had adapted this approach to his own style. His ad read something like this:

FULL PRICE

I will pay you full price for your property if you are willing to sell on flexible terms. Call J.B. 555-1234.

His approach was to attract prospective don't wanters and to *qualify them* on the phone. Then, if all seemed well, he set up an appointment with them in *his office* to discuss a sale. If that went well, he made an offer to purchase their property on the spot with a *subject-to-inspection clause* in the earnest money contract. He purchased as many as 20 homes this way (at last count) and those he could not handle he would sell at a slightly higher price to investors . . . in order to keep his cash flow going.

This is extremely innovative and gutsy . . . so I decided that if he could learn a trick or two from me, I could learn from him also. I began a similar program in my small city with an ad that reads as follows:

FULL PRICE
I will buy your property at full price if you are willing to sell on flexible terms (little or no money down). Call S.M. 555-1234.

(I added "little or no money down" so that the reader of the ad would understand what "flexible" means.) Such ads are not expensive in small local newspapers, although they may cost an arm and a leg in some of the major newspapers. But what counts is the results. It is not unusual to recieve a call or two a day, and sometimes as many as five calls a day. This indicated to me that there must be a real backlog of don't wanters out there if we can run a small ad in a very unknown column in the paper and still receive calls.

The basic response to any caller is that I will have to run an analysis on his property to see if it qualifies for my investment portfolio. The sellers are told up front that my definition of "full price" is a bonafide appraisal by an FHA appraiser. They can choose the appraiser and I will pay for it whether I decide to buy the property or not. I ask the seller information about the property which will give me a score using the *Point System for Nothing Down Property Selection* (included elsewhere in this volume).

Most properties offered through this method are higher-priced homes which I reject due to the problem of potential negative cash flows. This exercise has given me a different perspective on the reasons why people become don't wanters. I think I can say with this limited exposure that the reason most people give for their flexibility over the telephone is: Balloon payments due within one year. Negative cash flows created by high-interest second mortgages.

This might give you a warning about your own investing. . . I surely don't want you to become don't wanters because of imprudent analysis or hasty decision making.

I am still learning from this new source of don't wanters and will be fine-tuning this approach as the months go by, but I think that it holds some promise. People seem to respond to our legitimate ad because they see how *they can win* in the long run without having to lose face now. Don't wait to buy real estate. Buy real estate and wait!

Key to Success: Finding the Don't Wanter Seller

Richard J. Allen

The heart of the Robert Allen Nothing Down System (RAND, for short) is the art and science of locating the flexible seller or "don't wanter"—the person willing to sell using creative techniques. We call this finding process an *art* because it frequently depends on "feeling out" the leads and reading the ads "intuitively" between the lines. The process is a *science* because it depends on the recognition of specific, predictable clues that the investor comes to look for in familiar patterns of phraseology and frequency. The skillful RAND investor can scan the ads quickly and decide on the half-dozen most likely candidates for the next stages of the system—fact-finding, analysis, and negotiation.

How Does the Expert Read the Ads?

The editorial board of the *Nothing Down Advisor*—Robert Allen, Richard Allen, and David McDougal—took off for the hills one day to spend a few hours reviewing the whole process analytically from the viewpoint of someone trying to master the skill of ad-scanning. Together with researcher Paul Mero, they mapped out a system of ad categories based on the nature and frequency of specific clues as well as the likelihood of the ads paying off. Then, using an extensive sampling of major newspapers, they tested the frequency of ads by category in order to set up a predictability scale (see charts for the results).

The system of ad categories is summarized in the adjacent boxes. Categories I through IV apply to the newspaper classification "homes for sale," "condos for sale," and "investment properties (income properties)." Category V applies only to "homes for rent" and "condos for rent." Here are the details:

CATEGORY I is the most desirable type of ad—an obvious don't wanter

HOW TO READ THE ADS

CATEGORY I: BLATANT DON'T WANTER	CATEGORY II: PROBABLE DON'T WANTER	CATEGORY III: OPEN TO CREATIVE FINANCE
NO DOWN, assume 12½% on $67,000 home, 1¾ baths, 2-car garage. 3 bedrooms, newly re-modeled. 968-0337	KEARNS. $3,000 down, con-tract. 3 bdrm., 1½ bath, family room, frplc., fruit trees, fenced yd. $58,000. 463 PI. 466-0191.	BY OWNER: 3 bdrms; 1¾ baths, firepls; garage. Southeast loc. Contract $65,000. 261-4069.
BY OWNER. Several choice 2 and 3 bdrm. homes with exist-ing low interest assumable loan. Priced from $49,800 to $61,800. Will sell on R.E. contract.5% down, monthly payments from $450-$650 per month. Buy out owner's equity in 2 or 3 yrs. and assume low interest 1st mort-gage loan. Call for details and appt. 539-1506.	$5,000 TO ASSUME. $59,500. Gorgeous West Valley, 4 bdrm., split entry home. Fireplc., large, fully fenced and landscaped rear yard. $685 mo. on low in-terest loans. Owner-agent, 268-4027.	FOR SALE BY OWNER, will carry back paper, 966-5926.

CATEGORY V: LEASE OPTIONS

LEASE-OPTION. Convenient Sandy home, 3 bdrms., beautiful landscaping. $550. 572-2314.

CATEGORY IV: ANXIOUS TO SELL

OWNER DESPERATE. Has reduced price on his one bed-room condo from $34,500 to $30,900. Fireplace, pool, sauna. Eves 582-5603.

FORECLOSURE, by owner. Great buy. 969-2680.

with a *blatant* clue such as "nothing down," "no money down," or "no down" *OR* a *combination* of three or more good don't wanter clues ("low down," "anxious," "contract," "easy assumption," "flexible terms," "owner will carry," etc.). The down payment range for Category 1 is zero to 5%.

CATEGORY II is next in line, with two or three good clues, but less obviously flexible than Category I; more information is needed to verify the don't wanter status of the seller. Between 5% and 10% down fits here, together with the flexible "fixer upper" ad or the "anything goes" ad ("work for down," "services for down," etc.). "Owner-agent" ads that don't otherwise fit into the higher category also fit here since we suspect the agent might be flexible with his or her commission.

Categories III and IV are the least desirable, but still of interest.

CATEGORY III has only *one* clue, i.e. a clue that indicates a seller is probably amenable to creative finance (e.g. "owner will carry," "contract," "trade," "exchange," "creative terms," etc.). **CATEGORY IV** also contains only *one* clue, i.e. the fact that the seller is under *pressure* to sell (e.g. "transferred," "divorced," "anxious," "desperate," "distress sale," "foreclosure," "kick me I'm down," etc.). Such persons will probably be flexible, but we won't know for sure until we call.

The special **CATEGORY V** refers to homes or condos for rent and picks up on only one type of clue, i.e., "rent to buy," "rent to own," "lease option," or simply "option." Such a clue says dramatically, "I don't *need* any money down." Whether the owner will actually be willing to *sell* for nothing down is a matter for negotiation. But we know for sure that if he is willing to rent, he doesn't actually *need* the money in the event of a sale.

There are other special kinds of ads that will attract the attention of the investor who wants to generate cash or "contract income" by buying and selling a property quickly. More on this in another article.

With a little experience, you will be able to separate out the promising ads from those that consist mainly of real estate puffery. Reading about a home with gold-plated escutcheons or rare hybrid Jacaranda trees is interesting—but not usually productive for finding don't wanters. The true don't wanter will leave behind clues that say, *"I want out! Get me off the hook! Come and solve my problem!"* Frequently the little two-line ad is a better bet than the fancy two-incher. Watch out, too, for the tempting new home listing marked "nothing down" or "low down." More often than not such ads seek people who will be asked to qualify for low down FHA or VA financing and occupy the home.

Ad scanning can be fun if you have a serious purpose in mind—to find the responsive don't wanter who can help you achieve financial independence. What to *do* with a don't wanter after you find him is the subject for a future discussion. Happy detective work and let us know of ways to refine and improve our ad categories.

Don't Overlook the Smaller Cities and Towns

Richard J. Allen

Probably the most vital issue that faces the real estate investor—along with finding opportunities for creative financing—is the question of where to buy—location, location, location. The Nothing Down program encourages its graduates to buy solid "bread and butter" properties in neighborhoods that show promise of continual stability and growth. The idea is to keep the law of supply and demand working in your favor. There are many well-known factors that relate to housing demand: the acute national housing shortage, the upsurge in fuel costs which tends to discourage flight to the suburbs, the long-range growth patterns in various parts of the country. Now let's enlarge our perspective and consider yet another significant factor related to demand and the question of where to buy.

In his book, *Human Scale* (New York, 1980), Kirkpatrick Sale makes a strong case for the need to restore a "human dimension" in our political, economic, and social spheres—to redress the ills that beset us as a result of runaway "bigness" in all sectors of life. We suggest that you have a look at his chapter "The Optimum City" (pp. 192-208). Here are a few insights from those pages that might stimulate your thinking in regard to where to buy income property.

1. Great minds and planners from all cultures and epochs—everyone from Plato to Leonardo da Vinci to Rousseau and modern New Town planners in virtually all countries—are surprisingly in agreement that the optimum city size is around 50,000 to 100,000 people. When cities get much bigger than that—let's say above 150,000 to 200,000 and beyond into the metropolis range of millions—personal, social, and economic dislocations are more likely to abound and the qualities of civility decline.

2. The traditional doctrine that bigger cities are more "efficient engines of production" is being challenged in several crucial respects. For a variety

of reasons—congestion, the demand for shorter working hours, pollution, high energy costs in dense city centers, security problems, crime, higher land costs, higher taxes, etc.—big cities are becoming disadvantageous for business and production. Manufacturing is no longer monopolized by bigger cities because larger businesses, particularly since the 1950's, have been moving to smaller cities where costs are lower and residential areas more desirable for both workers and executives. Contrary to the prevailing theory, smaller cities, rather than bigger cities, are chalking up better scores in the areas of economic stability and efficiency in supplying municipal services.

3. According to polls taken over the last 25 years, people have consistently expressed a preference for small towns and cities over big ones. Only a handful like big city living; two-thirds of the people, if given the chance, would move to communities in the 10,000 to 100,000 range.

4. In recent years, many big cities have been losing population at an accelerated rate, while smaller cities and modest-sized urban areas have been gaining rapidly. The greatest losses have been occurring in cities over one million (and also in rural areas). The greatest gains have been in the range 10,000 to 100,000, especially 25,000 to 50,000.

5. Not only are people following jobs to the smaller cities, but jobs are following people there, too. Many younger, better-educated, more affluent people are first heading to the smaller cities and then seeking jobs there, thus creating a demand for jobs. Small city growth is therefore a result of both factors.

What are we to conclude from these observations? Since the long-range trend of the future seems clearly to favor the smaller city, followers of the Nothing Down program would do well to remain alert to the following possibilities:

1. Consider properties in smaller cities within a reasonable commuting distance from where you are living, especially in growth areas where demand will be high.

2. Smaller cities may well remain longer immune to rent control problems.

3. Smaller cities may well involve lower maintenance and utility costs as well as less vandalism.

4. Smaller cities may offer lower price levels needed to combat negative cash flows.

5. By looking in flourishing smaller cities nearby, you may be able to take advantage of accelerating appreciation trends.

This is not to say that splendid opportunities will not continue to attract the creative investor in larger cities. Such opportunities can and are being found every day by Nothing Down graduates and their like-minded colleagues in the biggest cities of America. We are only suggesting that we put things in perspective for the next five to ten years of investing and keep in mind the future needs and demands of tenants. It is demand, after all, that will dictate the optimum places to buy in the coming years.

"But Can You Buy Real Estate for Nothing Down in Syracuse?"

David A. McDougal

Last week, I received a telephone call from a newspaper reporter in Syracuse, New York. Our "Nothing Down" seminar had been in town that past weekend, and he was doing a follow-up story. His first question was, "Can you buy real estate for nothing down in Syracuse?" I said, "Of course you can." I then related briefly Bob's experience with the *Los Angeles Times* challenge in San Francisco, one of the toughest markets in the entire country, and of his incredible success. The reporter then said, "I read the newspaper article and know it works in San Francisco, but can you buy real estate for nothing down in Syracuse?" He was paying for the telephone call and seemed anxious to learn, so I spent the next 30 minutes explaining why I knew you could buy property for nothing down in Syracuse. I'm confident the modest group of Nothing Down seminar graduates we have in Syracuse will prove to everyone, including our newspaper reporter, that you can buy real estate there for nothing down.

It appears to be a law of nature that whatever the rule, we believe we are the only exception. People believe the world is round with the exception of the tiny place where they live and that part of the world is flat. If that line of reasoning were followed and everyone in the world looked out their tiny window, the entire world would appear to be flat. The problem is not with the earth, but with the limited vision and perspective of the viewer. Columbus envisioned a round earth long before the astronauts ever took a picture of it. The laws of aerodynamics existed long before the Wright Brothers ever flew, but it took the Wright Brothers to make man's travel in air a reality. People believed for a long time that it was impossible for a man to run a mile in less than four minutes. Then Roger Bannister broke the four-minute mile. Since then many have run the mile in less than four minutes and the world's record is broken on a regular basis.

The difference between the Wright Brothers and their contemporaries is they believed man could fly, they were willing to spend the time, work and energy necessary to develop the airplane, then they flew. Roger Bannister believed he could run a mile in less than four minutes. He was willing to spend the time and do the work necessary to succeed. It is no different with the Nothing Down principles of creative financing. Just because people believe you can't buy property for nothing down does not make it so.

Robert G. Allen believed you could buy real estate for nothing down in any city in the United States. He was so confident that the principles of creative financing were universal and could be applied anywhere in the country that he was willing to accept a challenge from the *Los Angeles Times* to prove his point in a city of their choosing. The seven properties he purchased in less than 56 hours in San Francisco are now history. The point is that Bob did something that had not been done before. There were those who believed that it couldn't be done, but Bob believed it could be done; and he did it. Now many others are following.

To the newspaper reporter in Syracuse, I say, "Your question to us concerning nothing down financing is like saying to the Wright Brothers, 'I know you can fly an airplane in Kitty Hawk, but can you fly in Syracuse?' "

One of my favorite nothing down success stories is about a young boy who in the late 1800's immigrated from Italy to the United States. He soon began peddling fruits to earn a living and later got a job as a hod carrier for brick masons because the money was better. He lived on practically nothing and saved everything he had. His name was Giovanni Deferrari. With no formal education but a great desire to succeed, this young man began investing in real estate. He bought or negotiated for small pieces of property wherever he could and when the time was right, sold wisely or traded up into larger pieces. He had the rare ability to be able to select property that invariably increased many times in value over a short period. Soon he was known throughout the Boston real estate establishment. He was a young man in his early thirties when he retired from full-time work and became totally independent. He rented a small apartment suite in the nicest part of town and lived very simply. He had no radio or T.V., owned no car and prepared his own meals. Once every month, Giovanni left his apartment on foot to visit the offices of many of the most important properties in the city to collect his rents. When he died in May of 1950, he left a small trust for his sister and all the rest of his money to unnamed charities. After his death, it was discovered that he had once given $1 million to the Boston Public Library. Giovanni was a man who believed you could start with nothing and succeed. One author put it this way: "Whatever the mind of man can conceive and believe, he can achieve."

Anxious Property Sellers Calling Buyers: Is Anybody Listening?

David A. McDougal

During the Depression millions of people were without work in the United States. Fathers were willing to try almost any type of honest work in order to earn a few dollars to provide food and shelter for their families.

One morning an ad appeared in the newspaper of a small midwestern town advertising an opening for a telegraph operator. All applicants were to apply in person at the telegraph office the following morning at a.m. When the doors opened at a.m., several men were already waiting for the interview to be held one hour later. By 8:30, the entire waiting room had been filled and men were lining up outside the building.

At approximately three minutes to nine, a gentleman from the very back of the room, one of the later ones to arrive, arose from his seat, walked toward the manager's door, and, without hesitating, walked in and shut the door.

Several minutes later the manager of the office came out with the gentleman who had just entered and announced that it was no longer necessary for the men in the lobby to wait any longer, for the position had been filled. Several men jumped to their feet and complained that they had not had an opportunity to apply for the job and had arrived considerably earlier than the man who had just been hired. They felt they had been dealt with unjustly and that it was not right that this man should have the job.

The manager stepped forward and said, "All of you had an equal opportunity for this job. At three minutes to nine I took my pencil and tapped out in Morse Code on my desk, 'If anyone waiting in the lobby can hear this message, come immediately into my office and the job is yours.' Only one individual answered that signal and I have hired him."

We don't know a great deal about the other men who showed up at the telegraph office looking for work that morning. I would imagine that several of them didn't even know Morse Code and came unprepared— hoping that through some miracle they might be able to learn the signals through on-the-job training. There were probably many there very proficient in Morse Code, some with years of experience and training behind them. They may have even been more skilled than the individual who obtained the job, but they weren't listening when the message came. If they were listening, they didn't act. That made all the difference.

We may observe several things about the individual who was hired for the job. First of all, he was technically capable; he came prepared. He knew Morse Code and was able to decipher the message. Second, when all others in the room were visiting and not tending to business, this man heard the signal above all other conversation and commotion in the room. He was alert and recognized the message. He was listening. Third, after hearing the signal, he acted; he did not wait; he didn't hesitate; he got up and quickly walked through the door.

Today, real estate is recognized for what it is—one of the greatest investment opportunities in all of America. The waiting room is filled with would-be investors anxious to purchase good pieces of income property. There are many people out there seeking the same nothing down deals which we describe. There are those professionals with more experience and perhaps more technical skills than we have. But all too often they are not motivated. They are not the ones listening. They are not the ones to respond when the message is sent.

Great real estate deals are not offered; they are made. We have all heard of deals that looked so good after they were done that everybody says, "I wish I could have found a deal that good. I would have bought it! I would have invested! I would have loved that deal!" But the deals don't look that good in the newspaper. They didn't look that good when the offer was first made through the multiple listing service. Someone recognized the need. Someone knew how to put it together. Someone knew how to make a good investment. Someone recognized the potential and realized the reward.

To the trained nothing down investor there are many great investments surrounding him. The possibilities are endless. The contract instrument allows infinite considerations in putting together a real estate investment. If we lack the technical expertise other investors have, we may compensate by seeking good, professional, competent advice and in working harder and putting forth a more consistent effort than those who have been lulled to sleep.

Compensating for our weaknesses is only a short-term solution. The long-term solution is to become proficient in every area of investing. We need to become experts in real estate tax. We need to learn all of the ins and outs of rental management. We must learn to negotiate our own packages, meeting our needs and the needs of the seller. We must learn how to write our own contracts and how to document our offers and learn to understand all of the aspects of paper financing. We ought to become knowledgable in the use of options, know how to take advantages of exchanges, and learn how to develop strong partnerships, even syndication capabilities should we decide to stretch our wings in that direction.

Is anybody listening? Can you hear the signals being sent out by anxious sellers all across America? By don't wanters looking for someone to buy their property? Like the man in the telegraph office, can you hear the quiet signals being sent out while all about you are missing the opportunity? It's been said that opportunities are never missed. Someone always takes advantage of them; if not you, someone else. The best real estate packages are not offered, they are made. They are created by individuals who know how to negotiate, who know how to finance, who know how to manage, who know how to solve individual needs and problems and who are listening. Can you hear the signals in your neighborhood? Are you listening?

What Else?

Jeff Horvitz

Recently, I had the pleasure of meeting with Bob and Richard Allen at their office in Provo, Utah, which I must say was a very exciting thing for me. I took it upon myself to fly to Salt Lake City from San Diego, California, and then to drive to Provo to visit the Allens. They were most surprised at why I would do this, but I felt it was the least I could do. Since attending the *Nothing Down* seminar in San Diego, I have acquired over $1 million in real estate and have a good deal more in escrow at the current time. Before attending the course, I owned about $1 million in property but I had not acquired anything for quite some time, over a year, in fact. The nothing down techniques that I had used myself had slipped away and I was becoming a doomsdayer like everyone else around me. "You can't buy break-even properties," "The appreciation has stopped," "The real estate crash is coming," were among the ideas I was hearing passed around both in and out of the real estate industry. A bunch of negative thinkers. Here were people who should know better, sitting around *waiting* for things to happen, for things to get better.

Well, I found out that you don't *wait* for things to get better, you go out and *make them better*. It wasn't until I took Bob Allen's seminar that this idea sunk into my head. I hate to sound foolish, but I felt a certain rebirth, a rekindling of some kind and I've been in high gear ever since. Setting down those goals, jumping in the water at the shallow end and getting wet, and having fun at what you're doing—this is what has paid off for me. It's simply a matter of *doing* what you *wish* you would do. With myself, I had been thinking for months about how I would like to acquire more property in order to build my estate faster so I might reach financial independence at the early age that I had hoped (I'm 29 now). I was like everybody else, sitting around thinking and not *doing*. Bob's course made me *do*.

Everything he talks about regarding don't wanters, flexible sellers, searching for good properties . . . is all true. But you will never know the delight and excitement of finding out it's true unless you push yourself out into the flow. I find good deals dropping into my lap because I just plug away. If a deal is going the wrong way, or it looks as if my offer is not going to work, I ask myself, "What else?" What else can I offer this seller? What else can he offer me? Maybe he has other property that can help solve his problem. Maybe I have other property which can help the deal out.

People would be surpised at the flexibility of sellers (they *are* people, you know—we'll all be sellers someday) if they would only sit down with that seller and find out what else can be done to close a transaction. I've found that when a property looks promising, there is always a way to put together the transaction if you try hard enough. The worst thing you can do is look at a real estate offer as a cut-and-dried situation. When you hear, "No," don't walk away. Look things over and find out the alternatives. Too many people I know will inquire about a property, they will hear the terms that the seller wants, and they will make a pre-conceived judgment that there's no way they can buy the property. This is the *wrong* approach! If there's good potential in the property and you can get on good personal terms with the seller, work it out. Explore all the avenues. I do this all the time and I am amazed not only with what I come up with, but sometimes the seller will offer things I never would have dreamed of. I've found that a real estate purchase is a fantastic encounter, a very creative experience, or it should be.

My best example of using this "What else?" approach has to be when I bought my first income property a few years ago. Three houses on one lot were for-sale-by-owner, as a sign indicated on the front lawn. They were located about a mile from my office and I thought it was a very good rental area. (I had just gotten my real estate licence eight months previous.) I called the owner and found out the price was $55,000 and he owed about $18,000 on a first trust deed. My dad told me to offer $1,000 (that's all I had) down and with my blinders on, I promptly told my father that he must be crazy. After arguing for a while, I wrote the offer full price for $1,000 down. I was nervous as I drove down to see the owner at another of his rentals. I was young-looking (23) and had about half a beard growing in on my face. I introduced myself and after a few minutes, he asked about my offer. I mentioned the $1,000 down and he said there was no way possible that he could sell that property to me for $1,000 down. He almost laughed me out of the place. I guess most people would have politely thanked him and moved on to the next property. However, I politely asked him, "Why?" What else would he need from me so we could close the deal? After about three hours, he accepted my offer of $1,000 down (taking additional security on a small condo I owned) and he also paid off the $18,000 existing first trust deed and carried the whole purchase price trust deed himself at 9% for eight years. I couldn't believe it.

I guess what it boils down to is this: in order to be creative, to use the techniques that Bob Allen has set down in his book, one has to really open himself up. Being out front, honest, and most of all persistent is what has really paid off for me in real estate acquisition, especially the last three months. I've had sellers give me dirty looks right from the start and let me know right off that they don't want to deal with me. I've ended up best of friends with the same sellers. I let them know who I am, they let me know who they are, and it always seems we get a lot more accomplished. All it takes is a positive attitude, an eagerness to close a deal, an excitedness about what you are doing, and *action* (you can't see results until you resolve yourself to the latter) and it just happens, you start to acquire real estate. Once again, I have to thank Bob for putting *me* into action. When you get out there and make things happen, it sure is fun to watch the results.

PART IV:

Analysis and Property Selection

Taking the Guesswork Out of Property Selection

Robert G. Allen

You may have heard of the "Greater Fool Theory." Let me assure you, the theory is in for hard times. The greater fool theory is simple. It assumes that real estate prices will go up, across the board, indefinitely... therefore, buy anything you can get your hands on, at any price. It assumes that you can never get burned because some fool, greater than you, will come along sooner or later to bail you out... at a higher price, of course. In my mind, the greater fool theory is pure speculation. It is risky and it is foolish. And in recent times, speculators have been learning that the greater fool theory has some major flaws in it. Since prices in most cities have not been rising as usual, a few speculators have been left holding a turkey or two with a balloon payment to make.

This doesn't mean ,of course, that real estate is dead or that the gloom and doomers and crash predicters are right... but, simply that in times of uncertainty, investors have to resist the temptation to speculate. Uncertainty creates opportunity, but you have to watch out for the pitfalls as well. Before you go out to sign your name to the wrong dotted line, let me give you three guidelines to help you become a Master Investor instead of a Greater Fool Speculator.

Point Number One: (which I have borrowed from a book entitled *Basic Steps of Using Private Money Financing* by Carlos Royal and Max Hollis) is just this, in a nut shell: *Don't use a creative financing to make a bad deal good. Only use it to make a good deal better!* This requires that you know what a good or bad deal is. Whenever I analyze the mistakes of real estate investors, I find a common tendency... a tendency to rush in where fools fear to tread, to use all of the fancy creative techniques to buy a bad deal with nothing down. Hurray! You just bought a piece of property you had no business buying, you answered the prayers of some don't wanter, and you perpetuated, at least for another day, the thought that the greater fool theory is alive and well. Finding a good deal is a process of sticking to the basics like Jack Nicklaus sticks to the basics of a good golf stroke. This brings us to our next point:

Point Number Two: *Establish some basic guidelines to use in the selection of property which you can use in your negotiation with the seller . . . to protect yourself against your over-optimistic attitude.* I have struggled with this principle in my own consulting. At least three times a week someone calls and wants to know if they should or shouldn't buy a particular piece of property. After going through all of the normal questions I have to come up with a "gut-feel"—yes or no. Sometimes it's not all that easy to accept or reject a piece of property on a pure gut feeling.

To help me in consultation and in my own investing I have developed a point system for analyzing any property. As you can see on the accompanying chart, the major decision factors in property selection are the five areas of property analysis taught in the basic Nothing Down seminar. Briefly, I judge each factor with a point system that gives one point for a poor rating, 2 for an average rating, and 3 for an excellent rating. For example, if a seller is not a don't wanter and is not motivated or flexible, I assign a point value of one. If the location is excellent I assign this a point value of 3 and so on. In a toss-up between poor and average or average and excellent, always choose the lower rating.

By adding up the total, you arrive at a Property Score. Any property with a score of #9 or more is acceptable. Less than nine is unacceptable. If you are buying a *lot* of properties with a point total of 9, 10, or 11, you are living the greater fool theory. You are speculating and not investing. The accompanying chart gives instructions as to how to judge whether or not a property is poor, average, or excellent. I also have given you my personal Ten Commandments of Property Selection, mostly made up of "Thou shalt not's." You may disagree with my way of looking at a property, but you should not be guilty of *not* coming up with your own system to meet your own investment goals. You will find that it takes away an enormous part of the guesswork, and gives you the courage to say "No" to an insistent Realtor or seller who doesn't understand your way of analyzing property. And it goes without saying that you shouldn't use this system to give you excuses not to buy . . . it should only give you more incentive to look harder for better deals.

Let's analyze a couple of properties to see how it might work in real life. At a recent seminar, a graduate came up to me to discuss a property that he had just located through a Realtor. He was excited and wanted to know what to do. Let's go through the question process point by point together

·PROPERTY SELECTION GRID·

	POOR	AVERAGE	EXCELLENT
1 SELLERS MOTIVATION AND FLEXIBILITY	**① POINT** Won't budge on price or terms. "Take it or leave it." Doesn't need to sell. Not anxious at all. In the driver's seat.	**② POINTS** Might consider a small discount in price. Needs cash for new house or property. Needs cash for bills, etc. May carry small second or contract but leery of unusual deals.	**③ POINTS** Needs cash for pressing items, i.e. behind in payments, etc. Or, doesn't need cash at all . . . has tax, management, transfer, time problems, or divorce, retiree, or investor looking for a solution without major need for cash. Flexible in price or terms.
2 LOCATION	**⓪ NEVER** No pride of ownership. Junk and debris in streets. High crime. No appealing shopping close by. Declining neighborhoods. Abandoned buildings and boarded up properties. Close to major streets, industrial areas, or commercial zones (across the street). Far from employment centers or commuter accessibility.	**② POINTS** May be clean older neighborhoods. Close to shopping, churches, schools, etc. but not very appealing. Working class tenants, neat, established. May be poor location on the upswing with pioneer fixer-uppers. Nicer inner-city neighborhoods.	**③ POINTS** Easy accessibility to all necessary amenities and transportation. Middle class, suburban neighborhoods. Not on busy streets. Cul-de-sacs ideal. Properties nearby very similar in price. Good foliage and landscaping except in brand new subdivisions. Only high class inner-city locations.
3 FINANCING	**① POINT** More than 15% down. Seller needs lots of cash and wants all of his equity. Or, property will have heavy negative cash flows for more than two years. Or, there will be a large balloon payment due in less than three years from date of purchase. **Consider only if price is excellent.**	**② POINTS** Financing required from an institution with up to 15% down of buyer's money. Credit checks. Institutional, secured loans for part of the down payment (high interest, high monthly payments). Seller carries small amounts. Cash required from buyer. Balloons due in less than 5 years.	**③ POINTS** Less than 5% of buyer cash involved. Seller carries most of the financing at lower than market rates with no balloons in less than 7 years. No negative cash flows projected beyond the first year. Contract sales, no credit checks.
4 PRICE	**① POINT** 10% or more above the reasonable market price. **Consider only if financing is excellent.**	**② POINTS** Within + or − 5% of market price.	**③ POINTS** At least 10% or more below market price.
5 PROPERTY CONDITION	**① POINT** **Consider only if price is excellent.** Needs major cosmetic and structural improvements. At least 10% of purchase price will need to be spent immediately to make unit rentable. Improvements do no significantly improve the rent roll because of quality of tenants and location. Improvements not to increase value more than 10% above purchase price. Usually associated with poor locations. Possible to find this property in excellent locations where prices are so high that improvements do not increase value but just make units acceptable to renters. Viewed as making a larger down payment (for improvements) and receiving an averaged priced property.	**② POINTS** This is the true fixer-upper! Cosmetic improvements would be nice but not immediately necessary. Costs not to exceed 5% of the purchase price. Cosmetic improvements immediately affect the value upwards and make the property more desirable, saleable, and attractive. Not much structural work (if any) is necessary . . . only paint, landscaping, drapes, and other inexpensive improvements. This type of property should not be bought if the buyer does not have the time or mental capacity to undertake supervision of improvements. This property can prove to be the most profitable in the short run. The worst house in the best neighborhood.	**③ POINTS** Newer property or older property with recent renovation. No problems, clean inside and out . . . good landscaping. New components to replace major items. May have been a recent fixer-upper project which is being sold by a don't wanter at an excellent price. No work necessary before renter moves in. Solid property with a hassle factor of zero. Quick closing, quick rent-up, quick cash flow.

- Analyze and assign a point value to each factor of a property.
- If in doubt about a point value always pick the lower number.
- Add up the numbers and totals.
- The lowest acceptable score is 9, the highest possible is 15.
- Greater fools always buy property in the 9, 10, 11 range.
- Great investors always buy property in the 12, 13, 14, 15 range.

TOTAL SCORE

and assign point values and come up with a Property Score. You'll begin to
see that it really helps.

First: Is the seller a don't wanter? How flexible is he? The answer: He is
not motivated. He has decided to sell if he can get his price and doesn't
need the cash but isn't interested in much flexibility. On a scale of one to
ten, he would score a 2 in motivation. In other words, he is poor in
motivation. Let's circle the number one.

Second: What about the location? Answer: It's a great location, excellent
by any standards. Let's assign a value of three and circle the three on the
chart.

Third: What about the financing? Answer: He wants $25,000 down on
each duplex (there are two of them) and a price of $100,000. That figures to
25% down on each. The remaining mortgage will be carried by the seller at
12% interest for five years with a balloon due at that time. Cash flow is
moderately good . . . which means only slightly negative. In other words, it
has good points and it has bad points. In doubt between poor and average
we pick poor and assign a point value of one. Circle one.

Fourth: What about the price? $100,000 per duplex is right on the market,
maybe a little high. We assign a value of two and circle the two.

Fifth: What about the condition of the propery? Answer: not so hot.
Needs some fix-up. It's rundown due to lack of proper pride of ownership.
Tenants are not so hot. Needs $5,000 to $10,000 of immediate fix-up after
the closing in order to bring up to minimum standards. Still, it's not that
bad. In doubt between poor and average we give it a poor rating and assign
a point value of one and circle the one on the chart.

Now let's add up the totals: One plus three plus one plus two plus one
equals eight. Minimum standards are nine. No, we don't want this
property. In addition to having this low a score, the property broke some of
the ten commandments. Let's review them.

1. *Never buy a property in a poor location . . . never . . . not under any
circumstances.* This property is in a good location, so it doesn't matter.

2. *Never buy a property with a point total less than 9.* This property has a
point value less than 9, i.e., 8. And that is one of the reasons we won't buy it.

3. *Never buy a property with poor financing unless it has an excellent price.* In
other words, if a property has a point total of 1 in financing, it must have a
point total of 3 in price. This property has a point total of 1 in financing and
a point total of 2 in price, and therefore we reject it.

4. *Never buy a property with a poor price unless it has excellent financing.* This
doesn't apply in the case of the property we are considering in our example.

5. *Never buy a property in poor condition unless it has an excellent price and
you have the capital, know-how (which can be hired), and mental toughness to*

want to improve a property. This property has a point of 1 in condition and 2 in price, and therefore it breaks the commandment.

6. *Never buy a property unless it has at least one excellent factor (score of 3).* This one does; it has an excellent location.

7. *Don't live the greater fool theory.* This theory states that properties in the 9, 10, or 11 range should not be purchased consistently or constantly or you are speculating and not investing.

8. *Never borrow partnership money to invest in a marginal property.* If you were going to borrow $25,000 to invest in this property, and it wasn't your money, you would be making a mistake.

9. *Never buy a property that has more than two poor factors, unless under the extremely rare circumstance of an immediate condo conversion planned to take place after the purchase.*

10. *Never buy a property unless you are committed to following through on the major and minor details of property management or hire a professional company.*

The only way I would consider this property is if it could be immediately converted to office condominiums directly after the closing. Otherwise, I would recommend no. Try this system on some of the properties you have bought lately to see whether you are buying marginal properties or not. Don't be disconcerted if you don't score as high as you would like. The point of this exercise is to help you in the future to improve your investor status and to avoid your speculator status. That brings us to the final point in this article.

Point Number Three: *The Hundred House Rule.* Bill Greene, the San Francisco investor, millionaire, and lecturer, teaches his students what he calls the Hundred House Rule. Here it is in his own words:

"Circle every ad for investment property located within half an hour drive from your home. Look at them carefully. For at least a month, look at a minimum of 25 offerings every weekend. The first exposure to the conventional market is your kindergarten. Don't buy anything. You are not educated yet . . . not until you have seen 100 properties. Just look. Ask questions. Make no serious offers until you have looked at at least 100 properties. Then make a low offer or a no money down offer on every deal you look at. After looking at 100 properties, you will then recognize an outstanding deal when you see it."

This sounds like a lot of work, but I wish I had had something like this when I got started. It pays off in handsome dividends from teaching you to avoid the speculator's greater fool properties . . . and to make real money as you continue your investment progress towards your first or second million.

I encourage you to use guidelines, use them wisely, and be successful. To review again: First, don't use creative financing to make a bad deal good. Only use it to make a good deal better. Second, have a system you use to separate bad properties from good ones. And third, if you are just beginning and don't know the difference between an apartment building and a motorcycle, try the hundred house rule . . . it builds confidence fast.

PART V:

Dealing With Negative Cash Flows and Balloons

Alligators and Balloons: The Hobgobblins of the Conservative Investor

Robert G. Allen

Sooner or later every investor will be faced with the problem of negative cash flow (hereafter abbreviated to NCF). It's a real world problem that requires real world solutions. But while we consider some solutions, let's keep things in perspective. We all prefer break-even or positive cash flows, of course, but a solid investment property with a manageable NCF is better than no property at all. Sometimes we have to endure the thorns in order to enjoy the roses. There's no mystery in that. What is really mysterious is why the conservative investor recoils in horror at the prospect of a $200 per month NCF but doesn't bat an eyelash in forking over two or three times that amount each month in unnecessarily high income taxes. Instead of recoiling in horror, he really needs to face the issue head on by considering some of the following ten solutions.

Solution No. 1: Keep Looking Until You Find the Break-Even or Positive Cash Flow Deals

If alligators scare you, don't buy them. You may have to do a lot more shopping, but break-even and positive cash flow deals still exist. We get reports from all over the country to prove this each month. One of our Los Angeles graduates has specialized in this approach. He uses the newspaper and telephone exclusively and won't even go look at a property until he finds a serious don't wanter with an income property he is willing to sell with at least a break-even cash flow. It may require hundreds of calls to weed out "unacceptable" properties, but he continues to persist. Within one month of completing our Nothing Down seminar he had purchased a duplex and an eight-unit building. Both were purchased with no cash down from flexible sellers. In the case of the eight-plex, the seller volunteered to take less monthly payment on his mortgage so that our graduate would have a $200 monthly positive cash flow.

While I was on a radio talk show some time ago in Columbus, Ohio, a listener called in to say that he had just purchased a duplex in a good location from a seller who accepted nothing down and a first mortgage at 6% on the entire purchase price. Needless to say, there was a positive cash flow. And this was in a time when the going bank mortgage rates were 14-16%. How does one "fall into" deals like this? You must be "out there, falling!" Seek and ye shall find . . . it just takes time.

Solution No. 2: Lower the Price or Raise the Number of Units.

If the property has an NCF, maybe the price is too high. It sounds logical. Therefore, either negotiate for lower prices (and hence lower payments) or shop around some more. In single family homes select the cheapest three-bedroom home available in a respectable neighborhood. Ideally the price should be below $60,000, even lower if possible. The higher the price above $50K, the higher the NCF. In cities where home prices are extremely high (i.e., L.A., Orange County, San Francisco, Washington, D.C., some areas of Chicago, etc.), the solution may be to look further out in the suburbs. Try to locate smaller communities outside major cities which have their own source of employment to create a demand for rental housing. I would avoid far out bedroom communities without employment centers; we still do not know the long range effect of $2 to $3 per gallon gasoline prices on commuters (although in his book *The Third Wave*, Alvin Toffler argues that as much as 30% of the future working force will work out of their homes with the aid of computer technology).

As for apartment buildings, it is normal to expect better cash flows from larger properties. The more units, the better the cash flow. The enormous demand for smaller income properties by beginning investors has driven up the prices of the smaller multi-units, thus affecting cash flows.

CASH FLOW RANGES

Single Family Homes	Apartment Buildings
30K 40K 50K 60K 70K Higher	2 units 4 6 8 10 20 100 Higher
Better	The Red Zone	Better
Cash	Great Probability of	Cash
	Negative Cash Flows	Flows

Solution No. 3: Improve Management — Raise Rents, Decrease Expenses, Increase Occupancy.

Sellers invariably say: "The rents are too low; a new buyer could easily raise them." In most cases this is just sales hype, but in rare cases the rents are in fact below market and need adjustment. This is an immediate cure for NCF's. Where this is not the case, there is still hope. A conservative investor often does not take into consideration that NCF's are usually a *temporary* problem. A few years of rent raises will convert the situation to positive cash flows that will be with you for a lifetime.

On the expense side of the ledger, many property owners handle their own maintenance and repairs as well as management. This saves hundreds of dollars. Personally, I have always preferred to use a professional management company. The higher costs have more than been offset by increased freedom and property appreciation. I'll take the thorns to be able to enjoy the roses.

Solution No. 4: Partners.

If you can't handle the NCFs, chances are someone else can . . . and would *love* to help you for a percentage of the future profit. If you have located an excellent low or no down property but are not strong enough to "carry" the alligator, look for one of your friends, business associates, family members, or RAND colleagues to become your 50/50 partner. Half a pie is better than no pie at all. I recall one young man in one of our California seminars who bought eight houses *all* with NCFs. Since he had purchased all of the houses $10,000 below market, he had no trouble finding *very* willing partners to help with the monthly payments.

Moreover, you might persuade a partner to come in with a large cash down payment, perhaps even pay down to an existing low interest rate mortgage. This will eliminate NCFs altogether and produce healthy front-end profits for all concerned. In another variation, David Read, our excellent seminar instructor, tells a story of how he eliminated his NCF on a condominium purchase by making a partner of the tenant. Since the condo had an NCF of $130 per month, he advertised in the paper with a "Rent to Buy" ad. Among those who responded, David chose an excellent prospect who was willing to pay the full mortgage payment (including the NCF) for two years in return for half ownership. After two years they can exercise a buy-out agreement, rent to someone else, or sell the property and split the profit. In the meantime the rents will nearly catch up with the NCF. A very creative solution!

Solution No. 5: Borrowing Negative Cash Flows.

Here's a gutsy solution for the very experienced investor! I know of an investor who has purchased over 30 single family homes in the $150-200K range in Northern California in the past few years. Of course, there are stiff monthly NCF's. How does he handle them? He and his two partners buy a house *each* month and pull money out of it with the second mortgage crank technique. Suppose they find a $150,000 home for sale by a flexible seller with a $50,000 first mortgage and $100,000 equity. They offer the seller $50,000 cash at closing if he will accept a $50,000 second subordinated to the new loan. Then they proceed to put a new loan of $110,000 on the property. Let me diagram that for you:

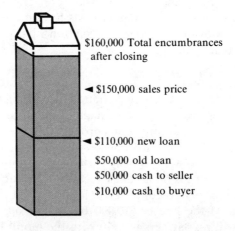

$160,000 Total encumbrances after closing

◄ $150,000 sales price

◄ $110,000 new loan
$50,000 old loan
$50,000 cash to seller
$10,000 cash to buyer

That's right. They pull out $10,000 cash from each monthly purchase (I'm guessing at the exact figures) to help cover the NCFs from the other properties in their portfolio, perhaps $300 per month negative on each of around 30 houses. Next month? The same story. Actually, every month they *have* to buy a new property. Of course, the sellers are made aware of the financing arrangements and the buyers have a well-established relationship with a local S & L for non-owner occupied loans. As you can tell, the above method is *extremely* dangerous, especially in times of tight mortgage money. We do not subscribe to over-finance techniques. But you cannot argue with $500,000 profit in the past two to three years, either. I mention this technique for only one reason: to get you thinking. There are a million ways to skin an alligator. You may have a situation which could be solved by a variation of the above techniques without any of the dangers. Put on your thinking cap!

Solution No. 6: Use Positive Cash Flows from Other Investments.

My first two 12-unit buildings became very good "friends." One property had an NCF of several hundred dollars a month. The other had a positive cash flow large enough to "feed" or support the first. A nice solution! As the years go by, the extra positive cash flows from your "seasoned" properties can help "fertilize" the new properties you buy each year.

Solution No. 7: Negative Cash Flow Kitty.

I'm writing this article in Detroit during my down-time from my book PR tour. In the Detroit paper this morning is an ad for a $36,500 7-room house in a good area. The owner is transferring and is asking zero down with owner financing. What if the seller needs $400 per month PITI and I can rent the house out for only $350? Do I have a $50 per month NCF? Maybe. The new tenant will probably bring with him first and last month's rent plus a security deposit. That's $350 plus $350 plus $150 equals $850. It's customary in a tight rental market to expect as much. But my first mortgage payment is not due for three days. That gives me $850 advance cash to put in my *Negative Cash Flow Kitty.* That would give me as long as 17 months at $50 per month. By then I will have raised the rent . . . goodbye alligator.

Solution No. 8: Structure the Mortgage Payments.

Never buy an income property without doing your homework! Never! If there is to be an NCF, you should know about it *before* you negotiate. Then you can ask the seller to structure the payments so that your negative is kept to a minimum. (See pp. 102-108 of my book *Nothing Down* for seven good alternatives to structuring a mortgage to avoid NCF. See also the Nothing Down seminar manual for a full treatment of the subject.) The point to be stressed here is getting breathing time . . . negotiate for *at least* twelve months lenient terms from the seller. This gives you the opportunity to check out the property, feel out the management situation, and see if you want to keep the property before payments are increased to the seller.

Solution No. 9: The Balloon Mortgage.

One of the alternative strategies encompassed under Solution No. 8 is the balloon mortgage. I have made this a separate section because it is so universally feared by most beginning investors. Let's create an illustration. You locate a beautiful home for $60,000 in a good neighborhood. The seller is a don't wanter but needs $4000 down. He has a $40,000 existing loan. He will accept a $16,000 second mortgage. As you check out the rental situation, you discover that you will have a break-even cash flow just making the seller's original mortgage payment of $425 per month without even considering the payments on the $16,000 second. What to do? I automatically ask the seller to accept *no* monthly payments on the second, with a balloon in five years. That eliminates the NCF, but of course the seller's note will grow in value over the years (almost doubling). However, if I have a positive cash flow from the rents in years 2, 3, 4, and 5, I can apply it toward the balloon payment due or spend it on other investments to carry *their* negatives (I lean toward the latter).

How do you convince the seller to carry a no payment note with a balloon? If he is a serious don't wanter there will be less problem. If he is borderline flexible, I just mention to him that the most conservative investments in the world are T-Bill accounts, CD's, and Money Market Certificates. *And if they don't make monthly payments to their investors, why should I?* Sometimes the magic works, sometimes it doesn't.

At any rate, in solving my NCF problem I have created a monster down the road in five years. This monster is sometimes frightening enough to scare the conservative investor. Let's look at the overall picture. In five years the home will be worth $100-120,000, depending on inflation, etc. Our loans will total $68,000—a $38,000 first mortgage plus a growing second (approximately $30,000). With a value of $100K that gives us an equity of $32K. Negative cash flow—zero. Maybe even a net positive cash flow over time.

What do we do in five years to reap this $32,000 crop of money? We have six alternatives:

1. Refinance the property
2. Sell the property to a new buyer and let him take care of the balloon
3. Refinance another property you own to pay for the balloon
4. Sell another property you own
5. Borrow from a partner in return for a percentage of the profits
6. Give the property back to the seller.

Will the owner mind if you give back the property? Will he report you as a bad risk to the credit bureau? I doubt it. After all, he now gets the $32K profit. He won't care a bit; in fact he might even be *hoping* that's what you will do. It's not desirable for you to lose the property, but at least your $4000 down payment is probably recouped over the years with positive cash flow. I doubt if this last alternative will ever be your fate, but even if it is... what is so bad about it? You have nothing to lose and everything to gain. Just for the record, however, let me give you four guidelines to use with balloon mortgages:

1. In negotiating terms, don't even consider using or suggesting a balloon until it's the last resort. Save that for last. If the seller is willing to accept a long-term loan, don't stop him.
2. Try to push the balloon due date at least five years into the future. Ten if possible. Balloons with short-term due dates are called "short-fuse notes" for a very good reason. If you want to make winter go fast, have a $50,000 note due in March. I have had a few of these, and it is not something I am going to repeat.
3. Always include an extension period in the balloon terms. If money is tight or impossible to obtain when the note is due, you should have 12 months to shop around. You can likely "buy" an extension by paying an extra sum in cash (i.e. a 10% reduction in the loan). That way you have an "out" which will enable you to handle things if the going gets rough.
4. Begin at least 12 months before the due date to arrange new financing or a sale.

The balloon solution is frightening to most, but it is the wave of the future. S & L's are already gearing up to offer "rollover" or variable rate mortgages that will need to be paid off or renegotiated every five years (like Canada now). Our fixed-rate long-term mortgage is soon to be the dinosaur of the financial world. Don't let a little balloon stop you. Get while the getting is good.

Solution No. 10: Let Bob Pay $50 Toward Your Next Month's Negative Cash Flow.

Send in your creative solutions to your NCF's. If it's truly unique, I'd be glad to pay you for the idea.

As a final note, NCF's are a problem you will have to face and solve on your own terms to fit your own personality. Think of negative cash flow as the "fertilizer" for your real estate garden. And keep your mind on the end results.

Maybe that will help.

In the meantime, God bless.

Don't wait to buy real estate; buy real estate and wait.

Keeping Air in Your Balloon Notes

Sam F. Hall

What would you say is one of the major hurdles to success for today's real estate investor? If your reply is "Coping with negative cash flow on a per-property basis," you'd be right on target. Negative cash flow is a two-sided sword. It's a major reason for investors to sell their properties and it is also one of the main reasons many investors won't buy a property.

A wide variety of negative cash flow remedies are available to the knowledgeable real estate investor. Unfortunately, only a small percentage of these solutions are ever utilized to any degree. The lack of expertise in eliminating negative cash flow can oftentimes be very expensive. In fact, many times it's the difference between success and failure. Relying on one or two negative cash flow remedies for all conditions will rapidly place you in a self-destruct mode. For the investor who relies heavily upon the balloon mortgage to negate negative cash flow, the following dissection of that technique, i.e., the *Straight Balloon Mortgage*, will hopefully keep you in control and out of hot water.

By definition, the straight balloon mortgage is any type of note in which no monthly payments are made, or the monthly payments are so small they won't repay the note in full before the term of the note is up. That sounds great, right? The catch to this, however, is that if you negotiate a balloon note into the purchase of a property, you'll be obligating yourself to make an oftentimes painful lump sum payment to retire the note at its expiration date. Of all the negative cash flow remedies available to the real estate investor, the straight balloon mortgage seems to be the most popular—which is rather ironic since this remedy often, through misuse or misunderstanding, becomes a major problem instead of becoming the solution to the problem.

Through experience, not all of which has been positive, I've come to compare the straight balloon mortgage to fire: It makes a wonderful slave but a terrible master. Granted, the straight balloon mortgage definitely has its place among the viable remedies in eliminating negative cash flow, but I can't put enough emphasis on the importance of using this technique wisely. An accurate perspective of when and how to utilize the balloon mortgage is a prerequisite to your success. Conversely, making emotional decisions concerning the financing of a property and using the balloon mortgage in an unwarranted situation is possibly the best way to facilitate a loss that could take years to recover from. I've often heard that adversity is an excellent teacher, but the logic I'm presenting here is that you need to learn from somebody else's mistakes.

Life is far too short to make inaccurate decisions, especially when it comes to your financial solvency. It should be well understood that balloon notes are by design and definition a *short*-term patch, *not* the *long*-term solution to cure your financial ills.

The very term "balloon note" should conjure up an image of a potentially-explosive situation. In order that you avoid the trauma of having a balloon note explode in your investing career, the following scenario needs to be considered before locking yourself into a short-term balloon note commitment.

Case Study

Tom was a novice investor who was aggressive but impatient to add to his investment portfolio. One evening, while reading through the "Income Properties For Sale" section in his local newspaper, Tom came across an ad that caught his eye. The ad read:

> **For Sale By Owner**
> Six-unit apartment,
> flexible contract terms,
> call after 6:00 p.m.

Naturally being aggressive, he was calling the seller at 6:00 p.m. sharp with high hopes that the seller would be motivated to sell his property on terms Tom could tolerate.

Instead of asking pertinent and penetrating fact-finding questions designed to determine the level of seller motivation, Tom was simply content to set up a face-to-face meeting with the seller for the next day. In the following conversation between Tom and the seller, see if you can detect the short-fuse trap being set on an unwary investor.

Tom: What do you think your property is worth?
Seller: Oh, I need about $185,000 to sell.
Tom: How much equity do you have in your property?
Seller: I owe about $100,000. That gives me about $85,000 in equity.
Tom: What are your contract terms?
Seller: I need $10,000 down, but we can structure the wrap-around contract on the $175,000 balance so you don't have a reverse cash flow.
Tom: You mean on your $75,000 equity balance you'll be flexible.
Seller: Sure! I need to sell the property . . .
Tom: What are your terms on that $75,000 equity?
Seller: Well, I pay about $1,100 per month on the first mortgage, and the rents generated by the property are about $1,500 per month. What do you think about $10,000 down and my equity balance accruing at 12% from closing, due and payable in 12 months?
Tom: Do you mean with $10,000 down I won't have any payments at all on your equity balance for a whole year?
Seller: That's right.
Tom: If I can realize a positive cash flow in today's market and don't have to pay you out for a year, I think we've made a deal.

The following diagram illustrates the transaction at closing.

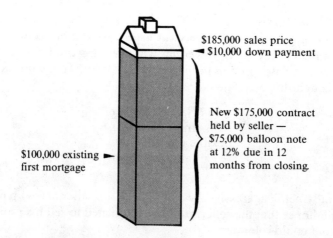

$185,000 sales price
◄ $10,000 down payment

New $175,000 contract held by seller —
$75,000 balloon note at 12% due in 12 months from closing.

$100,000 existing ► first mortgage

Are you wishing you could find a seller that was as flexible as the one Tom located? Let's look now a little deeper into this transaction and see what happens to overzealous investors who don't do their homework and commit themselves to balloon notes, or as aptly referred to by seasoned investors: *short*-fuse notes, i.e. they have a way of blowing up in your face.

Well, after closing the transaction, Tom was the proud owner of a six-unit apartment building, a property he could be proud of to have in his portfolio. After about six months of ownership, Tom decided he ought to start thinking about the balloon note coming due. He started half-heartedly checking the market for new financing for his apartment, thinking he had plenty of time to fulfill the contract terms.

Another two months passed and Tom realized he had better get serious about the note he was obligated to pay, but mortgage money was tight and getting tighter all the time. He soon learned his six-unit apartment building was a commercial loan property and commercial funding was next to impossible to obtain.

Thirty days before Tom's balloon busted, he called the seller to discuss his dilemma. If you ever want to see an otherwise congenial seller lose all sense of humor, just call him thirty days before his note is payable and say you're having difficulty. As you may have guessed, all heck broke loose when Tom said he wasn't going to be able to make good his balloon note payment.

It seems the seller also had a short-term note coming due and needed cash, not excuses. The bottom line here is that Tom, through a lack of knowledge and planning, lost the property through foreclosure, lost his $10,000 down payment, and lost, I'm sure, many good nights' sleep, but I can almost guarantee he did gain the experience to be cautious with balloon notes in the future.

If the previous example injected a little twinge of fear concerning balloon notes, then I accomplished exactly what was intended. You see, fear is a very natural protective instinct. If you can become motivated by a well-controlled, well-understood fear, the value judgments you make will be based on logic and reason and most likely will be accurate decisions. If, however, you make decisions based on the emotional involvement concerning a specific property, contrary to the facts, then unfortunately you have what I call a "built-in failure mechanism."

To turn that failure mechanism off in dealing with balloon notes, you need to keep in mind the following guidelines. The balloon note technique should be used only as a last choice. Remember, balloon notes do have a sneaky way of falling due at the most inconvenient times. I once heard an investor comment that if you want the winter to really fly by, all you have to do is commit yourself to retire a balloon note in twelve months, due in March. If the balloon-note technique seems to be the only viable solution for your investment needs, I would *strongly* suggest that the balloon fall due in **not less than** five to seven years. Five to seven years will give the property time to grow in appreciaiton, the property itself being, of course, the best source of repaying the obligation. Along with the negotiated five-to-seven-year balloon, it is always a wise idea to incorporate a clause in the final documentation that the seller will be amenable to a grace period if mortgage money is impossible to find. In order that the seller agree to this extension, you'll most-likely have to put up some type of sweetener, such as a token payment every six months or so, until you can locate a willing lender. And let the balloon-note holder do some checking for you on his own. He may be able to find financing for you. It's in his best interest to do so.

With the previous guidelines and suggestions in mind, let's see how the balloon note technique can be used wisely. The following example will illustrate how an educated investor deals with having to use the straight balloon mortgage.

Case Study

Through a friend, Rex found an eight-unit apartment for sale by a gentleman who, according to Rex, would be willing to be quite flexible.

Understanding that the term "flexible" means different things to different people, Rex said he would check into the property that evening. Rex called the seller with only fact-finding in mind. In talking with the seller over the telephone, Rex realized the seller was highly motivated, which could lead to a potentially profitable transaction. That evening Rex made an appointment to meet with the seller the following day. (Note: Rex made a value decision over the *telephone* as to the motivation level of the seller before he made an appointment to begin the negotiation process.) The negotiation process that ensued the following day followed this format:

Rex: Tell me again why you're selling the complex.

Seller: I don't really want to sell, but I've obligated myself and I need the cash.

Rex: You mentioned over the phone that you want $240,000 for the property. How did you arrive at that price?

Seller: I've done some checking with a broker friend and he seems to think that's a fair price.

Rex: I understand you have a great deal of equity in the property.

Seller: With a sales price of $240,000 and an existing first mortgage of approximately $88,000, I've got about $152,000 equity.

Rex: Last night you mentioned you wanted to carry the contract-for-deed. What kind of terms are you suggesting?

Seller: Well, I've got to realize at least $20,000 cash as the down payment.

Rex: With $20,000 down, you'll carry the balance of approximately

$132,000?

Seller: Yes.

Rex: The banks would pay you between 5% and 7% on your money if they had it in a savings account. What do you think about carrying the $132,000 balance at 10%?

Seller: That sounds good to me.

Rex: The operating statement indicates the rents are $225 per unit, times eight units, which equals about $1,800 gross income. Is that correct?

Seller: That's correct, but the rents should be raised.

Rex: It's my policy to buy a property using the existing income information. If you were buying, wouldn't you do the same?

Seller: I guess so.

Rex: If we multiply the gross rents by 35%, that would give me a monthly expense of about $630. Is that pretty close?

Seller: That's about right. Maybe a little high.

Rex: $1,800 gross income minus $630 monthly expenses gives us about $1,170 per month NOI and you said your existing first mortgage payments are at $926 per month PITI (Principal, Interest, Taxes, and Insurance) Correct?

Seller: According to my calculations, that will give you a net positive cash flow, on a monthly basis, of $244.

Rex: Now, what about the balance of your equity? How would you like to be repaid?

Seller: I'd like to amortize the note over 25 years at 10%, but I want to be cashed out in ten years.

Rex: That's going to pose an immediate problem in that your monthly payments would put this property into an extreme negative cash flow.

Seller: I understand that, but what else can we do? I really need to be cashed out in ten years.

Rex: What if I could cash you out in five years?

Seller: That's great, but how can you do that?

Rex: This is my plan. If you'll accept a straight balloon mortgage, i.e., no monthly payments but your principal accruing at 10%, I'll cash you out in five years.

Seller: No monthly payments for five years? I don't think I can live with that.

Rex: You said you wanted $240,000 for the property. Would it persuade you any to go along with my proposal if I offered you $250,000 for the property?

Seller: $10,000 more than I am asking? Now you've got my attention.

Rex: Then you're receptive to the five-year balloon?

Seller: I think we can work it out.

The following diagrams illustrate the transaction at closing and again in five years when the balloon note comes due.

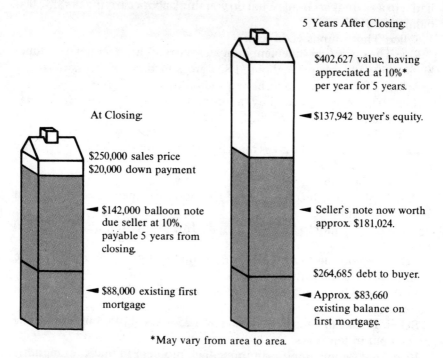

5 Years After Closing:

$402,627 value, having appreciated at 10%* per year for 5 years.

◄ $137,942 buyer's equity.

At Closing:

$250,000 sales price
$20,000 down payment

◄ $142,000 balloon note due seller at 10%, payable 5 years from closing.

◄ Seller's note now worth approx. $181,024.

$264,685 debt to buyer.

◄ $88,000 existing first mortgage

◄ Approx. $83,660 existing balance on first mortgage.

*May vary from area to area.

As the previous diagram indicates, in five years the seller's balloon note is now worth approximately $181,024. The increase in the original note is often a powerful inducement for the seller to accept a five-to-seven-year balloon note, so show the seller what his balloon note will be worth at the expiration date of the balloon at some point during the negotiation process.

Although the seller's note grew during the duration of the mortgage, the previous diagram also points out that the property itself gained substantially in value—that being the justification and the rationale behind using the balloon mortgage for the buyer.

Summary

If the balloon-mortgage technique is to be used, the repayment method should be firmly and realistically established. Alternatives for repayment should be considered and a decision made as to which avenue will be taken before the final documentaion and subsequent closing. The approaches include refinancing the subject property (or other property you own), selling the subject property (or another one you own), renegotiating terms with the seller from the outset for a rollover provision, or bringing in a partner. The least pleasant alternative is to return the property if the balloon cannot be met. As unpleasant as it may sound, sometimes the logical thing is simply to deed the property back to the seller. Granted, you'll have lost the property, but you'll have saved your credit.

Conclusion

Although caution and sound judgment should be used when implementing the balloon-mortgage technique, it remains a viable solution in alleviating negative cash flow.

Two Novel Solutions for Negative Cash Flows

Richard J. Allen

Creative real estate investors need to be vigilant in guarding against the dangers of negative cash flows, particularly where property values might not be rising as quickly as in the late 1970's. The number of solutions to the cash flow challenge is limited only by the imagination and creative reach of the investor. Here are two case studies to illustrate the principle of innovation in real estate:

One of the Nothing Down graduates in San Bruno, California, has acquired a condo in Honolulu, his residence in San Bruno, and, most recently, a four-bedroom home in Fairfield, California. The rental home, priced at $76,000, had a first mortgage of $56,000 at 8½%, which was assumed. The remaining $20,000 came from the proceeds of a second mortgage at 12% secured against the buyer's own residence.

Problem: Since the house rents for $450 per month, and the payment on the first mortgage is $546 per month, there is a considerable negative cash flow even before the second mortgage is factored in.

Solution: He pulled not $20,000, but $30,000 in equity out of his home, putting $10,000 of it into a finance company where it draws 8½% interest computed daily. (A high-yield liquid asset account would have been even better!) The payments on the second are $500 per month. Total payments are thus $1,046 per month, leaving a negative of $596. But the kitty is available to draw on if needed while the buyer works out other solutions.

Creative afterthought: He asked himself what he could do to avoid drawing on his $10,000 kitty to cover the negatives. Solution: He rented out three rooms of his own four-bedroom, three-bath residence at $200 per month per room. The $600 per month proceeds offsets the negative cash flow in the rental home. This solution works best for single people with large homes — but it just goes to show that creativity knows no bounds.

Another graduate in the San Jose area reported to us recently an alternative approach for dealing with negative cash flows. He had acquired a rental property priced at $117,000, using the financing indicated in the sketch below:

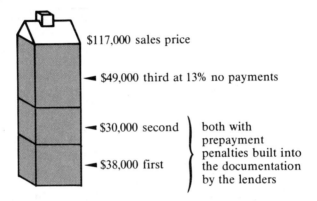

$117,000 sales price

◄ $49,000 third at 13% no payments

◄ $30,000 second ⎫ both with
                   ⎬ prepayment
◄ $38,000 first   ⎭ penalties built into
                     the documentation
                     by the lenders

The total monthly payment (first and second) is $1,374. With rents of $625 per month, the negative is $749 — not too comfortable.

Solution: He placed an ad to attract a tenant who could pay $1,000 per month in exchange for a partial equity position. Someone promptly responded to the ad by asking if he would be willing to sell outright. He agreed, under the condition that the party would pay him $5,000 down and leave him on title with a 20% equity position. The deal was consummated and his benefit was to realize a good share of his anticipated profit up front while still retaining part interest in the property. There is more than one way to skin an alligator.

Questions and Answers on Cash Flow Management

Richard J. Allen

Question

"I have just closed on a nothing down single-family home with rent potential of $650 and mortgage payments of $950. Would equity sharing be a good technique for taking care of the negative?"
PK, San Francisco, CA

Answer

Equity sharing is certainly one way of covering the negative. However, the first reaction we would have to your question is this: One of the fundamental tenets for successful creative real estate investing is to see the broad picture before you act. The best time to cure a potential negative cash flow is at the point in the negotiation where you are structuring the financing, not afterwards. It is easy to acquire property for nothing down—anyone can do it! The trick is to package the nothing down purchase so that the negatives are controlled from the very beginning.

In the situation you are describing, there is a $300 negative. How might this have been cured ahead of time? Assuming that you are making payments to the seller on a carry-back note, would one or more of the following techniques have applied in your case?

1. A long-term balloon with no payments at all for at least seven years;

2. Payments on the carry-back structured so that the payments on the first mortgage plus the payments on the carry-back would either equal the rent income or not exceed it by more than is tolerable to the buyer (this is sometimes called "reverse paper" or "walking the paper backwards;" the shortfall on the payment is actually added to the principal each month);

3. Interest-only payments on the carry-back each year so that the buyer

has time to locate other sources of income;

4. Stepped interest rate system that starts with modest payments and climbs each year until a pre-negotiated plateau is reached;

5. Delay in payments on the carry-back for a period of time, perhaps one year, so that the buyer has a chance to consolidate the operation.

There are many other techniques that could be looked into. Using partners might be the most expensive route to go (since you frequently have to give up an equity position as reward). However, this is sometimes the answer to a stubborn negative. The partner not only puts up the down payment (perhaps buying down to the first mortgage) but also covers the monthly negative, if necessary. Where the tenant is the partner (tenant equity sharing), he or she pays the negative each month and also takes care of minor maintenance. As in all partnership deals, you have to make sure the paperwork is done with the help of competent legal advice. If you go the tenant equity route, make sure you put the closing off long enough to find the right tenant-partner. It hurts to go into a deal with a vacant property! Of course, tenant equity sharing is possible only where the negative does not elevate the total monthly payment too far above the local rental market. An alternative is to look into the long-term lease option where the negative is paid by your tenant as part of a future down payment on the property.

Whichever the way you go, keep in mind the following statement by Robert Allen:

"You show me a *successful* real estate investor, and I'll show you someone who has mastered the fundamentals . . . Show me an *unsuccessful* investor, and I'll show you someone who has refused to invest time and money into learning the *basics.* That's the key."

Question:

"I am negotiating on a beautiful home on which the seller is willing to carry 100% on 1st, 2nd, and 3rd trust deeds. However the rates have 5-, 4-, and 5-year balloons respectively. I feel that I can handle the balloons as they come due by refinancing. Is this dangerous thinking on my part?" *S.P., Denver, CO*

Answer:

In our opinion, any refinance strategy for dealing with balloons that doesn't include some very solid contingencies from the outset is risky in this volatile market. Balloons of four or five years are bordering on short-fuse these days. It is tempting to succumb to a seller's tolerance for a 100% "paper out," but a creative buyer should resist any terms that go beyond the buyer's ability to perform.

What contingencies are available other than refinance? Possibilities include provisions for "rolling over" balloons at the option of the buyer if refinance becomes difficult, or converting balloons to amortizing rates (probably with the addition of some sweeteners like a paydown on principal). Such contingencies must be built into the arrangement from the outset. Alternate plans might also include the availability of partnership funds from the outset to solve balloon problems where refinance becomes difficult.

The best contingency of all is to negotiate the balloons entirely out of the picture. We like Barney Zick's 5-10-15 formula for carry-back financing: 5 years no payments (interest accruing); 10 more years interest-only annually; then 15 more years to fully amortize the balance. Not all sellers will accept this approach! But many will buy a lesser variation when they see they must play according to your creative rules.

PART VI:

Understanding the Principles of Win/Win Negotiating

Negotiation: How to Make Your Weaknesses Look Like Strengths

Robert G. Allen

A clergyman goes to his superior and asks a simple question: "Father, may I smoke while I'm praying?" The superior denies his request emphatically. After thinking about it, the same clergyman approaches the superior again with another request: "Father, excuse me for bothering you. May I pray while I'm smoking?" To this the superior replies, "Of course my son. You must have a prayer in your heart at all times!"

Didn't the clergyman ask exactly the same question?

I love that story about negotiation because it illustrates three very important principles of the negotiating process that are often overlooked:

1. The importance of understanding the motivations of the other party (fact finding).

2. The importance of a win-win attitude, where all gain.

3. The importance of persistence.

Not only are these three principles important in negotiation, but they are essential to the little or nothing down buyer since the nothing down offer is often perceived by the seller, his agents, or the banker as either 1 an insult, 2 financially irresponsible, or 3 socially unacceptable.

Obviously, the nothing down buyer must have some techniques for making his weaknesses look like strengths or he or she will never succeed.

Let's begin with principle #1 and apply it to the nothing down context.

One. The Importance of Understanding the Motivations of the Seller.

A. Finding the don't wanter seller.

Negotiation is a process of satisfying needs. "When there is an imbalance of needs (i.e., weak buyer vs. seller who doesn't *need* to sell) between parties, the one with the most basic need (the buyer) must somehow provide himself with leverage in order to narrow the disparity. A disparity or lack of needs puts a damper on getting others to negotiate," says Henry H. Calero in *Winning the Negotiation.* It should stand to reason that the "weak" nothing down buyer should first attempt to find a real estate seller whose need to sell quickly (motivated by fear) outweighs the need to wait and find a strong buyer who can satisfy his need for security.

The nothing down buyer is not only looking for financial leverage but psychological leverage also. If you want to increase the chances of your success, *don't negotiate until you find the don't wanter seller!*

B. Engage in fact-finding to discover seller's hot buttons.

Almost all of the very important fact-finding is done on the telephone. I never look at a property to buy unless I know that the seller will be flexible. Otherwise, it is a waste of everyone's time. Most of the time the seller will reveal many of his motivations in the initial newspaper ad. Here is the copy of an ad for a property I bought with $100 down recently:

> DECORATOR'S deluxe one bedroom
> Furn. apt. 6575 W. 4 Ave. $35,900 low
> down owner will finance or rent $375
> owner-agent 595-3111

This ad was full of clues. The property was in good condition according to the ad. It was furnished, which would allow me to sell the furniture as part of a splitting technique to raise some cash for the down payment if necessary. It was in the right price range, so negative cash flows wouldn't be a major problem. The seller was advertising "low down!" And he was interested in either a renter *or* a buyer. This is a blatant clue that tells me that money is *not* the motivating concern. He doesn't need the cash. And finally, we are dealing with an owner/agent, which indicates that the seller is likely not afraid of a creative offer... and there will be no commissions to have to worry about.

You can tell that the negotiating job to buy this property was not very difficult. All the seller was interested in was a motivated "buyer," and since I am always motivated to buy property on my terms, I bought it within 24 hours after reading the ad in the paper. The seller did not ask me for any identification, for any job verification or credit information. You see, once you find the don't wanter, the rest of the job is much easier.

But most ads are not as blatant. Finding the motivation takes some in-depth questioning. The initial telephone contact with the seller is important. You must not be afraid to ask questions that will help you to understand why the seller is a don't wanter. If the ad states that the seller is "motivated," then your first question will be, "What do you mean by motivated?" If the ad says, "Will consider low down," your first question will be "How low is low?" If he says low to him means $5,000, then you will ask, "What are you going to do with the money?" If there have been other offers ask, "Why did you refuse the last offer?"

This questioning process must reveal to you just how motivated the seller is. Why is he selling? Does he really need money? Are tax savings important to him? Would a quick closing be important to him? Is he motivated by greed... would an extra $1,000 tacked onto the price motivate him enough to lower the down payment he thinks he needs?

Remember, you are in the driver's seat here. Most "weak" nothing down buyers feel that they have no right asking these kinds of questions. They feel this way because of their guilt and their assumption that they are taking advantage of a seller's problems. Not so. The seller is the one who paid for the ad. He *wants* you to call. He is thrilled to respond to your questions. And besides, he doesn't know who you are, so what do you have to lose? Let the seller talk. And listen with your heart! The more you know about that seller, the more prepared you are for the next stage in the negotiation.

Two. The Importance of the Win/Win Attitude.

The next step in the negotiation process is the face-to face meeting of the buyer and seller. As soon as you determine that the seller is flexible, then waste no time in visiting the property and the seller. You snooze, you lose as they say.

A. Break down seller's barriers.

One of the best ways to break the barrier that exist between buyer and seller is to visit the seller in person. I have always found this to be effective for me. Even if there is an agent involved, you need to arrange a face-to-face meeting. "Although an agent is often desirable in one's own cause, it also follows that in negotiations it is best to avoid dealing with the adversary's agent. If at all possible, deal with the principal... Always... deal with the man who signs the checks." writes Gerard I. Nierenberg in *The Art of Negotiating.* The obvious reasons for this are:

— the seller's agent doesn't understand creative financing.
— anything new or different will be suspicious.
— the seller's agent does not understand the seller's motivations because he is not as skilled as you at perceiving them.
— it is easier for the seller to dismiss your offer without you present.
— the offer may not be in the best interests of the agent.
— the agent may not be as skilled or motivated as the buyer in pointing out the benefits of the offer to the seller.

There is no question that the agents often resist our attempts to visit with their clients under the pretext of "not bothering" the seller. You must persist. If the agent is adamant, then look for another property or another agent. The only exceptions to the above rule would be 1 if you are dealing through an agent who has been through the Nothing Down seminar or understands creative financing, or 2 if you are presenting "all cash" and low price offers.

What happens when you visit the seller in person? You have an opportunity to prove yourself to him . . . to show him that you are on his side . . . to practice the win/win philosophy . . . to show him that you are not an "unscrupulous buyer" but an honest, upright, concerned, trustworthy individual.

Fear is a powerful emotion. I will try my best to dispel the fears of the seller about me by making small talk about the property. I may notice something of interest and suspend active negotiation in order to pursue it. All of this talk teaches me important information about the seller and his motivations. I am trying to be his friend, whether I buy his property or not. I may ask tough questions about the condition of the property or the seller's situation, but they are always prefaced with a statement that clarifies why I am asking the question or detoxifies the question so that it is not so blunt. For example, "Mr. Seller, I know that it is none of my business, but it would really help me know how to buy your property if you would share with me what you are planning to do with the down payment," or "Mr. Seller, I'm not trying to be overly critical, but the appliances in this unit don't seem to be in very good condition." I think I have learned over the years that "the stronger the tactics, the greater the resistance," as Calero says. This is a slightly different approach than that explained in my book *Nothing Down* in the chapter on negotiation.

You see, if I am negotiating from a position of weakness then the only thing I have going for me is the trust I can generate with the seller. *This is my strength!* (Moral strength is more important than financial strength.) After all, why would anyone sell his property to a stranger with little or nothing down? That's just the point! When the seller is finished negotiating with me I am no longer a stranger, I am a friend. He knows that I will not take advantage of him because I let him know subtly that he can trust me. I don't rock the boat. I try to help. I give him advice. I try to be part of the solution instead of part of the problem. I don't use tough, unfamiliar vocabulary such as "trust deeds" or "wrap arounds" . . . but more common words like "security" and "collateral." A confused mind says no. I try never to let him get confused. I don't try to impress him. I try to bless him. All of this is part of the win/win attitude. It is sensitivity. The three most important rules in negotiating are listen, listen, and listen. You catch more flies with honey than you will with vinegar.

Once you break down the barriers with the win/win attitude you will launch into the negotiation of the hard points. This is an area of compromise. In order to inspire flexibility in a seller, I must also be willing to be flexible.

B. The art of compromising.

The first rule in compromising is to be generous on the little things and stingy on the big things. What are the little and big things? Let's break them down into tangible and intangible benefits for the seller which are found in any negotiation.

Intangible benefits	Tangible benefits
—freedom from hassle of management	—cash down payments
—ability to leave (transfer)	—monthly payments
—starting a clean slate	—interest rate
—saving face, good name	—closing date
—saving credit	—tax advantages
—freeing up time for other more important pursuits	—cutting losses
—liability on the mortgage	—security or collateral
	—balloons, future money
	—closing costs
	—price
	—percentage of profits from future sale

The most important things in the above lists are 1 down payment, 2 monthly payments. I am willing to compromise on the other items (within reason). I am willing to pay more than the seller wants in order to get my terms (monthly payments). I am willing to pay a higher interest rate if the seller will carry his note with no monthly payments and at least a five-year balloon. I am willing to close immediately if that is important to the seller. I will pay all closing costs. I will give him additional security in the form of a blanket mortgage... as long as I can negotiate a low down payment or a low monthly payment or both.

I give up the things *that don't cost me much now* in order to obtain the benefits I seek. I have to be persuasive with the seller to convince him that he wins if he does things my way. And I have to be quick to point out the intangible benefits that he will obtain. These intangible benefits are sometimes more important than the tangible ones. As negotiators, we need to be sensitive to spot the "hot buttons" that motivate the seller.

For example, in one negotiation in Washington, D.C. some time ago the seller and I were stuck on a point. He had agreed to a $2,000 down payment and an $8,000 note for the rest of his equity ($50,000 two-bedroom condo) but he wouldn't put his name to the dotted line. I probed deeper. Why? He had another buyer who would pay $10,000 in cash *and* assume his V.A. loan so that he could have his entitlement benefits restored. There were two issues here: 1 cash, 2 V.A. benefits. I proceeded to attack the first issue. What are you going to do with the $10,000 you *might* get from the buyer (I say "might" because a bird in the hand is worth two in the bush). He was going to invest the money in a C.D. at 13%. I gave him an alternative: I'll raise the price by $500 and give you a note for 15% interest. As a further incentive, I explained how, unlike the cash offer, my note would not be taxable since he would receive no cash from me. This would give him a better return on his investment. He could not argue . . . he was an accountant. As for the V.A. benefits, I agreed to find a partner who would enter into the purchase with me to insure the seller that his V.A. benefits would be restored. I only would have to find a renter to whom I would give an ownership in the property (⅓ or ½) for the privilege of using his V.A. benefits. The seller agreed that my logic was sound and that he would sell to me after conferring with his attorney.

The art of compromising is in understanding the seller's needs enough that you can show him *alternative* solutions to his problem. Look at the following chart:

Sometimes these alternatives don't work. It may take other tactics. Here are some which may help.

1. Lay-the-Cards-on-the-Table Approach. If the seller doesn't seem to budge from his inflexible stand, he may be moved by honesty. We, of course, are always honest, but we don't reveal *all* of our cards until necessary. If nothing seems to work, lay your cards on the table. "Mr. Seller, I don't have the $20,000 necessary for the down payment (or I can't afford the monthly payments). But I'm an honest and hard-working person. You don't really *need* the cash. I can solve your problem immediately. And you can help me get into the property. It's win/win. What do you say?" This appeals to the *emotions* instead of to *logic*.

2. Student/Teacher Approach. This approach appeals to the seller's ego instead of to his logic. "Mr. Seller, if you were to go about amassing a fortune in real estate, how would you do it?" Or you might say, "Mr. Seller, how did you get your start?" This works well if you are young and/or inexperienced. These weaknesses can then appear as strengths since the seller may agree to sell his property to you to teach you a lesson. The old and wise seller takes the young and inexperienced buyer under his wing and shows him the way. Don't laugh. I've both bought and sold real estate with this approach.

"I Need More Money Down!"

Seller Says (Or Gives Clue)	Buyer Gives Alternative
A. Investment Conscious: I'm going to invest my proceeds so I need a cash down payment.	1. I'll raise the price/lower the terms. 2. Give you higher interest rate. 3. Give you percentage of profits from future sale.
B. Debt Conscious: I need to pay some debts.	I'll assume your debts.
C. Property Conscious: I need cash to buy my next property.	If I could find you a property to buy with nothing down, would you sell yours with nothing down? (This is a difficult alternative, but does work, especially if you *need* the property.)
D. Security Conscious: Why should I sell to your with little or nothing down? What assurance do I have that you will take care of it?	1. I will give you a blanket mortgage on another property that I own (or that my partner owns). 2. I'll prove to you that I am honest and have excellent references.
E. Small Bills Conscious: I need only a few thousand for small bills.	1. credit cards. 2. rents and deposits. 3. partners. 4. Realtor's commission borrowed.
F. Tax Conscious: I am worried about taxes.	The smaller the down payment, the lower your tax bill.

"I Need Monthly Payments."

Seller says:	Buyer tries for smaller or no payments:
A. That's just the way it's done. Everyone asks for monthly payments.	Not so. Look at banks: the most conservative of institutions don't pay monthly payments to their investors. Gold? Stocks? Etc.
B. I need the monthly income.	1. Look at tax consequences of receiving the cash. 2. If you sacrifice and let the money compound, you could double your money in _____ years. 3. I can't afford to make heavy negative cash flows. 4. Don't squander your money on monthly income when you can have a huge future balloon payment.

3. Share-the-Problem Approach. Sellers are more receptive to creative deals when they know *why* the offer is different from more conventional financing methods. Studies have been performed which prove that people respond better to requests when there is a reason included, *even* if the reason given is a poor one! That's why telling the seller that the monthly payments will "kill" your monthly budget just *may* work as an approach. It's worth a try. You never can tell what a seller will do until you ask him. So ask. Share your problem with him and let him be part of the problem-solving process. All of us love to help. Let the seller help you for once.

Three. The Importance of Persistence.

Let me mention five quick points in closing!

A. Don't die of thirst just inches from the fountain!

Or, to quote Calero again, "Many negotiations are constantly on the verge of collapse."

Just knowing this should take some of the pressure off and give you the courage to probe and dig deeper to find solutions that work for both parties. Don't give up too soon just because you feel the seller is offended by your offer. Keep trying. Many a negotiation has been saved from the jaws of defeat by a last-minute solution to the seller's problem. "When one side does not acknowledge needs, the other side has to show persuasively that such needs do exist and that there is great value in satisfying them," Calero adds. Dig deep.

B. "No" means, "I don't understand." The seller is often confused by the creative offer. Rehearse the offer. "Mr. Seller, let me understand this. You say you won't accept my offer because you don't like the nothing down part. But you told me earlier that you didn't need the cash. Could you help me understand what I did wrong?" In other words, "What's bugging you?"

C. "It can't be done" means "I've never done it," or "I don't know how to do it." Sometimes the seller's agent needs to be educated, too. If all parties involved can see *how* the offer works to the *advantage* of both the buyer and the seller and the agent, the success is more probable.

D. Don't be stubborn, be persistent. "The difference between a persistent negotiator and a stubborn one is that the former keeps trying different approaches, while the latter sticks to only one," Calero maintains.

E. Optimism is the root of persistence. I *know* that I can buy real estate with nothing down because I understand the law of averages. "If you throw enough spaghetti against a wall, some of it has got to stick" (Joe Girard). If I look and call enough don't wanters, I *have* to find a nothing down deal, no matter how lousy a negotiator I think I am. That is why I persist. Many an optimist has become rich simply by buying out a pessimist. And so it goes!

Creative Negotiation: What Experience Has Taught Me

Wade B. Cook

Times have changed. The economy has changed, but people haven't changed and neither have their needs, If one looks past high interest rates and prices and looks into the basic reason real estate is such a good investment in spite of everything, then he will see that the disadvantages actually create advantages.

The advantage created is this. The same "set of facts" that might make a property seem out of reach actually creates a "set of facts" that make it an even better investment — better in terms of leverage, tax shelters, and control of appreciation.

Let me be more specific. If you're looking at a four-plex for $100,000, you will deal with its purchase more cautiously.

You want to maximize the most out of your cash, so you offer a lower price with less down and at a lower interest rate. The less down, aspect lets you leverage higher, consequently the leveraged cost of your tax benefits, equity appreciation, and income is enhanced.

Now is not the time to back off and wait. Now is the time to turn these disadvantages into advantages.

Solutions to problems are as varied as the problems themselves. Creativity is the word used to explain buying properties through unconventional sources. The owner wants to sell, you want to buy, in steps come imagination and creative techniques and "voila," a purchase is made.

Understanding is the watchword. Understanding the seller's problems. Understanding your goals. Understanding the process of lining these two up. The following eight points are lessons I learned over the years, lessons that helped me be creative, lessons that helped me get the job done.

1. People do things for their reasons, not yours. This was taught to me best on one occasion when I was selling a house. I had used bank loans to complete extensive repairs on the house. Everything was remodeled inside and out! New carpet, drapes, paint, roof, landscaping, cabinets, fireplace, etc. I was so proud when it was completed and I wasn't surprised a bit when it sold the next day. After negotiating the deal, I asked the lady what made her buy it. My chest was six inches bigger while waiting for her answer, but then it deflated when she said, "I've always wanted a double stainless steel kitchen sink." That was probably the only thing in the house that I hadn't repaired or replaced.

If you want to buy or sell, you need to ascertain the seller's reasons.

2. People act in their best interests. I had periods of investing when I was buying and processing up to six properties a month. Of all those deals, there was rarely a time where what first presented itself as "the reason" actually was the "whole truth and nothing but the truth." I'm not saying that anyone deliberately lied to me, but I learned quickly that almost all people are very intelligent. And the closer the problems get to home (their home) the more intelligent and cautious they become. Good! That's the way it should be. If anyone thinks that he'll get rich by running around "stealing candy" from unsuspecting people, he has a powerful lesson to learn.

I have watched many people who thought they could circumvent this law of honesty. They cannot and did not. We do reap what we sow.

I've come to the point where I would rather do business with a sophisticated person. When we both understood what was in each other's best interest, a deal could be put together. This lesson helped me learn and use my most powerful lesson which is explained next.

3. Use the Golden Rule. One time I came across a lady who wanted desperately to move out of a house. Her husband had died six years before and the house had gone steadily downwards and finally into a state of disrepair. She had a teenage daughter and together they had found a nice apartment with a swimming pool. I told her that her price wasn't high enough. She said, "I know I could fix this and that and get it up in value, but I don't want to. I hate this place and want out. I'm half-moved now. Just give me the $800 and promise me I won't have to worry about the back payments." We drew up the papers and she left satisfied. And for the first time in a long time, she could relax and enjoy life.

She didn't want anything down, but that could not have been right. I put myself in her shoes and felt that $800 was fair. She was thankful for this, and I was glad that we both got what we wanted.

I mentioned before that people are intelligent. When I first started investing, I thought maybe I could learn something about a property that the seller didn't know. This might be true in terms of potential or my tax advantages, etc., but rarely is it true in terms of present value or current rent prices. After my first deal I dispelled that notion and started hoping for really intelligent people to do business with.

It was with these people that I prospered and I'm confident they did, too. Call it the win/win philosophy or whatever you like, but the concept does ensure success.

4. People will not trade their certainties for uncertainties. If you're proposing an unfamiliar concept, you'll have to spend extra time educating the seller. And this will be time well spent if he ends up feeling good about you and your offer.

For example, you just meet the seller and even though he doesn't know you from Adam you make him an offer to pay him a little money two years from now then start payments to him after that time. *And,* you also want to secure this amount against another property later on — a property that he doesn't know from the Garden of Eden. Can you wonder that he'll be apprehensive? Take time with him until he feels comfortable.

5. Tension is lessened with time. The longer you can spend with the seller, the better the relationship becomes. This is best described in the following graph:

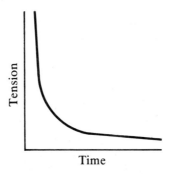

At first meeting with no time elapsed at all, the tension is high. As time progresses, the tension is lessened. I'm not advocating spending hours talking about the weather, but there are many things that can be discussed that will uncover mutual areas of interest, building rapport. Later, many things you've learned will be helpful in your negotiations.

Also, there will be times when several meetings will be needed over a period of days or weeks. That's okay. The end result is worth it, not to mention the new friend you'll have.

6. Ask a lot of questions to avoid surprises. Use a questionnaire form and fill it out completely. If this form is filled out properly *and* you have all the information, then you are in a position to create a "golden rule deal." The reason I mentioned "all the information" is that many times I would get to a closing and find out about one more little encumbrance that the seller forgot about, or the interest rate and payment you're assuming is not exactly what he said.

It's not fun to have surprises in the investing business. To ensure that you don't have any surprises after you make your offer, ask questions like the following:

"Mr. Jones, can we go over your file to make sure we haven't missed anything?"

"Did you take out any other loans while you've owned this property?"

"Might there be any other liens from suits, divorces, car accidents, or whatever that you can think of?"

Stay a step ahead by having all the information.

7. Be loaded with alternatives. Be prepared with several alternatives. These shouldn't be presented like, "Well, you don't like this one; how about this one?" Use one as a springboard for another. Have many tools in your toolbox. "When all you have is a hammer, every problem becomes a nail." (Steve Bird). To get the job done, you'll almost have to be a pharmacist: a pill for every ill.

8. Creativity and persistence. Creativity is not some magic formula that brings success and happiness. I know several people who were considered creative by almost everyone. "He's so smart." "He puts together deals that no one can." "He's bought over $5 million dollars worth of real estate and he started with nothing." Sound familiar?

But close inspection of the methods of operation of these successful investors shows something that is always overlooked. That something is the persistence that went into their success. "Sure he got a good deal, but do you realize it's been two months and 18 other rejected earnest monies before he got this one?" "Sure he's successful, but he works 60 hours a week."

The deals are there, but like selling, it's a numbers game.

Let me put down some numbers of this game. You look at ten properties and make earnest monies on six. Three out of the six are seriously considered but only one is accepted.

The only way to control and get the one is by processing the ten. Results take time, time spent processing the numbers.

When the final tally is taken, the investors that are called creative will be the persistent ones.

Conclusion

These lessons are integral parts of the finding, negotiating, and buying process. If the big fish gets away, it's probably because of the negotiating process. It behooves all of us to strengthen this step. Strengthen it by conceptualizing how it can be better for us individually, and then developing a good style that comes from practice and experience.

"If there's a way, take it; if not, make it."

How Do You Know the Seller is Telling the Truth?

Richard C. Powelson

Many years ago when I was selling real estate for a living in Aurora, Illinois, one of my favorite sayings was, "All buyers are liars and so are sellers." This is, of course, not universally true, but it is a reminder that we have to be on our guard. As a Realtor, it was my job to find out who was telling the truth and many times I was fooled. As a buyer, how do you know if the seller is telling you the truth?

What do you do if the seller is pretending to be a "don't wanter" and is just chomping at the bit to get you to buy his property? He knows all the right answers to your questions and you end up making him an offer. Do you have any protection in case this happens?

Richard J. Allen's book *How to Write a Nothing Down Offer* is essential in helping you to determine just how honest the seller might be in your case. It is essential because it tells you how to protect yourself in case the seller is lying. There are certain clauses that I personally use for my own protection and I'd like to share several with you. These, coupled with Richard Allen's suggestions and guidelines, should remove whatever doubt you may have as to the seller's honesty.

We start out, of course, by asking questions. Once we have determined that the seller is a don't wanter, we do our investigation and make our written offer and include our "weasel" clauses. I try keep these clauses as simple as possible to avoid arousing suspicion on the part of the seller. My favorites are: *subject to my partner's approval, subject to a "soil" test, subject to financing suitable to the buyer,* and *subject to an appraisal.*

It's hard to argue with a clause *subject to an appraisal or soil test* so I seldom have any disagreements over these two clauses, especially if I agree to pay for the appraisal. I don't always get an appraisal, but I like this clause because I can use it to back out of a purchase if necessary.

In addition, I like to buy without personal liability so I always include the "Exculpatory Clause" and buy "subject to" any existing financing. Your protection in using these two clauses is that if for some reason the seller did lie to you and you end up losing the property, they take the property but don't take you! The Exculpatory Clause reads as follows: "The liability shall be limited to the property itself and shall not extend beyond this." Every once in a while a seller will object to the use of this clause, stating that he wants me on the note personally. My reply is: "Oh, I thought the property was worth the money. If you don't have any confidence in your own property, why should I? If you will reduce your price, I'll be happy to sign personally." Most of the time, this eliminates that problem. By buying "subject to" you of course do not agree to "assume" the mortgage itself, only the payments. You have no personal liability in case of default.

This gets you into the property without personal loss, but what if the seller has lied to you about the income and expenses? In this case, your loss could come in the way of loss of down payment or result in a negative cash flow when the seller told you it was a positive cash flow. Do you have any protection if this happens? If the seller is carrying any or all of the financing for you, yes, you do have some protection by using the "Performance Clause." It reads as follows:

"The debt service, net of any impounds for taxes and insurance, shall be $ _____ per month, but not to exceed _____ percent (_____%) of the net operating income, subject to an independent audit."

Simply put, if the net operating income is $11,000 as stated by the seller, your mortgage payment to him is a percentage of that amount, say 80% or $8,800. If the net operating income falls short of the $11,000, then your payment is reduced by that amount. You might also suggest to the seller that if the net operating income goes up, you'll increase your mortgage payment by that percentage.

What does this accomplish? It overcomes any doubt that you might have as to what the income of the property might be and it guarantees that you will always have a positive cash flow regardless of economic conditions.

You have weasel clauses to allow you to check your "fears," special clauses to give you personal liability protection, and the performance clause to insure a positive cash flow. So what if the seller isn't telling you the entire truth? If you have done your homework properly, which includes a warranty of property condition, you should have no worries. As Robert Allen would say, "Don't wait to buy real estate, buy real estate and wait!"

You'll Never Know Until You Ask: A Case Study in Creative Negotiation

Richard J. Allen

Bob and Carolyn O'Brien of St. Louis shared ths one: In the presence of the listing broker, Bob did some "fact finding" with a woman who was offering her $120,000 home for sale. The lead-off question from the "Nothing Down" list made the broker sit up and take notice: "How much did you pay for the house?" But the seller obliged willingly with the information. Among the other questions, which horrified the broker but elicited "yes" answers from the seller in each case, were these:

Q. Would you be willing to carry 100% financing on your home?
A. Yes.
Q. Your home would need some remodeling in order to suit our family needs. Would you be willing to loan us around $30,000 for the improvments at around 11-12%?
A. Yes.

(And this next one takes the cake for chutzpah.)

Q. Unfortunately, we already have a second mortgage on the other property. Would you loan us the money to pay off the second so that we can put on a new second for you?
A. Yes.

Conclusion: The O'Briens were speaking with a don't wanter. Second conclusion: the O'Briens have courage. As it turned out, they decided the property didn't quite suit their needs, so the woman sold it to another party—for nothing down, of course.

Even so, the O'Briens' approach underscores an important principle for us all to follow: you never know what a seller will say until you ask. It is vital to ask the important questions first in order to identify flexible sellers and avoid wasting your precious time with sellers who are not don't wanters. It takes courage, but that is what financially free people are made of.

PART VII:

Understanding the Techniques of Creative Finance

An Alternate Strategy: The Robert G. Allen Nothing Down System

Richard J. Allen

In his slender book *New Think*, Edward de Bono makes the statement: "It may be so difficult to escape from a dominant idea that it becomes impossible without outside help" (New York: Basic Books, 1968, p. 33).

The world of real estate has been governed for years by one dominant strain of thought, i.e., in order to buy and hold property successfully, the average person must have excellent credit, a strong financial statement, good income, lots of money for a substantial down payment, and strong collaborative support from the hard-money lenders. With the coming of the days of economic austerity, those who agreed that income property was the finest of all investments found they could not hope to participate in owning a larger piece of America under the dominant rules that had obtained hitherto. New patterns were needed if the cash-poor but creative individual was to break into the world of property ownership.

High-orbit investors had long been aware of creative techniques for acquiring property with minimum capital of their own. Out of the exchange movement of the Fifties and Sixties—especially in California—formulas for nothing down purchases became the rule of thumb. But such alternative approaches to buying real estate were mostly confined to the private circles of the highly sophisticated investor or real estate professional. The average Joe was still burdened with the dominant ideas of high down, hard money, and heavy credit. How could he hope to participate in America's most beneficial investment?

How, except through outside help? There had to be a way to escape from the domination of conventional ideas. One of the most important popular contributors to that escape—and perhaps the most important—was Robert G. Allen, whose book *Nothing Down* (Simon and Schuster, 1980) remained on the prestigious New York Times Best-Seller list longer in

1981 than any other hard-cover non-fiction work except for Milton Friedman's *Free to Choose.* Over 715,000 copies of *Nothing Down* have been sold to date. Some 950,000 people nationwide have attended the widely advertised free lectures on the Nothing Down System and over 95,000 are graduates of the famous two-day Robert Allen Nothing Down Seminar. It would be hard to estimate how many hundreds of thousands, perhaps millions, have taken note of Robert Allen's famous line: "Fly me to any city. Take away my wallet. Give me $100 for living expenses. And in 72 hours I'll buy an excellent piece of real estate for nothing down."

What accounts for the rather phenomenal success of the Nothing Down movement nationwide? From its humble beginnings in August of 1977, the Nothing Down Seminar has grown to be America's most popular educational offering on the subject of creative finance in real estate. The only explanation for this success is the fact that the RAND System offered deliverance from the strictures of conventional approaches. At last the general public had access to techniques and formulas that would permit the acquisition of a real estate portfolio under the cashless conditions that prevailed toward the end of the Seventies and into the Eighties.

Robert Allen became, in effect, the major force for popularizing creative financing in America. It was my good fortune to become associated with this movement in 1979, when my brother Robert invited me to leave the academic world of meditative serenity and venture with him into the world of educational entrepreneurship on a grand scale. My task would be to assure the educational and organizational quality of the nothing down product and to assist in the program for "taking the message" to the American public.

If there was something of the missionary spirit at work in the way we went about our task, it was a conscious effort to place the program in the context of values that had contributed fundamentally to the American way of life—initiative, self-reliance, creative thought, mutual support—values that would strike a familiar chord in the minds of the cross-sectional audience we wanted to reach. The response was overwhelming. What came to be known as the "win/win" approach to real estate investing had immediate appeal to readers and seminar attendees. The nation-wide network of RAND graduates organized into "RAND Groups" continued the task of expanding awareness of new techniques and practicing principles of peer support and creative problem-solving. Additional seminars, books, tapes, newsletters, and hot-line advisory opportunities were introduced for those with specialized needs. In 1983 the RAND network was expanded as a professional investors association under the title The American Congress on Real Estate,™ or ACRE™ for short. The objective of the movement was to make it possible for anyone—anyone, that is, with the desire and the will—to become successful as income-property investors. As of this writing, some measure of success has been realized. Graduates are acquiring nothing down property at the rate of over $1 billion worth per year — and climbing. As the many case studies show, the acquisitions program in general is progressing without undue burdens of negative cash flows and balloons. Here is a program that works!

The organizational framework that I recommended for the Nothing Down System—the one that was eventually adopted—is summarized in the chart below. Details are available in the seminar manual for the Nothing Down Seminar. The basic task of laying the foundation consists in appropriating an open and creative mind-set, establishing realistic goals, targeting "bread and butter" properties in good condition, identifying "don't wanter" (i.e., flexible) sellers, and doing one's homework in analyzing all important aspects of the property. The transaction is then completed by means of the appropriate win/win strategies of negotiation, financial problem-solving using the nothing down system of fifty basic creative techniques (organized according to the nine flexible sources of down payment capital), and seeing to it that the closing is accomplished in as risk-free and professional a manner as possible. The "harvesting of the money crop" can proceed in a variety of ways depending on one's goals and circumstances. Whatever the individual patterns decided upon, all must of course proceed on the basis of action—"Mastering the Art of Becoming a Doer." The entire program is summarized in Bob Allen's formula: "Don't wait to buy real estate; buy real estate and wait."

What follows is a series of brief vignettes summarizing all fifty of the Nothing Down techniques of the program categorized by sources of capital (plus options):

1. The Seller	6. Hard-Money Lenders
2. The Buyer	7. Underlying Mortgages
3. The Realtor	8. Investors
4. The Renters	9. Partners
5. The Property	10. Options

The Nothing Down System is one way investors can escape a dominant conventional idea and replace it with a new gestalt—one that is more in tune with the needs of our modern age. Complete details of the illustrations used in the following outline are available in the book *How To Write A Nothing Down Offer.*

Robert G. Allen's
Nothing Down System
of Creative Real Estate Investing

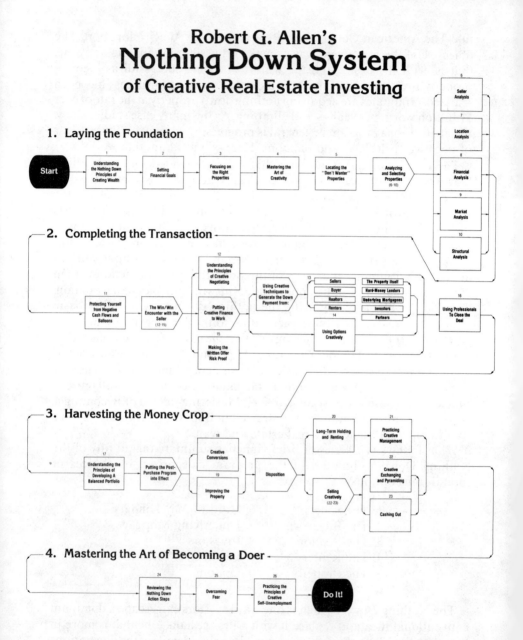

1. THE SELLER

Among the nine major sources of down payment funds for property acquisition, the seller is no doubt the most important. If the buyer has done his selection job well, he will be dealing with a person who is anxious to sell and therefore flexible with financing arrangements. The seller will need to take on a role that might be new for him—that of lender. But if the buyer is sensitive to the needs of the seller, he will foster trust and see to it that both parties win. (Lending can, after all, be a lucrative business with its own slate of benefits, even for property sellers.)

This section reviews eight nothing down techniques involving seller financing.

Technique No. 1 The Ultimate Paper Out

An investor in Milwaukee was able to acquire a $48,000 triplex from a banker who not only arranged for a new low-interest first mortgage, but carried back virtually all the remaining equity in the form of second at below-market rates. Another investor in West Palm Beach, Florida, picked up a single family home for $66,500 by putting on a new first and having the anxious seller carry back all the rest of his equity ($36,500) for five years, no payments, no interest. Both of these investors were using the technique known as "The Ultimate Paper Out." Here is how it works.

When we are talking about buying or selling a piece of real estate, we are really talking about the problem of defining and dealing with the seller's equity. Equity as a concept is straightforward enough. Everyone knows that it represents that portion of the value of a property that is not encumbered, that belongs lock, stock, and barrel to the owner. But equity is a fluid concept. It can be specified only in relation to that mysterious and shifting quantity called the "fair market value." The owner has dreams about an equity of such and such—usually an optimistically high number. But the truth of the matter is that market forces determine his equity by determining how much his property is really worth at any moment in time. The members of the market club—you and I—gang up on the poor old seller and say, collectively, "You have a nice little place, but we've taken a vote around town, and the best we could come up with is a price of such and such." At that moment in time, the seller's equity is defined, and the problem becomes how to transfer to him value equal to the equity involved.

The majority of sellers, of course, will want to hold out for a selling price at the high end of the scale. They want their equity to be overweight. No one can blame them for that. But among the army of sellers in the marketplace at any given time, there are always a few—perhaps five percent or less—

who say to themselves, "We like our equity and want to preserve it and derive benefit from it, but we are very anxious to sell. So anxious in fact, that we might give up some of that equity in order to get rid of the property quickly." Alternately, these don't wanter sellers might be thinking, "I don't really feel like discounting my equity for a quick sale, but I would be willing to wait until later for a part or all of my equity to be converted to cash."

And that is the issue when it comes to "papering out" a deal. After the seller and the buyer have determined what equity is involved, the next step is to decide how soon the equity is to be converted. It all boils down to a matter of patience. The seller with infinite patience (and infinite desperation) will say, "Here's my equity; take it all and just get me out of this place." In a case like that the selling price is equal to the liens. But such cases are rare.

The next best situation is the case in which the seller says, "Here's my equity; pay me for it when you can. Let's work out the schedule." That is the technique referred to as "The Ultimate Paper Out." All of the seller's equity is converted to paper before it is converted to cash. When the buyer takes over the property, he gives the seller paper for his equity and obligates himself to redeem the paper according to mutually agreeable terms.

Not all sellers will agree to an "Ultimate Paper Out." But creative buyers should always ask. You never know exactly what the seller is thinking or how anxious he really is to sell. Perhaps only one seller in twenty will be willing to enter into a nothing down deal; and of these, perhaps only one in ten will agree to an "Ultimate Paper Out." That means that Technique No. 1 will show up in only one out of every 200 creative deals. But it does happen from time to time— much to the surprise and delight of the creative buyer.

Technique No. 2 The Blanket Mortgage

The key to using the seller as lender in a real estate transaction is trust. The seller has got to trust us to pay him his equity according to the terms of the agreement we work out with him. The conventional way to "buy" trust is to give the seller a large cash down payment. That way he knows that we will not likely walk away from the property. We are going to stay around and take care of our obligations; otherwise the seller will be able to take back the property, and we will lose not only that big cash down payment but also any appreciated value above the seller's equity.

But how do we develop trust when there is little or no cash put down on the property? How does the buyer make the seller feel secure in such cases? Often the buyer can develop personal trust with the seller simply on the basis of personal qualities and win/win attitudes. In such cases, the security of the subject property itself is sufficient to close the deal.

In some instances, however, a little extra is needed to remove lingering suspicions on the part of the seller. That is where the blanket mortgage comes into play. In any mortgage or trust deed arrangement, there are two basic documents that are prepared: one is a note given by the buyer to the seller setting forth the terms for converting the equity to cash; the other is a security agreement in which the buyer says to the seller, in effect, "If I don't perform according to the terms of the note, then you can take back the property." In a cashless or near cashless transaction, the security of the subject property may not be enough to satisfy the seller. Therefore, the buyer may choose to secure the note with additional collateral—not only the subject property but also additional property (equity) he may have in his portfolio. The note itself stays the same, but the security agreement is changed to increase the collateral and build trust with the seller. Naturally, the buyer will want to arrange to have the seller release the additional collateral as soon as the subject property appreciates to a predetermined value or as soon as the buyer has proven himself to be dependable and prompt in making his payments.

The blanket mortgage technique is not among the most frequently used in creative finance. The buyer hopes to build trust without having to tie up his other equities. Still, when a seller needs that extra bit of persuasion, the blanket mortgage technique can come in handy.

For example, one creative investor we know of recently acquired a nice four-bedroom, three-bath home for $75,000. The investor put a new first on the property (which was nearly free and clear) and had the sellers move their remaining equity ($35,000) to another property owned by the investor. To build trust will the sellers, the buyer granted them a blanket mortgage that also included his equity in another rental property he owned. Although the buyer did not put any of his own money into the deal (the bank provided all that was needed), he was able to persuade the sellers to agree on the basis of his neck being on the line with the blanket mortgage.

Technique No. 3 Life Insurance Policy

There is another strategy the buyer can use to persuade the seller to play lender in a transaction. As in the case of the blanket mortgage, the key is building trust. What if you say to the still somewhat incredulous seller, "Since you are permitting me to pay off your equity in cash over a period of time, how would it be if I took out an insurance policy in the amount of the note and made you the beneficiary? That way you will feel secure that the note will be paid off no matter what."

This technique is not usually necessary; still, it is an inexpensive way to build trust if the seller cannot quite see it your way and needs just a bit more persuasion.

Technique No. 4 Contract or Wrap-Around Mortgage

An Albuquerque investor recently bought a triplex for $69,300 by putting down $1,300 and having the seller accept a contract for the remaining $68,300, 10.75% interest for 35 years, payout after 12 years. The contract "wrapped around" a small underlying first mortgage. Similarly, an investor in Springfield, Massachusetts, acquired an $80,000 free and clear single family house by putting a small sum down and having the seller carry back the rest in the form of a contract. These are variations of the technique referred under various names such as "contract," "wrap-around," or "owner carry back."

This technique is one of the most frequently used creative finance tools. It is the foundation of seller financing. Rather than refinancing the property or formally assuming the existing mortgage, the buyer uses a contract as the purchase instrument. Technically he does not get title to the property until he has performed according to the provisions of the agreement. In effect, he says to the seller, "I'll pay your equity off in installments over time. And as soon as I have paid everything off, you will give me the deed for the property, and it will be mine. In the meantime, I will act as the owner by taking over the management and getting all the tax benefits and the appreciated equity above what the property is worth at the time of purchase. Of course, all the expenses in the meantime are mine as well."

If the property is free and clear at the time of purchase, the seller pockets all the installment payments on the contract. If there are existing encumbrances on the property, then the contract is referred to as a wrap-around contract or wrap-around mortgage. It "wraps around" the existing first and subsequent mortgages or trust deeds. When the seller receives the installment payments, he has to first make payments on the existing notes before he can pocket the rest. The advantage to him is that the interest rate on the total wrap-around contract will be higher than on the underlying loans. Therefore, he will be making an interest spread on the underlying part of the note — not a bad deal for a seller-turned-lender. In addition, he will be able to spread his capital gains profit out over time rather than receiving all of it during one year. The tax advantages are considerable. With the recent liberalization of installment sale provisions by the IRS, sellers have great leeway in how contracts are set up for maximum tax benefits. A competent tax accountant can spell out the details.

The advantage to the buyer is that he does not need to come up with a large cash down payment. Frequently a moderate amount down will close the deal. In addition, the interest rates acceptable to sellers are usually far below conventional market rates for new financing.

In practice, a contract sale is handled by an escrow company, which holds the pre-executed deed from the seller in favor of the buyer until the latter satisfies the terms of the contract. Generally the escrow or title company will also hold a quitclaim deed made out by the buyer in favor of the seller, which is to be released to the seller in case of default. It is in the best interests of the buyer if the escrow company is also empowered to receive his installment payments and take care of making the payments on the underlying loans before disbursing the balance to the seller. That way the buyer can be assured that his money winds up in the right places.

An alternative form of the "contract/wrap" technique is the situation where a buyer takes title subject to the existing financing (agrees to take over the seller's obligations) or goes through the formal procedure of assuming the existing financing (qualification, credit checks, transfer of title). The buyer then signs a contract with the seller for the equity above the existing loans and makes payments according to a mutually agreeable schedule. The seller's equity is covered by a note secured by the property itself. The usual term for this arrangement is "owner carry back." The term refers to the fact that the seller carries back paper to cover the unpaid equity on his property. Terms on the paper are negotiable and vary from case to case.

Technique No. 5 Raise the Price, Lower the Terms

Seller financing has already become a convention for real estate transactions in the decade of the 1980s. Currently nearly two-thirds of all home sales involve contract sales or assumptions with owner carry-back second-mortgages. Tight money conditions always foster seller financing of this type. Yet even though the concept of "seller as lender" is no longer foreign to the American way of real property transfer, there are variations to the game that give creative buyers the advantage over the competition.

One such variation is the important technique called "Raise the Price, Lower the Terms." Simply put, this technique calls for the buyer to offer the seller more than he is asking for the property in exchange for flexibility with the terms. For example, one investor we know of recently took an interest in a Jacksonville, Florida, estate house with adjoining triplex. He offered to raise the sales price by $5,000 if the seller would lower the down payment requirement and accept payments over 15 years. By using this technique, he outpaced the competition and won over the seller despite the hue and cry of all the relatives in the background.

Technique No. 6 The Balloon Down Payment

An investor in Milwaukee recently bought a small rental home for $35,000 by putting on a new first of $15,000 and having the seller carry back the rest (no payments, no interest) after a small down. The seller would do so only after the buyer agreed to pay out the indebtedness after five years. The buyer of a $245,000 7-plex in Lake Worth, Florida, assumed the existing first and induced the seller to carry back the remainder of his equity after the $50,000 downpayment (obtained from a partner) in the form of a second at 12%. The seller agreed, but only on the basis of a ten-year payout of the balance of the second. Both of these investors were using the technique referred to as a "balloon" mortgage.

It is not uncommon for seller-financing arrangements to include provisions for a balloon payment in the future. In fact, balloons are an important inducement to get the seller to play the part of the lender in the first place. Knowing that the major part of his equity is coming in the near future, the seller is willing to carry the financing at rates below the conventional market. Occasionally a seller is willing to amortize the entire amount of the carry back over a long period of time — fifteen or twenty years or longer. Most of the time, however, the seller wants to be paid off sooner, in fact, as soon as possible.

And that is the danger the buyer must beware of. Short-fuse balloon notes can rob the buyer of health, sleep, and sometimes the property itself. In theory, the time of the balloon payment should be far enough away to take advantage of interim appreciation. Property values and rents must grow enough to permit a refinance solution to the balloon payment.

But what if local property values — particularly during a period of sustained high interest rates and sluggish real estate sales — do not grow as anticipated? The buyer may be forced to sell the property, or another piece of real estate in his control to pay off the balloon. Alternately, he may have to bring in an equity-participation cash-partner to bail him out, thus giving away important benefits. In the worst case, he might have to give the property back to the seller and lose all his investment.

Despite its liabilities, the balloon payment technique can be a valuable way to get into a property for little or nothing down up front. Buyers should resist pressures to accept anything less than five years for payout. Seven years or more would be preferable.

Technique No. 7 High Monthly Down Payments

This technique is a variation of Technique No. 4, "Contract or Wrap-Around Mortgage." Usually a contract sale requires at least a token down payment to substantiate the good faith of the buyer and put a little cash into the pocket of the seller. Sometimes a hefty down is required, in which case funds have to be "cranked" out of the property (Techniques 32 and 33) or a cash partner must be brought in (Techniques 43, 44, and 45).

But what if the buyer has nothing at all to put down except an income that gives him the ability to make monthly payments of several hundred dollars toward the purchase of a piece of property? Perhaps the seller would permit him to purchase the property now and make high monthly payments over a couple of years until a mutually acceptable down payment had been constituted. It never hurts to ask.

Technique No. 8 Defer the Down Payment with No Mortgage Payment

There are endless variations of how seller financing might be set up. Here is one more which could prove useful under certain circumstances. A seller of a free and clear property who needed cash down only to build trust in his buyer might be induced to forego rental income for a few months while the buyer accumulated enough to put together the required down. It is not a common opportunity, but it has happened in the past and will happen again in the future — perhaps to you.

This technique, together with the other seven described and illustrated in this section, should stimulate creative buyers to take advantage of seller flexibilities in financing. Seller financing, after all, is one of the major sources for down payment capital.

2. THE BUYER

The second area of flexibility in solving the problem of down payments has to do with the buyer's own resources. "But," you say, "if we are trying to spare the downtrodden, cash-poor buyer from coming up with down payments in the first place, why bother to look to his personal resources?" The reason is that buyers often overlook valuable resources right under their own noses. They frequently have personal property, talents, expertise, or equity resources that could be used to acquire desirable income-producing property without the need for cash. And sometimes they even have cash or inheritances that could be applied — there's no shame to that, if you have the money at hand! This section reviews ten techniques in the area of buyer flexibility.

Technique No. 9 Your Own Savings and Inheritances

Practitioners of the Nothing Down System sometimes get the notion that putting their own money into a deal is somehow tantamount to failure. Nonsense! If you have it, use it; but use it with skill and creativity. The conventional buyer with $25,000 to spare will go out into the marketplace and plunk the full amount down on a single property. He might find a nice rental home worth $60,000 with a $35,000 mortgage. His first instinct is to take his $25,000 and cash out the seller. There will be no contract payments or balloon mortgages to worry about. Very likely there will be a modest positive cash flow after expenses and debt service are taken care of. He is happy watching his rental unit appreciate in value.

By way of contrast, the creative buyer takes his $25,000 and distributes it over, let's say, five rental homes worth a total of $300,000. By using a combination of creative acquisition techniques and strategies for avoiding negative cash flows, this buyer puts down only $5,000 on each of the homes. He must be careful to structure his deals advantageously, but the outcome is that he controls the growth of five times the real estate for the same amount of investment. His yield will, therefore, be much greater.

In either case, the best approach might be to use the cash resources as collateral to borrow down payment funds. That way, the cash assets can remain in the hands of the buyer and earn a substantial amount of interest. The same might be true of coming inheritances that would be acceptable as collateral on loans.

Technique No. 10 Supply the Seller What He Needs

The question of seller needs is a complex one. Often buyers resort to sophisticated psychological observation and strategic interrogation in order to penetrate the seller's wall of secrecy. That is fine as far as it goes. But the best approach is nearly always the direct one in the form of one simple question: "What do you need the money for?" There are more subtle variations, such as, "What do you plan to do with the proceeds of the transaction?" But it all boils down to the same thing — letting the seller know that you can solve his problem best if you know what he plans to do with the cash coming to him as a result of the sale.

Often the seller has consumer needs that the buyer could satisfy by carrying the necessary amounts on charge accounts or credit cards. In this way, the immediate upfront cash needs are spread out over time. Frequently the seller will be anticipating financial obligations that will require a set amount of cash each month beginning at some time in the future. If the buyer is on his toes, he can help the seller translate the down payment into installment payments that can be taken over by the buyer in lieu of a heavy cash down payment.

One buyer we know of in Stanford, California, gained insight into the seller's need for future day-care funds and persuaded her to reduce the down payment by $13,500 in exchange for his providing monthly payments toward her day care for the next thirty years at very low interest. He was able to supply the seller what was needed and spare himself a heavy down payment obligation.

Technique No. 11 Assume Seller's Obligations

Often a seller is planning to apply down payment funds to debts he may have or payments that may be overdue. If the buyer can arrange to assume these debts and then pay for them over time, he can avoid having to come up with the down payment funds all at once.

One Cleveland buyer of a small rental home was able to take care of the seller's arrears mortgage payments and utility bills and then cover some consumer debt obligations through installment payments. The result was the relaxation of the up-front cash requirements for the transaction.

Technique No. 12 Using Talents, Not Money

A buyer will often have professional expertise that can be "traded" in lieu of down payment funds. Contractors, painters, landscapers, health-care professionals, lawyers, Realtors, insurance agents, car dealers, merchants — all of these can provide valuable services or discounts that could be used in place of down payments. The potential list is not restricted to professional consideration either; sometimes a supply of plain elbow grease can help swing a deal in the absence of funds.

One beginning investor we know of was able to assume a seller's obligations and work off part of the debt by providing maintenance and management services for the creditor. As a result he picked up his first investment property—a mobile home—for nothing down.

Technique No. 13 Borrow Against Life Insurance Policy

In an age of oppressively high interest rates, it is inconceivable why people will leave assets lying around unused in the cash-value accounts of their life insurance policies. But many do it, not realizing that for a pittance (perhaps as low as five or six percent interest) they can pull those funds out of their policies and apply them to other investments.

For example, a Eugene, Oregon, investor recently put together a deal on a duplex by taking the property "subject to" the existing first, having the seller carry back a sizeable second for five years, and generating the $8,000 down payment by borrowing it from the cash value of his insurance policy at 5% interest. Another investor in San Jose, California, set up a transaction involving a $57,500 single family house by assuming the existing first of $25,400, planning to put on a hard-money second in the amount of $20,000, and having the sellers carry back the rest in the form of a third. However, when he went to put on the second, the lenders required him to come up with 10% down in the form of cash. He solved this problem by going to the cash value of his life insurance policy and borrowing $5,800 at 5% interest. The amount needed from the hard-money second was now only $14,200, and everyone was happy. The beauty of insurance loans of this type is that the principal need not ever be paid back (except out of the death or annuity benefits of the policy).

Technique No. 14 Anything Goes

Down payments need not be in the form of cash. We have already seen how professional services can be used in lieu of cash. The same is true of personal property that the buyer might offer the seller to satisfy down payment needs. Cars, boats, furniture, art, clothing, musical instruments — anything acceptable to the seller might be used. We have even heard of pets such as rare monkeys or valuable cats being used as down payments.

One buyer in San Diego acquired a luxurious new home by using gems — diamonds, rubies, and emeralds — as the down payment. For another investor we know of, five truck loads of topsoil did the trick. Anything goes if it satisfies the seller's needs.

Technique No. 15 Creation of Paper

An investor in Sacramento, California, picked up a clean SFH for $56,000 as follows: assume existing $28,000 first mortgage, assume existing $7,700 second due in 7 months, have Realtor carry back a third for $2,500, have seller carry back a note on another property owned by the investor in the amount of $11,600, put down $6,000 cash (borrowed from credit union). By having the balance of the seller's equity carried back in the form of a note secured on the other property, the buyer was able to put his equity in the other property to use and leave himself in the position to be able to refinance the newly acquired property with a new hard-money second in order to retire the existing balloon second and pay off both the Realtor and the credit union. In fact, he had a kitty of $6,800 left over to handle the negative cash flows for several years. The central strategy in this deal was "creating paper" against the other rental property already owned by the buyer.

Frequently a cashless buyer can solve down payment hurdles by applying the value of his other equities to the deal at hand. If the seller is amenable, it is a simple matter to prepare a note secured by the buyer's equity in other properties and hand it to the seller as all or part of the down payment on the subject property. In effect, the buyer says, "I don't have the cash to give you as a down payment, but I can give you this note in exchange for your equity. The note will generate payments to you on mutually acceptable terms. I will maintain the collateral property in **excellent condition as security for the note.**" Then the buyer has a trust deed prepared in favor of the seller to back up the trust deed note.

What the buyer has done is magic — he has created paper out of thin air. But his paper has value. It is solid consideration for the seller's equity and is used in good faith in lieu of all or part of the cash down payment required. If the seller is dependent on such an exchange to consummate the deal but hungry for the cash just the same, he can always sell the note at a discount for cash (Technique No. 40, explained later on).

Not only is the Creation of Paper technique valuable in property acquisition, it permits the complete leveraging of a buyer's other holdings. Usually commercial lenders will lend only up to 80% of the value of a collateral property. If an owner wants to borrow against his assets at levels higher than 80%, he can readily create paper against the top 20% value and use it for exchange purposes. Rarely will a seller ask for credit checks or complicated paperwork to back up such a technique.

Technique No. 16 The Two-Way Exchange

In the Creation of Paper Technique, the buyer retains ownership of the property used to secure the note given to the seller as down payment on the subject property. In an exchange, the seller actually receives the buyer's property in exchange for his own. Title transfers.

Buying property by means of an exchange, if correctly done, provides great benefits in the form of tax deferrals. Section 1031 of the Internal Revenue Service Code permits trading of properties without triggering taxation on the gains. This is one of the single most important strategies in building up a real estate portfolio.

One Milwaukee investor we know of recently traded his $170,000 7-plex for a more desirable $280,000 12-plex by means of a two-way exchange. In another illustration, the owners of a free and clear $150,000 home in Palo Alto, California, traded this property for three other homes in the area and enhanced their tax and cash-flow situation. There are countless variations of this type of exchange going on all the time.

Technique No. 17 The Three-Way Exchange

The principles are the same as in the two-way exchange except that the seller, while anxious to get rid of his own property, is not willing to accept the buyer's property in exchange. However, if someone with a property acceptable to the seller is willing to take over the buyer's property, then everything will fall into place. The end result is the same as a simple exchange except that an extra link is added to the chain. theoretically any number of links might be added. As a result, the business can get complicated. But the outcomes can be spectacular.

Technique No. 18 Lemonading

In exchanging parlance, lemonading refers to the technique of adding cash to a property that, for one reason or another, has not sold as readily as the seller had hoped (a "lemon"). The new package of property-plus-cash is then offered in exchange for any acceptable package on the market. With the cash sweetener added, the lemon is supposed to become more palatable to the marketplace —"lemonade."

3. THE REALTOR

The third major source of down payment capital is the Realtor. By convention, most people assume that the real estate commission for listed properties is a fixed cash element of a transaction and that a seller is responsible for paying it. In fact, the commission is not fixed in any of its dimensions: rate, form, or source.

Like almost anything else, the percentage rate for calculating the commission is negotiable. Indeed, there would be legal problems if the real estate industry were to publish uniform fixed rates. Moreover, there is nothing written dictating that one must pay a commission in cash and cash only. Of course, almost all real estate professionals would prefer cash. It makes a deal clean and tidy and allows one to buy bread for the family table.

However, most informed agents know that some transactions may involve commissions in the form of paper — promissory notes that may provide for monthly payments or a single payment balloon note at the end of an acceptable period. Generally the time involved does not exceed a year or two. Occasionally the commission may be in the form of a share of ownership, with cash emerging upon sale of the property down the pike. Still other possibilities include commissions paid in personal property. In Techique No.14, the agent recieved a beautiful 0.81 carat diamond for his services. He was delighted, as are most agents who shrewd enough to realize that a commission in an alternative form is better than no commission at all.

One of the important techniques available to the buyer who is interested in reducing the cash down payment for a deal is the technique of "Borrowing the Realtor's Commission" (No. 19). While it is true that according to current agency practice, the seller pays the commission, the buyer is at liberty to negotiate alternative arrangements with either the listing or selling agents (or both). If the buyer can induce the agents to defer the commission, the down payment can be reduced by the same amount because the seller's immediate obligation is relieved.

Who pays for the deferred commission in the final analysis? It is negotiable. If the buyer can strike a nothing down deal with the seller paying the commission over time, all the better. In many cases the buyer himself assumes the seller's obligation (Technique No. 11) and pays the deferred commission. Occasionally they share.

The whole point is that the flexibility of the Realtor may be an important factor in whether the deal comes together. Since the commission is usually the largest cash obligation of the seller in a transaction, the power of this technique cannot be overestimated.

There are examples that illustrate how "Borrowing the Realtor's Commission" works in practice. In one Albuquerque transaction we heard of recently, the seller of an 8-plex arranged to pay $3,000 of the commission on a note, the balance being paid in the form of a real estate contract invested in the deal by the buyer's partner. The two notes not only constituted the entire commission, but the entire up front cash needs as well. In another deal, this time in St. Petersburg, Florida, a 35-unit motel and restaurant were acquired using, among other approaches, the technique of borrowing $30,000 in commissions ($15,000 in the form of a personal unsecured note signed by the buyer, and $15,000 in the form of a third mortgage on the buyer's home). Similarly, a note for the commissions was instrumental in closing a deal on two duplexes acquired by an investor in Homestead, Florida. This techinique is very frequently used. As a matter of fact, our research among the Robert Allen Nothing Down investors shows that as many as 20% of the transactions involve some degree of Realtor carry back of commissions.

4. THE RENTERS

In nearly every real estate transaction involving rental property, the renters are instrumental in helping the buyer with the down payment. Of course, they are not aware of it. And few buyers are conscious ahead of time of how important the role of rents and deposits is to their success in reducing the cash down payment.

Technique No. 20 Rents

Since rents are paid in advance, a buyer who closes on the first of the month when rents are due stands to receive the gross rental income for that month. The first mortgage payment is generally not due until thirty days after closing, so the buyer has a thirty-day breather. His immediate cash down payment obligation has therefore been offset by an amount equal to the rents.

Technique No. 21 Deposits

The situation with tenant security deposits is similar. It is not uncommon for the landlord to require the tenant to pay an amount equal to the first and last month's rent as a damage deposit. If a property is sold, the deposits are passed along to the new buyer. Unless state law prohibits the co-mingling of deposit funds with the rental accounts, the buyer can effectively use the deposit funds given to him at closing as an offset to the cash down payment obligation. Of course, when a tenant moves out, all or part of the deposit must be returned. If the new buyer is a wise manager, he will require a buffer period before returning the deposit. This will give him some protection against the possibility that the tenant may have neglected to pay some bills and will allow him meanwhile to find a new tenant who can add to the deposit kitty.

Virtually every real estate transaction involving rental property has the potential of providing access to these two techniques. For example, the buyer of a $325,000 mobile home park in Cheyenne, Wyoming, was able to raise $8,000 of the $25,000 down payment from tenant rents and deposits in a recent transaction. We know of another case from our Los Angeles files where the buyer of a 72-unit apartment complex received $7,000 in rents and deposits at closing to apply to the transaction.

5. THE PROPERTY

The fifth source of down payment capital is the property itself. The buyer who is on his toes learns to recognize aspects of a given property that might be sold off to raise funds for the purchase. The variations are endless — everything from fixtures to parts of the land itself. There are two techniques that belong to this category.

Technique No. 22 Splitting Off Furniture and Other Items

Two years ago, one of the Nothing Down graduates in Florida was $5,000 short of funds needed to purchase an option on a valuable tract of land near Orlando. While wandering over the property one day pondering how he might come up with the necessary capital, he noticed a large area overgrown with beautiful ferns of the type one finds offered for sale in florists shops. Since problems often lead to creative solutions, he put two and two together and arranged to split off the ferns to raise enough money to bring the deal together. Today, the property is being developed into a multi-million dollar recreational park, all because of a patch of ferns — and a creative mind.

Technique No. 23 Splitting Off Part of the Property

In some cases a given property is structured so that parts of it — extra lots or individual buildings — can be split off and sold to raise funds for the acquisition. Here is how it worked recently for an investor we know in West Bend, Wisconsin. He had located an attractive single family home on a large lot with a package price of $99,000. Since he needed to come up with a hefty down payment, he resurveyed the property and established two lots on either side of the house. By the time of closing one lot had sold for $15,000 and the other for $10,000, contributing the bulk of the down payment to acquire the property in the first place. It was all taken care of in a simultaneous closing.

6. HARD-MONEY LENDERS

Hard money refers to funds borrowed from banks under strict conditions of qualifying and repayment, generally at market interest rates. Soft money from sources like sellers comes more cheaply, with terms that are generally much more flexible. For that reason, creative buyers tend to exhaust soft money sources before turning to the banking industry. Nevertheless, hard-money lenders are an important, if not indispensible source of down payment capital to which buyers, sooner or later, must turn. This section outlines eleven techniques for using hard-money funds in creative ways.

Technique No. 24 Small Amounts of Money From Different Banks

Investors getting started are well-advised to cultivate their credit at several banks in their area. Often credit can be built up quickly by borrowing small amounts from different banks and lending institutions and then repaying the loans promptly, even ahead of time. The strategy is to build up credit in sufficient amounts so that funds will be available when that promising deal suddenly surfaces and cash is needed quickly.

Technique No. 25 Cash-By-Mail Companies

Certain specialized lending institutions and finance companies appeal to executives and other well-qualified borrowers through ads in flight magazines and professional journals. The advantages are privacy and speed.

Technique No. 26 Credit Cards

In the past little while we have learned of two cases involving small properties (in this case mobile homes) where the buyers contributed the down payments by using credit cards. In one case an investor raised $500 for the down payment on a 12' × 60' Flamingo which then rented out for a $137/mo. positive cash flow. In another case a fortunate buyer in Phoenix picked up a spotless two-bedroom Schultz mobile home by putting down $1,700 borrowed on a revolving charge account.

Except in unusual cases where the investor has acquired dozens of credit cards and uses them in a strategic and coordinated way, the amounts of cash generated by this technique are not generally large. However, where the buyer comes up a few hundred (or even a few thousand) dollars short, credit cards can make the difference.

Technique No. 27 Home Improvement Loans

Often hard-money funds borrowed to complete improvements to a property can relieve the pressures on cash-poor buyers and rejuvenate accounts set aside for down payments and fix-up. Allocation of home improvement funds has to comply with the lender's policy, of course. For example, in a recent Kansas City, Missouri, transaction we heard of, a $6,000 long-term Title I Home Improvement loan was an important ingredient in the over-all acquisitions process of a single family house.

Technique No. 28 Home Equity Loans

Even in tight-money times, there are mortgage and finance companies willing to make second-mortgage loans secured by the equity in a buyer's home. Often the beginning investor will get his or her start in this way. We know of a couple in Arizona who used a $20,000 home equity loan to acquire two single family rental homes and get their investment ball rolling. They even came out with a modest positive cash flow.

Technique No. 29 Refinance Boat, Car, Stereo, or Other Personal Property

Hard-money lenders are often willing to loan money secured against valuable personal property. In a counseling session recently, a client was asking how to come up with the last $2,000 needed to consumate a deal on an excellent condo. He had no family, no partners to turn to, and no more money in savings that he could use, but he did not want to pass up the deal. I asked whether he owned a car or truck. He replied that he owned a new Datsun pickup free and clear. "Why don't you try to refinance the truck for $2,000?" I suggested. A light went on, and he headed for the banks to see what could be done. Not all lenders will welcome him with open arms, but he will eventually find one who will.

Technique No. 30 VA Loans

For the buyer who qualifies for a Veterans Administration loan, the down payment on a property is quite manageable —zero! VA loans are also possible even if the qualifying borrower is buying a duplex or 4-plex with the idea of living in one of the units. Anyone can assume a VA loan with a minimum of hassle and cost (around $50). That leaves energy to spare for dealing creatively with the down payment challenge.

Technique No. 31 FHA Loans

Buyers who want to acquire their own residence for little down will find a loan guaranteed by the Federal Housing Administration to their liking. Down payments can be as low as 5%, although the FHA, like the VA, is particular about the quality of home they will accept. FHA loans are always readily assumable with a minimum of hassle and cost (around $50).

Investors who are sensitive to the modern problems of negative cash flow will keep their eyes open for properties with assumable FHA and VA loans. Due-on-sale clauses are never a worry with such loans, and the interest rates are usually somewhat lower.

Technique No. 32 The Second Mortgage Crank

This technique is one of the foundation stones of creative finance. Named by Robert G. Allen, the second mortgage crank is a strategy that will work equally well with fussy sellers as well as don't wanters. The term "crank" is an old exchangor's term that refers to the process of generating hard-money funds by originating new loans against a property. One speaks of "cranking" money out of the property in this way. Here's how the technique works.

The buyer looks for properties that are free and clear or have relatively low loan-to-value ratios. A new hard-money first(or second) is obtained in order to generate enough money to satisfy the seller's needs. The remainder of the seller's equity is carried back on terms that are mutually agreeable. None of the cash comes out of the buyer's pocket. Naturally, the hard-money lender's policies and requirements will have to be satisfied. It may be that the carry back will have to be secured by another property in the buyer's portfolio in order that the subject property will have no secondary financing (anathema to most hard-money lenders who are asked for refinance funds of this type).

Because of the importance of this technique, let us give you several examples from our files of how it has been used successfully by investors in the past year or two. A buyer in Chico, California, acquired four SFH's for $159,000 by taking the property subject to an existing first mortgage of $64,000, then putting on a new hard-money second for $55,000 (out of which the down payment was generated), the balance of the obligation to the seller being carried back in the form of paper against another investment property. In another situation, an investor in Oklahoma bought two SFH's by putting on a new first mortgage (proceeds to the seller) and having the seller carry back the rest in the form of paper secured by the property. In both cases, the down payment was "cranked" out of new hard-money encumbrances against the property, rather than out of the buyer's pocket. There are countless other illustrations for this technique, which becomes all the more important in periods of lowering interest rates and easier access to bank funds.

Technique No. 33 Variation of the Crank: Seller Refinance

In some instances it might be difficult to persuade conservative lending institutions to refinance a property or provide secondary financing as part of a "crank" purchase. They may regard the substitution of collateral on the owner carry back as too complicated. To them, it might seem as though the owner carry back still looks suspiciously like an encumbrance against the subject property (even though the mortgage has been moved to another property).

One variation of the second mortgage crank technique calls for the seller to refinance his own property and then pass the new loan on to the buyer. No one at the bank is going to object to his refinancing his own property or putting on a new second mortgage. In this way the seller's needs for cash can be taken care of, the balance of the equity being carried back in the form of a second or third mortgage.

A case we heard of in Tucson recently is a good example of this alternative approach to the second mortgage crank. The seller agreed to obtain a $12,000 hard-money second to generate needed capital before the property was passed on to the buyer, who in turn gave the seller a third mortgage for the remaining equity.

Technique No. 34 Buy Low, Refinance High

This is the old "buy low, sell high" strategy transferred from the stock market to creative real estate. The basic strategy is to locate a property discounted substantially below market levels and then refinance it with a new hard-money first in order to achieve higher leverage or generate funds to satisfy the needs of the seller (and buyer as well). This technique is particularly suited to tight-money times where negative cash flows can be a deterrent to investing.

A woman investor from California recently put herself in a position to **make $1.5 million on 180 discounted townhomes in Arizona by using the** "buy low, refinance high technique." A buyer in Pennsylvania was able to pick up $10,000 in instant equity by refinancing a discounted duplex acquired for nothing down. When he goes to sell the duplex, he can "sell high" and convert the equity to cash. Still another investor in Tulsa picked up three duplexes for $165,000. Since they were appraised at nearly $240,000 for all three, he was able to put on a new first mortgage at a high enough level to generate over $30,000 cash to buyer at closing. When he goes to sell, he can convert the rest of his profit to cash. And so it goes with "buy low, refinance high" technique.

7. UNDERLYING MORTGAGES

The seventh area of flexibility in acquiring property for nothing down is the area of underlying mortgages. Three vital questions for the analysis phase are: What mortgages (trust deeds, liens) are there against the property? Who holds them? Would these holders of underlying mortgages be flexible with their assets? In most cases the mortgagees are banks; for that reason conventional wisdom assumes that there will be no flexibility whatsoever. Hard-money lenders, after all, are "tightwads" who never yield on the terms of their loans. Conventional wisdom is usually correct in this, and yet even hard-money lenders can soften up if it is in their best interests to do so. The unprecedented rise in interest rates in the last few years has caused some agencies and institutions to develop flexibilities with their mortgage holdings that can benefit real estate investors.

With private mortgage holders, the opportunities for creative finance techniques are even greater. The mortgagees may be sellers who have accepted paper back for part of their equity when they sold the property. Now they are receiving payments over time, sometimes at interest rates far below the current market. Often such private mortgage holders realize that their assets are not well invested in relation to current investment opportunities and yields, so they become open to suggestions from creative buyers who present more beneficial solutions to the problem.

This section outlines five techniques from this area of flexibility.

Technique No. 35 Use Discounts from Holders of Mortgages

The basic approach to the private holders of underlying financing is this: "Mr. Mortgagee, you are receiving monthly payments on this note at a moderate rate of interest, and you must wait patiently until the note is paid off. Would you not rather have this mortgage redeemed for cash right away?" If the holder of the mortgage is willing to discount his note for cash, the buyer can look for new financing to put on the property in order to pay off the existing private mortgage. The strategy is to have enough refinance funds to pay off the private mortgagee and still have sufficient funds to take care of part or all of the down payment needed to acquire the property in the first place. It might turn out that the private mortgage holder will be willing to discount only a part of his note for cash. Perhaps he would respond to the idea of taking part in cash (at a discount) and the rest in new secondary financing above the refinance mortgage, possibly with an improvement in his interest rate or other terms.

There are many variations to this technique, but the basic idea is to redeem the underlying mortgage at a discount for cash (using borrowed funds), with the balance being applied to the down payment. For example, a buyer of a rental home in Los Angeles had induced a seller to take back a single-payment second of $11,000 for three years. After the closing, the buyer approached the seller and offered to buy back the second for $7,000 cash. When the seller agreed, the buyer borrowed $10,000, paid off the note, and had $3,000 to offset the small cash down payment he had made to get into the property.

Technique No. 36 Moving the Mortgage

A mortgage consists of two basic documents: one is a note setting forth the terms for paying back funds that are borrowed; the other is a security agreement that provides collateral for the loan in case of default. The security agreement promises, in essence, to back up the performance of the borrower in repaying the note. If the buyer fails to live up to his commitments, then the lender is entitled to the collateral (property) pledged as security for the loan.

What conventional wisdom fails to grasp is the idea that while the terms of the note are fixed, there may be dozens of ways to satisfy the security needs of the seller other than using the subject property itself as collateral. As the procedures of Technique No. 36, "Moving the Mortgage," will make clear, it is always wise in negotiating a real estate purchase to include a "substitution of collateral" clause in the purchase agreement. Such a clause allows the buyer to substitute other collateral as security for the note in the future, subject to the approval to the seller. It is sometimes possible, even after the fact, to induce a seller or the holder of an underliyng mortgage to "move the mortgage" to another property (substitute other collateral). Frequently sweeteners are needed to get the job done — an increase in the interest rate or the principal amount, an improvement in the position of the note (e.g. from, third to second or from second to first), an increase in the amount or quality of the collateral,etc.).

Why is it beneficial to move a mortgage? The key is this: if property owned by a buyer can be definanced (freed of encumbrances, in this case by having the existing mortgages moved to other properties), then the buyer will be free to put new financing on the property and "crank" out funds that can be used, for example, as down payments. Alternately, the definanced property can be sold to raise capital for the same purposes. Now here is the twist that boggles conventional wisdom: What if the down payment funds generated in this way are used to acquire the very property to which the mortgages we have been talking about are to be moved? Is it possible to arrange for a simultaneous escrow involving both properties? Certainly!

Here's an example from the community of Olaho, Oregon. An investor acquired a 10-plex in the following way: using funds he had cranked out of an earlier investment property, he bought a SFH whose owners were willing to accept security for their carry back against the 10-plex our investor wanted to acquire. He then traded the definanced SFH to the owners of the 10-plex, who in turn put new financing against the SFH to get capital they needed. Brilliant!

In another transaction in Evergreen, Colorado, the problem was not one of generating cash for the down payment but rather in assuming a first mortgage without violating the policy of the lender prohibiting secondary financing on the property. The buyer simply induced the seller to carry back the difference on a note secured against other properties. By moving the mortgage off the subject property, the buyer prepared the way for a future refinance or dale to raise capital for the next big deal.

Technique No. 37 Creative Refinance of Underlying Mortgage

In general, the only flexible holders of underlying mortgages are private parties. Hard-money mortgagees are for the most part not cooperative when it comes to techniques discussed in this section. However, there is one aspect of underlying financing where even the hard-money people are beginning to show flexibility: refinance. The unprecedented flight of interest rates in recent years has left financial institutions holding large portfolios of undesirable low-interest mortgages. With the advent of high-yield money market funds, deposits in savings and loan associations have been withdrawn in record amounts, making the situation even worse. The result is that the lenders are desperate to rid their holdings of the older, low interest loans made in yesteryear. A symptom of the malaise is the aggressiveness of many banks in upholding the due-on-sale provisions of conventional loans made during the last decade. they want those loans paid off or assumed at higher interest rates.

The current situation will bring about a softening of hard-money hearts in the interests of institutional solvency. One major example of this has already become policy. The Federal National Mortgage Association, which holds a vast portfolio of home mortgages acquired from lenders around the country, is offering to refinance their own mortgages at rates below the market for both owner-occupied as well as investment situations. Since they will go as high as 90% for owner-occupants and 80% for investors, the program offers interesting possibilities for the creative buyer. FNMA calculates the new interest rate on the refinanced loan by averaging the yield on the old amount with the yield on the added amount according to an internal formula. The combination is always lower than the market rate. Although FNMA guidelines must be met, buyers should consider taking advantage of the opportunities the refinance program offers to raise funds.

The Fannie Mae program is not the only "creative refinance" opportunity available. Many primary lending institutions around the country are devising innovative ways to divest themselves of unprofitable low-interest loans in ways that might be beneficial to investors. Investors should explore opportunities for working creative deals with lenders in their own areas. The next period of time will be marked with increased hard-money flexibilities that could lead to win/win deals for everyone involved.

Of special interest also are the R.E.O.'s — "Real Estate Owned" properties that the lending institutions have had to take back through foreclosure and now want to get rid of. Foreclosure activity increases during tight-money times, and investors should cultivate relationships with lenders who might be very anxious to sell R.E.O.'s to them on soft terms.

Recently in Freemont, California, one buyer used the program to generate $15,000 toward the down payment on a condo. The existing

FNMA first at $41,000 was refinanced at $56,000, with the excess proceeds going to the seller. The new interest rate was 12.25%, far below market levels at the time.

Technique No. 38 Pulling Cash Out of Buildings You Own But Don't Want To Sell

Many variations in the basic approach of dealing creatively with holders of underlying mortgages are possible. Here is one other example — of how a creative investor might pull investment funds out of a property without actually selling it. Let's suppose that a private party holds a mortgage against a property our investor wants to keep. He needs to raise investment capital, but a refinance of the property would not net a large amount of cash because most of the proceeds, let's suppose, would go to pay off the existing private mortgage. What can he do? Perhaps the private mortgagee would agree to share the proceeds of the new loan with the investor and take back the balance in the form of a new second mortgage against the property. The investor may have to sweeten the deal (perhaps in the form of a higher interest rate, higher monthly payments, or a shorter pay out period), but at least he gets to keep his property and achieve his goal of raising capital.

Technique No. 39 Making A Partner of the Holder of an Underlying Mortgage

What other ways are there to induce a private mortgage holder to cooperate in creative arrangements such as moving the mortgage? One could offer to give the party one-half interest in the property if he would release his mortgage so that a refinance could take place. Out of the refinance would come the funds to buy the property from its owner.

Short of an equity position, one might offer the holder of an underlying mortgage a higher interest rate in exchange for certain concessions that would facilitate the purchase. In a recent Sante Fe, New Mexico, transaction, one buyer came up against a non-assumable private mortgage on the property he wanted to buy. By giving the holder a three point interest increase, he eliminated the hurdle and bought the property. In effect, the holder became an investment partner who said, "Help me make more money and I will see to it that you get the property." The variations are endless.

8. INVESTORS

In the eighth area of creative financing flexibility, we turn to investors for help with down payments. Our interest is in a particular kind of investor — the kind specializing in buying and selling second trust notes. When a note is created, it tends to have a life of its own. It can move from master to master as it continues to generate monthly payments in accordance with the terms its originators gave to it. The person to whom it is first given — as for example in a real estate transaction where the seller carries back paper on his equity — can turn around and sell it in the marketplace for cash. In order to convert it to cash, he will have to sell it at a discount, anywhere from, say, twenty to fifty percent, depending on the nature of the note, how "seasoned" it might be, its collateral, etc. But the seller is willing to do this for the privilege of having at least a major part of the face value of the note in the form of immediate cash.

It is the marketability of the note, as well as the difference between its face value and its cash value, that makes it interesting to real estate buyers. There are two major possibilities to keep in mind. If a buyer can acquire second trust notes in the marketplace at a discount, and then use them at face value as down payments on real estate, he has effectively picked up the difference between the discounted value (cash value) and the face value. That difference has now been converted to equity in the property he has purchased. and since the note traded into the subject property is secured by another piece of property altogether, he can "crank" funds out of his newly acquired real estate to take care of buying the note in the first place. It is a remarkable chain of events that can yield handsome rewards.

The other major role for second trust notes in creative real estate is generating cash for the seller who needs more down payment than the buyer can provide. The following technique illustrates the approach:

Technique No. 40 Selling of Second Trust Notes

If a buyer cannot supply the seller with a large enough cash down payment, he can give the seller a note — fully secured by the property — with a face value just large enough to yield the required cash proceeds when sold to an investor in the marketplace. Of course, the buyer has to make payments on the note according to the terms agreed upon, no matter who holds the note. Alternately, the buyer can give the seller a note secured by another property in the buyer's portfolio. the same process of selling the note at a discount can be used to generate the cash needed by the seller. By moving the mortgage, however, the buyer has the advantage of fully leveraging other assets that may have already been encumbered beyond the threshold tolerated by commercial lenders. He also can now "crank" funds out of the newly-acquired property more readily since it is left with less secondary financing or none at all.

Here's how it worked recently in a Phoenix transaction. The buyer of a $65,000 SFH gave the seller two notes for his equity, one of which was sold by the seller at a discount to raise the needed down payment cash. The other note remained as a third with a single-payment balloon after three years.

9. PARTNERS

The ninth area of flexibility in creative finance is the use of partners. For those who rationalize their investment inactivity on the basis of having no money, no credit, no financial statement, no equity, etc., Robert Allen has the following response: "If you don't have it, someone else does." The strategy is to make that someone your partner if you cannot bring the deal off in any other legitimate way. Assuming that the buyer has exhausted all other areas of flexibility, there are many *quid-pro-quo* arrangements he might use to involve a partner. Five of them are covered in this section. section.

Technique No. 41 Borrow Partner's Financial Statement

Many investors without strong financial statements feel they must approach sellers with fear and trembling. Not necessarily. If the deal requires partnership support in this area, a successful investor will add to his team the strength he needs and go into the marketplace with confidence.

For example, a creative buyer in Albuquerque induced a seller to discount an 11-plex by over 20% and carry most of his equity on a wrap, largely on the strength of his partners' financial statements. Both of the buyer's partners happened to be millionaires, not bad company to keep when facing an experienced seller.

Technique No. 42 Borrow Partner's Money for Down Payment

Frequently an investment partner can be persuaded to loan the buyer all or part of a down payment. The loan may or may not be secured by a trust deed on the property. In any case, the buyer who is just short on funds for the down payment is probably better off to avoid giving the partner an equity position in the property unless absolutely necessary. Equity sharing partnerships are costly when calculated over the entire life of the investment.

Two case studies in this section show how investment partnerships can contribute to the success of real estate purchases. In one St. Charles, Missouri, transaction, an equity sharing partner on a 4-plex deal was able to raise $5,000 of his contribution by borrowing it from his mother. The buyer of a 6-plex in Seattle did a similar thing. His mother came up with $10,000 as an investment to help him buy the property. (It was not just a case of maternal support – the women were shrewd investors who received a good return on their money.)

Technique No. 43 Borrow Partner's Money for down Payment Until Your Money Comes

In this variation, the partner does not have to leave his cash investment tied up in the property in exchange for an equity position: he gets it all back plus interest as soon as the buyer can put together the cash. The partner puts his money to good use and still comes out with part interest in the property.

Technique No. 44 Your Cash Flow/My Equity Or Some Combination

Often the partner provides something other than cash to make the deal fall together. There are many illustrations of this technique. For example, a partner in a SFH transaction in Southern Florida recently provided property to which a created second mortgage was moved. In another Florida case involving a large motel, a partner was brought into the deal because he had some stock that was used as collateral in order to borrow $20,000 essential to the deal. Like Bob says: "If you don't have it, someone else does."

Technique No. 45 You Put Up the Cash; I Put Up the Time and Expertise

This is the most common partnership arrangement. In exchange for cash needed at the front end, and sometimes cash to offset negative cash flows and balloons, the partner receives an equity position in the property.

In a case from our Atlanta file, for example, a beginning investor with only $100 rent money in his pocket was able to close his first deal using $2,000 from a partner. In a recent San Diego case, a father and son team located a partner with the $7,000 needed to get into a condo. Somewhat bigger stakes were played for in a Los Angeles transaction completed by one of our colleagues in the recent past: the buyer lined up several partners to provide the cash needed ($148,000) to close on a 72-unit property. Regardless of the amount invested by partners, the principles are always the same.

10. OPTIONS

This final section treats a group of special creative finance techniques that permit a buyer to gain control of significant amounts of real estate with little down, even though ownership may be months or years away – if ever. The principle is simple: the person buying the option gives the seller a sum of money in exchange for the right to buy the property at a given price within a defined period of time. The buyer benefits by locking in the price and gaining control of the property without a large investment. The seller benefits by retaining the tax advantages of ownership while locking in the sale at an acceptable price or picking up the option money in the event the buyer decides to back out.

The Nothing Down System includes five variations of the option

Technique No. 46 The Rolling Option

In this approach, a large tract of land is optioned piecemeal by the buyer. Rather than taking control of the whole package at once, which would be very expensive, the buyer purchases a segment for development or resale while at the same time buying an option on the next segment. The option can then be rolled from segment to segment until the whole package is developed or the option dropped.

Technique No. 47 Equity for Options

Other assets besides cash can be used as an option payment. Personal property (cars, trucks, equipment, collectibles), equity resources, and even services can work just as well.

Technique No. 48 Sale Option Back

What if a property owner needs to sell a piece of property now in order to raise capital but wishes he could eventually have it back to take advantage of predicted appreciation and future growth? What can be done for him? The "Sale Option Back" technique is cut to order: the seller disposes of his property at a moderate discount but with the option to buy it back within a specified time frame at a price fixed now. Whether or not the option is exercised, the buyer wins; and the seller has the choice of getting his property back if future conditions develop as planned.

Technique No. 49 The Earnest Money Option

Every Earnest Money Agreement is an option. For a short period of time, the potential buyer has control of the disposition of the property. If he fails to follow through as agreed, he loses the earnest money (option payment)

as liquidated damages. Meanwhile, if he has executed the offer to purchase in his own name with the additional phrase "And/Or Assigns," he can choose to sell his interest in the property to whomever he will. If he has struck a good bargain, it is possible the assignment of the earnest money rights to some other investor could be very profitable.

Technique No. 50 Lease With An Option To Purchase

This is the most common form of the option. Buyers who don't have enough cash for a down payment or who wish to build up a portfolio of properties using this technique can use their available funds as option money and then maneuver for purchase later on. Meanwhile, if monthly payments have been carefully structured, the buyer (optioner) might be able to pick up a little extra cash on sub-lease payments.

There are numerous examples of this technique, which is used frequently by investors. For example, the buyer of a 14-plex in Bremerton, Washington, initiated his program recently with a six-month lease option. The reason? He did not yet have the down payment funds, and besides, the seller needed to hold the property a little longer to qualify for long-term capital gains. In a Nashville, Tennessee, purchase, a home buyer we know picked up an estate property for $1,000 on a six-month lease option. The breathing room permitted him to get together the down payment needed for closing. And so it goes.

The important thing to remember in applying these techniques to advance your own real estate portfolio is that not all of them are essential to your success. Find the approach that suits your needs and matches your resources and goals. Most purchases we have researched across the country involve combinations of one, two, three, or four of these techniques. Many times an investor will hit on just the right approach for his/her situation and use it over and over again. It becomes a "cookie cutter" that punches out the "dough" time after time.

Best of luck in putting these powerful and effective tools to use!

Magic With Mortgages

Robert G. Allen

Understanding the intricacies of mortgages must begin with a basic understanding of what a mortgage is. It is simply the use of two instruments: 1) a note between buyer and seller spelling out the terms of a loan with designated payments, interest rates, and due dates; and, 2) a collateral or security agreement which allows the holder of the note to seize the property pledged as collateral if the terms of the note are not met as agreed upon. When these two documents are combined together we refer to them as *a mortgage*. For centuries there have been certain conventional ways of using mortgages for the purchasing of properties. It has been generally agreed by the powers-that-be (bankers, lawyers, real estate brokers, sellers, etc.) that to obtain a mortgage it is imperative to abide by a set of unwritten rules or assumptions such as:

1. To obtain a mortgage you must have at least some and preferably all of the following:

- excellent credit
- a steady job with future (and at which you have worked for years)
- lots of cash for down payments
- a wonderful financial statement

2. For some reason, obtaining a loan or mortgage through a financial institution is somehow preferable to having a seller carry back a mortgage.
3. Mortgages, once they are originated, are forever rigid, cast in concrete, and, of course, completely riveted to the property collateralized.

Obviously, under these sets of assumptions you can readily see why, although it was the dream of our parents' generation to pay off a mortgage, it is now the dream of our generation just to be able to *get* a mortgage in the first place.

And you can also see why those of us who are preaching a new gospel of creative financing are being looked down upon as if what we were teaching would be more appropriate in the pages of the *National Enquirer.* At any rate, what I am getting to is simple. The 1980's will be known as the decade of creative financing. Mark my words. Those of us who understand the little-known secrets of manipulating mortgages will do well—not only in our buying programs, but also in our investment and cash flow generating programs. What we are teaching may be seen by some as being on the fringe of respectability but it is definitely smack dab in the middle of profitability. And that is the subject of this article. *What are some of the best-known secrets of the trade with regard to mortgages—and how can the layman learn to use them profitably?*

Secret Number One. Banks aren't the only sources of mortgage money.

This secret is not much of a secret to those of you who have taken the Nothing Down Seminar but to most of the world this is a revelation. I read in an article recently that up to a few years ago about 65% to 75% of all mortgages used for the purchase of homes were originated through banks, savings and loan associations, and mortgage bankers. The rest involved seller financing. As you can well guess, these numbers have been reversed in recent years as anxious sellers are being forced to become lenders in order to sell their properties. This opens up worlds of opportunity for the real estate entrepreneur. As I so graphically proved in the *Los Angeles Times* $100 challenge, there are plenty of sellers who can be shown win/win ways to selling their properties to "conventionally unqualified" buyers. The reason that this is so is because most sellers can be shown flexible alternatives to solving problems which are radically different from the rigid rules of conventional financing. Sellers who are considering carrying paper don't have to involve stodgy loan committees comprised mainly of security-conscious employees worried more about making themselves look good than about solving problems. Creative financing is built upon a philosophy of problem solving. That is why it is so powerful. It is not perfect, but it works in many cases. The secret then is to use as much seller financing as possible. It is cheaper. It is easier to obtain. The terms are better. And we can build some wonderful advantages into the clauses of the mortgage which build marvelous future benefits . . . as I will now explain the second secret.

Secret Number Two. Mortgages don't have to be riveted to the collateral property.

Let me elaborate. In conventional lending the only way to change the collateral for a note is to pay off the old loan and write a brand new loan on another property. In creative financing, we just revert to the basics. Since a mortgage is just a note and a property to collateralize the note . . . it is an easy step to convince a seller that if his money is secure it shouldn't matter which property we choose to collateralize the loan. The key here is the word *security.* "Mr. Seller, I want you to be secure in the money that I owe you. You have chosen to have your security on the property which I am buying from you. But in the future, if I should find a property which seems to offer you more security in terms of greater equity or better condition and location I wouldn't think that you would object, would you?" This is the kind of dialogue which leads up to the use of the *substitution of collateral clause.* I insert the following clause into all of my contracts and earnest money offers:

"The seller hereby agrees to accept a substitution of collateral for the amount of this note by moving the mortgage (or trust deed) to another piece of property which the buyer shall designate. The seller shall have the right to inspect such property to insure the security of the collateral and shall give his approval to make the substitution of collateral, which approval shall not be unreasonably denied."

If the seller doesn't agree to the clause but agrees to my other terms, then all is well. If the clause is accepted, then the fun begins. I recently bought a four-unit building where the substitution of collateral clause was accepted by the seller (after getting approval of his attorney). The details were as follows:

Property worth	$110,000
Mortgage	54,000
Equity	56,000

The seller carried back a second mortgage for his entire equity with absolutely nothing down. The payments on the loan were structured at $300 per month for the first year, $400 per month for the second year, and $500 per month for every year thereafter until a five-year balloon came due. This was essentially less than interest only . . . but helped out immensely with negative cash flows. We offered to let the seller use other property for a blanket mortgage (another little-known technique for creating trust without spending cash) but at the closing it was never mentioned. We also included a clause that if after five years we so decided we could extend the mortgage another year with the payment of a non-refundable payment of $1,000. This gives us insurance in the event we can't obtain financing for a while . . . it's what I refer to as a procrastinator's clause.

But the best clause is what I call the *Santa Clause.* It is, of course, the substitution of collateral clause. The seller has agreed to move the mortgage at any time in the future as long as he has an opportunity to inspect and approve the collateral. This opens up great doors for me. Let me run through what I have in mind for this property. I will begin looking for another property immediately. I will be looking for a special kind of don't wanter . . . the wholesale don't wanter who wants lots of cash but who doesn't care (and may even suggest) a significant discount in his equity to raise the needed cash. Let's create an example. Suppose I find a property worth $150,000 where the seller wants out— needs cash of $25,000 immediately. He has a loan of $90,000. He knows that by accepting cash of $25,000 he is effectively selling his property for $115,000, but no matter . . . he wants out. Where do you get the $25,000 from? There are several alternatives such as: 1) borrowing from the property worth $150,000. This raises some problems about timing and ability to finance a non-owner occupied property that you are buying; 2) borrow from a partner and then refinance the property you buy later; or 3) use the substitution of collateral technique (No. 36 in the Nothing Down System) that you have already prearranged with the holder of the $56,000 mortgage on the four-plex. This alternative may prove to be the best since it combines these benefits:

Discounted Property

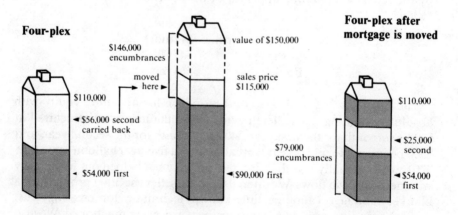

● You can have already made arrangements for a quickie loan through your banker on the four-plex subject to you finding a suitable property to move the second mortgage to. The critical factor here is timing. You need to close fast to take advantage of these kinds of wholesale opportunities.

● The holder of the mortgage which you wish to move can be shown ways to want to cooperate readily with your request by offering him such sweeteners as a higher interest rate, a larger monthly payment, a cash payment upon the move, a larger mortgage amount upon the move, or a better and more secure property to collateralize his loan. This should be pre-arranged with the seller so that there will not be any hang-ups when the time comes.

● There will be no necessity of trying to get the seller of discounted property to "play games" in order to get a new loan on his property. The last thing a serious don't wanter wants to do is to help you arrange for financing. He wants cash, now, and no Mickey Mouse tricks.

To recap, then, we make an offer to buy the discounted property for $115,000 with $25,000 quick cash dollars and take over his payments subject to the new loan. We approach the holder of the mortgage on our four-plex and show him the property and obtain his permission to move his $56,000 loan to the new property upon closing. He will now have a second mortgage above the existing $90,000 first mortgage. The total encumbrances equal $146,000, just a little better security position than before . . . but we can sweeten the pot by increasing the interest rate by a point to make it palatable. Then we make arrangements for our friendly banker or finance company to loan us $25,000 cash with a second mortgage against the four-plex. The new situation on it will look something like this: Old loan first mortgage of $54,000 with a new second mortgage of $25,000; total loans equal $79,000. (Less than the 80% loan-to-value ratio.) We have the loan prearranged . . . just waiting for our money to pounce on (so to speak). Of course, we obtain a new property with a discount of $35,000 without having to sell any of my properties to raise cash. The best part of this arrangement is that once the seller has become accustomed to doing this once, he shouldn't mind doing it again if the benefits are right. And so, the next year, when our conscience sears us to action again, we simply have to go to him and remind him that *it's that time of year again . . . the time to move his mortgage!* And off we go again, to find the bargain of the year using someone else's cash . . . and, mind you, our second-mortgage holder loves us for it for we are providing benefits for him that he could not have received elsewhere. And that's win/win.

Some miscellaneous secrets.

I would think that you would be wise to include the following clauses in all of your mortgages in the future. The benefits should be obvious.

The stutter mortgage. Jimmy Napier taught me this one. When creating your mortgages, always include the right to miss a payment each year without any penalty. If your rental home is vacant one month you may decide that it's time for you to let your mortgage stutter. Anything is negotiable.

On all mortgages you give (when you are buying) you should retain the *first right of refusal* to buy your own mortgage from the mortgage holder in the event he should decide to sell. For instance, suppose in our example above that the seller decides to discount his $56,000 second for $35,000 in cash. Wouldn't I want to know this? Maybe I could refinance the property for enough to pay the $35,000 and own it outright. (Thanks again to Jimmy Napier.)

Always try to retain the right to *extend a balloon mortgage* by at least one year beyond the due date with the payment of a non-refundable fee or any other sweetener such as a raise in interest rate. Of the last five properties I have bought, we were able to negotiate this clause on two of them. That helps me to not have too many balloons coming due in the same year.

Try a *subordination clause.* This simply states that the buyer has the right to place a new first mortgage on the property and that the seller agrees to subordinate his loan to this new mortgage upon the payment of a certain amount. I met a fellow in Tucson who loves to use this on his fixer-uppers. He finds a property which he can buy with nothing down but which needs substantial work. He fixes up the property and raises its value. Then he refinances and pulls out all of his fix-up cash plus some extra and the holder of the second loan moves his mortgage up to accommodate a new loan. When you need some cash, it's always nice to know that the second mortgage holder on at least one of your properties will be cooperative in letting you borrow against your equity if you throw some cash his way.

There are infinite ways to solve problems with mortgages if you have the ingenuity and drive to learn and practice them. Good luck . . . and happy borrowing.

Three Old Ways to Make Money in Real Estate... And One New One

Robert G. Allen

There are three major ways to make money in real estate investments. The first is as old as the hills. It was first espoused in a meaningful way by William Nickerson in his landmark book *How I Turned One Thousand Dollars into One Million Dollars in Real Estate in My Spare Time.* This book appeared, I think, in 1960 and has been a steady seller ever since. It is, in my opinion, the best nuts and bolts book that has ever been written on real estate investing with perhaps the sole exception of *Nothing Down.* (Did you expect me to say anything different?) Albert J. Lowry's book, *How to Become Financially Independent by Investing in Real Estate,* plays fairly much the same tune. The formula in these two books by Nickerson and Lowry is simple. Take a property which needs "cosmetic" work, fix it up, and sell or trade the increased equity for a larger unit. The paper profit in these transactions is created through sweat equity... physical improvements in the property which thereby make it rent for more money and thus make it more valuable to a new investor.

I think that I have been fairly clear over the years that "there are no calluses on my hands." In other words, I have neither the skill nor the inclination to find run-down properties and fix them up for profit. Although many of our students do well following this route and I wouldn't discourage them, it just doesn't seem to be my cup of tea.

The second major way of making money in real estate is the "Buy and Hold" philosophy. Rather than turning a sow's ear into a silk purse, this philosophy says buy an already excellent property in a good location with as favorable price and terms possible...rent it out and hang onto it forever. Why sell the goose that lays the golden eggs? Slowly, the property will increase in value with inflation, and as the rents are gradually increased, the cash flows will become substantial. It is a get-rich-slow program. My book *Nothing Down* ends with the following quote:

"Don't wait to buy real estate. Buy real estate and wait."

The profits from this program are harvested in five to ten years down the road by either selling or refinancing your portfolio and reinvesting the proceeds into automatic pilot investments which produce cash flow as opposed to equity growth.

A prudent acquisition program of one or two single family homes per year would fit nicely into this philosophy, and no matter which of the major routes to real estate wealth you choose, I highly recommend at least a bare minimum buy and hold program.

The third major route to real estate wealth is the buy low/sell high routine. The object is to locate extremely flexible "wholesale" sellers who need lots of cash but who will significantly discount their equity. This type of investor makes money "on the way in" by picking up immediate profit. He doesn't need to "fix up" the price of his investments... he buys the price down. He doesn't use "sweat equity," he uses "brain equity." His time is not spent in manual labor, his time is spent hunting for bargains. The profits from this type of investing are harvested either immediately or are left in the property for later harvesting depending on the temperament and the tax situation of the investor.

Now, this approach usually takes some cash; but if you understand the Nothing Down philosophy, an investor can always raise the cash through a myriad of sources if the deal is good enough.

These three major routes to real estate wealth rely upon equity growth in some fashion. The fix-up route creates equity value by improving cosmetic appearance. The buy-and-hold route relies on inflation to drive prices up and thereby create an equity position for the owner. The buy-low/sell-high route counts on immediate equity growth through bargain hunting. All of them seek to increase a seller's equity and therefore his wealth. This equity can then be converted to cash or other forms as the owner chooses.

Recently, there have cropped up advertisements in every major city in the country, announcing a new (actually, it was used extensively in the depression) way to create equity quickly. You have probably heard of builders who are willing to sell their remaining properties at *zero interest* with 60 or 72 equal monthly payments. The buyer of the property ends up with a unit free and clear at the end of a five-to-seven-year period of time. In other words, the rapid build-up of the buyer's equity is realized because all monthly payments are applied directly to principal . . . with **zero interest**. Let me quote you some actual figures from an ad I read recently:

ANNOUNCING OUR NEW INTEREST RATE:

0%

WITH TOTAL OWNERSHP IN 6 YEARS!
NO INTEREST PAID EVER! NO BALLOONS EVER!

That's right — now you can own a 1 or 2 bedroom condominium Free and Clear in 6 years! Here's how easy it is: Pay just 20-40% down (depending on unit selected), make monthly no-interest payments of $510-$550, and in 6 short years you own it free and clear. No more payments! Sound like a great deal? It is! We are fighting back against today's high cost of home financing. For example:

0% Mortgage		16% Mortgage (today's rate)	
Sales price	$52,500.00	Sales price	$ 52,500.00
30% down	$15,750.00	30% down	$ 15,750.00
Mortgage balance	$36,750.00	Mortgage balance	$ 36,750.00
Monthly paymt. for 6 years	$ 510.41	Monthly paymt. for 30 years	$ 494.20
Total $ paid over 6 years	$36,750.00	Total $ paid over 30 years	$177,896.00
Total interest costs	$ 0	Total interest costs	$141,146.00

In addition to all of the benefits mentioned above, as of this writing, you are still allowed a 10% interest rate tax write-off by the IRS.

Now, wait a minute! This sounds too good to be true. I'd better go look at these units. And sure enough, the builder, desperate to unload some extra inventory, has agreed to zero interest. We'd better figure out just how good a deal this really is. Let's see, what would the rate of return be on an investment of $15,750... supposing I had that much cash on hand or could get it somehow?

First of all, what about the cash flows? Well, you could probably rent out the two-bedroom unit for just a little bit less than the mortgage payment of $510.41. And then there would be taxes and insurance to consider. Roughly, our out-of-pocket negative cash flow would be at least $100 per month for the first two-to-three years... and then it would be break even or positive from then on. We'd probably have to invest another two to three thousand dollars in this negative cash flow over the holding period. But this would be tax deductible... or at least a portion of it would be. The rate of return would be negligible.

Then, what about equity build-up? Since there is no interest payment, the entire payment is applied toward principle. That means that $510.41 multiplied by twelve or $6,124.92 is applied toward reducing the loan. And on an investment of less than $17,000 (down payment plus negatives) I get a first year return of 36%. Now, that's not too bad! I dare you to find a reputable stock broker who can consistently earn you 36% on your money.

Then, what about tax benefits? Well, since all of the payment goes to principal, there is no interest to deduct... and therefore the entire payment is taxable. But the ad said that the IRS will impute an interest rate of 10% on these types of transactions... under the assumption that the builder had raised his price to compensate for the lack of interest (which he might have done). If we are allowed to impute an interest rate of 10% on the balance of $36,750 (and it would be wise to run this by your accountant), then at least $3,650 of the $6,124.92 that we paid on the loan is deductible. That leaves a principle amount of about $2,500 which is not deductible. But there is depreciation on the unit to take into account. This unit can be depreciated over fifteen years giving a first-year depreciation of approximately $5,000. That means that there would be a slight tax shelter available, even discounting the zero interest situation. Since the return on investment from tax shelter would be less than 5%, let's ignore it.

Now, what about appreciation? If the unit appreciated 10% from $52,500 to $57,750, our return on our invested dollars in the first year would be $5,250 divided by our first year investment of approximately $17,000 or about 31%.

Our total return including equity build-up and appreciation would be over 67% in the first year. It would decline thereafter but would still remain significantly higher than what other investments could produce. Even if we are conservative and assume no tax benefits and no appreciation, the average return on investment over the six years is over thirty percent. And the compounded rate of return is over twenty percent. And that is assuming no appreciation or tax benefits!

Clearly, this is not a get-rich-quick type of investment, but it gives a safe return on investment and produces a property free and clear of mortgages in six years which will continue to produce cash flow virtually forever. A true money machine in a relatively short period of time.

If a person had $100,000 cash to invest in six of these units and had the patience to manage them, he could end up owning six free and clear units in six years—worth, at conservative estimates (8% per year), over half a million dollars and capable of generating a free and clear retirement income of between $3 — 4,000 per month from then on. And this income would be inflation adjusted... and partially tax sheltered with the units' depreciation.

Now, I realize that there aren't many people with $100,000 sitting in their bank accounts. But I thought I would open your minds to some possibilities.

Let's assume that you not only don't have $100,000... but you don't even have $15,750 for even one unit. The next question I will ask is: Can you borrow the down payment using another piece of real estate as collateral?

Suppose you don't have the cash, but you do have some equity. You could borrow against your available equities. A loan of $15,750 would cost you in the neighborhood of 15% per year... and if you were lucky enough to negotiate a ten-year term on the loan, your monthly payments would be about $300 per month. (If you are in California, you would also have to pay some front-end points... the money seems to cost a bit more there.) You could then buy a unit, using your borrowed dollars as the down payment, but you would have to sacrifice and cut into your monthly budget enough to pay the $300 payment on your new loan. But if you are in a high tax bracket anyway, the $3 — 4,000 per year spent repaying this loan would be entirely deductible. I realize that this would produce a negative cash flow... but have you considered just how much the IRS causes you to pay in monthly taxes? Isn't this a negative cash flow? And in six years the unit will flow positive cash flow when the first mortgage is paid off... leaving you with a remaining balance on your borrowed down payment of just over $10,000. If you applied all of your rent money to this loan, it could be paid off in less than two years more. And you would end up, in less than eight years, with a free and clear unit and no more loan on your equity. That's something to consider.

Now, suppose that you have no cash and no equity to draw upon. (An unlikely situation, I'm sure.) And these deals are just sitting there, tempting you. What can you do?

The Nothing Down system was designed specifically for situations like this. Remember the motto of a Nothing Down investor?

If I don't have it (money, credit, equity, income), someone does!

Could you find a partner who would take the tax benefits, as small as they are, plus a twenty percent return on his money in exchange for the use of his money secured by the property you will buy? If you are still skeptical, do you think that there are people out there in this marketplace who would like to earn between twenty and thirty percent on their money? If you doubt that there are, just count up the money in money market certificates... over $150,000,000,000 by last count. And what are money market funds paying? Under 10%. I think that you could find someone who would give up the liquidity of a money market fund for the extra return in a well-selected property. I'll let you mull this one over. If you want more information, reread the section in my book *Nothing Down* concerning partners and how to find them.

As a final note, if there is any question about the future appreciation of our real estate investments, maybe we should be looking at other alternatives to increasing our equity. The more you think about the zero interest option, the more it will entice you.

Recession Tactics: Specific Ways of Making Money in a Sluggish or Declining Real Estate Market

Robert G. Allen

I'm amused. Every time the economy dips into a recession, it seems I can't open up the paper, watch the evening news, or go to any national investment conference without some expert telling me how lousy, risky, and downright awful real estate is as an investment. I can't help but laugh out loud sometimes. The level of ignorance is abysmal. Let's look at what happened during 1980 during our last major recession:

Gold lost 63% of its value.
Sliver lost 85% of its value.
The stock market lost 20% of its value.
The bond market only worth 63 cents on the dollar.
Diamonds nose-dived despite DeBeers monopoly control.
I won't even talk about commodities.
Even the all-mighty Money market Certificate was down 24%.

And in the midst of all of this carnage, the median price of single-family homes in the United States increases by a mere percent or two... and all of the world tells us how bad real estate is! Who are they trying to kid?

This report is my answer to those who would scare you into doubting your decision to invest in real estate. I'm going to show you how the average real estate investor can run circles around any of the major investments... and can do it with nothing down. And how the smart real estate investor can make a fortune even in times of recession... no matter what happens to real estate prices.

This is in response to the many investment experts around us who, for some reason or other, feel that real estate is a bad investment. Since real estate appreciation slows considerably during recessions these experts always predict that "the game is over." Nothing could be further from the truth. The game never ends; it just starts all over again in a great cycle with another set of rules depending upon the ups and downs in the economy. And those who know that rules will have many years of profit taking . . . while those who listen to the doomsayers will sit on the side-lines and watch.

Let's start with a basic formula. Buy Low/Sell High.

Have you ever heard that before? It has been assumed that the only way you can make money in real estate is to buy low and sell high. Obviously, if real estate isn't appreciating it is not a good investment.

Wrong!

There are dozens of ways of making serious money in real estate investing besides the old Buy Low/Sell High After Appreciation formula.

Ten of these ways are listed as follows:

1. Buy High/Sell Low.
2. Don't Buy (Option).
3. Buy High/Sell High.
4. Buy Low/Fix-Up High.
5. Buy High/Sell One-Half High.
6. Don't Buy/Sell High.
7. Buy Low/Don't Sell.
8. Buy Low/Refinance High.
9. Buy High/Zero Interest.
10. Buy High/Condo Higher.

As I will show you, not one of these formulas relies on future appreciation. In fact, you can forget about future appreciation altogether. If inflation or the laws of supply and demand drive the prices of our real estate holdings upward over the years, then we can count this as additional icing on the cake . . . but in essence, we don't speculate that this will happen. Because real estate operates in an imperfect and inefficient marketplace, we can make our money "on the way in" and not have to wait for appreciation to carry us to profit.

Let's take the basic Buy Low/Sell High formula and have some fun with it:

Formula Number One. Buy High/Sell Low.

I have always said that one of the ways to be successful in anything is to do the exact opposite of what the world is doing. So let's take the tried and true formula Buy Low/Sell High and reverse it. Let's Buy High and Sell Low. If you were to do this with any other investment, you would lose your shirt. But real estate is a different story. I am going to show you how to buy a property for $100,000, sell it for $80,000, and still make a $10,000 profit. That's right . . . to sell a property for $20,000 less than its purchase price and still make $10,000. And it will be win/win, of course. Have I got your attention?

Let's start with a seller of a $100,000 property. I pick $100,000 for ease of illustration. For the same reason, this property will be free and clear. The seller is not a don't wanter but he is slightly flexible. He wants $20,000 down and is willing to carry the balance of $80,000 on a long-term, amortized loan. In the slower market place during recessions, he has to carry paper, or he may not be able to sell. He might even accept a $5,000 price reduction for a quick sale. He places his ad in the classified section of his local paper. He is actively seeking a person to give him $20,000 cash plus $80,000 paper in exchange for his house.

In the same marketplace, advertising in the same classified section (although on a different page) are dozens of individual sellers of paper. For example, you might find in the Mortgages or Trust Deeds for Sale section of your paper a person who owns an $80,000 mortgage that looks fairly similar to the one that the above house seller is willing to accept. This mortgage holder sold his property several years ago, carried back a mortgage, and has been receiving monthly payments regularly ever since. The property which is the collateral for the loan has increased significantly in value, thus enhancing the security of the loan. The seller, for whatever reason, wants to sell this mortgage for cash. Because of market forces, he will probably part with his paper and be happy to receive 60% of its face value or $48,000 cash. Sometimes less.

Interesting. One person is looking for paper. And another person is willing to sell it . . . at a discount. Is there a way that we could get these two people together and profit from it in a win/win way without investing any of our own money? The answer is "yes".

Let's go to the seller of the paper and obtain a 45-day option to buy the paper for $48,000. You explain that you will need some time to arrange your financing. You try to tie up the right to buy the paper at a discount so that you will have time to put all of the pieces together.

Then you go to the house seller and make him an offer. You offer to give $20,000 cash down plus an $80,000 mortgage secured by another piece of property. The seller has already agreed to accept paper against his own property. The crucial link in this whole process is to get him to accept an existing piece of paper secured by another property (the paper that you can buy at a discount) instead of a new piece of paper secured by his own house.

How do you get a seller to accept a substitution of collateral? You show him the benefits . . . and there are many.

First of all, the existing $80,000 paper has a proven track record. You can show the seller a history of regular monthly payments being made over a several-year period of time. That is much better than your promise to make payments on a new mortgage. The paper is "seasoned" . . . as they say in the business.

Secondly, the collateral will probably be better on the existing loan than on a new mortgage. In other words, the seller will be more secure with an existing loan on a more valuable property with a proven track record than with a new loan on his own home.

Not everyone will accept this substitution of collateral, but enough people are willing to make it well worth the time and hassle to find them.

The next step is to get a loan against the $100,000 house. Since the property is free and clear and since the seller has agreed to accept an $80,000 loan secured by another property, that gives us a marvelous borrowing opportunity. Let's put an $80,000 loan against the seller's house. The $80,000 loan proceeds will be dispersed as follows:

$48,000 to the seller of the discounted mortgage. He collects his money and walks away happy. Win/win.

$20,000 to the seller of the house. He collects his $20,000 cash plus an $80,000 mortgage secured on a property other than his own. He gets what he wanted without any dickering in price. Win/win.

$2,000 cash for closing costs to obtain the new loan. The bank makes a new loan, makes some fees, and has adequate security for the new loan. Win/win.

That leaves us with dispersals of $70,000 from the $80,000 loan proceeds. Where does the remaining $10,000 go? If you like, you can send it to me . . . but I expect that you'll just pocket it yourself.

Let's review, then. The house seller got what he wanted. The banker got what he wanted. And you ended up with $10,000 in cash plus a $20,000 profit in an investment home. With nothing out of your pocket . . . and of course, no balloon payments. Not bad for a month's work. Some Americans don't do as well in a year's time.

But suppose you don't like the thought of renting out this home, managing tenants, and paying the negative cash flow that will obviously be a part of this new, high-interest-rate first mortgage you had to obtain. Well, let's complete the circle in a win/win way. Do you suppose that at this very moment in your city there are people who still buy real estate the old-fashioned way . . . putting up a large down payment and refinancing at high interest rates? Although this seems ridiculous to us, knowing what we know, there are still hundreds of conventional buyers in the marketplace. In fact, I'll wager that there are dozens of buyers at this very moment who are buying $100,000 houses in your city . . . who are using their hard-earned $20,000 cash down payments and are agreeing to obtain high-interest first mortgages. They don't like it . . . but they don't know of any other way. Let's give them an alternative. Let's advertise our newly-acquired property in the following manner:

Nothing Down and
Guaranteed Twenty
Thousand Dollars Below
the Market

Do you think that headline might attract a few buyers? The conventional buyer who was willing to put $20,000 down and buy at market price can now keep his $20,000 cash and buy a property $20,000 below market. He buys your property with nothing down simply by assuming your mortgage. In one swift move, he has increased his net worth by $20,000 and still has his cash left to buy something else with . . . probably something that goes down in value like furniture. Do you think that this is win/win to him? Of course it is.

So the end result is we buy a property for $100,000 and sell it for $80,000, pocket $10,000 cash, *and everybody wins.* This is not an overfinanced scheme with pyramids of unstable debt. This is conservative for everyone.

Now you might say that this is an awful lot of work just to make $10,000 cash. But if you had a system of doing this once a month . . . it might be worth the effort. I know a lot of people who make a third this amount and work twice as hard to get it. Are you one of those?

I know that I haven't been able to touch on the minute details here... but there are answers to all of your questions. The best source I know of is in a tape package by one of our guest lecturers, Joe Land. And that brings us to our next formula.

Formula Number Two. Don't Buy.

You heard me right. If you are afraid of what is going to happen to real estate in the future, don't buy it. I'm not being facetious. I really mean it. Instead of buying it and assuming all of the obligations of debt, why don't you specialize in option techniques. Don't buy, just option. Let me give you an example.

One of our Million Dollar RAND Table winners related this example at our annual conference. (By the way, I would like to see you at your next conference.)

They located a don't wanter who had bought a home in the Sunbelt. He lived in New York and had given this property to his daughter who had died in the meantime. He was trying to sell it for the exact amount he had paid for it . . . $78,000. He learned that he had paid too much for the property. It was worth perhaps $70,000. There was a mortgage of $48,000. If he were to leave this property on the market, he would have to make perhaps six more monthly payments of $461 PITI, plus commissions, plus wear and tear on his vacant property. It was a real lose/lose situation for him.

Our students made the following offer. Instead of buying the unit, they would lease it from him for $400 per month with an option to buy it in four years for $78,000. Why did he accept it? He realized that he would be able to take the yearly tax shelter (averaging over $6,000 per year) from the unit to offset his $61 monthly negative cash flow ($732 per year or less than $3,000 in four years). Since he was in the 50% tax bracket he would save well over $3,000 per year in taxes, have no management headaches and no selling hassles. It was a quick solution to his problem. Why did our students like it? They rented the property out for a $75 per month positive cash flow immediately. As the years go by, they will increase this cash flow. If the propety doesn't appreciate in value, they will not exercise their option to buy. I'll bet they will be able to negotiate an extension from the same owner. If the property does appreciate, they will exercise their option and pay the seller off to realize their profit. Either way, they don't care if the property goes up or down in value. They win now, or they win later. They just have to wait four years to see how much.

Study my book, *Nothing Down,* for more ideas about options.

Formula Number Three. Buy High/Sell High.

How can you buy a property for $100,000 and sell it for $100,000 and still make a profit? It depends on the kind of profit you are trying to make. Sometimes you are not interested in making capital gain. Perhaps you are more interested in positive cash flow. Well, how can you generate positive cash flow when you don't sell at a profit?

It all depends on the terms you can negotiate.

Let's suppose you locate a retail don't wanter who doesn't want to discount his price but will be willing to sell flexibly . . . with nothing down. And carry soft paper for his equity. It is a $100,000 home with a $60,000 first mortgage at 8% assumable. The seller has $40,000 equity and is willing to carry his balance at 10% for twenty years. The payments on the first and second equal about $860 per month including principal and interest. Now, you could rent this out for about $600 per month with a $300 per month negative cash flow, or you could sell it again. Suppose you put it back on the market, again for nothing down to attract more buyers. You are offering bargain terms: Nothing Down and a wrap-around contract for the entire $100,000 balance at only 12% for 30 years. No assumption problems. No balloons. No stringent qualifying. (You will, of course, do some checking.)

The payments would be $1,028 per month for the next thirty years. The payments on the underlying loans would be less than your incoming payment by about $170 per month. Mind you, this is not a king's ransom. But it is positive cash flow without management headaces. And when the underlying loans are paid off within twenty years, the final ten years of payments would come to you directly . . . all $1,028.

Now, this may sound like a lot of work to generate some cash flow. After all, you have to find a seller *and* a buyer in order to pull this off. That's why you always run your ads in the paper advertising for people who want to sell flexibly. At the same time you can continually run an ad offering to sell a home for nothing down with bargain interest. If you don't happen to have a home which fits their criteria at the moment, put their names on the waiting list. And call them when you do have something to offer them. Try to do the buying and selling in the same escrow to avoid extra costs. Put contingencies in both your buying and selling contracts, making either transation subject to the terms and conditions you set to make you feel comfortable.

How does this technique work? Rather than looking for bargains in prices . . . concentrate on finding bargains in terms. And then you take some of the cream off the top and sell the same property at the same price (more if you can get it) but with a higher interest rate which still is a market bargain.

Formula Number Four. Buy Low/Fix-Up High.

As you may already know, I have never been a great fan of the fix-up process. Just the idea of buying a run-down property and working to upgrade it cosmetically sounded like too much work for me. But there is a lot of sound, legitimate money to be made through this process as our Lowry/Nickerson friends are quick to point out.

I have recently taken on a project which has shown me these benefits first hand. Several years ago I bought my first major apartment building. It was an old twelve-unit property built in 1928. I bought it from a don't wanter for about $5,000 down with the balance on a contract at 9.75% interest for twenty years. It was a grand old building with a classic architectural style and large balconies overlooking the main street in our city. It was excellently located a block from the county court house and a major shopping area. I continued to operate this building as apartments for about five years, but it gradually became obvious that this 50-year-old building would have to have some major work done to keep it alive. Since its true highest and best use is commercial office space, and since I have always had it in the back of my mind to convert this property one day into my corporate offices, we decided to do the conversion. We began gutting the apartments to make way for the facelift. And our Allen Group offices moved into a brand new building.

Now, this conversion process was not easy... and cost more than twice as much as the original projections... but there were significant benefits. First of all, the building is worth significantly more money as a new office building so all of this work has added substantially to my net worth. Secondly, all of the renovation qualifies for federal tax credits as work done to renovate older buildings. With the new tax law in effect in 1982, I can take a 20% investment tax credit for every dollar spent to improve this property. If I can get this building to qualify as a historical building on the national register, I could increase the investment tax credit to 25%. This alone will save me about $40,000 in taxes. And that is a welcome present on April 15.

Obviously, the fix-up route is a harder route. But the benefits are there and should not be over looked.

Formula Number Five. Buy High/Sell One-Half High.

Equity participation is sweeping the country. And I can see why. The benefits are obvious.

My first use of the equity-sharing formula happened about two years ago while I was doing some PR for my book *Nothing Down* in Miami. I had an evening free, so I decided to see if I couldn't buy something. I read an ad in the paper which had some good nothing down clues in it:

> Deluxe one bedroom
> condo. Fully furnished.
> Rent to own. Low Down.
> Owner-agent. $35,900.
> Call 555-4321.

I called and found out that they would settle for $1,000 down and a contract for 30 years at 12%. I thought that this was too good to be true, so I made arrangements to go look at the property and couldn't resist buying it. I gave the owner $100 deposit and a $900 postdated check to be cashed at closing which we set for about three weeks.

But I had several problems to overcome. First of all, there was the management problem. How was I going to manage this unit from 2,000 miles away? Secondly, there would be a small negative cash flow of about $50 per month. I decided that I would rather own one-half of this property with no negative cash flow and no management hassles, instead of owning

100% of this property with all of its negative cash flows and management responsibilities. I easily found a partner by offering one-half ownership for, you guessed it, nothing down. Ths new partner found a new tenant who gave the normal first and last month's rent plus a deposit. This amounted to $1,250, which was conveniently used as the down payment to buy the unit... I didn't have to use my own $1,000 after all. Therefore, I now owned one-half of a nice condo in Miami with no management hassles and little or no negative cash flow for nothing down. I haven't had one iota of trouble for the past four years.

It was win/win for my partner and me. If the property doesn't appreciate rapidly in value, we will still be able to split the tax and cash flow benefits over the years.

This gives you a brief idea of the reasons why the concept of equity sharing is growing so rapidly. Around the country, smart investors are sharing the wealth by selling one-half ownership of certain properties to qualified partners or part-owner occupants. The investor wins by having reduced negative cash flows and management problems. The partner wins by receiving half ownership in a property for little or no money down. There are legal bugs to work out in many states, but the benefits are worth the trouble.

Formula Number Six. Don't Buy/Sell High.

Is it possible to sell something you don't own at a profit and not go to jail for it? John Schaub thinks there is. And those of us at our first annual Nothing Down convention in the Bahamas listened in amazement as he shared this formula with us. The key to using this formula is the option. Let's suppose we locate a seller of a $75,000 single-family home who is trying to get out from under the property. He has a $50,000 first mortgage with payments of $550 per month. The property is vacant. The seller has moved to another city. Every month that goes by ... he has to continue feeding his pet alligator. He is getting more and more anxious to do something which plugs this black hole in his financial statement. Enter the creative investor. We offer to lease his property for three years at $550 per month if he will give us an option to buy his property in three years for $75,000. We also want terms for the eventual purchase in three years. We agree to assume the seller's first mortgage loan of $50,000. For the seller's $25,000 equity, we agree to pay $5,000 cash each year plus 12% interest until the entire $25,000 is paid in full. The seller is not thrilled with the option price or terms, but he is thrilled with the guaranteed lease arrangement. By accepting this offer he cuts his losses and can begin to sleep better at night. He agrees.

Once the option is negotiated we proceed to sell the property. Our ad in the paper will read:

Nothing Down
Buy beautiful home for
$80,000 with nothing down
and only 12% interest.
Payments $822 per month.
Call Bob. 555-1234.

When the buyer is found, you explain that the payments are $822 per month for three years. After three years he will either have to refinance the property and pay you out, or he can assume your underlying loan and agree to the payments which you have... $5,000 per year until the equity is paid out.

How do you profit from this? You get to keep the difference between $822 (the monthly payment to you) and $550 (your lease payment) for a total of $272 per month. In addition, you have built-in $5,000 profit for yourself down the road. Instant cash flow to you plus future profit.

How does your buyer profit? He is able to buy on excellent terms.

Once again, you profit without having to worry about whether or not real estate appreciates.

Formula Number Seven. Buy Low/Don't Sell.

We run a regular ad in the newspaper in the Real Estate Wanted Column of our local newspaper. We offer to pay full price for single-family homes if the sellers are willing to sell for nothing down. In this way we have the don't wanters looking for us instead of us looking for them. Early in December, one seller called us and offered to sell us his $60,000 duplex. he was moving, was behind three payments in his mortgages, and couldn't stand his property anymore. He asked us to please take it off his hands. We asked him what he wanted. He said he would be thrilled if we just brought his payments current... he would walk away from the remaining equity if we would close quickly. We analyzed the situation. There were two mortgages on the property totalling $48,000. They were both assumable. The payments totalled about $500 per month. He was behind three payments. After closing costs, it would cost us about $2,000 to bail him out. The property was rented with about $100 per month negative cash flow. We reasoned that the $2,000 investment would yield an immedite $12,000 equity which is about 600% return on our money immediately... not bad. In addition, it would provide excellent tax benefits.. and the negative cash flow problem would be solved by the gradual raising of rents over the next few months...

and then it would be a positive cash flow property forever. There were no balloons to worry about. In essence, I could keep it forever without worrying about appreciation . . . it would continue to pump out positive cash flows to me and my posterity as long as we owned it. In due time the loans will be paid off, and the cash flows will be even better.

Once again, real estate pulls through with flying colors.

Formula Number Eight. Buy Low/Refinance High.

In times like these, are there sellers whose need for cash is greater than their need to sell at a profit? In other words, are there bargains out there for those who have lots of cash to invest? Say, "Yes".

Just as in the previous example, one way to find these bargains is to advertise in the Real Estate Wanted Column of your local newspaper. You will indicate in your ad that you have cash and can close quickly for the right property. Suppose you receive a call from a seller who has a $60,000 property. It has an assumable $30,000 loan against it bearing payments of $250 per month at 8.5% interest. The seller needs to move and needs immediate cash. He is willing to reduce his price significantly for a fast cash sale. You offer him $15,000 cash, and he accepts. You close and now become the proud owner of a property you bought at $45,000, which is worth at least $60,000. But you have a problem. You used all of your available cash to invest in this one unit. You can rent it out for $500 per month and have about a $250 positive cash flow per month, but you would still like to be able to invest. You go to your local finance company and ask them for a second mortgage against this property you have just acquired. They appraise it and agree to lend you 80% of value which would be up to $48,000. You take out a loan for $18,000 at 20% for fifteen years with monthly payments of $316 per month. You walk out of the closing with your original cash of $15,000 plus a bonus of $3,000 as profit. But your combined payments of $250 and $316 will give you about a $75 per month negative cash flow. You could eliminate this cash flow problem by either the slow process of raising rents over the next few years, or you could sell one-half interest in the property to your tenant if he agrees to make all of the payments. This is the equity sharing way of getting rid of a negative cash flow in a win/win way.

You have your original investment back in your pocket ready for the next investment. You put $3,000 cash in your pocket as an immediate profit plus the $12,000 equity profit in your property. At this rate, who cares about future appreciation?

Formula Number Nine. Buy High/Zero Interest.

Builders all across the country are using the zero-interest method of unloading their unwanted excess inventory. It has significant benefits to the buyer. To recap, using an actual example from a builder's ad, the builder agrees to sell his $60,000 condo to us. We put $20,000 down, and the builder agrees to finance the $40,000 balance at zero percent interest with monthly payments of $650 per month for the next five years.. at which time we will own the property free and clear of any mortgage. Granted, we have to come up with the $20,000 as a down payment (it could be borrowed). And we will have a negative cash flow. (Do you now make a negative cash flow to Uncle Sam every month?) But the fact that the property will be free and clear in five years offers some major benefits for retirement planning that can't be over-looked. If we discount appreciation altogether, our $20,000 investment "earns" $7,800 per year (850 x 12) or 39% each year... which is not too shabby.

It's something to think about.

Formula Number Ten. Buy High/Condo Higher.

In my book *Nothing Down* I tell of a ten-unit apartment building which I bought with a partner for $30,000 down (his money, of course). We paid $22,000 per unit. We then got approval through the city to turn these apartment units into condos and sold the condos for $33,000 per unit with $5,000 down (enough to recoup our original $30,000 cash plus pay Realtor fees). We carried the paper. It generates $880 per month profit to us for the next twenty-five years. And it was relatively simple because we sold the units with excellent terms at a price that was about $5,000 below the market. They sold like hotcakes.

If you want to review some of the details, see page 204 in my book.

So there you have them . . . ten ways of making money in real estate without worrying or speculating on the future appreciation of real estate. Believe me, there are dozens of other ways. Keep your chin up. Keep looking for those bargain prices or those bargain terms. As Joe Girard says, "If you throw enough spaghetti against the wall, some of it is bound to stick."

Recession Tactics:
A Footnote

Richard J. Allen

Recently the following question was posed by an investor on the telephone: "Could you clarify Formula Six in Bob's article, 'Specific Ways of Making Money In A Sluggish or Declining Real Estate Market' (May 1982, page 3)? He writes, 'Once the option is negotiated we proceed to sell the property.' How can you sell something you have not yet closed on?" *CM, Annapolis, MD*

Answer

Formula Six in Bob's series of ten zero-appreciation techniques is called, "Don't Buy/Sell High." This is an option approach that John Schaub teaches. Essentially, the buyer purchases an option on a property with favorable terms, then turns around immediately and sells an option on the same property to another buyer, but subject to the first option. Under the conditions of the second option, the selling price will of course go up to assure a built-in profit, and the monthly payments meanwhile will be higher than on the first option. In effect, our first buyer never really buys the property: it is bought (at a higher price) by our second buyer under conditions of the second option (hence the term "Don't Buy/Sell High") The stick figures will summarize the details:

First 3-year option

Second Option (also 3 years)

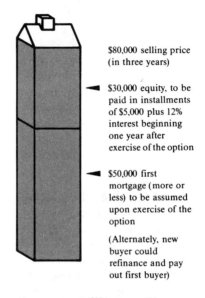

$75,000 selling price
(locked in for
three years)

$25,000 equity, to be paid
in installments of $5,000
plus 12% interest
beginninge one year
after exercise of
the option

$50,000 first mortgage
to be assumed upon
exercise of the option

$80,000 selling price
(in three yeurs)

$30,000 equity, to be
paid in installments
of $5,000 plus 12%
interest beginning
one year after
exercise of the option

$50,000 first
mortgage (more or
less) to be assumed
upon exercise of the
option

(Alternately, new
buyer could
refinance and pay
out first buyer)

(Lease payments $550 per month)   (Lease payments $822 per month)

Life Without Inflation

Richard J. Allen

Can a Nothing Down creative investor make it without the benefits of inflation to help boost property prices? The answer to the question is a rousing "Yes!" The basis for the answer is the word "Creative."

Demand for real estate is expected to remain acutely high throughout this decade. As long as people must find ways to satisfy that fundamental need, there will be an opportunity for investors to profit in their roles as problem-solvers—if they can stay creative and flexible.

Robert Allen demonstrated what creative flexibility means in his article "Recession Tactics: Specific Ways of Making Money In A Sluggish Or Declining Real Estate Market". Bob outlined ten different approaches for profiting from real estate during a zero-appreciation period. The buy/sell matrix included here shows some of the possible combinations of those approaches.

With some creative thought, you can come up with other approaches that might work for you in a flat market. (An example is buying and selling time-shares rather than property—currently a burgeoning business now that the first big generation of time-share opportunities is being sold out.) The message is clear—life without inflation can still be profitable for the creative investor.

What does this mean for you as a real estate investor? If the growth pattern in your area is flat, pay particular attention to the alternative formulas in Bob Allen's "Recession Tactics" article (summarized in the chart above). If the growth pattern in your area is still strong, be prudent and use your best judgment as to the techniques you use to acquire property. You can never go wrong pretending that the growth may not last and act accordingly. It reminds me of a story my father used to tell about the advice of an old Indian Chief: "When weather good, always take coat.

	DON'T SELL	SELL LOW	SELL HIGH
BUY HIGH ►	☐ Keep only half, sell half interest to equity partner ☐ Buy from builder with zero interest and own free and clear in five years ☐ Buy with discounted paper, then refinance and hold	☐ Buy with discounted paper, then refinance, take profit, and sell low	☐ Buy, then sell on contract for cash flow ☐ Sell half to equity partner, keep half interest ☐ Buy, then convert to condos and sell
BUY LOW ►	☐ Buy discounted properties and hold for cash flow ☐ Buy discounted properties and refinance high ☐ Fix up and hold for cash flow	☐ Buy, then sell on contract for cash flow	☐ Buy, then sell on contract for cash flow ☐ Fix up and sell for profit
DON'T BUY ►	☐ Buy option only, follow through with purchase later if profitable		☐ Buy option only, then sell for cash flow on option subject to first option

When weather bad, suit yourself."

What is the long-term prospect for inflation? Despite jubilant victory cries over the defeat of inflation, our perspective is that we are only going through a lull in the storm. We had better keep our coat on, so that we don't relax and lose our shirt. With huge federal deficits coming up the hopes of keeping inflation's ugly head down for very long are not good.

The government will either have to borrow from the economy to make up the difference, or (most likely) create the necessary capital through the fractional reserve banking system or by printing it. Either way, the likely outcome seems clear: life without inflation is a short-term prospect.

Meanwhile, creative investors can take comfort in the fact that the Robert Allen Nothing Down System is flexible enough to work in any economic climate—with or without inflation.

Positive Cash Flow Formulas in Real Estate

Robert G. Allen

Real estate is often looked upon as a wonderful capital gain investment with fantastic tax shelter benefits. But it is rarely regarded, especially by neophytes, as a powerful cash generating investment. In fact, real estate is widely maligned as being just exactly the opposite . . . a negative cash flow alligator. Thus, cash-poor investors shy away from real estate . . . which is exactly the opposite of what they should be doing. (A common human tendancy, I might add.)

As I have often said, real estate is a multi-faceted investment . . . a miracle of flexibility. It will do for you financially just about anything you want it to. If you want appreciation, tax shelter, equity build-up or cash flow . . . or any combination of these . . . you can find a formula which will solve your needs. But you have to be specific. If you want appreciation, choose formulas which are suited for appreciation. If you want cash flow, you need to use cash flow formulas. The mistake most investors make is using appreciation formulas when what they really need is cash flow.

Take, for example, the case of a beginning cash-poor investor. He can barely keep his nose above water, couldn't even think of handling a negative cash flow, and would be devastated by any unexpected expenditure such as a major roof repair. And, despite these strikes aginst him, he buys big chunks of real estate hoping for the big long-term bucks when it is those little short-term bucks which hold the key to his success or failure. He doesn't need a million dollars in five years. He needs an extra $300 per month now. And when he has *this* problem solved maybe he will be in the right frame of mind to think about the future.

Perhaps a better approach is for a cash-poor investor to take things one step at a time. Rather than marching out into the cold, cruel world of investments to make a quick fortune, he should look upon his real estate operations as a sort of part-time job with a goal to have his real estate activities (you'll notice I didn't say "investments") generate for him a comfortable cushion of monthly cash flow plus a few small chunks of cash to be used later on in his investment program. The primary goal is to generate cash or cash flow to enhance the financial strength and stability of the investor (I really should say "employee").

I am trying to make the distinction between "investor" and "employee" to reinforce the fact that real estate is technically not an investment... it is a business. And those who treat it like an active "hands on" business generally prosper while those who treat it like a passive "arm chair" investment are the ones who moan and groan the loudest about how lousy real estate is as an investment. It is lousy as an investment, but it is simply marvelous as a business. (I hope that doesn't confuse anyone.)

The purpose of this chapter is to catalog a few of the many cash flow generating techniques and formulas that are available. Go for the cash flow first, then build up a cash pool and when you are ready you can go for the capital gains.

To make this a little more realistic and useful to you, let's assume that you are a cash-poor investor (who isn't?) with a steady job and fairly good credit rating (more of a rarity these days). You are living from paycheck to paycheck. You want to invest in real estate but don't dare because you don't have much margin for error. You would feel more comfortable if you had $10,000 in cash and a four or five hundred dollar per month surplus income.

Question: How could you use your knowledge of real estate investing to help you reach your comfortable cash flow goals within a six-month period of time?

Let's try it.

The first step is to write down our goals. Let's get the subconscious mind on our side.

Secondly, devise a plan. There are five major ways to squeeze cash or cash flow from real estate:

1. Buy it right and lease it out.
2. Buy it right and sell it.
3. Lease it right and sublet it.
4. Option it right and sell the option.
5. Buy discounted paper right and sell it.

The essence of all of these cash flow-generating categories is becoming an expert in finding bargains, wholesale situations, and re-marketing those bargains to the public at retail. That's what free enterprise is all about.

Let's examine each one in turn.

1. Buy It Right And Lease It Out.

What do I mean by buying it right?

In order for you to buy a home, for instance, and have a positive cash flow of at least $100 per month you would need a perfect combination of the following ingredients:

- low price
- low interest rates on mortgages and/or
- deferred payments on mortgages
- a high rent-to-value ratio

What is the probability that you will find an inexpensive home that you can buy for 60 cents on the dollar with nothing down which has a low interest rate, long-term assumable loan? Not very great. And this probability is reduced even further if you don't live in a city with an abundance of cheap housing (Sorry for those of you living in major cities like Los Angeles, Washington, D.C., Honolulu . . .).

But this doesn't mean that it is impossible. If you have chosen to buy wholesale properties and rent them out for cash flow (and you happen to live in areas of the country where this is more feasible), then you should gear up a program which will increase the probability that you will be successful. Here are the six things I would do, if this were my formula:

A. Become an expert in foreclosures. Visit every sale.

B. Visit every savings and loan association, finance company, bank or credit union in my area and ask to speak to the person in charge of "real estate owned" or the bank Repossession Department. Ask to study their portfolio of repossessed properties. Look for properties in lower price ranges which could be purchased below market with below market financing offered by the lending institution.

C. Make a thorough study of the rental market in your area. Learn what is in demand and what is not. Get a feel for what properties are renting for, what deposits are asked, etc. The more you know, the easier you will find a blind spot . . . that area of the market which is in short supply making the rents higher and the properties easier to rent out.

D. Place an ad in the paper in the Real Estate Wanted section of the classified advertising that you are in the market to buy property at full price but on the condition of extremely flexible financing. Don't be disappointed if you have very few calls. You need to be advertising. How can you catch fish if you don't have your bait in the water?

E. Do a thorough study of prices in your city. How can you know what is wholesale if you don't know what retail is?

F. Volume is the key. I'm sure that you would have to sift through a hundred properties before you found one that even came close to your needs. All sources of properties should be combed. MLS books, Realtor contacts, reading ads in the newspaper and generally circulating in the right circles (apartment owners associations, local investment groups like RAND, exchange groups).

2. Buy It Right And Sell It.

Once you have found a bargain property you may decide not to rent it out for cash flow. You may choose to sell it. And if you sell it you have two choices. You can sell it for a higher retail price and pocket the cash as your profit. Or you may decide to sell for full price with a small or no down payment and retain your profit in the form of a note with monthly cash flow coming in to you over a period of years. There is no secret to this.

But if I had decided to make the buying and selling of real estate for cash flow profit, I would be sure to do the following:

A. Read Wade Cook's book, *How To Build A Real Estate Money Machine.* It is a classic on the subject.

B. Search out five of the top experts in your market place who are entrepreneurs in this area. Take them to lunch. Find out what their cookie cutter is.

C. Develop a list of investors to whom you can sell your properties. You may wish to start with Realtors who deal with investor clients who are looking for good deals. Get in the habit of finding excellent buys which you can tie up for a few dollars and re-market to these investors for a small cash profit. The better the deal and the lower your mark-up, the faster you will be able to turnover your properties. And turnover is critical.

D. Advertise in the paper. You may even wish to include a clause in your purchase agreements that will give you ample time to market your properties before you close.

E. Set aside a fixed time each week for searching for new properties.

A footnote to this approach: check with your attorney concerning local regulations on "investor" versus "dealer" status. Make sure your activities accord with local regulations and give you the greatest tax benefits.

3. Lease It Right And Sublet It.

Many beginning investors shun this approach because it doesn't involve ownership. But ownership is not what is critical. Control is critical. And when you have a lease on a property, you control it... at least partially. For instance, let's suppose you locate a beautiful three-bedroom home which is available for lease for $400 per month . . . but which is worth perhaps $550 per month on the open market. The seller is desperate to get it rented out because of the monthly payment. He agrees to accept just enough to cover his mortgage payment of $400 if you will agree to a long-term lease of three years with the right to renew for two extra years. He is thrilled to have the headache taken care of. You proceed to find a new tenant and sublet the property to him . . . for $500 per month. Notice that you don't charge full market rent. You charge less than market to attract a solid tenant who has an incentive to move in and to stay there. The positive cash flow accrues to you for the management trouble.

You can make this even more attractive by asking the seller of the property for a lease with an option to buy. By negotiating a good future purchase price, you can increase your profits. But the key to this formula is the cash flow. In essence, you are in business to find property which is underrented and your job is to re-rent it for a profit.

If this formula interest you, you would do well to take the following steps:

A. Visit every rental property firm in your area. Establish relationships with these companies. They are looking for good rentals for their customers, who usually pay a fee for the service. You will need a ready source of renters for a fast rent-up of your units.

B. Become thoroughly familiar with the rental customs of your area. What are the best areas of town? Will people pay more for a furnished apartment? Are one bedrooms more in demand than three bedrooms?

C. Join the local Apartment Owners' Association. Learn all you can about tenant laws and rights. You will need to walk a thin line from time to time.

D. Study carefully the Houses and Apartments For Rent columns of the classified section of your local paper. Call on the new ads daily. If this is going to be your part-time job, you better be the best there is.

4. Option It Right And Sell Your Option.

In my book, *Nothing Down,* in the chapter on options, I talk about a $30,000 profit I made on the sale of an option on a tract of ground. To recap briefly, I found an excellent piece of property which was owned by a major church. They had been trying to sell but had not generated the kind of offers they wanted. I was informed that for $2,500 option money they would give me the right to buy this 4-acre parcel in one year for $200,000. It was in a prime location, I knew the area well, and felt that the price was low. I brought in a partner to put up the $2,500 cash (nothing down to me, of course) and sold the parcel about nine months later to a developer for $275,000. The church received a better offer than they were able to generate by themselves and I was able to split a $75,000 profit among my partners.

What made this profit possible? Of course, my knowledge of the value of property, my decision to act and my ability to find a suitable buyer. If you want to make money in options, you should be prepared to comb the market for super bargains, have the money to tie up the properties you find, and be prepared to market the property you control up until the final bell. Options are a relatively open field and not much has been written about them. I can only point you towards what exists in my own book about them. If you know of a good book that deals with the subject in depth, drop me a line. I would like to read it.

5. Buying Discounted Paper Right And Selling It.

Let me say briefly that I feel that the field of discounted mortgages is the greatest opportunity for creating wealth in a real estate-related field of any that I have studied. Billions of dollars of owner carried-back financing was created in the years 1979-1982. That means that we will see a good portion of this paper flooding onto the discounted paper market in this coming decade.

How do you make money in discounted mortgages? The same way you make it in real estate. You hunt for bargains and don't wanters. You negotiate for profit. For example, suppose you find a holder of a note with a face value of $10,000 with monthly payments of $143 per month at 12% interest. It is completely amortized over a ten-year period of time. He decides that he wants cash instead of this steady income stream. How much cash would you be willing to pay him for his note? The market place would pay him about 65 cents on the dollar... or about $6,500. This would yield the investor in the note about 24% on his invested dollars. Not bad, eh? Yes, but what if you don't have the $6,500 in cash to buy this gem? Well, what do you think all of those money market fund investors are doing with their money these days now that rates are down from their highs of 17% to around 12% or less? Do you think some of them would flee the safety, security and liquidity of money market funds if you offered them 20% on their money? You tell them that for $7,400 you will sell them your interest in a note which will yield them over 20% per year for the next ten years. Not too bad! Well, if you bought (or optioned) the note for $6,500 and sold it for $7,400 ... that means $900 in your pocket without having to risk or invest a lot of your money. I think you are getting the drift. There are some problems with securities laws in certain states.

I just wanted to give you a taste and tell you how excited I am personally about this area.

As a summary, then, we had a goal to make $10,000 plus a monthly income of $400-500 within a six-month period of time. How would I go about this, now that we have reviewed the many areas of potential cash flow?

I would go immediately to a lease/option formula, placing emphasis on generating cash flow. I would attempt to find two houses in the lower price ranges that I could lease and sublet out for immediate cash flow. This would take two to three months.

Next, and perhaps simultaneously, I would look for bargain properties which could be bought and immediately rented out for cash flow. I would want to buy it at a wholesale price to build up an immediate equity position to borrow against later. I would concentrate on finding one such property in a six-month period of time.

I would want to find, purchase, and resell two to three bargain properties purchased at least 20% below market and sold within a short period of time thereafter. Two of them would be sold for nothing down at 90% of the value, with the profit being carried back in the form of a note with monthly payments. For instance, suppose I found a home valued at $75,000 which could be bought using nothing down techniques for $60,000. I would resell it for $67,500 (below market) with fantastic terms retaining my profit in the form of a $7,500 second mortgage or interest in a wrap around. The payments on this note could feasibly be $100 or more per month. It would take the full six months to comfortably accomplish this, but the $200 per month minimum cash flow would be very helpful. The third bargain property I would buy and sell in order to generate a $5,000 cash profit.

A final lump sum of at least $5,000 would be generated by using Joe Land's technique of buying discounted paper and trading it for real estate. See the chapter on recession tactics under formula #1 for more details. Joe also has an excellent set of tapes which I have listened to and highly reccommend. They are available through our bookstore.

I feel comfortable that following a general program like this would comfortably yield you $10,000 in cash as well as $400-500 in monthly positive cash flow.

I hope this is helpful to those of you who have heretofore kept out of the real estate market because of those negative cash flow fears.

What is a Wraparound?

Richard C. Powelson

In these days of creative financing a term that is probably the least understood is that of "Wraparound" or "All Inclusive Deed of Trust." I have been teaching this term and how to use it for some seven years now but I still find that attorneys, Realtors, lenders and common everyday investors just don't understand what the term means or how to use it. Yet it really is very simple, and, if used properly, is a dynamite way to sell your property, or is a valuable tool to use in buying. Let's take the confusion out of "wraparound" once and for all.

Example: A $100,000 property. The Seller wants a $10,000 down payment but is willing to take the balance of $90,000 in the form of monthly payments. You offer him a promissory note for this $90,000. As collateral or security for this note, the seller asks you to sign an instrument called a "mortgage" ("deed of trust" in certain states). This instrument describes the security involved and spells out the terms of repayment. This instrument is signed in front of a notary public and is recorded at the courthouse. Once it is recorded it becomes a lien against the property. Simply put, the seller acts as the lender for the buyer instead of a savings and loan becoming involved.

If there are no other liens recorded against the property then this mortgage becomes the first such lien recorded, making it a First Mortgage. If there is already a mortgage recorded against the property then this becomes secondary to the already-recorded instrument. If there is just one mortgage recorded, then this becomes a Second, if there are two mortgages recorded, then this becomes a Third, etc. In other words, a mortgage is called a First, Second, or Third, etc, because of time of recording. Such designations normally appear on the instrument.

Let's go back to our example of the $100,000. If the property is free and clear then the note secured by a mortgage is a first mortgage. If the property has a loan of, say, $40,000 on it, secured by a first mortgage on the property, then whatever is recorded after this instrument is called a second or subordinate mortgage. A buyer can buy, taking over the first of $40,000 and offering the seller a note for $50,000 for the balance of the $90,000 owed, or $60,000 if it is a nothing down offer. This $50,000 or $60,000 mortgage is recorded and the seller's collateral is a second on the property. The buyer now owes two notes, one for $40,000 and a second for $50,000. The buyer pays the first mortgage payment and also has to pay the seller on the second mortgage. This technique of seller "helping" with financing has been around forever and is understood and accepted by almost everybody.

The difference between this method of financing and the "wraparound" method is that instead of the buyer taking over the first mortgage and assuming the payments, the seller remains responsible for this first loan. The buyer makes one payment, not two, and his note is for $90,000, not $40,000 and $50,000 as it would be if he takes over the first mortgage. This $90,000 note secured by a mortgage is called a "wraparound" simply because it wraps around or includes any existing financing already there. A buyer owes $90,000, whereas the seller owes $40,000 but is owed $50,000 by the buyer. A buyer would still owe $90,000 if he took over the first but he would owe it in two notes, not one as he does with a wraparound.

Once again, a wraparound mortgage or all inclusive deed of trust is called that because it includes any other financing already on the property. Now, let's look at title and why a buyer and seller should consider using a wraparound.

When a property is purchased, the buyer can pay off the seller in one of four ways:

1. He can obtain a new loan for the purchase price, less his down payment and pay the seller his price in cash. If there is a loan on the property the seller must take from his proceeds enough to pay off this loan. Example: $100,000 price, $40,000 existing loan, terms of all cash. Seller nets $60,000 after paying off old loan.

2. A buyer may take over the existing loan or loans on the property and pay the seller the balance in cash, or in the form of a note. In this case the buyer assumes responsibility for the $40,000 loan, which to the seller means the same thing as his paying it off. The $60,000 balance can come in the form of cash, note or a combination of both. If the seller takes part of the $60,000, or all of it, in the form of monthly payments secured by a note and mortgage, then this mortgage is recorded and is security for the note.

3. The seller can act as the lender and remain responsible for the $40,000 first mortgage, taking back a note for enough to include this $40,000 plus

whatever balance the buyer still owes. If he does this he can sell to the buyer on a wraparound.

4. The seller can sell to a buyer on a "Contract for Deed." Either way, the seller remains responsible for the existing loans on the property. The major difference is who is in "title."

When a property is sold and deeded to the buyer at closing, the note secured by a mortgage is called a "wraparound mortgage." The seller could foreclose just as any lender could. When a property is sold but title does not pass at closing and instead the contract is recorded, then the note held by the seller is secured by the contract. The seller remains as the "legal" title holder and the buyer has what is called an "equitable title."

Even though the buyer does not have legal title to the property, he can still take all the tax benefits of ownership plus sell the property if he wants. The only thing he can't do is deed the property to somebody else without first obtaining title himself. Yes, he can create notes against his equity also. He can sell to somebody else on a contract, too. In this case, his purchaser would owe him and he would still be responsible on his note.

Important: If you ever get involved in a contract or wraparound, either as a buyer or a seller, be sure you get legal advice and help. This is not a normal sale and lots of problems can occur if you don't understand what you are doing or how to protect yourself. On the plus side, however, selling and buying this way is perfectly safe and a recommended way of doing business in today's market place.

Problem: The question I get every week is, "What if the seller doesn't pay the first mortgage payment. What is my position as a buyer?" In other words, the buyer pays the seller on his $90,000 note but the seller doesn't pay the existing lender on the $40,000 note. What happens? If this takes place, the buyer loses or has to bring current the first mortgage balance or loses his entire investment. I realize this doesn't sound fair but this is the way it is.

Solution: Hire a third party or escrow company to both collect from the buyer and pay the mortgage payments. In this case, the buyer pays the escrow company on his one note and the escrow company pays the first mortgage holder and sends any funds left to the seller. Now both parties are protected.

Remember, a wraparound mortgage means that the seller "deeds" the property to the buyer and takes back a note secured by a mortgage on his property. The seller is no longer in title and now acts as a lender. The buyer is now the legal title holder. Under a contract sale, the seller remains in title and the contract is recorded indicating that the buyer is buying and if he performs then at some future date the deed will be recorded. The buyer has an "equitable" title interest in the property. While one is called a "wraparound" and the other a contract for deed, they both "wraparound" any existing financing and are treated the same except for who is in title.

Which is best, contract or wraparound? State laws dictate this most of the time. In some states it's best to sell on a wrap while others suggest you use a contract. The contract-for-deed sale is not as likely to trigger the due-on-sale clause if done correctly so some prefer this method. Naturally, the recent decision by the Supreme Court upholding due-on-sale clauses makes it all the more essential to get legal advice before proceeding and by all means protect yourself as far as making sure the existing loans are being paid current. I personally prefer to always be in title so I buy on a wrap and sell on a contract.

Equity to Paper to Cash: A Case Study

David Read

Recently, I found myself in need of a new personal residence. Being an instructor for Bob Allen, I felt I should acquire it with nothing down, naturally. In fact, it would be nice if I could put some cash in my pocket at the same time.

What Did I Want?

1. Three bedrooms, two baths, with a garage or carport.
2. Nice neighborhood.
3. Good amenities (fireplace, pool, tennis, and recreation room).
4. No down payment.
5. Good appreciation potential.
6. Preferred condo with grass but no outside maintenance.

What Did I Have?

1. Cash (but can't use it).
2. High monthly income (I could qualify for a new loan). Remember, I just came off 13 years of creative unemployment where I couldn't qualify for an outhouse with a conventional lender.
3. I had an investment property (house) that I had owned for about four years that had about $25,000 gross equity ($75,000 Fair Market Value and $50,000 loan).
4. Excellent credit.
5. I also had a Realtor working for me who knew the market very well.

My Realtor found the following property: A nice three bedroom, two bath condo with good amenities in an excellent location. It belonged to a little old lady who was going to live with her daughter. She owned it free and clear. My Realtor had tried to list the property, but the lady and her daughter wanted to sell it themselves. They didn't need any help. A comparative market analysis showed the property to be worth about $75,000. The seller wanted $70,000 with $35,000 down.

I suggested to my Realtor that she introduce me to the seller and if I bought the property, I would pay a $500 finders fee. She agreed!

The Seller's Objectives:

1. Sell the property. (She no longer was able to live alone).
2. Get as much cash as possible (it's safe!).
3. She would carry up to one-half of the equity at 11%, interest-only for three years.

My Offer:

I'll give her $70,000 cash, if she'll buy a note I have for $20,000 cash. She said, "Dave, I would love to give you $20,000 cash for your note, but I don't have it!" I said, "That's OK. I don't have $70,000 cash for you either, but I'll show you how we can both get the cash we want... I'll qualify for a new 90% owner-occupied loan with a conventional lender. But I don't have the other $7,000 for a down payment until you buy my $20,000 note." She told me if I gave her the $63,000 loan proceeds, she could buy my note and I could give her an additional $7,000 out of the $20,000. I agreed!! (Actually, the title company did it in escrow.)

This is how it looked:

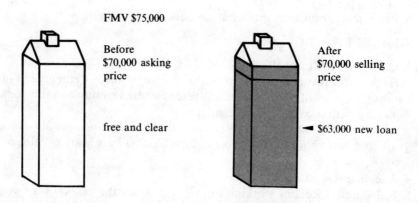

FMV $75,000

Before
$70,000 asking
price

free and clear

After
$70,000 selling
price

◄ $63,000 new loan

I really enjoyed my visit with the bank. They said, "Where is your down payment?" I told them it will come from the note the seller is purchasing from me. They said OK.

Now where did I get the note? Right out of my typewriter. Remember the little house I wanted to put a second on? Well, the seller agreed it would be perfect security for this new note.

The results were benefits:

Dave's Benefits:

1. I got the property I wanted with nothing down.
2. I put $10,972 cash in my pocket at closing—I'm so easy, I paid the closing costs—the difference between $20,000 cash and $7,000 down payment after costs.
3. I financed my investment house with a 90% loan. No points, interest-only at 11%, all due five years. (Better than a bank.)

Seller's Benefits:

1. She sold her property.
2. She received $50,000 cash, not $35,000.
3. She got her price.
4. She got a $20,000 note, interest-only with monthly payments, all due in five years.

With interest rates at all-time highs, I don't think you can do a Second Mortgage Crank technique without asking for a sharing of the wealth. Do it honestly, ethically and never over-finance.

"I'd Like to Buy Your Property – I'll Give You My Personal Note For The Down Payment."

David A. McDougal

During the Revolutionary War, Richard Jackson was caught and accused of treason against the patriots of the American Revolution. He readily admitted to the charge and was confined to a small country jail from which he could have easily escaped. After a couple of days in jail, Jackson asked the sheriff if he might be released to work by day to provide for his family, promising to return every evening to be locked in jail. His reputation was so well-known for honesty throughout the community that the sheriff agreed.

Each day for several weeks, Richard Jackson worked by day providing for his family and returned in the evening to the jail. After six weeks had passed, the time came for Richard Jackson's trial in Springfield before the Massachusetts council. Again, he told the sheriff that it would be needless trouble and expense for the sheriff to travel that distance and that if he were released, he would travel to Springfield for his own trial. On his way to Springfield Jackson met Mr. Edwards of the council of Massachusetts. When asked where he was traveling to, Jackson responded, "To Springfield, Sir, to be tried for my life." Jackson and Edwards finished the trip to Springfield together.

At the end of the trial, the evidence was complete and Richard Jackson was sentenced to be hung. Before dismissing the trial, the head of the council asked each member if there were any reason why Richard Jackson's sentence should be suspended. Man after man responded that they could see no reason why Jackson should not be hung until the last man was questioned, Mr. Edwards. He told of his meeting with Jackson in the woods and after relating that incident, the council voted unanimously to free Richard Jackson and drop all charges. Richard Jackson's integrity had saved his life.

Our integrity may be among our greatest assets in purchasing property, especially when we want to purchase it with no money down. During Richard Jackson's era, a man's word was his bond. Many important business transactions were agreed to and enforced over a handshake with the legal documentation never taking place. It has been reported that Colonel Sanders, who built the Kentucky Fried Chicken empire, began by traveling from restaurant to restaurant sharing his recipe for southern fried chicken with the owners. At the end of their meeting, he asked for a nickel per chicken for every chicken sold using his recipe. If the restaurant owner agreed, the recipe was exchanged, they shook hands and Colonel Sanders was on his way to another restaurant.

If we buy real estate today with a large cash down payment or are able to secure the property with a mortgage against other real estate property that we own, the buyers feel secure and know that if any default takes place, they come out far ahead. But if we don't have large equities in other properties and we don't have large cash amounts available to us for the down payment, we must convince them that our personal note is something of value. We have to build up a relationship of trust every time we put together a nothing down deal. We must convince those people that we are as good as our word.

There's an old proverb that says good will is built up with a thousand good deeds and lost by just one bad one. That is often true with our integrity and our credit. As a small boy, my father taught me to always pay my bills and debts on time. He said his credit was very important to him. That was when he had no money and had to work very hard to make the payments on the property that he had purchased. Today, he can take his signature to any of several banks and make a withdrawal of several hundred thousand dollars on that signature.

Often we buy rental property from people we have purchased property from before. Where we have honored all of our payments and made good on our personal notes, they are anxious to do business with us again and even willing to give us better terms than the first time around because that relationship of trust has been built. If that trust has not been established and we have been late with our payments and not honored the commitments that we made, we have very little chance of purchasing additional property. Establishing trust is imperative not only with those we purchase property from, but also with additional friends and referrals and references to whom they may lead us. These people may also be willing to sell their property under the same terms and circumstances because they have been happy and satisfied with the deal we negotiated with them.

Today, people who negotiate contracts with no intention to repay and honor them are called con artists. Occasionally we read editorials in the newspaper from people comparing the Nothing Down approach to con artistry. Our greatest protection against misrepresentation of creative financing is based in our win/win philosophy and so honoring our commitments that those people with whom we do business have no reason to question our integrity nor our motives.

Sir Thomas More was one of the most outstanding men that England has ever produced. When the King of England sought to get a divorce from his wife and break away from the Church of England, Sir Thomas More was in line to become Prime Minister of the country. His conscience would not allow him to support the King and he reamained silent when questioned about the issue. Sir Thomas More's reputation of honesty was so well-known throughout the kingdom that when he remained silent on the topic, it was reported that that silence roared throughout England. Sir Thomas More was eventually beheaded by the King because he could not in clear conscience speak in favor of his divorce in denouncing his Church.

It is not my intent that any individual should lose his head over his property. My point is that we ought to be so well known for our win/win philosophy and integrity that anyone in our community would be willing to do business with us because when we put together a deal, he knew we were standing behind it and intended to do everything possible to honor those commitments. With that kind of reputation it would not be difficult to approach any don't wanter in any of our communities and offer our personal note as down payment.

The Creative Use of Real Estate Commissions: Or, Why My Real Estate Agents Love to Work With Me

Wade B. Cook

There came a time in my investing that I needed to surround myself with a more dedicated, upbeat team of professionals. Creativity was becoming the byword of real estate investing and I not only needed someone who could put together creative deals, but someone who could be creative with his own interests.

When my program heated up I was purchasing two to five houses a month. It was hard to continually find houses to fix up and quickly resell. To keep up this volume, the idea to "buy right in order to sell right" became all-important. Often the only thing that stood in the way was the large down payments required to close the deals.

At this time I met an agent named Mort. He was aggressive and had a good business sense. We closed a traditional deal wherein he received his 6% commission. We got to know each other pretty well during all the paperwork and I found out he was ready to go on his own as he had just passed the broker exam. At this time, though, he had an arrangement where he was paying $300 a month for office expense and used another broker's services—not having to split commissions.

Mort and I went to lunch one day and hashed out an investment strategy. The gist of it was that Mort would find properties for me and then take his commissions on contract. (Actually, we used a deed of trust.) The terms of the contract would be that the monthly payments would be one per cent repay, meaning that if the commissions were $2,000, the monthly payment would be $20. All notes were to bear an interest rate of 11%.

Both of us were reluctant at first. I didn't want to impose on him because I knew how important getting cash would be to running his business. He had the same fears, but took the attitude that he would squeeze in a few deals for me in between his regular activities.

Nothing happened for about a week and then he called with several houses to go look at. I made offers on four and two were accepted. His commisions were $2,800 and $4,900 (this was a duplex) and the next month he started receiving his $28 and $49 checks.

During this time he had one other house close and that kept him going. The second month he found two more houses and then by the end of the month one more came along. The first two closed and his net income picked up by another $95. He needed some cash so he discounted the very first $2,800 note for 60% of its face value, netting $1,680. At the end of his second month he had:

- Cash of about $1,800 (from the sale of the contract plus the other monthly payments).
- Equities of $14,400.
- Monthly payments still coming in at $144 per month.
- Sold one other house that he had found for me but that I didn't buy (it was to close the next month).
- Sold one other house to me that would be closing the next month.

Already Mort was taking a second look at this M.O. He put me on the front burner and both of us started cooking. He took me to lunch again for the prime purpose of asking me if I could pick up my purchases to four a month instead of two.

I told him that I would have to close the deals quicker and always get the keys upon acceptance of earnest money (if the properties were vacant). He found a different escrow and title officer that could process the transactions in two or three days. We were in business.

Two days later we looked at eleven properties. I made offers on eight. Mort said that four of the eight were really shakey, but because he was taking his commissions on notes, it left almost all of the down payments free to go to the sellers. He literally plastered together four of the deals.

These eight were all smaller houses, but still his commissions totalled $25,600, netting another $256 a month.

There must be something to the expression that activity breeds activity. It seems that the sheer volume of these transactions created other sales for Mort. He was beating the streets for me and uncovered two other houses that he sold to others and had closed within two months.

This happened month after month. Mort sowed and then reaped more than he ever imagined.

By this time a lot of things started happening; so many, in fact, that I couldn't keep track of them.

I knew the deals that he was putting together for me, but had no idea of all the other properties that he was processing because of these contracts.

I don't know all that he did, but we talked often enough for me to find out the following:

1. One day he came across four four-plexes that required $5,000 down. The man wanted Mort to sell them for him. Mort knew a good deal when he saw one and attempted to buy them for himself. The man was a doctor and was to the point of exasperation with the tenants and his managers and seriously wanted to unload them. He would have taken zero down but he wanted to make sure that his buyer had something to lose if he walked away. Hence the $5,000. The purchase price was $300,000, which was even below market value. Mort didn't have the $5,000 cash but he sure didn't want this one to get away. He knew too many things could happen with even a two-or three-day delay. He made an offer to the doctor of $10,000 down, using three contracts (they actually totalled $10,450 when the exact figures were researched). He told the doctor of his 60 cents on the dollar sale, and also mentioned that the profit portion of the monthly payments from these contracts would be able to be claimed as received. They both agreed and the papers were drawn.

The doctor carried the contract on the balance and Mort now had sixteen units which were all full, except one. The doctor had trouble worrying about the places, but not Mort. He moved his wife and himself into the vacant unit, and almost immediately started making over $800 a month off the rents, and he bought tons of tax benefits with this purchase.

2. The second big thing that happened to Mort happened right after they moved into the four-plex—he found his dream house. Both he and his wife were exhausted from moving but they would have done anything to get into this house. The seller was about as creative as a big bank; the only thing he wanted was cash for his equity and the underlying loan was not assumable in any way, shape, or form. It had as many clauses as Macey's at Christmas time.

The only solution was a new mortgage. Things didn't look so good. Mort had everything going against him during the first half of the loan interview: only a broker for a short time; his income wasn't that steady; and most of all, this S & L didn't like real estate agents. He thought he was wasting his time but then the loan officer started asking about his other assets.

He brought out his portfolio of contracts and rentals and paraded them in front of her, and the whole atmosphere changed. Remember, Mort had only been operating like this for about five months but already his contract and rental equities totalled over $160,000. The loan officer almost got dizzy turning around so fast! The loan was approved. They moved in a week later. I didn't mention one other exciting aspect of this deal. The house was worth $125,000. The seller was afraid of the market and also needed to move as his company had already transferred him. He lowered the price to $90,000 to Mort if Mort could get the money within a month. It took only three weeks and everyone walked away with a smile.

3. Mort had sold four other houses to me by this time and he took all of these contracts and traded them on a 12-plex. I don't know all the details. I asked him about it once and he just smiled.

4. Mort had a knack for finding good deals, usually in real estate, but sometimes in cars. He found a man with a Mercedes for sale at a price way under value. He wanted $4,000 cash but took a $5,000 contract. He got the equities, their monthly payments and the advantage of being able to claim the profit on installment sales. Mort drove away in a nice Mercedes.

5. I know that several times other agents would throw good deals at him because they weren't flexible enough with their agent/broker relations to swing them—in walks Mort and gets the cream. As a matter of fact, his activities led him into so many creamy deals he should have opened a dairy. Once in a while he would sell properties that included other agents. If they needed cash for their commission, he would make arrangements to pay them and take the whole contract himself. As a matter of fact, the Mercedes mentioned before was purchased with just such a contract.

6. Once in a while all investors run into problems. Mort was sued by a tenant. The matter was solved before any litigation in the courtroom, but chalked up $920 in lawyer fees. He didn't want to pay him in cash so he gave him a $1,400 contract. Everyone was happy.

7. Mort was now to the point that he started buying contracts. He would find houses for me and try to get anyone having underlying loans to discount the equity and sell them to him.

One other thing that needs to be mentioned here is that Mort was able to claim his commissions as he received them (treated a lot like installment sales). He received the benefits from some of the contracts as if they were cash—like in some of his trades. It was great to see that, even after all his wheeling and dealing, he paid no taxes.

Many other agents wanted to get involved with him and with me. They could see the large amount of activity that we were creating. Mort wanted all of this business himself. He felt he had pioneered a new system that others had laughed at him for. Now he was making good money and he wanted to keep it that way. While his cohorts were running around doing the bidding of banks and government agencies to get one deal closed he was closing five to six. He felt it was his gold mine and guarded it carefully.

Economic necessity or financing restrictions have posed a real problem and forced some agents to move in this direction. The ones that see the whole picture and utilize this method along with their other activities really stack the deck in their favor. Mort didn't want me to let the cat out of the bag, but it needs to be let out. Creativity indeed has become the byword.

I don't see much of Mort these days. We've both moved on to bigger and better things. He was doing a lot of traveling, looking at big complexes all over the country.

We both learned a lot from each other. We used to joke about the expression, "If you'll do for two years what most people won't do, you'll be able to do for the rest of your life what most people can't do." He made this come true. He was a card that wanted to hold all the cards, and he did. Together we stumbled upon a way that let him build up his deck faster than either of us thought possible.

Now, a few years later, people still ask me to analyze Mort's success. I can do so best by using the exact words he said to me just after closing three properties in one day. He said, "I have everything now that I've wanted: steady income, nice home, travel, opportunities to find and buy good deals, and one heck of a great financial statement that really means something in terms of income, and I wouldn't have it at all if I had not stuck my neck out and sold real estate in this different way.

"All of the other good things that I own have their foundation in my taking my commissions on contract."

Real Estate is Changing – Are You?

Wayne Phillips

I would like to share with you my favorite story, "The Touchstone."

During the days of the great library of Alexandria, there was a terrible fire that destoyed all the books, save one. Since this book wasn't a work of art, nobody wanted the book except a poor man. So this poor man purchased the book for a couple of pieces of copper.

Upon returning to his home and reading the book, the man came across a parchment in between the pages. Written on this parchment was the magic of the "Touchstone." You see, the Touchstone looked like any other pebble except in two ways. One, when you picked up the Touchstone, it would be very warm. And two, if you took the Touchstone and touched it against ordinary metal, the metal would turn to gold.

The parchment said the Touchstone could be found along the shores of the Black Sea. Now this poor man became very excited and realized that if he could locate the Touchstone, he would be wealthy beyond his wildest dreams. So the poor man sold his house and belongings, placed his family in the care of his neighbors, and set off for the Black Sea.

Upon arriving at the Black Sea, the man saw millions of pebbles that all looked the same. He figured that when he picked up a pebble, and it was cold, if he threw the stone back onto the ground, he may very well pick up the same pebble hundreds, perhaps thousands of times. So he came up with a plan, and a simple one at that. He would reach down, pick up a pebble, and if it was cold, throw it into the sea. So he went to the shore, reached down on the first day and picked up a pebble; it was cold, and he threw it into the sea. He reached down again, picked up another pebble; it was cold, and he threw it into the sea. And so on and so on for the rest of the day.

This went on for a week, a month, then a year, then three years. He would reach down and pick up a pebble; it was cold, and he threw it into the sea. Finally one day, the poor man reached down, picked up a pebble, and it was warm, *and he threw it into the sea.* He threw the Touchstone into the sea! He threw away his dreams and goal of becoming wealthy into the sea. Why did he throw the Touchstone into the sea?

He threw the Touchstone away because he had formed the *habit* of picking up a pebble and throwing it into the sea. He lost sight of his objective and didn't focus on his goal of looking for the Touchstone, a warm pebble, the magical stone that would turn metal into gold, and turn his life from that of poverty into that of riches.

Now you are probably asking youself, "What in the world does this story have to do with real estate?" Well, the point I'm making is simple. Let's not allow the habits we've formed in the past to prevent our being effective in the new real estate market of the 1980's.

Let's be flexible enough to be open to new ideas and possibilities as we encounter them in today's marketplace. Just because techniques and formulas worked for us in the past doesn't mean they will be effective for us today in the 1980's. I've recognized the problems in today's marketplace. Negative cash flows, large down payments, balloon payments, high interest rates, high sale prices. I've recognized these problems and have found the solutions to these problems. Now, I didn't wake up one morning, and presto, was enlightened and had the answers to all of today's problems with real estate. I had a problem. I had a terrible heating-fuel problem. A $10,000 per month problem to be exact. And I had to find the solution to this problem in a hurry.

One of the great things about the real estate business is that when you are out there looking for deals, reading the ads, talking with sellers and real estate agents, looking for that don't water, sooner or later, you are going to come across that *proverbial super bargain.*

And that's what happened to me back in October of 1980. I located a super bargain, a 31-unit garden apartment complex in a very nice area of Baltimore, Maryland. I negotiated a $200,000 sales price, with only a $2,000 (1 percent) down payment, with the seller carry-back first mortgage at 8 percent interest for 30 years. Now that was the good news. The bad news — guess who was paying for the fuel oil? That's right, the owner. So the very day we purchased the complex, we had to have 5,000 gallons of heating oil delivered.

You see, back here in the East, most of the properties use oil to heat the buildings. So we had to find a way to pass the cost of heating this apartment complex onto the tenants, where it should be.

We marched down to our friendly banker with whom we had excellent relations, and requested a $75,000 second mortgage so we would be able to install 31 separate gas-forced warm-air furnaces, and 31 separate gas-fired hot water heaters, one for each of the apartments. We were turned down. Now, I was a little disappointed, and angry as well, because I felt that the $3,500 per month cash flow over and above the mortgage and heating bills would have been more than enough to pay back the $75,000 we needed to borrow.

So I did a great deal of research and found out that in each state in the United States, there is a Housing Finance Agency. This state department, like our federal government H.U.D. (Department of Housing and Urban Development), manages the state-wide programs that help foster decent and affordable housing for all citizens. I'm sure you've read in your local newspapers many times that your state had just passed a $50 million bond issues for first-time home-buyers at *low interest rates!* Well, that's one of the many functions and programs this state agency has.

I inquired about the possibility of there being a government loan program for investors who wanted to bring their property up to local code standards and who wanted to install new heating systems. To our delight, I was told: yes they did. They had a "special" program for investors with a maximum loan up to $200,000 at eight percent interest and with 20 years to repay the loan.

To make a long story short, we got a loan for $120,000 to install the separate heating furnaces and gas hot water heaters. In addition, the government officials requested that we install a new 10-year guaranteed roof, and security doors and doorbell intercom system, which we gladly agreed to.

Now, Uncle Sam just doesn't give you the check for $120,000 and hope that you do the work. They inspect the property, and give you a draw (usually 10% of the loan amount) after, say, ten percent of the work is completed. Well, that's understandable.

But the heating, plumbing, and electrical people wanted a large deposit before they started work, and of course we didn't have any deposit money. We had a loan for $120,000, but no money for a deposit so the work could get started. In order to stay in control of the work, I decided that I would be the contractor, since the contractor is the one who actually receives the money after the draws have been approved by the government officials.

So we were stuck in a Catch 22. We had the loan, but not the money to start. Guess what? We marched down to our friendly banker again, and asked for another loan, this time showing him our commitment letter from the city for the $120,000, and, folks, in less than 10 minutes, we had $75,000 deposited into our business account. That was the easiest loan we ever made. Out of this money we paid the plumbers, etc., their deposits. The $75,000 loan from the bank was paid back by the draws from the city, as the work got completed.

Now, a beautiful thing happened as the work was completed. We had borrowed $120,000 from the city, because this is the figure that the city estimators said it would cost to complete all the work.

However, after all the dust had settled and the work was completed and inspected and approved by the city, it only cost us $90,000. This left us with $30,000 in tax-free money. The $30,000 was tax-free because it was borrowed money, and you don't pay taxes on borrowed money. Yes, even Uncle Sam allows us to make a profit.

At the time, I was a very successful drummer, having been voted 7th best drummer in the December 1979 issue of *Downbeat Music Magazine* awards. But $30,000 cash at one time was more money than I made performing during one year. The urge was too great. I retired from the music business and went full time into real estate looking for deals. So after pocketing 30 "big ones", I went out looking for every apartment property that has central heat and/or hot water. (Please note: central heat/hot water is where there is one furnace/hot water heater servicing more than one dwelling unit.)

As time went on, I had located many properties that needed fix-up and rehabilitation. And by doing a lot of research, I learned about and used many of the local, state and federal programs to purchase, rehabilitate and renovate properties. I found out about the more than $2 billion dollars worth of government real estate giveaways available to all of us. Boy, was I excited.

You see, by looking for a solution to my heating problem, I discovered the many fantastic programs our government has for real estate. I had found the ultimate motivated seller — Uncle Sam.

I never again had to worry about negative cash flows, high interest rates, balloon payments, or high purchase prices. By utilizing the many different government programs, I would never have to be concerned about any of those problems again.

I've learned two things about making money. One, if you really want to become wealthy, you must have the ability to borrow big bucks. Not the type of dollars we get when a seller finances his or her property you purchase (that's called "soft dollars"), but the kind of bucks we can put into our pocket, and live on, survive with, buy things with, and invest with.

The second thing I've learned is if you want to make money in real estate, you *must* have staying power. You must have the ability to stick with it through the tough times as well as the good times. Translated into plain English, you *must* have Cash Flow.

That's what my program that I've developed is all about. *Cash flow* and *the ability to borrow big bucks.* It is easy to get big loans approved from Uncle Sam. Try borrowing a couple of million dollars from your local bank. Try borrowing even $50,000 from the local bank. And with the many programs I deal with, the government will not allow you to have a negative cash flow. I even have Uncle Sam mail me my rents. And best of all, I pull out those tax free dollars to live on, to grow with, and to hire the best people that money can hire with the cash flow my program deals with.

Even if you do not own your first house, I have a program for you to get you into your own house for little or no money and with 30-year mortgages and no balloon payments, and at low interest rates. Even if you only want to borrow as little as $7,500 to fix up your home or rental property, I have a program that will fit you. Or if you are after the big game, there are even bigger and better programs for us.

I am so excited about this fantastic program that I've developed, that I want to get out there and help everybody. It's win-win for everyone. Uncle Sam wins, because I am helping Uncle Sam reach his goal of having decent and affordable housing for all Americans. Our neighbors win because there is more better and affordable housing available for them. The city/states win, because the improved buildings will result in higher property taxes, thereby increasing our local/state tax basis. And, of course, we win, as we increase our net worth and make a buck, which is our motivation.

The one thing that has blown my mind about my How to Get Government Loans program, is that I'm the first person to write, teach, and talk about the dynamite programs in a comprehensive way.

This year is going to be the best year for all of us. I am looking forward to meeting you, and hope to see you at one of the many personal appearances I'll be making this year. If you do nothing else after reading this article, I hope it has enlightened your awareness to the possibilities out in the real estate market-place today, and that you'll learn more about How to Get Government Loans. The special five-year depreciation write-offs, 25% investment tax credits, and all of the other incentives Uncle Sam has for us, that we can either keep for ourselves, or sell the tax benefits to others for big bucks in our pockets.

Second Mortgage Crank: What the Lender Needs to Know

David Read

During periods of high interest, investors sometimes have a hard time with lenders in obtaining new loans. It is important to know what the lender needs to ask you when putting on a new loan. For the purposes of illustration, let's talk about a new FHA non-owner occupied loan (investor loan).

There are two very important questions a lender will ask in order to qualify you for a non-owner occupied loan:

1. Where is your down payment?
2. Is there any secondary financing?

The answer to these two questions can make the difference as to whether you obtain the loan or not.

Q. Where is your down payment?

A. The seller has already received it in the form of an exchange.

Q. Can you verify that?

A. Of course, the seller will be glad to send you a letter stating he is satisfied with the down payment and has it in his possession (or in escrow).

Q. What is the market value of the down payment?

A. The seller has agreed to accept it but if you want an appraisal I will be glad to obtain one from an independent appraiser.

The appraisal can be a bit complicated. You should use someone who has some ability in assessing value. For example, if you are giving a note and trust deed to a seller as his down payment, a letter from a secondary mortgage broker should be sufficient. A banker would also be a good appraiser. Please remember that these people may require large discounts if the notes do not have fairly hard terms (high interest rates, short due dates, large monthly payments). However, with a little work you should obtain appraisals that will satisfy any lender. One of the big mistakes that many people make is giving the lender too much information, so only answer questions to which they have a right to know the answer. Do not educate them.

Q. Is there any secondary financing?

A. No.

This is the only acceptable answer to this question. Let's review the way this can be answered correctly.

1. When the seller indicates he will carry some of the paper, make sure it is not secured against the property you are financing. Use other property you own or a partner's property or personal property or an unsecured note.

2. Ask the seller to refinance and then you will mortgage him out.

3. Use a cash account and put the second trust deed against the property after you close. Trust the seller, don't make prior arrangements with him.

4. Buy the property on a contract with a short due date (6 months to 12 months) then refinance your own property. (Works well with fixer-uppers.)

Knowledge makes you free and any buyer armed with this information should be able to use the second mortgage crank technique as one of the very best ways of obtaining residential real estate with nothing down.

The Seller Paid Me $11,000 to Buy

Richard C. Powelson

I'll never forget the time a student called to tell me about his first real estate purchase. Naturally, I asked him if he had been able to buy with nothing down. He retorted, "Not only did I buy with nothing down, but the seller paid me $11,000 to buy it!" My curiosity got the best of me and I asked, "How did you do it?" His reply broke me up. "I really don't know—all I did was make the offer as you suggested and he accepted it."

Nor will I forget the delightful real estate lady that I had in a class in Orange County one time. In these supposedly hard times of high interest rates and buyer resistance, she was making more money than she ever had and was eagerly looking forward to learning more techniques that she could use as a real estate salesperson. In fact, she had sold 16 houses in the last two months to just two investors. And, in each case, the seller got his cash requirement, she got her commission, and the buyer was paid $10,000 to buy.

Neither will I forget the personal pleasure I recently experienced when I learned that my son had just purchased his own home and was paid $1,800 for buying it.

What do these three examples have in common? In each case the buyer was paid for buying and in each case the technique used was the same. What's the technique? It's called "*rebate.*"

When we think of rebates, we generally think of car dealers who are using this technique to generate sales. They don't discount the price of the car, but do offer cash back to buyers as an incentive for them to purchase a car. In other words, a car buyer buys with no money down and is paid back cash for doing it. This is an accepted practice. Lenders feel comfortable it, car buyers like it, and, of course, the car dealers improve their sales because of rebates. If it works so well with cars, why not consider it for real rebate transaction (or any real transaction, for that matter).

Is this a method of 110% financing? NO, it is not. Remember, the property is worth $100,000 but the seller is willing to 'discount' his price in order to find a buyer.

The only loser is the 'alligator' who finds himself without money to eat!

Fun With a Note

Donald M. Berman

I purchased a $7,100 note payable: $67.50 including 8½% interest. I paid over $5,000 for it. Payments would be coming in for a little over 16 years. My yield was 14.66% (remember this was way back when that was a good interest rate).

Three months later I bought a 4-plex using some cash plus this note at face value. I made a $2,000 profit on an investment of $5,000 in 3 months—a return of 142.3%!

Five months later, I bought that same note back from its new owner. I paid him $5,000. How much do I have in the note? $3,000! (Although I paid $5,000, I made $2,000 which is now in my equity in the 4-plex.) Everybody with me? My yield has now increased to 26.57%.

I went out to the payor, the guy making the $67.50 payments, and offered to reduce his interest rate from 8½% to 4½% if he would be willing to increase his payments from $67.50 to $135.

Any benefits to him? Let's see:

> Originally $67.50 x 188 months = $12,690. P&I
> New $135.00 x 57 months = $7,695. P&I
> (new note of $7,000 at 4½% interest with
> $135 monthly payment will amortize in 57 months)

The savings to the payor is roughly $5,000 P & I, plus the property serving the note will be free and clear in under five years, instead of 16 years. Good deal? You bet! The payor thought so, too. The yield has now increased to 48.31%.

Why? The return on an investment, called a yield, is based upon the amount of payments and the time frame over which the investment is returned. Look at this:

If you received $100 interest plus your principal of $1,000 back at the end of 12 months, you have had a 10% yield, right? If the borrower pays you the full $1,100 which he agreed to pay you, but he gives it *all* back to you in six months, you can clearly see that your interest (or yield) has gone up significantly due to the rapid return of the money. (Your yield in this instance would be around 20%.)

Next, I went to a friend, let's call him Jay, who had money in C.D.'s. At that time his C.D.'s were paying him 7%. I offered to sell him half interest in my $7,000 note for $3,500 and pay him 9% interest . . . 2% better than the bank. In order to increase his comfort level, since I knew there was no risk but Jay didn't, I agreed to subordinate my half interest in the note to his half. That means, if something went wrong, he would get all his money out before I got one red penny. He thought that was a good idea.

Let's look at this now:

Monthly payments coming in	$135.00
Jay gets $75.69 (to amortize	
$3,500 over 57 months at 9%)	75.69
	$59.31

I get $59.31 for 57 months plus, since I'm only into the note for $3,000 and I get $3,500 from Jay . . . I net $500 in pocket (the best place).

That's the good news.

The bad news is:

A. My calculator refuses to calculate a return on my minus $500 investment; actually I lie to it and say I paid one dollar! and,

B. This has just about driven my accountant totally bananas!

Now here's how the story continues. Last fall I was stalking a single-family home in our Multiple Listing Book. I knew the property. It was run down. (Realtors call it "Rough!") This one was Very Rough! Not only did it need tender loving care, it needed rescuing from poor design and an elderly couple's poor taste. "Poor taste" doesn't begin to describe it; every room had different colored carpeting (including the kitchen which had indoor/outdoor carpeting in a paisley, quilt-like pattern). I must admit, though, the multitude of colors did find support from the varying colors of the appliances—there were three: a harvest-gold, seriously-dented dishwasher, a coppertone refrigerator and an oven of the most hideous aquamarine color you can imagine. All of which clashed terribly with the bright-green-patterned wallpaper.

The countertop was white with gold flecking. The gold flecking did serve to set-off the frequent burns liberally scattered. The sink had once been white enamel. It was now streaked with bare spots and water stains. On the upper level (living room, dining room & kitchen) there had been built a four-foot-wide deck along the entire rear of the house with two sliding doors serving as access, one in the dining room, one in the living room.

That would not have been bad, but somebody had, quite amateurishly, attached paneling to the railing, and angled windows from the top of the railing to the eve of the house. The angle was such that every time it rained, water seeped onto the deck, and the linoleum which had been used as floor covering was warped and water-stained beyond salvation.

Each window in the house had different window treatments running from low quality sheer to lower quality bamboo. The house had four small bedrooms made even smaller by dark colors—the worst had one wall entirely covered with a dark-green, lush, tropical-jungle scene (I'm sure you've seen the one!). The bathrooms, of which there were three, rivaled the rest of the house for attention—a potpourri of color!

The grounds can best be described as a "compound"—for somebody had constructed around the entire perimeter, front and rear, a six-foot pecky-cedar fence. It, needless to say, was in ill-repair. The lawn had long since gone to wherever it is lawns go after children and animals have finished with them.

Needless to say, the property was not a decorator's showplace. But it *was* the worst property in a nice neighborhood . . . and that usually means opportunity!

The property had been listed for many months with no takers. There had been lookers, who, as I understand it, usually left holding their sides against the pain of their laughter.

The current owner was a divorcee living with her two children. She had owned the house for less than a year and couldn't afford it—never could. She was behind in all her bills including the mortgage which was several months in arrears. She was on the verge of losing everything.

The property had been listed for $115,000 but over the last few months had been coming down—but still, no takers. Currently, she was asking $100,000. I kept hearing about it each week at a broker's meeting. Boy, I sure sensed opportunity. But, why hadn't it been snapped up? What was I missing?

I cornered the seller's broker, Mary, and discussed it some more. She said the seller was going to lose the property and was at wits-end.

"If you snooze . . . you lose!"

"Let's go, Mary," I said, courageously. "Let's write an offer."

And we did:

I offered the seller $90,000:

$10,000 cash, (which she needed for her bills).

$8,000 valued acre of land I owned in New Mexico.

$6,200 existing note (Mr. Wolf).

$65,800 takeover of existing financing.

I also agreed to pay the brokerage commission to Mary. (I asked Mary which she would prefer. A note for $3,000 or $2,000 cash. She chose the cash. That served to increase my purchase price to $92,000.)

Mary shook her head incredulously at this offer. She said, "How am I going to tell the seller about a lot in New Mexico?" I said, "Mary, for all you know, this woman has had a life-long dream to own property in New Mexico. You know better than to think for anybody!" Do you know what the seller said upon learning of the lot in New Mexico? "You know," she said, "I've always wanted to own property in New Mexico!!!" She accepted the offer.

Now the plot thickens . . .

While we were still in escrow, I asked Mary to ask the seller if she would rather have cash instead of that $6,200 note. Mary called me the next day and said Suzanne (the seller) wanted to think about it. I heard nothing further until the day after closing when Mary called and said Suzanne wanted to know if I still had interest in buying the note. I said I did but I'd only be able to give her $3,000 cash for it. I thought a moment and quickly added, "$500 a month for six months, no interest." Silence! Mary cleared her throat and said "Okay, I'll tell her." She didn't sound too excited. Mary called the next morning and said "I don't believe it. She accepted your offer." Mary still shakes her head every time I see her.

I got my note back and still haven't missed a payment. I'm starting to get concerned, though; the note pays off in fourteen years. It'll be a great loss to me. I suppose, though, I could always lend Mr. Wolf some more money.

Oh, by the way, concerning the house I bought. . . I hired an out-of-work carpenter friend for $11 an hour and had him remove the fence in the front, and move part of it to the side. We knocked out a wall between the dining room and living room to open the upstairs some; dropped the ceiling in the kitchen and put in recessed fluorescent lighting, replaced the appliances with new ones (all of the same color!), pulled up the old carpet throughout and replaced it with better quality (one color). We pulled the homemade deck-enclosure off and extended the deck ten feet. We replaced the countertop and bought a new stainless steel sink. I had a painter friend remove wallpaper here and there, remove the cork squares in the one bedroom, and paint the interior.

Actually, the finished product looked quite nice.

All in all, the rehab cost me just under $9,000, a pleasant and unusual experience. These things usually come in over budget and I had originally projected $10,000.

The house, of course, was vacant for the sixty days it took to do the work so I had two mortgage payments to make.

Before the house was completed and ready for occupancy, I had lined up a tenant interested in a lease-option. The tenant put up $5,000 in cash for an option to purchase the house from me for—are you ready?—$127,000, after one year (long-term capital gains treatment). The monthly lease payments are $1,000 which is $250 more than it should rent for. I've agreed to apply the $250 excess to the purchase price. This tends to encourage the buyer not to change his mind . . . more and more so each month.

To exercise the option the seller must put up an additional $10,000 in cash. Let me recap the numbers for you.

Purchase Price	$90,000
Mary's Commission	2,000
Closing Costs	900
Subtotal	$92,900
Less Discount on Note	(3,200)
Total Cost	$89,700

My Cash Outlay:

$10,000	To Seller
2,000	To Mary
900	Closing Cost
9,000	Rehab Cost
1,200	Two Months mortgage pmts.
$23,100	

Cash Income Next 12 Months

Lease Payments	
@ $1,000 per month	$12,000
Option Consideration	
To Exercise Option:	5,000
Additional Cash Required	10,000
Gross Receipts	$27,000
Less Mortgage Payments ($600 x 12)	(7,200)
Net Cash Return	$19,800
Sales Price if Option is Exercised	$127,000
Less Total Cost	(89,700)
Profit Before Tax	$37,300

Well, if the tenant exercises his option, and I can't believe he won't, it looks like I'll end up leaving $3,300 in the deal, but after we apply his down payments to the purchase price he'll still owe me $109,000, and since we've wrapped the existing loan at a higher interest rate, I'll be making $481.86 per month for the next four years, when a balloon payment for the balance of my equity will be due me.

All in all, a fairly satisfying transaction.

Thank you Mary . . . you, too, Mr. Wolf!

Equity Sharing
to the Rescue

Donald M. Berman

Master sergeant Bryon F. had purchased an older house in Reno. The house, probably 16-17 years old, was on a corner lot in an older, well-established residential neighborhood. As the lot was large enough and the zoning was right, Bryon, a carpenter by trade, had intentions of some day adding a small house on the back side of the property (hopefully, in the not-too-distant future) with the ultimate view of bringing his aging and ailing parents out to Reno . . . closer to his care and support.

Bryon had acquired the property from a fellow serviceman who had been transferred shortly after buying the house. It was an easy transaction for Bryon . . . the seller said, ". . . take over my loan and the house is yours." The loan was a brand spanking new V.A. loan —scarcely under $76,500, which was what the seller had paid for the property a few months before. (As I'm sure you'll recall, V.A. loans are usually 100% loans.) This was a clean deal for the seller — a fast sale, no commissions to pay — and an equally easy transaction for Bryon — a $35 assumption fee (in those days; now it's $45) and no qualifying.

Bryon promptly rented the house to a couple of nice young gals for the most it would bring— $450 a month, which wouldn't have been bad except his payment on the brand new V.A. loan was $902 a month P.I.T.I. Bryon felt he could live with the negative for awhile, for once the new house was completed, he reasoned, he'd be able to bring his parents out to Reno from upstate New York and, certainly, that would make it worth the sacrifice.

Several months went by, interest rates continued to be annoyingly high, making constuction costs prohibitive; the $902 payment, though, did come around with depressing regularity — seemingly faster each month! (Time is truly relative, isn't it? Have you ever noticed how rapidly time goes by when you're feeding an alligator . . . and how agonizingly slow it is when you're on a diet?) In addition, one more problem presented itself: Jackie, Bryon's wife, who had, at best, only been luke-warm about the old house anyway, now began making noises like… "No way am I going to live in that dump!" or words to that effect!

That was Bryon's state of confusion and concern when he called me. My wife and I and Bryon and Jackie have been long-time friends. We were next-door neighbors for many years and have retained a close and warm friendship. Bryon wondered whether I had interest in taking him out of ownership as it didn't seem like he'd be able to turn Jackie around and the $452 negative was eating on him.

I didn't know how to break this to Bryon, but I don't like $452 negatives either! But, wait a minute. This is a nothing down deal. That makes it good, right? WRONG! Not even slightly right! Buying nothing down properties without being able to solve the problems, as many people have already discovered, is not creative finance, it's "CREATIVE BANKRUPTCY!" Getting in "Skinny" appeals to me — always has — but a $902 note payment on a property that rents for $450 is a bit like dancing with a gorilla . . . you go wherever he leads you!

I do believe, however, where problems exist, opportunity is abundant — that is, — if we're good enough. We have to exercise the right side of our brains — the creative side, so they tell me. We must first identify the problem, collect all the components, tally all the plusses, determine where the obstacles are then set our minds to work on a solution. If one exists — and surely one must — we'll find it.

I'll share the secret with you. I'll tell you what the biggest obstacle to our success is and will forever be. I call it Berman's "Ant" Law. Berman's "Ant" Law says, —"Success is absolutely assured if you'll but *avoid negative thinkers.*" You might not know this but there is an army out there, a never-ending army of small-thinking people who lay awake at night thinking up all the reasons why nothing works at anything. People like this must be avoided at all costs. Tell them what you're going to do and they will recite verbatim the 2,704 reasons why you won't do it, and they'll tell you all 2,704 within 3 minutes, eight seconds (and that's not even the record. The record is held by a 73 year old ditch digger — still working — in Duluth — time verified at 2 minutes 14 seconds.) Watch their eyes as they speak. Note the passion as the irises narrow… not to mention the scorn and ridicule. And each time you pass them you'll get a reminding look and a barely perceptible nod of the head.

If you wish to succeed, at anything, maintain a positive outlook and deny entry to your world of any negative thoughts or negative people.

Bryon's house intrigued me. Could I somehow solve the negative cash flow problem? Let's see what I have to work with. An old house in acceptable condition. The highest rent it will command at the moment is $450 — no apparent way to increase that rent. A large enough lot to accommodate two more units with the proper zoning. A loan less than eight months old at 13% interest with payments of $902 principal, interest, taxes and insurance a month. An easily-assumed loan and a very willing seller. I can buy this property worth $76,500 with less than $50 down! I guess that about covers it. Now what?

Maybe I could bring in a partner on some sort of shared-equity basis and get him to pay the negative. $452 × 12 = $5,424 per year. That's a lot of negative. After calculating the tax benefits that would be available to a partner to offset the payments he'd have to make, I didn't think there was enough to encourage anybody to say yes.

How about building out the other two units? That might work. I spoke to a builder I knew. He estimated it would cost between $65,000 and $70,000 to build a small duplex which I calculated I'd be able to rent for $350.00 each side. It didn't take me long to figure with interest rates at 18% (if I was lucky) my negative after the construction dust settled would be even worse than before. Significantly worse! Even if I could borrow it all — highly doubtful — $65,000 at 18% over 15 years would take payments of $1,046.77, an additional $346 negative on top of the $452. That's not a viable solution.

Where to now, people? Anybody have any ideas?

I do! I have to cut the debt service on the new financing. I have to get those payments down to $450 less than the rents we'll receive from those new units. That means two things: 1. I have to lower construction costs, and 2. I need to bring in an equity investor so that I don't have to borrow as much.

I approached my builder friend. "Sam," I said, "have I got a deal for you. I'll make you a 25% partner in this project in exchange for your skills. I want you to design and build a duplex for time and materials only (no profit!) and I want you to be responsible for all maintenance in the project for the five years I anticipate we'll hold it." I explained that I'd arrange the financing — a combination of an equity-investor and a loan — and I would manage the property and the partnership for the duration. Sam estimated he'd be able to build out the duplex for around $55,000 at cost. Perfect! Sam accepted.

Next, I approached a doctor friend and said, "Mike, have I got a deal for you!" Dr. Mike agreed to put up $62,000 cash — $30,000 as an investment and $32,000 as a loan at 17% interest with interest-only payments of $453.33 monthly for which he became a 50% partner in the project. Since the duplex was expected to be worth $90,000 to $95,000 upon completion it looked like we had a profit going in of maybe $33,000 to $38,000, half of which was to be shared by Mike. Further, Sam's 25% position and my 25% position were subordinated to Mike's 50% (which is only fair since Mike is putting up the bucks) and, when we go out of ownership five years down the road, Mike gets his $62,000 before Sam or I get penny one.

Let's look at the numbers and the benefits:

Construction Phase

Cash raised	$62,000.00
Cash needed for construction	55,000.00
Cash left over for reserve	$ 7,000.00

Monthly Cash Flow Analysis

Monthly Debt Service	
First Mortgage	$ 902.00
Mike's Second Mortgage	453.33
Total Debt Service	$1,355.33

Monthly Rents

Existing House	450.00
New Duplex ($350 X 2)	700.00
Total Rents	1,150.00
Monthly Negative Cash Flow (First Year) (To be handled from reserve)	($ 205.33)*

Projections

Year	Debt Service	Rent	Cash Flow*
1	$1,355.33	$1,150.00	($205.33)
2	1,355.33	1,265.00	(90.33)
3	1,355.33	1,391.50	36.17
4	1,355.33	1,530.65	175.32
5	1,355.33	1,683.72	328.39

*(assuming 10% annual increase)

Property Value at Completion of Duplex —

$ 76,500	House	
90,000	Duplex	
$166,500		$166,500
Projected Value at End of Year (E.O.Y.) Five (assuming 10% annual appreciation)		$268,150
Mortgage Balance E.O.Y. Five		75,033
Balance Available for Distribution		$193,117

Distribution:
Dr. Mike
(Return Of Investment)   62,000

$131,117

Dr. Mike
(Return On Investment — 50%)   65,559
Sam   (25%)   32,779
Me   (25%)   32,779

In addition to the profit potential, please note . . . that's a positive cash flow starting in the third year. And what about the tax benefits? There is well over $18,000 of tax write-offs in the first year. Do you suppose Dr. Mike, who is in a 50% tax bracket, could use his half? Note, too, that inasmuch as I couldn't get the new debt-service low enough to entirely offset the negative cash flow, I used the "over-borrow" technique. I borrow $32,000 from Mike thus picking up an additional $7,000 to be used as a reserve for the negative cash flow and maintenance.

Was this a win/win transaction? Let's see: Sam is in for nothing down . . . he used his expertise instead and owns 25 percent. Dr. Mike is in solely for the interest he would be losing on the $30,000 were it still in his Certificate of Deposit. The other $32,000 is a loan and, as a matter of fact, is earning him a higher rate of interest than he was getting in the C.D. He owns 50 percent of three units with a profit going in, a very low risk and no management to worry about.

And me? Well, I too, am in for my time and expertise, own 25 percent with its attendant benefits plus one more thing . . . didn't I help my friend, Bryon? By the way, in case you're wondering, I suggested Bryon stay in the project with me and use his carpentry skills — after considerable thought, he declined.

How Lease-Options Maximize Benefits From Rental Houses

Robert J. Bruss

My favorite method of buying and selling single-family rental houses is the lease-option. It's the most under-used home finance technique because real estate agents hate lease-options and discourage their use. The reason is the agent doesn't earn all his sales commission until the option is exercised.

Lease-options are a great way to control property when buying. But they are also advantageous during ownership by (1) cutting or eliminating negative cash flow, (2) renting houses quickly in two hours or less, (3) assuring top quality tenants who treat the house as their own, and (4) giving the owner tax-free option money.

How a lease option works:

A lease-option is simply a combination of a lease (usually for one to three years) and an option for the tenant to buy the property during the lease term. Although the lease conditions are the same as for regular leases, the option terms can be as creative as the owner and tenant desire. A good lease-option form is available from Professional Publishing Corporation, 122 Paul Drive, San Rafael, California 94903. A copy of that form is contained in the "Nothing Down" seminar materials.

The exact purchase terms should be spelled out in the option. The hardest part is setting the option purchase price at what you think the house will be worth at the time of option expiration. From experience, I've learned to set it at least 10% above today's market value rather than to use a vague, problem-causing term such as "Purchase price to be determined by appraisal at the time of option exercise."

To protect both buyer and seller, it's also important to spell out the purchase terms in the option. If the seller will carry back a first, second, or wrap-around mortgage, put those terms in the lease-option so nothing is left to doubt at the time of option exercise. Specify interest rate, monthly payment, and any balloon payment. However, I will not allow my options to be recorded (only one tenant ever asked) because it clouds the title if the tenant doesn't exercise the purchase option.

Lease-option advantages to rental house owners:

Whether you buy your rental houses on lease-options, or use another "Nothing Down" technique, the lease-option has its greatest advantages during ownership when you want to keep the house rented. If you've ever had a vacancy which lasted more than a week or two, you've probably worried about finding a tenant. The lease-option solves that problem and many others too.

To illustrate the lease-option advantages for the owner, let me use an example of a house I lease-optioned in August, 1980. I paid the outrageous price of $135,000 for a two-bedroom house (with seller financing, naturally) in a desirable area of San Mateo, California. I call it "Fernwood" because it's located on Fernwood Avenue!

After closing the escrow on a Thursday, I decided to advertise the house for rent the following Sunday on my typical lease-option. That was a mistake and a waste of time. Never, never, never show a house that isn't cleaned up and ready to rent. Renters have little imagination. They can't visualize how desirable a home can be. During my Sunday open house (the hours of 1 to 3 p.m. are best) at least 50 people inspected the house but not one asked to fill out a rental application! I should have gone fishing instead.

By the next Sunday, however, the house was all painted, carpets cleaned, and ready to show. At the second Sunday open house, I took three rental applications, each accompanied by at least a $100 deposit check. One applicant wrote out a $1,650 deposit check (and it didn't bounce)! It's best to accept more than one application since applicants often phone on Monday morning to say they've changed their minds. After checking the applicant's credit and rental history, get the lease-option signed by the tenant.

How to structure the lease-option:

My primary purpose for using lease-options on my rental houses is not to sell the house. It is to get maximum, above-market rent to cut or eliminate my negative cash flow. For example, this $135,000 house would rent for $625 per month. But I got $750 for it on a lease-option. I could have obtained $800 per month, but I'm not greedy.

Tenants gladly overpay rent for a lease-option because it guarantees them a chance to try out their home for a year while they save up for the down payment. The ironic thing about lease-options, however, is most of my tenants don't exercise their purchase option. But they will ask for extensions for another year, which I gladly give, at an increased rent and increased option purchase price, of course.

The 12-month lease-option usually works best. Although I used a 36-month term on "Fernwood," most prospects fear a lease over 12 months. Since I build in price increases in a 36-month lease-option, many prospects resent the fact that I will increase my profit by 10% each year until they exercise their purchase option.

Special methods of lease-option rentals:

To easily market your lease-option rental, the first step is to write a short newspaper want ad. I prefer the headline, in bold type, "$1,650 MOVES YOU IN—OPEN SUNDAY 1-3 PM." Then I describe the house, use the words "Rent applies to purchase," and give the address. Don't give the rent or your phone number. This ad gets the prospects to show up at the designated time without disturbing your peace and quiet at home. Run the ad under both "Houses for Sale" and "Houses for Rent" to get maximum response.

At the Sunday open house, give each prospect a typed information sheet. You can get these quick printed for a few dollars. This sheet saves having to repeatedly give all the details over and over again to each new visitor. I greet each prospect, hand them an information sheet and then disappear to the kitchen (where they can fill out a rental application on the counter) for the "closing."

Let the prospect inspect the house and grounds alone. After inspecting, he'll find you to discuss any questions. Don't haggle over rent or terms. You'll find a few sharpies who love to bargain. If you set your price and terms right, you won't need to change them.

In addition to a description of the house and its special features, my information sheets contain the rent and lease-option details. I specify the following conditions:

1. Rent must be paid each month no later than three days after the due date or the purchase option becomes void and the ½ rent credit toward the purchase price is forfeited.

2. The purchase option cannot be assigned or sold without the owner's permission.

3. The lease cannot be assigned or sublet without the owner's permission (which will not be unreasonably withheld).

4. The tenant may cancel the lease at any time (thereby cancelling the option).

5. Owner extends the special purchase finance terms only to the original tenant and he reserves the right not to extend these terms to any sublessee or assignee.

6. When the purchase option is exercised, the property is to be sold in its then "as is" condition with no warranties or representations by the seller. Owner shall pay for routine maintenance, except on appliances, until the time the option is exercised.

7. Tenant shall receive a copy of the latest termite pest control clearance report at time of signing the lease-option.

8. Normal escrow and title insurance procedures will be used at the time the tenant exercises his purchase option.

Consideration for the option:

Some owners insist on a big "consideration for the option" of several thousand dollars at the time of signing the lease-option. I don't. I take only $1 for the option. Such option money is tax-free until the option either expires or is exercised (it then applies toward the purchase price).

But I do insist on a big security deposit. For example, to move into "Fernwood" cost the tenant $750 first month's rent plus $900 security deposit ($1,650 total) to move in.

Down payment at time of option exercise:

At the time my tenant exercises his purchase option, he must make a cash down payment. I set this amount based on (1) my initial investment in the property, (2) capital improvements added, (3) any negative cash flow expected during the lease term, and (4) a little extra. To exercise the "Fernwood" purchase option, for example, costs $20,000 cash down payment. The balance of the sale price goes on a wrap-around mortgage for a few years when a balloon payment is due.

How to set the option purchase price:

When setting my option terms, I establish a "target price" which I want to obtain if the tenant exercises his purchase option. Should he exercise the option, I then make the transaction into a tax-deferred IRC 1031 exchange. But for purposes of explaining the lease-option, the target price is all that matters.

"Fernwood" cost me $135,000. If the tenant buys it in a year, I want a $19,000 net profit. But I set the first year's option price at $158,500 to give the tenant credit for half his rent paid toward the purchase price. This rent credit is extremely important to the tenants. In one year, $9,000 rent will be paid of which $4,500 is credited toward the purchase price, giving me a $154,000 net sales price. Not too bad for a year's work!

The reason for waiting a year after purchasing a property before allowing the option to be exercised is to make the sale profit long term capital gain. During the year, that tenant will beg, borrow, but hopefully not steal, the $20,000 cash down payment so he can exercise his purchase option. But if he doesn't, he'll just keep renting. The option purchase price goes up in the second and third year of the 36-month lease-option. In the future, however, I will use only a 12-month lease-option as it's much simpler to explain to the tenant.

While there are many variations on how to set up your lease-options, this is an outline of the procedures which I have evolved to make them work smoothly. Once you get in the habit of renting your houses on lease-options, you'll find there's no better way. Lease-options are in strong demand in most areas. You'll find they offer the best way to operate rental houses with little or no management work because the tenant considers himself the "owner" of your house. It's amazing how much better care an owner takes of his property than does a tenant.

How Long-Term Lease Options Overcome Due-on-Sale Clauses

Robert J. Bruss

In the previous article, the benefits of the short-term lease-option were discussed. These benefits for the owner include (1) obtaining high-quality tenants, (2) earning higher-than-market rent to minimize negative cash flow, and (3) easy sale of property which is otherwise difficult to sell. The short-term lease-option benefits for buyers include (1) control of property with little or no cash, (2) lock-in the purchase price of a property which is appreciating in market value, and (3) minimum monthly cash outlay for rent.

The short-term lease-option, usually one to three years, is primarily a sales or marketing device. I used it to buy my home (while I arranged permanent financing) and I use short-term lease-options to rent and sell properties too.

Now let's shift our focus to the long-term lease-option which has an entirely different purpose. The only time to use a long-term lease-option is when the existing low interest-rate mortgage on the property you want to buy or sell has a legally enforceable due-on-sale clause.

The long-term lease-option blocks the lender's ability to "call" the mortgage when ownership of the property changes hands. Using this technique, the deed and fire insurance policy remain in the seller's name. As a result, the lender has no proof that legal ownership has changed. So the lender can't "blackmail" the new owner into either paying off the old mortgage or agreeing to an increase in its interest rate. The happy result for the buyer is the mortgage's old low interest rate is retained.

In many states the land contract (also called a contract for deed, contract for sale, agreement of sale, uniform sales agreement, and dozens of other names) is widely-used to accomplish the same results as the long-term lease-option. But in other states, such as California, land contracts have serious disadvantages which are overcome by the long-term lease-option.

I've been using long-term lease-options since 1970 and have never yet had a lender try to accelerate using the old mortgage's due-on-sale clause. Some mortgage firms give the lender the right to accelerate if a lease-option is created, but I've never heard of a lender enforcing this threat. As a practical matter, it's virtually impossible for the lender to document the lease-option so there is no basis for acceleration. (However you should become fully informed concerning the trust agreement involved and consult competent legal counsel before acting.)

The long-term lease-option theory. The theory of the long-term lease-option is that it is the equivalent of a sale. The buyer has all the tax and other benefits of an owner. The seller treats the sale as an installment sale (if the seller isn't helping finance the sale, use an unrecorded deed rather than a long-term lease-option).

The basis of long-term lease-option theory was IRS Revenue Ruling 60-4 now superceded by Revenue Ruling 72-85, which concluded that a 30-year lease-option is the tax equivalent of a sale. IRS Regulation 1.1031 (a)-1(c) further recognizes a lease of 30 years or longer as the same as a sale for exchange purposes. Numerous court decisions back up this view. The leading case on the subject is Oesterreich v. IRS, 226 F2d 798.

To summarize this theory, if it looks like a sale, smells like a sale, and acts like a sale, it must be a sale as far as the IRS is concerned.

Although the IRS regulations and the court decisions talk about long leases as being the equivalent of a sale, some cases hold that lease terms of less than 30 years are sales if all the sale attributes are present. Just to be safe, however, I use a 30-year lease-option term.

How a long-term lease-option works. To illustrate the long-term lease-option, here are some details of one I did in January, 1981. I've owned the property since 1968 and it produces about $200 per month cash flow. It is a three-unit building with a first mortgage from a federal savings and loan association which aggressively enforces its due-on-sale clauses. If I wanted to increase my depreciation, of course, I would have traded for a larger depreciable building.

My purpose for disposing of this property is to increase my cash flow income (since depreciation from other properties provides sufficient tax shelter). The buyers, a young couple with good jobs who have lived in one of the apartments for three years and who have added improvements at their expense over the years, were eager to buy the property. But they lacked cash for a down payment.

A long-term lease-option solved the problems. We agreed on a $130,000 sales price with $1 down payment (called "consideration for the purchase option"). The buyers pay $1,228.75 monthly rent. This is the sum of the monthly payment on the old $53,425.01 first mortgage ($463) plus $765.75 per month payment on their $76,574.99 promissory note to me for the balance of their purchase price. If I had needed cash from the sale, I could have added a second mortgage to the property before the sale. After considering all their income tax savings, and rent income from the rental units, the buyers will have a net annual housing cost of less than $3,000 per year.

Results of long-term lease-options. The happy result is that the buyers now own affordable housing which they formerly rented. The result for the seller (me) is I've increased my cash flow from about $200 per month to $765.75 and cut my management time. By the way, the promissory note provides for periodic adjustment of its interest rate in case we have continued hyper-inflation.

The only party not benefiting from this transaction is the mortgage lender who would have increased the interest rate from 9.5 percent to 14 percent if title had been transferred. When the buyers want to sell, the lease-option is assignable. Or they can obtain the deed anytime they want, simply by converting my $76,574.99 promissory note (secured by the lease-option contract) into one secured by a second mortgage on the property. Of course, when the buyers do that, the mortgage lender will raise the interest rate to market level, so the buyers have no incentive to acquire the deed.

How to create long-term lease-options. There are no standard forms for long-term lease-options. Have a real estate attorney draw one to meet the terms of your transaction, as negotiated in the normal manner using a deposit receipt or purchase agreement. Here are some of the important terms the lawyer will put in the long-term lease-option.

(1) Names of the buyer and seller (called lessee and lessor), (2) legal description of the premises, (3) the lease term, (4) consideration for granting the lease-option (any amount from $1 up), (5) monthly rent (sum of the current mortgage payment plus payment owed to the seller on his promissory note) and details of place of payment, late charges, balloon payment (if any), and other terms of buyer's payments to seller, (6) premises use not to increase fire insurance hazard or be illegal, (7) insurance policy to remain in seller's name but be purchased and paid for by buyer, (8) buyer to maintain the property and not commit waste, (9) buyer to pay utilities, property taxes, and other operating expenses, (10) property sold in its "as is" condition with no warranties now or in the future, (11) nonliability of seller for injuries on the premises (public liability insurance covers this risk anyway), (12) the lease-option can be assigned, (13) buyer's failure to pay rent terminates the lease-option, (14)

arbitration of any disputes, (15) manner of giving notice to the other party, (16) the lease-option is binding on heirs of both parties and can be passed by will, (17) time is of the essence (deadlines must be met), (18) effect of eminent domain proceedings by government, (19) the option to purchase and how it can be exercised during the 30-year lease term, (20) buyer is informed of the first mortgage's acceleration "due-on-sale clause" and agrees to assume that loan if the lender accelerates, (21) tax consequences of the sale giving buyer tax deductions and seller an installment sale, (22) buyer's recordation of a memo of the purchase option (but not the lease), (23) provision for modifications, (24) acceptance by paying rent, and (25) witnessed (notarized) signatures of the buyer (lessee) and seller (lessor).

Simplicity. Although this may seem complicated it isn't. The closing of this sale took about 30 minutes in a lawyer's office to prorate the taxes, rents, mortgage interest, and other items. From the seller's viewpoint, this long-term lease-option is better than a land contract because if the buyer doesn't make his payments he can easily be evicted. From the buyer's viewpoint, he buys with the benefit of the old low-interest mortgage, gets all ownership benefits except the deed, and can even obtain title insurance if desired.

A final note: be sure when using an aproach such as that outlined above that you become fully informed concerning the full range of legal implications involved. Consult competent legal counsel. Where questions of legality or ethics remain, one is always best admired to search further and locate properties (with FHA, VA, or other assumable conventional mortgages; etc.) where creative transactions are possible without recourse to strategies for avoiding due-on-sale concerns. Still, there are many instances where long term options can result in successful deals favorable to all parties concerned.

The Best of All Worlds...
A Sandwich-Lease With
a Purchase Option

Donald M. Berman

As Bob Allen has so ably demonstrated many times in these pages and elsewhere, real estate need not appreciate as dramatically as it has been (and still is in most parts of the nation in spite of what the doomsayers would have us believe!) in order for it to be a superb vehicle to where ever it is we want to go. The marvel of it all is real estate can be all things to all people. Look at it this way. There are only four economic benefits of a real estate investment. They are Income, Depreciation (now called "cost recovery," but old habits sure die hard), Equity-buildup and Appreciation. Not all four exist in every real estate investment and not every real estate investor wants or needs all four.

Therefore, to be effective all we need do is determine which of these benefits we are after, then structure the transaction to get that particular benefit. In this respect, it's much like renting a car. Have you ever noticed ... it doesn't really matter which formula that particular rental agency uses, it's going to cost $44.95 a day to rent that car! Whether they get you there by the daily rate, by the mileage, by the gasoline, by the insurance or whatever — who cares? — you can bet it's going to cost you $44.95 a day!!! Well, a real estate transaction is no different: it's all in how you structure it.

Since many of us are just now embarking on our investment journey and as it probably wouldn't hurt to have a few extra bucks coming in each month, let's look at an excellent cash-flow producing technique: The Sandwich-Lease with a purchase option.

The beauty of this technique is it will work on office buildings, commercial properties, apartment buldings, single family houses — anything that from time to time goes vacant. Here we'll look at its application on a single family hourse. I should mention that Bob Allen touched on Lease-Options briefly in a recent article he wrote for the *Advisor* but I thought we might explore it in-depth . . . deeply massaging the numbers to see just how powerful a technique it really is.

The premise . . .

Open any newspaper to the classified section and look at the "Houses for Lease" or "Houses for Rent" section. You will discover every eighth or ninth ad says "Lease With Option To Buy" or "Purchase Option Available" or words to that effect. You will discover, as I have, that not every person with a unit for rent sets out to provide the populace with affordable housing. Many individuals have accidentally painted themselves in a corner by innocently buying a new home, never expecting to have "this much difficulty" selling their old home. Some people have been victimized by fate: picture the recent widow trying to sell her no-longer affordable home . . . or the recently-unemployed wage earner (10.4% of the work force at this writing) . . . or the couple vainly trying to sell their home here because they've had a job transfer and hubby has been living and paying rent (or another mortgage) on the other side of the planet . . . or somebody that's just down on his luck. You may add to this scenario if you like. The list goes on and on. The point is this: these people are making mortgage payments on vacant or unaffordable properties and would prefer not to! they want out and are asking for our help. So, let's help them!

Here's what we ought to do . . .

Call each ad indicating an option to purchase is available. "Mr. Owner, my name is   . In order not to waste your time or mine, would you please give me the address of the house you have advertised. I'd like to drive by and look at the neighborhood and the house from the outside. If I have further interest, I'll call you back." Generally, the owner will be appreciative of our consideration of his time. Here's what we are looking for . . . a run-down property in a nice residential neighborhood, the worst looking property on the block. One that's been vacant for awhile — the longer, the better. We are looking for a motivated owner.

Let's say we find just such a property. It's a nice residential neighborhood, all right, (and that's very important!) but boy, what a house: let's see . . . there are shingles missing from the roof, two windows are broken, several torn and missing screens, needs paint side and out, the landscaping has gone to seed . . . got the picture? It's a mess . . . and that's perfect!!!

Let's interject some financial data about the property, shall we?

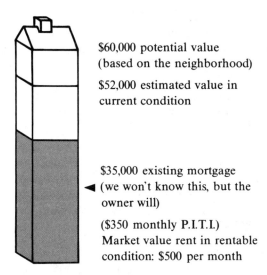

$60,000 potential value
(based on the neighborhood)

$52,000 estimated value in
current condition

$35,000 existing mortgage
◀ (we won't know this, but the
owner will)

($350 monthly P.I.T.I.)
Market value rent in rentable
condition: $500 per month

Now, let's call the owner and set up an appointment *at the property* (lest he forget what it looks like!). When we arrive at the appointment we'd certainly want to be well-groomed, driving a clean auto (no pick-up trucks or motorcycles!). Let's look business-like and successful. People generally like dealing with successful people.

The dialogue . . .

"Mr. Owner, it appears you have need of a decent tenant." (A mastery of understatement in itself!) "I understand from the neighbors you've been vacant... what? four, five months, huh? Well, I might consider doing the following:

" . . . enter into a long-term lease . . . say five years;

". . . if I did, since I always pay my rent on time, I'd be willing to add a severe penalty clause in case of late payment;

". . . I'd accept the property in 'As-Is' condition meaning you wouldn't have to spend 'nickle one' to fix it up;

". . . as a matter of fact, in consideration of the option to purchase I'll use my own money, time and expertise to repair and renovate *your* property;

". . . in addition, I'd take on the responsibility for all minor maintenance . . . . let's say up to $200 for parts and labor in any one occurence;

". . . and, you know what, I'll put up the customary security deposits. Would that hold any interest for you, Mr. Owner?"

Would it hold any interest for him? Are you kidding me? Picture this: He's got a property that's been vacant four months, looks like the entire

Russian Army bivouac'd there for six weeks and we're asking if this holds any interest for him! Of course it holds interest for him!

"What would a situation like that be worth to you, Mr. Owner?"

"Er... what do you mean?" he says.

"Well, I'm a professional investor. For me to be willing to enter into an agreement of this sort, there'd have to be something in it for me."

"Er... something in it?"

"Yes, I'd like a small discount off the rent."

"What's small? And off of what rent?"

"I don't know... say 15% off of market value rent."

"What do you think market value rent should be?" He asks.

"Based on the neighborhood and the checking I've done... I'd say it would be around $500 a month."

Now, what's going through his mind? He's doing the arithmetic, right? "Let's see," he says. "15% off of $500 is $75. That still leaves me $425 — a $75 a month positive cash flow — and I've got this great tenant."

While this is going on, you want to reinforce it: "Mr. Owner, I'd like you to think about this:

"For five years:

... No more empty house;

... No more looking for tenants;

... No more wasted time showing the house to every Tom, Dick and Harriet;

... No bothersome maintenance calls Saturdays, Sundays, holidays — at all hours, day or night...

"Think of it...

"For five full years this will virtually eliminate your day to day headaches."

What do you think? Have we strong appeal?

He says, "OK. I can live with that."

Good. "Now, Mr. Owner, your ad says 'Lease-Option.' We need to discuss the purchase option."

What do you suppose he will agree to on the sales price? — In its current condition it's worth maybe $52,000 to $53,000. (I suspect he's going to want more.) What if he won't agree to anything less than $60,000. Would you do it? Of course you would. Never fight price, fight time. If the owner wants too much, get a six-year lease, seven years, whatever. Let's say in this case the owner wants $60,000...

"OK. Mr. Owner, you're tough! This property is not worth $60,000 but... OK, I'll tell you what... I'll agree to $60,000, but where I come from, it's customary that if I exercise my option a portion of my monthly payments should go toward the purchase price."

"How much?" he asks.

"A small amount — let's say, $50 a month."

He agrees.

"One more thing. Mr. Owner, and I think we're pretty close to a transaction . . . in its current condition, this house is not fit for habitation; I'd like a three-week moratorium on rents — I need some time to clean the place up."

He agrees to that.

Let's see what our agreement looks like:

We've agreed to a five-year lease with payments of $425 per month; we have the right to purchase the property over the next sixty months and, if we do, $50 per month will go toward the purchase price; we're responsible for minor maintenance up to $200; we've retained the right to sublet (under no circumstance should you ever give up the right to sublet . . . it's too valuable!).

Now let's see what happens:

We jump in, pick up all we need from Sears, K-Mart — paint, paneling, tools, etc. — three weeks later, eight pounds lighter (which wouldn't be all bad for some of us) the house is neat and clean, more importantly, it's rentable. Concurrently with doing the fixup, we've been running an ad. Are we going to sub*rent* this unit or sub*lease* it? (You bet, sub*rent* it! . . . we never *lease* anything!)

The first year all we can get is market value rent — $500 per month. What are we going to do next year and each year thereafter? Raise the rent 10% (to use round numbers) so the next five years will look like this:

1st Year	$500 × 12 =	$ 6,000
2nd Year	$550 × 12 =	6,600
3rd Year	$605 × 12 =	7,260
4th Year	$665 × 12 =	7,980
5th Year	$731 × 12 =	8,772
	Total Rents	$36,612
Less lease payments (425 × 60)		25,500
	Gross Profits	$11,112
Less an occasional vacancy and some maintenance expense (guesstimate)		2,000
	Net Cash Flow	$ 9,112

"Wait", you say, "Nobody will ever pay you those rents." Before you do, reflect first and tell me in your wildest dreams ten years ago you could imagine yourself making the mortgage payments you presently are or paying the rent you do. Rents have to go up . . . that's a fact of life!

Let's see . . . so far we've made about $9,000 and we don't yet own this property. Now let's exercise our option and buy this thing.

What did we agree on? A purchase price of $60,000 with $50 per month of our payments going toward the price — ($50 × 60) that's $3,000 — so we owe the seller $57,000. Right? Where's that going to come from? (How about from the property itself; let's hit the lenders.)

After we rehabilitated the property it was worth $60,000. Look what 10% annual appreciation does:

Value at end of Year 5   **Situation after New Financing**

$96,630 potential value

$60,000 value at ◄ beginning (after rehabilitation)

$96,630 value

$77,300 new loan ◄ (80%)

Loan Proceeds	$77,300
Less Loan Costs (approx.)	2,300
Net Proceeds	$75,000
Less Amounts Due Seller	57,000
TAX FREE Cash for Buyer	$18,000

What else do we have? How about $19,330 equity in our newly acquired house!

Let's recap:

Cash Flow	$ 9,112
Net Cash After Refinancing	18,000
Equity	19,330
	$46,442

People, if we divide that by sixty months, we'll find we made an average of $774.03 per month and

... THAT'S ONLY ONE HOUSE!!!

Try doing that once every three months and see how long it takes us to retire!

Let's take it a step further.

Why couldn't we approach a suitable tenant and say: "Mr. and Mrs. Tenant, one of the problems I remember having when I was a renter was that I never felt like spending too much money fixing up the house I was renting. Why should I improve the value of somebody else's property?... A property which might be sold out from under me, forcing me to move. So I never decorated the way I might have liked to and, consequently, I never truly could call it 'home.' Since I'd like the two of you to be comfortable here and never have to worry about that, for an additional $25 per month, I'd be willing to give you a 'first right of refusal' to buy this house if I should decide to sell." If they like that idea, there's additional revenue.

Or, even further:

Why not hedge our bet. We're hoping for inflation down the road to add to our coffers. But what if we're wrong and the property doesn't go up in value, have we lost anything? No. We just won't exercise our option — which is our prerogative — and all we would have is the $9,000 cash flow, which you'll admit is not a bad wage for managing a little house. Keeping the old "bird in the hand" philosophy in mind, would we be wise taking a little more now in lieu of a "maybe" higher profit down the road? Try this dialogue:

"Mr. & Mrs. Tenant, how would you like an option to buy this property at the end of five years at an agreed price a *guaranteed* 10% below appraised value? I'll sell you an option for ... say $2,500 cash and an additional $100 per month rent, all of which we'll apply to the purchase price plus. Since this will probably become your home, you take care of the minor maintenance ... "

You've got the picture. In effect the tenants are not paying anything additional (unless they do not wish to exercise their option). All you've managed to do is get your profit sooner. If inflation does the 10% thing we've learned to count on, we've given up 10% of the appreciated value of the property as we've agreed to sell it for $86,967 (96,630 — 9,663). We've essentially traded a higher (potential) future profit for a guaranteed additional income of $8,500. A good trade-off, maybe!

How about win/win? Has what we've been looking at been win/win? Let's see:

. . . The original owner had a problem which was causing stress — a problem, we should note, we didn't cause. We solved his problem, gave him more than his property was worth at the time we went into the transaction — agreed price was $60,000, the property was only worth $52,000. We gave him a positive cash flow for five years virtually management-free. We gave him five years of tax write-offs. And we gave him peace of mind. (What value do you want to place on peace of mind?)

And the tenant with the sub-lease-option? He locked in the right to buy from us at a guaranteed 10% profit if he chose to do so, with all his extra payments applying toward the purchase price.

All in all, a profitable day's work for everyone involved.

The last observation I'd like to make is this . . . as wonderous and powerful as options are, they are loaded with risk. Please see that any option agreement you enter into is drafted by a competent real estate attorney. If you do these little jewels haphazardly, I promise you, at best, expensive litigation, probably a total loss of profit and, without a doubt, sheer exasperation.

Questions and Answers on Creative Finance Techniques

Richard J. Allen

Question:

"How does a blanket mortgage work, and when is it used?"
HH, Philadelphia, PA

Answer:

Blanket mortgages are not difficult to understand once you have the nature of a mortgage clearly in mind. A mortgage consists of two basic documents: a note and a security document. The note sets forth the terms governing repayment of the loan, and the security document provides recourse for the lender in case of default, i.e., the lender can proceed to take over the collateral property if the borrower does not satisfy the terms of the note. A blanket mortgage is one in which the security document provides collateral on more than one property, not only the property being bought, but also one or more properties in which the buyer has an equity interest.

Why would a buyer provide more collateral than is technically required to cover the amount of the loan? The primary motivation for doing so is to build trust with the seller. Especially in transactions where little or no money is put down, the blanket mortgage can serve as a trust-building arrangement. The seller knows that he has recourse not only to the property he is selling, but also to additional property put up as collateral. He knows that the buyer has his neck on the line and will more than likely perform faithfully on the agreement.

Naturally, the buyer will want to set up the deal with the provision that the extra collateral will be released from the mortgage upon certain conditions, e.g., prompt and faithful payment of the mortgage for a specified length of time (perhaps twelve months) or anytime an appraisal of the property shows that it has attained a target level of value above the selling price.

A blanket mortgage is not difficult to set up. A dependable title company or attorney can draw up the necessary papers. The seller will probably want verification of the buyer's equity interest in the added collateral.

Question:

"The Nothing Down System refers often to partners. Do you have any advice for the person just starting to line up partners for future deals?"

Answer:

Partners can be an invaluable asset to the creative investor by providing capital to close a deal or offset negative cash flows and balloons. The best general advice for beginners *or* experts is to draw up a legal partnership agreement in advance specifying *exactly* what each party is to do and what benefits are to accrue. It was never said any better than in these words from a rather well-known American: "Partnerships often finish in quarrels; but I was happy in this, that mine were all carried on and ended amicably, owing, I think, a good deal to the precaution of having very explicitly settled, in our articles, every thing to be done by or expected from each partner, so that there was nothing to dispute, which precaution I would therefore recommend to all who enter into partnerships; for, whatever esteem partners may have for, and confidence in each other at the time of the contract, little jealousies and disgusts may arise, with ideas of inequality in the care and burden of the business, etc., which are attended often with breach of friendship and of the connection, perhaps with lawsuits and other disagreeable consequences."

Who said it? Benjamin Franklin in his *Autobiography* some 200 years ago. Still excellent advice for the wise businessman.

Question:

"Is a lease-option arrangement a good way to get around the due-on-sale dilemma?"
L.G., San Antonio, Texas

Answer:

When it comes to due-on-sale, the best approach is to be the best informed. Find out what the trust agreement (mortgage agreement) has to say on the subject. Sometimes the agreement prohibits even lease options. Find out what current practices are in your area and with the lender in question. Make sure what they say about the existing "non-assumable" loan is true: sometimes the lender has sold the note to another party or institution in such a way as to render the loan assumable as is or with only a slight bump up in interest rates. (We heard of two cases like this in the past several weeks.) Where the terms are favorable, most investors would prefer an assumption to a lease-option because they come into title and enjoy clear-cut tax benefits. An assumption puts them into the driver's seat with less chance of being challenged. On the other hand, a lease-option doesn't require any qualifying (the seller seldom asks for it) and puts you in a position to sublet the property with a margin of profit. Whether the lease-option is a panacea for the due-on-sale, however, is a matter to be decided by the investor in conjunction with good legal counsel. Perhaps the best advice is to go into a deal having worked out the figures as *if* an assumption were necessary just to make sure everything fits your circumstances if that becomes an eventuality.

Question:

"I am interested in buying real estate using second trust deeds and mortgages. Where can I find sources and outlets for secondary paper?"
E. H., Salt Lake City

Answer:

Many newspapers have a classified ad section for "Mortgages and Contracts." If your paper has such a section, call on some of the ads and talk to the professionals who are in the "paper" business. They can acquaint you with the market in your area. Some Realtors, also, specialize in "paper." Make some inquiries to a few real estate offices and find out who the specialists are. One of the most difficult ways to find "paper" is also one of the most rewarding: go down to your local county courthouse and make a search of the records having to do with mortgages and contracts. You may put your finger on "seasoned" low-interest notes that could fit right into your plans. If all else fails, you could always put your own ad in the paper offering to buy (or sell) second trust deeds and mortgages.

Question:

"I have a basic idea of what is meant by the term "moving the mortgage." Could you explain this term a little more in depth and give an example of the proper wording to use in a note?"
L.P., Pittsburgh, PA

Answer:

The legal terminology for moving the mortgage is called "The substitution of collateral." This means the seller agrees to accept a different piece of property as collateral for security on the note you owe him. This technique increases your flexibility for borrowing against unborrowable assets, creates a pyramiding potential, and frees up a piece of property that you can sell to raise cash for your buying program.

An example of a "substitution of collateral" clause is:

"The seller agrees to accept a substitution of collateral for this note at any time in the future as long as the seller has the opportunity to inspect the new property and confirm that his note would be adequately secured. This approval will not be unreasonably withheld by the seller."

Check with a reputable title company in your area on local procedures and documentation.

For examples and further information you might want to review the section in chapter eleven of *Nothing Down*.

Question:

"I own four 4-plexes covered by a single trust deed. There is a fairly low 9½% assumable first against the properties. I would like to pull around $32,000 out to apply toward additional investments. Would it be best to refinance with a fixed-rate mortgage at a high interest rate or go for a somewhat lower variable-rate mortgage?"
J.G., Vero Beach, Florida

Answer:

Perhaps neither. That 9½% assumable first may be worth its weight in gold, particularly since the announcement of the Supreme Court decision upholding federally-chartered lenders in the due-on-sale dispute. What could you do to buy additional investment property without refinancing? You might consider putting on a hard-money second; naturally, the interest rate will be high, but the impact would be somewhat offset by the lower interest first. Alternately, you might consider creating paper against the equity in the 4-plex package. Frequently, flexible sellers will accept notes created in this way in lieu of cash down on their properties. Another variation on the same theme calls for the seller to carry back paper for all or part of his equity and have the paper secured by your 4-plexes (moving the mortgage). There are other ways to put your equity to use. In a pinch you could create a note against it and then sell the note at a discount to raise the cash you need. It is always possible, if the right opportunity comes along, to exchange your properties into other deals that would bring greater tax benefits and greater cash flow.

If refinance is your bag, shop around to find the lender who will give you the best deal. Interest rates have fallen off in recent months. However, we just don't know with any degree of certainty what future interest rates will be. The financial institutions are acting as though rates over the long term will continue to be high. They are probably correct. If rates were to decline, then the lower interest variable rate would seem to us attractive now. If rates were to go up, your current fixed-rate long-term loan might begin to seem like a bargain. To us, the best approach clearly would be to preserve your low-interest assumable first and hold it as a resale bargaining chip when you go to sell.

PART VIII:

Making Written Offers That Are Risk-Free

"I Agree/You Agree:" How to Write Risk-Free Offers

Richard J. Allen

In our research with the graduates of the now famous Robert Allen Nothing Down Seminar, we have learned that the average Nothing Down investor will have to make five formal offers—usually on five different properties—before achieving one purchase. If the purchase is truly a nothing down purchase where 5% or less of the buyer's own funds are used as a down payment, it takes more like ten formal offers to hit pay dirt. One young man from Southern California who acquired over $800,000 worth of real estate within two months of taking the seminar (all with nothing down) had to make 50 formal offers to attain his goal.

There is a lesson there. No offers. No purchases. Many offers. Many purchases. Simple! But naturally it is more than just a numbers game. The offers have to be skillful offers, based on careful analysis and astute use of creative finance principles. The buyer and seller have to agree on terms that will lead to win/win outcomes and then find the language to preserve and formalize their agreement accurately.

For some, the challenge of putting their signature to paper is very nearly an insurmountable barrier. There is something awesome and forbidding about that little dotted line just daring you to scrawl your signature along it—daring you to state irreversibly the commitment: "I do!" For those who cannot bring themselves to formalize their commitments, goals will ever remain fantasy. Such people will have to content themselves with dreams of financial independence. The actuality will always remain out of reach.

Real estate purchases require people to say: "I do." Transactions never take place without a formal commitment to action on the part of both buyer and seller. At some point in the process of fact-finding, analysis, and negotiation, both parties must see things fall in place and sign on the dotted line. There must be action—action based on the best information available and the most skillful planning for the future possible under the circumstances.

Graduates of the Nothing Down Program are currently buying real estate at a rate of around $20 million worth per week—over $1 billion worth per year. At an average purchase price of $100,000 per property (as validated by an independent university study on the program), that amounts to 200 properties per week. Based on the offers-per-purchase formula mentioned earlier, it would take between 1,000 and 2,000 offers weekly to achieve that level of success in buying. That means that your colleagues in the Nothing Down Network will be making from 125 to 250 formal offers *today* (based on an eight-hour work schedule) and between 15 and 30 offers during the *hour* it takes you to peruse this material. In fact, chances are that some wiseguy "nothing downer" made a spectacular offer during the minute or two it has taken you to read this section of the book. His chances are one in five to achieve success and one in ten to achieve a true nothing down deal. Without making the formal offer, his chances of achieving anything are exactly zero.

The same as yours. It's all a matter of making good offers—many good offers—enough offers to achieve your explicit goal. If you want to buy one excellent nothing down property per year, then somewhere along the line you will probably have to make around ten good offers, around one per month. If you want to buy four excellent nothing down properties per year, then get ready to sharpen your pencil at least once a week. It will take that many formal offers to achieve your goal. If you decide to go for broke and buy $1 million worth of single family homes during the next year without using your own money (around one per month), then you can expect to make a good offer every three days. Of course, if you have the fortune of stumbling across that spectacular multi-million dollar package of homes just ready for the asking, you can take care of your goal with a single successful offer. However, such luck is rare and is usually the result of countless hours of preparation and searching.

Once the Nothing Down Practitioner is persuaded that there is no alternative but action, that offers *have* to be made on a regular basis, then the next step is to examine the principles of how to make the offers as risk-free as possible. That is the purpose of this article. If we could set up a few safety nets below the cliff, then maybe more people would get up the courage to jump off. It doesn't take much instruction in the art of contingency planning before even the most risk-averse begin to come out of hiding.

The notorious document at the heart of the issue is the Earnest Money Receipt and Offer to Purchase. It has various aliases in different areas of the country, among others: Purchase Agreement for Real Estate, Purchase Contract and Receipt for Deposit, Deposit Receipt and Contract for Sale, Preliminary Purchase Agreement, Sales Agreement and Receipt for Earnest Money, Deposit Receipt and Agreement, Agreement for the Sale of Real Estate, Sale Agreement and Receipt for Earnest Money, Earnest Money Receipt and Sales Contract, Commercial Purchase and Sale Agreement, Deposit Receipt and Purchase and Sale Agreement, etc., etc.

It all boils down to the same thing—a legally binding written agreement signed by both buyer and seller committing them to the sale of a specific piece (or pieces) of real estate according to specific terms. To show good faith in entering the transaction, the buyer pledges something of value that commits him to action and shows his earnestness in the matter.

Even though the intent and substance of the preliminary agreement is the same throughout the country, the form and wording in various jurisdictions can vary widely. Some versions of the document are also protected by copyright. Therefore, we have designed our own version for use in this article. Our model may not be a paragon of documentary perfection, but it is at least straightforward and comprehensive enough to serve as an adequate instructional tool for examining the principles of making risk-free offers. Here is the masterpiece we came up with after examining counterparts from all areas of the country and conferring with competent legal counsel:

UNIVERSAL EARNEST MONEY RECEIPT
AND OFFER TO PURCHASE

"This is a legally-binding contract; if not understood, seek competent advice."

1. Date and Place of Offer: _____ 19_____ ; _____
                                                                  (city)   (state)

2. Principals: The undersigned Buyer _____
agrees to buy and Seller agrees to sell, according to the indicated terms and conditions, the property described as follows:

3. Property: located at   _____
                       (street address)   (city)   (state)

with the following legal description:_____

_____.

including any of the following items if at present attached to the premises: plumbing, heating, and cooling equipment, including stoker and oil tanks, burners, water heaters, electric light fixtures, bathroom fixtures, roller shades, curtain rods and fixtures, draperies, venetian blinds, window and door screens, towel racks, linoleum and other attached floor coverings, including carpeting, attached television antennas, mailboxes, all trees and shrubs, and any other fixtures,

EXCEPT_____ .

The following personal property shall also be included as part of the purchase: _____ .
At the close of the transaction, the Seller, at his expense, shall provide the Buyer with a Bill Of Sale containing a detailed inventory of the personal property included.

4. Earnest Money Deposit: Agent (or Seller) acknowledges receipt from Buyer of _____ dollars

$_____ in the form of ( ) cash; ( ) personal check; ( ) cashier's check; ( ) promissory note

at _____ % interest per annum due _____ 19_____ ; or other _____

as earnest money deposit to secure and apply on this purchase. Upon acceptance of this agreement in writing and delivery of same to Buyer, the earnest money deposit shall be assigned to and deposited in the listing Realtor's trust

account or _____ , to apply on the purchase price at the time of closing.

5. Purchase Price: The total purchase price of the property shall be _____ dollars $_____ .

6. Payment: Purchase price is to be paid by Buyer as follows:
Aforedescribed earnest money deposit . . . . $_____

Additional payment due upon acceptance of this offer . . . . $_____

Additional payment due at closing . . . . $_____

Balance to be paid as follows: _____

_____

_____

_____

_____

7. Title: Seller agrees to furnish good and marketable title free of all encumbrances and defects, except mortgage liens

and encumbrances as set forth in this agreement, and to make conveyance by Warranty Deed or_____

Seller shall furnish in due course to the Buyer a title insurance policy insuring the Buyer of a good and marketable title in keeping with the terms and conditions of this agreement. Prior to the closing of this transaction, the Seller, upon request, will furnish to the Buyer a preliminary title report made by a title insurance company showing the condition of the title to said property. If the Seller cannot furnish marketable title within thirty days after receipt of the notice to the Buyer containing a written statement of the defects, the earnest money deposit herein receipted shall be refunded to the Buyer and this agreement shall be null and void. The following shall not be deemed encumbrances or defects: building and use restrictions general to the area; utility easements; other easements not inconsistent with Buyer's intended use; zoning or subdivision laws, covenants, conditions, restrictions, or reservations of record; tenancies of record. In the event of sale of other than real property relating to this transaction, Seller will provide evidence of title or right to sell or lease such personal property.

8. Special Representations: Seller warrants and represents to Buyer (1) that the subject property is connected to ( ) public sewer system, ( ) cesspool or septic tank, ( ) sewer system available but not connected, ( ) city water system, ( ) private water system, and that the following special improvements are included in the sale: ( ) sidewalk, ( ) curb and gutter, ( ) special street paving, ( ) special street lighting; (2) that the Seller knows of no material structural defects; (3) that all electrical wiring, heating, cooling, and plumbing systems are free of material defects and will be in good working order at the time the Buyer is entitled to possession; (4) that the Seller has no notice from any government agency of any violation or knowledge of probable violations of the law relating to the subject property; (5) that the Seller has no notice or knowledge of planned or commenced public improvements which may result in special assessments or otherwise directly and materially affect the property; and (6) that the Seller has no notice or knowledge of any liens to be

assessed against the property, EXCEPT _____ .

9. Escrow instructions: This sale shall be closed on or before_____ 19_____ by_____
or such other closing agent as mutually agreed upon by Buyer and Seller. Buyer and Seller will, immediately on demand, deposit with closing agent all instruments and monies required to complete the purchase in accordance with the provisions of this agreement. Contract of Sale or Instrument of Conveyance to be made in the name of

_____

10. Closing Costs and Pro-Ration: Seller agrees to pay for title insurance policy, preliminary title report (if requested), termite inspection as set forth below, real estate commission, cost of preparing and recording any corrective instruments, and one-half of the escrow fees. Buyer agrees to pay for recording fees for mortgages and deeds of conveyance, all costs or expenses in securing new financing or assuming existing financing, and one-half of the escrow fees. Taxes for the current year, insurance acceptable to the Buyer, rents, interest, mortgage reserves, maintenance fees, and water and other utilities constituting liens, shall be pro-rated as of closing. Renters' security deposits shall accrue to Buyer at closing. Seller to provide Buyer with current rental or lease agreements prior to closing.

11. Termite Inspection: Seller agrees, at his expense, to provide written certification by a reputable licenced pest control firm that the property is free of termite infestation. In the event termites are found, the Seller shall have the property treated at his expense and provide acceptable certification that treatment has been rendered. If any structural repairs are required by reason of termite damage as established by acceptable certification, Seller agrees to make necessary repairs not to exceed $500. If repairs exceed $500, Buyer shall first have the right to accept the property "as is" with a credit of $500 to the Buyer at closing, or the Buyer may terminate this agreement with the earnest money deposit being promptly returned to the Buyer if the Seller does not agree to pay all costs of treatment and repair.

12. Conditions of Sale: The following conditions shall also apply, and shall, if conflicting with the printed portions of this agreement, prevail and control:

_____

_____

_____

_____

_____

_____

_____

_____

13. Liability and Maintenance: Seller shall maintain subject property, including landscaping, in good condition until the date of transfer of title or possession by Buyer, whichever occurs first. All risk of loss and destruction of property, and all expenses of insurance, shall be borne by the Seller until the date of possession. If the improvements on the property are destroyed or materially damaged prior to closing, then the Buyer shall have the right to declare this agreement null and void, and the earnest money deposit and all other sums paid by Buyer toward the purchase price shall be returned to the Buyer forthwith.

14. Possession: The Buyer shall be entitled to possession of property upon closing or _____ , 19_____ .

15. Default: In the event the Buyer fails to complete the purchase as herein provided, the earnest money deposit shall be retained by the Seller as the total and entire liquidated damages. In the event the Seller fails to perform any condition of the sale as herein provided, then the Buyer may, at his option, treat the contract as terminated, and all payments made by the Buyer hereunder shall be returned to the Buyer forthwith, provided the Buyer may, at his option, treat this agreement as being in full force and effect with the right to action for specific performance and damages. In the event that either Buyer, Seller, or Agent shall institute suit to enforce any rights hereunder, the prevailing party shall be entitled to court costs and a reasonable attorney's fee.

16. Time Limit of Offer: The Seller shall have until _____ _____ ,19_____
                                                              (hour)   (date)
to accept this offer by delivering a signed copy hereof to the Buyer. If this offer is not so accepted, it shall lapse and the agent (or Seller) shall refund the earnest money deposit to the Buyer forthwith.

17. General Agreements: (1) Both parties to this purchase reserve their rights to assign and hereby otherwise agree to cooperate in effecting an Internal Revenue Code 1031 exchange or similar tax-related arrangement prior to close of escrow, upon either party's written notice of intention to do so. (2) Upon approval of this offer by the Seller, this agreement shall become a contract between Buyer and Seller and shall inure to the benefit of the heirs, administrators, executors, successors, personal representatives, and assigns of said parties. (3) Time is of the essence and an essential part of this agreement. (4) This contract constitutes the sole and entire agreement between the parties hereto and no modification of this contract shall be binding unless attached hereto and signed by all parties to the contract. No representations, promises, or inducements not included in this contract shall be binding upon any party hereto.

18. Buyer's Statement and Receipt: "I/we hereby agree to purchase the above property in accordance with the terms and conditions above stated and acknowledge receipt of a completed copy of this agreement which I/we have fully read

and understand." Dated _____ 19 _____ . _____
                                                                                                    (hour)

Address _____   _____ Buyer

           _____   _____ Buyer

Phone No: Home (_____) _____   Business (_____) _____

19. Seller's Statement and Response: "I/we approve and accept the above offer, which I/we have fully read and understand, and agree to the above terms and conditions this day of

_____ , 19 _____ . _____
                                                              (hour)

Address _____   _____ Seller

           _____   _____ Seller

Phone No: Home (_____) _____   Business (_____) _____

20. Commission Agreement: Seller agrees to pay a commission of _____ % of the gross sales price to _____

_____

for services in this transaction, and agrees that, in the event of forfeiture of the earnest money deposit by the Buyer, said deposit shall be divided between the Seller's broker and the Seller (one half to each party), the Broker's part not to exceed the amount of the commission.

21. Buyer's Receipt for Signed Offer: The Buyer hereby acknowledges receipt of a copy of the above agreement bearing the Seller's signature in acceptance of this offer.

Dated _____ , 19_____   _____ Buyer

                                                          _____ Buyer

Commentary on the Universal Earnest Money Receipt and Offer to Purchase

The 21 divisions of the document address the following questions, all of which are centrally important to the transaction:

1. When and where is the offer made?
2. Who is involved in the transaction?
3. Which property is involved and exactly what is included in the sale?
4. What is the amount of the deposit and in what form is it given?
5. What is the purchase price?
6. How is the price to be paid?
7. Can the seller deliver clear title to the property?
8. Can the seller attest to the quality of the property?
9. When and how is the closing to take place?
10. Who pays for what at the closing?
11. Is the structure free of termite problems, and if not, how to proceed?
12. What special conditions of the sale are there?
13. Who is liable for the property from the time of acceptance until the closing?

14. When can the buyer have possession of the property?
15. What happens in case the buyer or the seller fail to comply with the terms of the agreement as promised?
16. How long does the seller have to accept or reject the offer?
17. What general agreements are binding on the parties to the agreement?
18. Is the buyer willing to accept the agreement as stated?
19. Does the seller accept the offer?
20. What commission is involved, and how and to whom is it to be paid?
21. Does the buyer acknowledge receipt of the final signed offer?

If the verbiage to answer all those questions had to be written out and negotiated from scratch every time an offer were made, buyers and sellers would be smothered in the paralysis of analysis and never get much done. Fortunately, a preprinted form such as the one reproduced above takes care of most of the boilerplate basics—all of which are important—leaving spaces for the optional items constituting the heart of the offer. Let's examine the earnest money form step by step and see how it can be filled out using risk-free entries.

1. **Date and Place of Offer.** Everyone can get this far on his or her own without the slightest tinge of fear and concern.

2. **Principals.** Here the name of the buyer is filled out but with the addition of the vital words "and/or Assigns." If "John Doe" appears on this line, then John Doe must follow through with the purchase. But if "John Dow and/or Assigns" appears there, then John Doe may, at his option, assign the agreement to someone else prior to closing and let that someone take over the purchase. What if you strike a spectacular bargain on a piece of property and then an associate, to whom you mention it, wants to step in and take over your interest? With the words "and/or Assigns" to back you up, you could effectively "sell" him your interest in the property and perhaps realize a handsome profit. Your "interest" in the property is effectively the earnest money you put down and the right it gives you to control the property according to the terms of the agreement. An earnest money agreement is, in fact, a short-term option to purchase: (Technique No. 49 in the Nothing Down System of creative finance). In most cases John Doe has every intention of following through with the purchase himself, but those two extra little words, "and/or Assigns" enlarge his options and add an element of insurance to the undertaking. It is possible, after all, that circumstances may on occasion prevent John from following through on his plan to purchase the property. He may be forced to assign his interest and needs the legal right to do so.

3. **Property.** If the legal description is not available to you at the time, you may enter the street address and add the words "to be supplied prior to closing" or "Escrow Agent authorized to add legal description to the agreement." An example of a legal description as recorded in the official records might be: "Lot 23 in Block 16 of Joseph Strator's 1st Addition to the City of Midvale, as per plat recorded in Volume 7 of Plats, Page 78, records of Everett County." As you can see, that is not something you might have access to as you are sitting there writing out an offer on a property that is in high demand.

The rest of Item No. 3 is boilerplate identifying as part of the offer anything that might be attached to the property. It is important to list separately any unattached items you hope to acquire as part of the property, e.g., refrigerators, ranges, furniture, wall-hangings, and so on. Such personal property might be depreciable for tax purposes at a faster rate than the improvements; therefore, Item No. 3 requires the seller to provide a bill of sale inventorying such items.

4. **Earnest Money Deposit.** The buyer can use as earnest "money" any consideration acceptable to the seller. The payment is usually in the form of cash (checks). However, many buyers prefer to use non-interest-bearing promissory notes made out in favor of the seller. If the buyer backs out of his commitments, then the seller has recourse through the note, which must be paid according to the terms agreed on. If the deal goes through as planned, the note is retired in favor of the payment schedule agreed to in Item No. 6. Paying the earnest money via a note has two advantages: no cash is tied up during the process of purchasing the property, and the buyer can offer a larger sum. One of the Nothing Down graduates in Los Angeles who specializes in multi-unit apartment buildings, makes it a practice of using $5,000 earnest money notes when submitting offers. The generous amount of the notes impresses the sellers.

If cash is used (currency, checks, etc.), the buyer should put down as little as possible and still stay within the "trust comfort zone" of the seller. Sometimes $100 will suffice; sometimes it will take $500 or more to demonstrate to the seller that there is a sincere desire to follow through with the purchase. The deposit should be held by a third party—in the real estate broker's trust account or in the trust account of an attorney or escrow officer. If the amount of deposit is small and no agent is involved, letting the seller hold it might be a gesture of trust that could elicit similar flexibilities on the part of the seller.

It is also possible to make an earnest "money" payment in the form of personal property: a car, a boat, a stereo, a piece of equipment—anything perceived by the seller as having value. Naturally the buyer will need to measure the value of personal property against the risks involved.

5. **Purchase Price.** This figure will represent either the outcome of a process of negotiation already completed, or it will represent the buyer's opening figure. Beginning investors will often attach their risk-sensitivity to this figure. They prepare to do battle down to the penny in order to feel secure about the transaction. Actually, the price is in general not as important as the terms of repayment. One of the Nothing Down techniques, in fact, is called "Raise the Price, Lower the Terms" (No. 5). There is less risk involved if the terms are "soft," i.e., flexible in the interest rate, size, and frequency of the installments, and length of note, than if the price is a bit too high. Of course, in a "wholesale" transaction (one involving a heavily discounted property), the price may be very important if the buyer is cashing the seller out. The buyer has to offset his risk in providing a great deal of cash by insisting on a lower price (as much as 15 to 50% below market). It all depends on the situation at hand.

6. **Payment.** This item represents the most important aspect of the negotiation process. Once again, the parties may have agreed orally on the terms and are now providing formal language to prepare for closing. On the other hand, the buyer may be using the earnest money agreement as a tool for negotiation. The terms he is suggesting may be his opening salvo; in this case, he will want them to minimize risk to himself while avoiding insult to the seller with too high a degree of one-sidedness. This is the realm where only two rules prevail: "You never know until you ask" and "A lasting and satisfying deal is a win/win deal."

Sometimes the seller will insist on additional earnest money upon acceptance of the offer. If so, the form provides a place for the figure. The balance of the down payment, if there is to be any, is entered on the line "Additional payment due at closing." The balance of the sales price (after the down payment) is then expressed in terms of the combination of existing encumbrances and new arrangements for paying out the seller's equity.

What are the possibilities? Most transactions are completed using one or more of the following approaches:

(a) *All cash* (as in a wholesale deal)—this is easy to express.

(b) *Assumption of an existing encumbrance:* For example, "This purchase is subject to Buyer assuming and paying Seller's current first mortgage and note (first trust deed and note) held by ABC Mortgage Company with monthly payments on the approximate balance of $_____ to be amortized over _____ years and to include interest not in excess of _____ percent per annum, together with monthly allowances for estimated annual property tax and insurance escrows."

Commentary: In an assumption process, the buyer may have to deal with the original lender, who may want to increase the interest rate prevailing on the existing loan. By using the terms "subject to" and specifying a maximum interest rate ("not in excess of"), the buyer is adding a contingency clause to protect himself in the event the assumption terms of the lender are unacceptable. In the case of an FHA or VA mortgage, the loan will be assumable as is, and the terms of the loan can be stated in the earnest money without a contingency. The assumption process can also apply to a second mortgage (or second trust deed), an all-inclusive trust deed, a contract, or other existing encumbrance.

(c) *Purchasing the property subject to an existing encumbrance:* For example, "Buyer to purchase property subject to an existing first mortgage and note (first trust deed and note) of record in the approximate amount of $_____ , payable approximately $_____ per month, including interest at _____ percent per annum and allowances for estimated annual property tax and insurance escrows (PITI)."

Commentary: Purchasing a property "subject to" existing encumbrances means that no formal assumption takes place. The buyer does not go to the lender and pass muster according to the institutional policies for qualifying. What risk is involved in buying "subject to?" In the case of an underlying FHA or VA loan, none at all, since such loans are fully assumable. In the case of a commercial loan in which the trust document contains a "due-on-sale" clause (acceleration clause), the seller may be in violation of his agreement with the bank unless he requires the buyer to go through a formal assumption process. The recent Supreme Court decision in favor of the lender in such situations must be taken into account. There is still controversy on the subject. There are outspoken advocates on both sides. Friends of the banking industry claim that the banks have every right to force new buyers to qualify and pay higher rates of interest (plus assumption fees up front). Friends of the buying public claim that sellers have the right of "alienation"—the right to sell their property without restraint as long as the loans are not rendered less secure as a result. In this period of tight money, the banks and savings and loan associations are frequently very aggressive about accelerating their loans when sellers sell "subject to" and not through the "assumption" process.

What is the down-side risk for the buyer who structures his offers on a "subject to" basis? At the very least, he should be prepared (in the case of due-on-sale loans) to respond to a call from the lender to come in and qualify for the loan, pay additional points up front, and pay higher monthly payments due to a hike in the interest rates. In many cases, this penalty may be far more acceptable than to go after new financing at prevailing high rates of interest. In the case of assumptions and new loans, the lender may very well replace the long-term note with one based on a variable rate of interest. Buyers who are concerned about the legalities of the due-on-sale issue should consult competent legal advice before acting.

The example above had to do with a first mortgage. A "subject to" purchase can also apply to second mortgages (second trust deeds), all-inclusive trust deeds, contracts, or other existing encumbrances.

(d) *New loan:*

For example:

"This purchase is subject to the Buyer obtaining a new loan on the subject property from (name of lender) in the amount of $_____ payable in monthly installments of $_____ , including interest of not more than _____ percent per annum, amortized over a period of not less than _____ years, plus monthly allowances for estimated annual property tax and insurance escrows."

Commentary: The words "subject to" constitute an important element of protection for the buyer. If the new loan is not obtainable according to the terms indicated, then the buyer is not committed to proceed with the purchase. If the seller or the seller's agent is on the ball, he may want to eliminate the specifics from the statement and try to get the buyer to generalize the conditions by saying "at prevailing interest rates." The seller may also insist on a time limit for obtaining the new loan, using wording such as this: "Buyer agrees to make application for the new loan within five (5) business days after acceptance of this offer, and to advise the seller in writing within fifteen (15) business days after acceptance of this offer of his ability or inability to obtain said loan in accordance with the indicated terms and conditions."

(e) *Promissory note taken back by seller:*

For example:

"Buyer to execute promissory note in favor of Seller secured by first mortgage in the amount of $_____ , payable $_____ per month, including _____ percent interest per annum, amortized over a period of _____ years, balance all due and payable _____ years from the date of execution."

Commentary: This is the now popular owner carry-back arrangement so common during tight-money times. Security for the note, depending on the circumstances and local practice, could be in the form of a second mortgage (second trust deed), third mortgage (third trust deed), all-inclusive trust deed or wrap-around mortgage pertain to the situation where the agreement encloses or wraps around an existing encumbrance.

The example used above includes a balloon payment. Not all do. Transactions often involve owner carry-back arrangements with fully amortized notes. In today's strained real estate market, balloons of less then 5 years' duration are risky. Seven years or more would be advisable.

(f) *Contract:*

For example:

"Buyer to execute a real estate contract (land sales contract, installment land contract, contract for deed, etc.) in favor of seller in the amount of $_____ payable $_____ per month, including ____ percent interest per annum, amortized over a period of ____ years, principal and interest all due and payable ____ years from the date of execution."

Commentary: The word contract (and its variations) implies that the buyer must satisfy the conditions of the agreement before title actually passes. In practice, the buyer should see to it that the escrow agent prepares the deed in favor of the buyer and holds it in escrow. Escrow instructions signed by buyer and seller should provide for release of the deed to the buyer when the contract terms have been satisfied. If the seller is on the ball, he will insist that a quitclaim deed from buyer to seller be prepared and placed in escrow in case of a default.

The example above contains provisions for a balloon payment. Not all do. Some buyers are fortunate enough to negotiate a contract covering a fully amortized note.

By way of summary concerning Item No. 6 of the earnest money agreement, payment of the balance of the sales price (after the down payment) occurs through one or more of the following approaches:

(a) Cash
(b) Assumption of existing encumbrances
(c) Purchase subject to existing encumbrances
(d) New loan
(e) Promissory note taken back by seller
(f) Contract

There are several important security contingencies that the buyer can add to the financial terms where applicable in order to reduce the risk or enhance future options:

(1) **Substitution of Collateral.** A mortgage consists of two basic documents: a note covering the amount owing and the terms of repayment, plus a security document offering real property collateral to back up the note in case of default. Usually a note is secured by the subject property being purchased; however, it is always wise to negotiate the right to substitute other property acceptable to the seller at any time in the future. Here is a sample of a statement that could be added to the earnest money agreement giving the buyer that right:

"Buyer has the right to substitute collateral of equal or greater value on the second mortgage at any time, with the Seller having the right of approval."

The title company handling the documentation can provide the technical language to secure the right of collateral substitution. The right to "move the mortgage" from the subject property to another property acceptable to the seller permits the buyer later on is to pull money out of acquired properties or fully leverage others.

In many cases the substitution of collateral is explicit in the earnest money itself, as in this example:

"Buyer agrees to execute note in favor of the Seller for the principal amount of $_____ , secured by a first (second, third, etc.) mortgage (first trust deed, second trust deed, etc.) on a property located at _____ , amortized for a period of ____ years, payable $_____ per month, including interest of ____ percent per annum, balance of principal and interest all due and payable ____ years from the date of execution."

(2) **Subordination.** The buyer may have given a note to the seller secured by a mortgage (trust deed) in second position above an existing first mortgage (trust deed). And the buyer may wish for this note to remain in second position, even though he may wish one day to refinance this first. What is called for is a subordination clause similar to this one:

"Seller agrees to subordinate the second note and deed of trust to the first note and deed of trust or any replacement thereof."

(3) **Rollover Provision on a Balloon.** An important risk-reduction clause provides the buyer with the right to extend a balloon payment in case he is unable to comply at the time:

"Buyer shall have the right to extend the balloon payment, at his option, for an additional twelve months, provided a principal payment of $_____ is made to the Seller on the original due date of the balloon."

An alternate way of inducing the seller to accept the rollover provision might be to offer a higher rate of interest on the balance during the extra year. Whatever sweetener is used, the buyer must attempt to secure this extension privilege because of the unpredictability of the economy over the next few years.

(4) **Prepayment Provision.** It is important for the buyer to negotiate the right to pay off his obligations to the seller at any time without penalty in the event he should wish to sell. The following kind of stipulation should do the trick:

"Buyer may at any time and without penalty pay in full all amounts owing to the Seller under conditions and terms of this agreement."

(5) **Assumption Provision.** The buyer's note to the seller should contain a stipulation that the note and mortgage (trust deed) are fully assumable. This would allow the buyer to sell the property subject to his obligations to the original seller. The wording need not be complicated:
" . . . said note and trust deed to be fully assumable, with no due-on-sale clause."

(6) **First Right of Refusal on Note.** It is in the best interests of the buyer to negotiate the option of having the first right of refusal should the seller ever want to sell a note the buyer had given him. In this way the buyer might benefit from a discount purchase and also protect himself from undesirable holders of the note. Here is an example:
"This arrangement is contingent upon Buyer having first right of refusal on the third note and deed of trust if Seller should decide to sell the note."

In all of these terms pertaining to Item No. 6 of the earnest money agreement, it is important to seek competent professional advice concerning the wording and the implications of what is being agreed to. The above examples are only illustrations. There are many variations—interest-free notes, interest-only notes, notes calling for annual payments only, amortized notes with several intermittent balloons, etc. The best risk-reduction strategy is to consult expert advice as you go. Once the agreement is signed, it becomes a binding legal contract.

7. **Title.** In some areas of the country, it may be customary for the buyer to share in the costs of title insurance. However, this version of the earnest money agreement presumes that the seller will bear the full burden. That is where the negotiation should always begin. This section is an important contingency for the buyer. On occasion a title search will disclose problems with the title—liens or judgments that effect the marketability of

the property adversely. The boilerplate of Item No. 7 protects the buyer against such cases and provides an escape from the earnest money agreement if the title defects cannot be resolved.

8. **Special Representations.** Once more, this section contains important protections for the buyer and reduces the risk of the offer. After the section on utilities, there are assurances concerning the structural integrity of the building and its major systems, also a "clean bill of health" in regard to compliance with government agency regulations, freedom from future liens and assessments, etc.

9. **Escrow Instructions.** This item specifies when the closing will take place and which agency will provide third-party (neutral) escrow services. In some states, it is customary for the earnest money offer to specify that complete escrow instructions will be provided by the buyer and seller within a specified number of days following acceptance of the offer.

The matter of how conveyance will be made (in whose name and precisely how it is to be stated) is a legal question for the buyer to review with competent legal help. For purposes of the earnest money agreement, one might state "To be provided prior to closing."

10. **Closing Costs.** In this section, the responsibility of who pays for what at closing is spelled out. The escrow fees are divided equally between the buyer and seller in this version; however, everything is negotiable. The boilerplate can be changed to fit the circumstances by simply striking out what does not apply or adding different wording. In the case of changes to the printed text, both buyer and seller must initial the change to show their agreement.

11. **Termite Inspection.** Once again, an important contingency for the buyer. No one wants to wind up with a property that is going to collapse because of the work termites or other insect infestation.

12. **Conditions of Sale.** Apart from Section No. 6 on financing, this may well be the most important risk-reduction section of all. Here is the place to state whatever contingencies the buyer wants to use for his own protection. Some examples follow:

(a) Inspection and approval of buyer or buyer's partner:

"This offer is subject to inspection and approval of the property by buyer (buyer's partner) within 72 hours of seller's acceptance."

Commentary: Offers are frequently made prior to a thorough inspection. This contingency is an important escape clause for the buyer who finds that he does not want the property after all.

(b) Building Inspection:

"This sale is subject to a building inspection at the buyer's expense and with the buyer's approval within seven days of the acceptance of this offer."

(c) Repairs. The buyer may already be aware of needed repairs, in which case the following wording may be used:

"This offer is contingent on the seller completing repairs to the roof at seller's expense. Roof to be in good condition and watertight at time of closing." Etc.

(d) Exculpatory Clause. The buyer is well advised to insist on wording that limits his liability to the value of the property offered as collateral for the notes taken back by the seller. The point is to protect the buyer from personal liability, i.e., liability that could extend beyond the real estate collateral to his personal assets. The following is an example of an exculpatory clause of this type:

"The liability on the part of the buyer to satisfy the terms and conditions of the note(s) executed in favor of the seller shall be limited to the property securing such note(s) and shall not extend beyond this."

(e) Warranty Policy. In some cases the buyer is able to negotiate for himself the added protection of a warranty policy paid for by the seller. The following wording covers this for a single family home:

"The seller shall place on the property a one-year home warranty policy available through (name of company)."

(f) Cleanliness:

"Seller agrees to delivery the premises in a clean and orderly condition at the time of closing."

Note: There are many contingencies that might be warranted in the case of a particular property. The buyer needs to decide what is needed for his own protection. A fairly obvious limitation on the number of contingencies used in the offer is the need to avoid frightening the seller unduly. As Bob Allen says, "A confused mind always says 'No'."

13. **Liability and Maintenance.** An earnest money offer in force (signed by all parties) is a legally binding contract. Without Item No. 13, the buyer may be responsible to cover all or part of the damages that might occur to a property between the time of acceptance and the time of closing.

14. **Possession.** Not all sellers automatically vacate a property upon closing. This item protects the buyer by stating exactly when he is to have

possession. In some cases the buyer may work out a deal with the seller to let him continue occupying the premises for a period of time. The following wording added to the agreement would cover this point:

"Buyer agrees to permit seller to continue residence on the property following close of escrow for a period of time not to exceed ____ months and at a monthly rental rate of $ _____ . Rental agreement to be executed and signed at the time of closing."

15. **Default.** What happens if the buyer or the seller fails to perform according to the terms and conditions of the earnest money agreement? It is important for the protection of the buyer that his liability in case of default be limited to the earnest money deposit and no more. That is why this particular version of the earnest money receipt and offer to purchase contains the vital phrase:

"In the event the Buyer fails to complete the purchase as herein provided, the earnest money deposit shall be retained by the Seller as the total and entire liquidated damages."

In most preprinted earnest money forms this phrase is not present. Frequently the buyer's liability is expressed as being the amount of the earnest money deposit or a certain percentage of the gross sales price (for example, not more than 3%). It might be that the seller will want to retain the right to demand specific performance on the contract, i.e., have recourse to legal means (in addition to retaining the deposit) to force the buyer to comply. According to the principles of making risk-free offers, the buyer should insist on using the "total liquidated damages approach" stated in our model earnest money. Of course, the buyer should make the offer in good faith. Only a win/win deal will prove to be satisfying in the long run. However, if the seller is adamant about having the right of specific performance, it may be that this particular seller will be inflexible in every aspect of the transaction. If so, the buyer may want to take the hint and not follow through with the earnest money offer. There are plenty of don't wanter sellers out there to deal with.

16. **Time Limit of Offer.** This is another important risk-reduction provision to protect the buyer. It is also a wise negotiating tool. The seller cannot have forever to make up his mind. Sometimes an earnest money agreement will state that the seller has to give his approval "upon presentation of the offer." That is really putting the pressure on!

17. **General Agreements.** This is a collection of legal provisions placed in virtually every version of the earnest money form. Each provision has its

specific purpose in helping to make the contract accomplish the purpose intended by the buyer and seller. Of special interest is the provision of mutual assent and cooperation in effecting an IRS 1031 tax-deferred exchange. If the buyer should find a property meanwhile that he could acquire using the subject property of the offer as an exchange, this provision would facilitate the process. Once more, the presence of the provision is designed to expand the options of the buyer and limit his risks.

Items 18-21 constitute formal approval of the offer on the part of both buyer and seller. Item No. 20 covers the real estate commission, which, according to the current conventions of practice, is paid by the seller. Naturally, this item is also negotiable, and many transactions involve situations where the buyer assumes the responsibilities to pay the commission over time, usually in exchange for a reduction in the down payment. If this is the case, details should be spelled out under Item No. 6 of the earnest money agreement.

In all cases, the investor is counseled to get competent legal advice before signing the earnest form or any contract.

Questions and Answers on Making Creative Offers

Richard J. Allen

Question

"How do I get hold of local forms to use in my real estate transactions?"
J.S., Los Angeles

Answer

Blank forms for all aspects of a real estate transaction are available from larger office supply and stationery stores. We recommend that you get in touch with a reputable title company in your area. Title officers would not only have all the necessary forms but would also be able to explain to you what the phraseology means and what the local practices are. In most cases a title company will have an attorney on the staff to keep the legalities in order.

The present volume, makes use of a "Universal Earnest Money Receipt and Offer To Purchase" designed on the basis of research with many dozens of such forms from around the country. We include elsewhere in this book a copy of this form as an example of a preprinted offer that is set up with the security of the buyer in mind. Note especially Item 15 of the form which contains a buyer-oriented default provision limiting liability to the amount of the earnest money.

Question

"A seller wants to sell me his property on a contract but leave the contract unrecorded in order not to trigger a due-on-sale provision. Is this a wise thing to do?"
S.O., Oklahoma City

Answer

Leaving a deed or contract unrecorded is never a wise thing for the buyer to do because he would thereby leave his interest in a property unprotected. If the seller is less than honorable, he could sell the property again to someone else who could then have it recorded. Our careless first buyer would then be out in the cold, because the records would not show his interest in the property. He would be in for a costly court battle and may perhaps lose his investment altogether.

As to strategies for avoiding the due-on-sale provision: we suggest your energies are better spent seeking properties with assumable low-interest loans (FHA, VA, etc.) rather than taking the risks involved with due-on-sale. The other alternative, of course, is to seek properties that are free and clear of encumbrances, or even to negotiate with lenders to assume loans that would otherwise be accelerated. Oftentimes the lender will permit qualified buyers to assume after payment of a tolerable origination fee and a modest hike in the interest rate of the loan. If you do decide to buy a property with a due-on-sale loan against it, make sure you have excellent legal counsel and know the practices of lenders in your area. Make sure, also, that the offer spells out the responsibilities of both buyer and seller in the event of acceleration. For example, one transaction in the book *How To Write A Nothing Down Offer* provides a reduction of the interest rate on the carry-back note in the event the underlying loan should be accelerated (pp. 78-79).

Question:

"What does it mean to ask for 'first right of refusal' on a note?"
J.K., Springfield, Missouri

Answer

There are several contingency clauses that are wise to go after in structuring an offer with a carry-back note: rollover provision on a balloon, subordination, substitution-of-collateral, the right to repay the note, assumption privileges, and first right of refusal. The first right of refusal grants to the buyer the right to buy the carry-back note himself if the holder of the note (the seller of the property) should ever wish to sell the note at a discount on the open market. An example of a clause granting first right of refusal is as follows:

"This arrangement is contingent upon the Buyer having first right of refusal on the third note and deed of trust if the Seller should decide to sell the note."

Why is this clause useful? Because the buyer can take advantage of the opportunity to achieve savings through the discounting procedure. He also maintains more control of the financing on the property and avoids what could be a forced relationship with a new and less-flexible holder of the note.

Question

"What is an exculpatory clause? Could you give me an example of how the clause should be worded?"
M.L., San Francisco

Answer

An exculpatory clause is one that expressly limits a buyer's liability in case of default. Here are two examples:

"The liability on the part of the Buyer to satisfy the terms and conditions of the note to be executed in favor of the Seller as part of this agreement shall be limited to the property securing such note and shall not extend beyond this."

"Liability of this contract shall be limited to the property itself and not extend beyond this."

The purpose of the exculpatory clause is to protect the buyer's own personal estate from recourse by the seller. Recourse in the case of default is limited to the collateral property. No buyer should knowingly enter a transaction with default in mind, but it makes good sense to structure offers and contracts to prepare for all exigencies. As Jack Miller, a prominent investor, once put it while discussing this issue: "Why should any investments that I have made in the past incur a possible liability from any future investments?" In any case, the help of expert legal counsel should be sought when a buyer finalizes the written documents for a transaction. The small cost of legal help is a bargain when the stakes are so high.

Question:

"I transacted a lease-option deal with a buyer several years ago before the due-on-sale became an issue. Will my savings and loan make any concessions to me since this agreement was consumated way before they started to enforce the due-on-sale?"
B.S., Pomona, CA

Answer:

The place to start is to get informed about what is actually written in the trust agreement for the original note concerning due-on-sale. Some trust agreements accelerate even where lease-options are concerned. Then get informed about the current policies of the Savings and Loans in question—each lender will have a different approach to due-on-sale. Always get competent legal advice, especially where due-on-sale is concerned. Even where notes are accelerated, it is often possible to negotiate terms with the lender that are tolerable.

Question:

"I entered into a lease-option agreement with a seller six months ago, but have now found out that the seller has put a second against the property and is behind in his payments on it. The lease option was not recorded, there was no title insurance issued, and I have spent some $8,000 in improvements on the property. What do I do now?"
K.S., Boulder, Colorado

Answer:

The key now is to retain the services of a competent attorney. There may be a possibility of attaching a mechanic's lien to the property in order to recoup some of your investment. It is imperative to get legal counsel. As with most problems, hindsight is better than foresight. Options should be recorded in order to protect the buyer. Option agreements should preclude the seller's putting any further encumbrances against the property during the option period. The buyer should require notification of any default on the existing encumbrances. Great care should be exercised on the part of the buyer in making major improvements to a lease-option property until the option is exercised and the purchase is completed. At the very least, the buyer should arrange to have any cash outlay for improvements apply toward the eventual purchase.

Question

"I made my first offer on a condo. The offer was accepted the next day; however, in the meantime, I found out that my source for the down payment had dried up, with no alternatives available. What can I do to nullify the contract and what can the seller hold me liable for?"
J.L., Chicago

Answer

From time to time situations crop up that prevent one from closing on a property. That is why it is essential to include in the written offer a risk-reducing clause such as "Subject to obtaining financing acceptable to the buyer." It is always safest to spell out the terms of the desired financing in specific detail so that there is no question. In this way, your earnest money deposit will be protected in the event financing cannot be obtained and you cannot perform. It is also prudent to state in the offer that the earnest money deposit will constitute the entire liquidated damages in case of buyer default. This will limit the seller's legal recourse to the amount of the deposit and nothing more.

In regard to your specific question: in the absence of contingency clauses of the type listed above, your options are somewhat limited. You should carefully examine alternative sources for the down payment by reviewing the 50 Nothing Down Techniques. Have you exhausted the possibility of providing the seller with things he might need (cars, trips, covering existing debts, appliances, etc.)—things you could obtain for him on a deferred payment plan and deduct from the down payment? If a Realtor is involved, would he or she take back all or part of the commission in the form of paper (that the seller could pay over time or you could pay as part of the down)? Are there private underlying mortgages involved that might be the source of creative finance funds? Can you locate a friend, relative, associate, etc., who might serve as equity partner or investing partner by providing the down? Case Number 37 in the book *How To Write A Nothing Down Offer* tells of an investor who raised $5,000 from acquaintances by borrowing small amounts from them short term at healthy interest rates in order to raise the down payment for a home. There are practically limitless possibilities for enterprising investors. Have you tried them all?

If everything seems to fail, your only recourse may be to renegotiate with the seller. Perhaps he really does not need the down payment and only wants security. Could you offer him a blanket mortgage for a year until you have proved yourself? Could you negotiate a deferral of the down payment for a few months until you can locate other sources? You might even be able to persuade him to release you from the contract entirely, especially if very little time has elapsed since it was signed by him. Sometimes sellers will even return the deposit (even though they have the right to keep it under terms of the purchase agreement). It depends on the trust that has been developed between seller and potential buyer. Be sure to read very carefully the terms of the agreement you have signed. Consult a competent attorney. And above all, prepare your future offers in such a way that your risk is minimized or altogether eliminated.

PART IX:

Using the
Professionals
Effectively

An Open Letter to Real Estate Salespersons in the U.S.A.

Robert G. Allen

One of the top ten problems hampering the success of any Nothing Down investor is the problem of finding and qualifying don't wanters. This problem is not made easier by the fact that the whole real estate industry—the brokers, agents, and Realtors who make up the professional sales force of the nation—have been slow to come around to the realities of this new decade. The 1980's are and, with a brief respite in late 1982 and for much of 1983, will continue to be, plagued with high interest rates and tight money. Yet the real estate sales professionals, while handling by far the largest percentage of all real estate sales, have, in general, been slow to adapt to the new exigencies and develop a creative game plan for the future.

This article is designed to help alleviate this problem by speaking directly to Realtors and showing them a new win/win way to view the real estate market. If you seem to be having trouble working with your favorite Realtor, you should make a photocopy of this article for him or her to read... it may make your task a little easier.

Let me introduce myself. My name is Robert G. Allen and I am the author of the bestselling book, *Nothing Down: A Proven Program That Shows You How to Buy Real Estate with Little or No Money Down.* Whenever I introduce myself this way I automatically get a response something like this: "Did you say, 'Nothing Down'!? You must be crazy!" "You can't buy property with Nothing Down. It's impossible!" If any one of the above remarks crossed your mind as you heard about *Nothing Down*, I urge you to reconsider. I intend to prove to you in the next few pages how learning and using the creative financing techniques described in *Nothing Down* will (1) earn you more money each year, (2) help you to serve the needs of your clients better, and (3) keep you competitive in this changing real estate world. As a matter of fact, I will go so far as to say that if you *don't* learn creative financing, *you cannot survive in the real estate business in the decade of the Eighties.*

For so many years the tried and true formula for making a living in real estate went something like this: Seller wants to sell property. Seller wants all cash. Agent lists property. Agent finds buyer with lots of cash, strong financial statement, great A-1 credit and super job. Buyer gets property by coming in with a large down payment and refinances property. Seller gets all of his cash. Agent gets commission. All live happily ever after.

Well, guess what? That formula has started to change — and drastically. You should have noticed its effect on your income by now (unless of course you are one of the few creative Realtors making more money than ever). The formula now is altered to read something like this: Seller wants to sell property. Seller would like to have all cash. Agent lists property and advertises in paper to find A-1 buyer. Property sits on the market for six months. No one looks at it because of high interest rates, tight money, and general feeling that the economy is chronically sick. Seller gets impatient since he has already bought another property and now has two mortgage payments to make. Seller cancels listing with Agent #1 and re-lists with Agent #2 who promises more action (but who has about the same probability of success). Seller loses. Agent #1 loses. Agent #2 has about six months to figure out just how much he loses. Buyer loses because he doesn't buy the property, which will be more expensive in the future no matter what happens to rates and availability of money. And that is not the way to financial independence for anyone involved. This is a lose/lose formula.

How can we rewrite this undesirable formula and put in its place a realistic alternative? May I suggest to you the *Nothing Down alternative.* Agents like yourself all over this country are beginning to learn this alternative and are finding it does make them more money.

Nevertheless, there has been tremendous resistance to *Nothing Down* by the real estate industry. One of my favorite sayings goes something like this: "The trouble with people is not that they don't know, but that they know so much that just ain't so!" There is so much about *Nothing Down* that you have assumed is right but just ain't so. Here are three of the major complaints I hear frequently about *Nothing Down:*

1. It just can't be done.

2. No seller will sell his property with nothing down because it's not in his best interest.

3. No agent can recommend a nothing down offer because it is not in his or her best interest (underlying concern—how do I get my commission?).

Let's examine each of these three complaints.

1. It can't be done.

Whenever people tell me that it can't be done, I try to remind them that what they are really trying to tell me is they *don't know how to do it.* I have used the techniques described in my book to become a millionaire. It works! But I think the problem is really one of misunderstanding. What does *Nothing Down* mean? Nothing Down does not necessarily mean that the seller doesn't get a cash down payment . . . it simply means that the buyer in the ideal situation does not come up with the cash out of his own pocket. That's the key.

We have developed the Nothing Down concept into a regular science and the graduates of our nationwide Nothing Down investment seminar learn how to apply each of the 50 Nothing Down techniques in various circumstances to make real estate transactions come together. Our graduates learn the difference between conventional thinking and creative thinking. They learn how to turn the bad news of the current tight money market into good news by showing specific sellers how they are better off accepting creative offers rather than waiting for a conventional offer which may never come. Our graduates learn how to analyze the nine specific areas of flexibility of every real estate transaction to look for creative ways to solve the seller's problem. Every month our graduates meet together to discuss new ways of buying property with nothing down. We have established monthly meeting groups in most major cities in the United States. Based on reports from these groups, we are able to calculate that their purchases amount to several billions of dollars worth of real estate per year.

Nothing down not only works, but it is the wave of the future. As home prices continue to rise and as the current tight money market continues to persist (and I believe that it will be with us for years—bye-bye 10% interest rates), it will become necessary for the real estate industry to adapt quickly to the new unconventional ways of getting sales. Nothing Down is not some weird concept but it is the way things will be done in the years to come. Already we are seeing the major franchises like Century 21, ERA, and Realty World come out with their versions of creative financing labeled as Alternative Financing and Seller Financing. And still there is resistance!

I couldn't believe my ears a few months ago as I watched a local television talk show host interview a respected real estate broker. He asked the broker what he thought about "this new book on the market called *Nothing Down.*" The broker replied that in his long career in the business he had been involved in over $3 billion worth of real estate closings and had yet to see a nothing down deal. "Obviously," he replied, "the title of the book was designed to sell books and not real estate." I had to chuckle to myself when only a few weeks later the chairman of our group in the area where this broker had his major offices related to me how he had just closed on a transaction on a single-family home with absolutely nothing down... no cash in the deal whatsoever. And he had bought it through this broker's office! The trouble with people is not that they don't know but that they know so much that just ain't so!

2. No seller will sell his property with nothing down because it is not in his best interests.

The above statement is almost always true. And that is the key to our success. We know by experience that about 90% of all real estate sellers are *not* flexible. They want their price and their terms... and they are willing to wait to get them. This does not bother Nothing Down buyers because they have been trained to look for the other 10% of the sellers who *are* flexible. We call these flexible sellers *don't wanters.* A don't wanter is a person who doesn't want his property and is willing to be flexible in the sale of it. How many don't wanters are there in any given market? Literally thousands— right under your very nose every time you thumb through your MLS book. I have said many times, "Send me to any city in the United States. Take away my wallet. Give me a $100 bill. And in 72 hours I'll buy an excellent piece of property using none of my own money." The reason I can do this (and have done it) is because I know how to find don't wanters and can show these sellers over fifty ways of solving their problems without using any of my own cash. Don't wanters fall into four categories:

1. Those who don't care about cash . . . they just want out.
2. Those who don't need cash.
3. Those who don't want cash.
4. Those who need some cash but not all of their equity in cash.

Some examples include sellers with management problems (on rental investment properties), transfers, people behind in their mortgage payments, owners of fixer-uppers, people with time problems or health problems. Other examples are divorcees, retirees, investors and builders or wealthy owners who are more interested in rate of return than cash. Some people don't want cash because of tax problems. Other sellers need some cash to solve a particular problem but are willing to carry the rest. There are dozens of ways to solve a don't wanter's problem without using cash.

You might be wondering about our ethics. After all, aren't we taking advantage of these people with their problem circumstances? You will find in dealing with our graduates that they have been trained in what we call the *win/win* philosophy. In other words, we believe that all parties in a transaction must win. If we can solve a seller's problem in such a way as to reduce our down payment to zero, then everyone wins. We look for people who will be flexible enough to consider these kinds of offers. We try to show the sellers the benefits of doing things our way. For this reason, our graduates will often ask you, as a real estate agent, to let them visit personally with the seller to explore different ways of solving the seller's problems. We always find resistance to this modus operandi. Many agents have been trained to keep the buyer and the seller apart and to act as go-between. No matter what you have been told, this is not always the best way to get the buyer and seller to agree to terms. Having the agent act as a buffer go-between when creative financing is involved almost always creates distrust and places the buyer and the seller in an adversarial position. In essence, as an agent, you cut your own throat. Adversaries don't try to solve problems... and if you don't solve problems you don't make sales. We train our graduates to understand the sellers' problems and to approach them in a win/win way.

Let me go through a recent transaction with you to show you how win/win philosophy works in the real world. A friend approached me recently with a problem. She had her home on the market for sale in California. It was worth $160,000 — on the high side. After months of having the property on the market with absolutely no response, she began to worry. And to make matters worse, she located another home she wanted to buy in an excellent location... and she didn't want to lose it. What can she do to buy the new property and sell the old one? Let me diagram the situation for you:

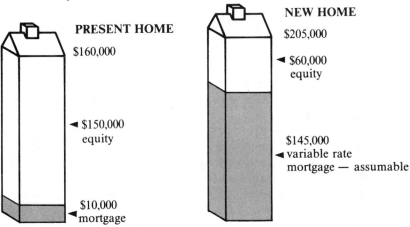

PRESENT HOME

$160,000

◄ $150,000 equity

$10,000 ◄ mortgage

NEW HOME

$205,000

◄ $60,000 equity

$145,000 ◄ variable rate mortgage — assumable

Both properties are listed with Realtors with normal commissions. The problem lies in the fact that she wants to buy the new home but has no cash to do it with. She is in competition with another couple who have made an offer to buy the same home, but their offer is "subject to sale" of their own home in another city. The seller of the new home wants to sell and we are told by his agent that he absolutely has to have all of his cash now. This is the way lose/lose attitudes are generated. Rather than listening to the conventional opinions of the agent involved, we made an offer to the seller as follows:

—We will buy your property now and take these heavy payments off your hands ($1,500 per month for a vacant home).

—We will give you $15,000 as a down payment (which we will borrow from a friend who owes us a favor—on a short-term loan until our home sells).

—We will give you a one-year balloon mortgage of $45,000 payable with monthly payments over the next 12 months at 1% per month. This is not contingent upon the sale of any other property.

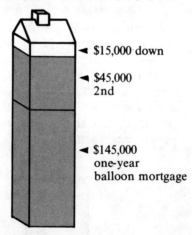

$15,000 down

$45,000
2nd

$145,000
one-year
balloon mortgage

The seller, being a reasonable man, saw the wisdom of this nothing down offer. (Remember, it is nothing down to us since the down payment is borrowed, although there will be cash involved.) He made arrangements with the Realtors involved (at our suggestion) that they only receive a part of their commission now and wait for the rest when the balloon would fall due. He received some cash now, rid himself of a bothersome monthly payment which only cut into his net profit, obtained a monthly payment of $450 for the next twelve months and a balloon of $45,000. He wins — and he knows it.

The buyer, my friend, also wins. She obtains her dream home now without having to wait for her sale and probably losing her dream home in the process. And the agents get some cash now and a promise of the rest in the future . . . which is better than nothing now and nothing in the future.

But we do have a problem here. My friend still has to sell her home. Remember, the market is absolutely dead. And she has a one-year balloon . . . and for an unsophisticated seller this is very scary (and with good reason). Our strategy is to let the home sell conventionally if possible, but if after a few months there is still no action, we will resort to creative financing in the sale of this property. Sure enough, three months go by with no action. We decide to shift to Plan B. I call the agent handling this property. (This is Agent #2 . . . Agent #1 gave up after six months.) I suggest something unorthodox. Let's advertise this property for sale with nothing down. That's right! Nothing down. The week before he had run an open house and had few if any lookers and no offers. I suggested that he run an ad stating that we, the sellers, would consider a nothing down offer to the right buyer. Result? The next weekend, after running this ad, he had 10 to 15 interested lookers and the following Thursday, four days after our new strategy went into place, we received two bona fide offers from strong buyers and accepted the best of the two. In other words, nine months of conventional sales techniques had produced not one acceptable offer . . . whereas four days of unconventional sales techniques produced a sale. Now, lest you think that I have taken leave of my senses, let me show you how all parties win in the following offer (the numbers were rounded off):

—Buyer will offer full price of $160,000.

—Buyer will come in with a full $30,000 down payment.

—Buyer will refinance the property for $130,000.

—After closing, the seller will agree to lend the buyer $45,000 of the proceeds of the sale and refinance and secure it by a second mortgage against the property being sold. This bears payment of $450 per month for three years and then a balloon.

—Buyer will place funds in an escrow account to guarantee that the payments on the second loan are made so that the seller feels secure.

This is how the results looked:

BEFORE

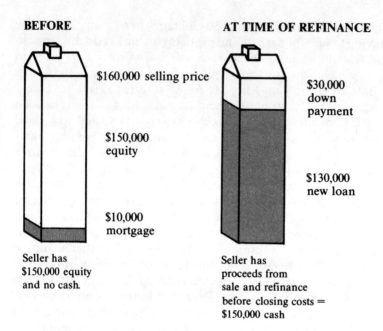

$160,000 selling price

$150,000
equity

$10,000
mortgage

Seller has
$150,000 equity
and no cash.

AT TIME OF REFINANCE

$30,000
down
payment

$130,000
new loan

Seller has
proceeds from
sale and refinance
before closing costs =
$150,000 cash

SEVERAL WEEKS LATER

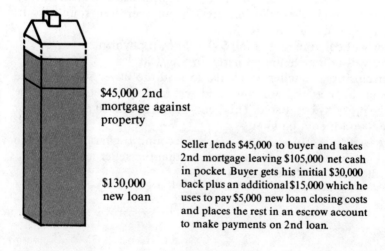

$45,000 2nd
mortgage against
property

$130,000
new loan

Seller lends $45,000 to buyer and takes
2nd mortgage leaving $105,000 net cash
in pocket. Buyer gets his initial $30,000
back plus an additional $15,000 which he
uses to pay $5,000 new loan closing costs
and places the rest in an escrow account
to make payments on 2nd loan.

Do you see how everyone wins?

Buyer gets new home for nothing down although he had to use $30,000 of his own money for a few weeks at the most. The closing costs for the new loan were even generated out of the deal... and money to make payments too.

Seller gets rid of property and payments. She gets $105,000 cash and a mortgage generating $450 per month for three years when it all comes due and payable. She also received a full price offer. She now can pay off her balloon payment and breathe easier.

Banker makes a new loan.

Realtors involved receive full commissions at closing.

For added seller protection I would advise using a qualifed real estate attorney to draw up the papers. in addition, the buyer should be checked out throughly and if possible should be required to provide addtional collateral to protect the seller in the event of default on the orginal loans by the buyer.

Let me repeat the last part. The Realtors involved received full cash commissions at closing. No commission-dectomies. No paper. Just cash. Is this offer in the best interests of the seller? In a word, she was ecstatic! Why couldn't someone have suggested this to her nine months ago and saved her nine months of anguish? She is totally protected by escrow agreements, cash in the bank, and the ability to fully check out the buyer and his financial strength. I have seen dozens of similar transactions go through with the same win/win results. And there are dozens of other creative financing techniques which help solve problems. For the life of me, I can't understand why more agents are not catching the vision of how to make more money and serve their clients better by using these kinds of solutions. I can tell you from first hand experience that the agents involved in this transaction explained above were flabbergasted to see how easy it was to put this together when both the buyer and the seller are counseled with the benefits of creative financing in mind. And that brings me to the next common complaint by unsophisticated agents about *Nothing Down*.

3. No agent can recommend a Nothing Down offer because it is not in his or her best interests (underlying concern—how do I get paid?).

As you saw in the previous examples, the agents received cash commissions at closing. In most cases, with nothing down deals, there will always be cash for the agents... and as a matter of fact, when you learn how to use these creative financing techniques described here, in my book, and in my seminar, you will be able to earn much more income than ever before because you are not stuck in first gear with conventional financing. And you will do your clients a greater service by opening up to them a whole new world of alternatives. It cuts down your advertising time, the number of calls you have to take, the number of people you have to show through any given property, and the number of calls you have to take from irate sellers.

However, there are instances in creative financing when you would do yourself a favor by not seeking to have your commission all paid in cash at the closing. One of the largest obligations that the seller has to pay off with the cash from closing is the commission cost. And, as you know, most buyers today don't have a lot of money for a down payment, although there are literally millions of young couples who earn a good income. Rather than trying to find qualified buyers with adequate down payments, it might be to your advantage (and ultimately to the seller's advantage) to offer to take your commission in the form of a note with monthly payments attached over a period of months or years. In this way, the seller wins since his property is sold more quickly ... the buyer wins because he is aided with his down payment. But where does that leave you? By offering to lend your down payments, you increase your client list and increase the probability of closing sales. If you could generate a $200 per month payment from a commission note on as few as five sales (which are now easier to put together) you could begin to take the uncertainty and insecurity out of the commission business.

I spent three years as a Realtor and know the pressure that one is under sometimes to put a deal together knowing full well that the monthly bills don't go away. You should get in the habit of building up a security blanket of monthly income notes to stave off the ups and downs in your income. You may even increase your business significantly by advertising that you will help buyers get into properties by lending them your commission. Your offer would be simple: If I receive my commission from the seller in cash I will charge a 6% fee. If the seller doesn't have enough to pay me in the closing, I will accept the buyer's note for a 10% fee. Try it. You'll see that it will increase your sales.

Well, as a final note in this discussion of the Nothing Down alternatives, let me make a few suggestions as to how to become a better, more profitable agent. One of the quotes which sank deep into my heart when I heard it goes like this:

"If you think education is expensive, try ignorance."
Derek Bok, President, Harvard University

What this means in a nutshell is there is so much about the business of selling real estate that you have taken for granted. The ignorance in this business is astounding. There is a whole new world open to you with the proper education. During 1976 and 1977, as I was just starting in the real estate business, I stumbled into an excellent seminar organization based in California which specialized in creative real estate. In that two-year period of time I attended something like 16 seminars (I can't remember the exact number anymore) and spent over $5,000 on a new education. This was, by far, the best thing I ever did for my career. Within three years I had made enough money to drop my license and devote full time to my own real estate investment program and teaching (which is what I really love to do . . . I never did love selling).

You need more education. It is the lifeblood of a successful agent's success. I urge you to learn more about creative financing. If you happen to run into one of our graduates of the Nothing Down system, don't turn him off by a negative attitude. Listen to him, let him teach you how everyone in the transaction can win with proper counseling. If you would like to learn more information about our systems or about other seminars given around the country by other excellent organizations, drop me a self-addressed envelope and I will send you my list of *Top Ten Best Seminars in the Country.* Good luck and God bless you. Let's get a win/win tradition started—and say goodbye to the good old lose/lose days.

What Do You Do With An Uncreative Realtor?

Robert G. Allen

It's time to talk again about a problem which I have ignored for too long.
I addressed it in another article, "An Open Letter to All Real Estate
Salespersons in the U.S.A." But the problem is not easy to solve. So let's
take it out of the "back burner" file again and face it head on . . . together.

Many of the people who take my seminar, or who have read my book,
report unbelievable resistance to nothing down concepts by the real estate
industry. I personally experienced this recently when I was asked to speak
to a group of Realtors belonging to a major national chain for which I have
an enormous amount of respect. The brokers were informed by mail that I
would be coming in to speak to all interested Realtors about creative
financing . . . especially the Nothing Down kind. The turnout to the
meetings was unusually small and the event coordinator couldn't figure
out why. Then he discovered that many of the local brokers had *boycotted*
the meeting. Some had not even informed their agents about the event for
fear of what they would learn. Can you imagine?! At first I was incensed . . .
outraged. I had flown two thousand miles to specifically teach these
Realtors practical techniques for increasing commission income with
creative financing. I thought of the proverb: "You can lead a horse to water,
but you can't make him drink." The trouble with these people was, I
couldn't even lead these horses to water to show how good it was. Once I
cooled down I began to look at it more objectively. These brokers, for
whatever reason, were obviously reacting to the concept of nothing down
the way almost everyone does when they first hear of it: disbelief. Being
practical people, they conjured up all of the reasons why this would not
work in today's marketplace and decided that they would rather stay in the
office than waste their time at a flaky one-day seminar. As I mentioned in
the previous article, most brokers have three main objections to the

nothing down concept when they first hear it:

1. It just can't be done ("I've never bought any property with nothing down so it is obviously impossible.")

2. It's not in the best interests of the seller ("Nothing down obviously means 'rip-off.' ")

3. It's not in the best interests of the Realtor ("Nothing down obviously means no cash commissions.")

As you and I know, all of these objections are false. You *can* buy real estate with nothing down. Every year our seminar graduates buy *$1 billion worth of real estate,* much of it with nothing down. Anyone who has attended my seminar knows about the win/win philosophy. Anyone who has read my book can find several nothing down techniques which can be used to help raise cash so that the Realtor, if there is one involved, can get paid in cash at closing.

The problem is in teaching the Realtor to understand that these things are true. And doing that is as hard for us as it was for Copernicus to convince the people that the sun did not revolve around the earth. Some people just don't *want* to learn.

With this in mind, let me give you three specific suggestions to keep in mind when looking for and dealing with Realtors to help you with your nothing down purchases:

1. Expect to be told that you are crazy.

All successful people run into this. At first your skeptics call you crazy when they hear what you are up to. And when you succeed they call you lucky. *"You can't get no respect."* You're either crazy or lucky. But if you let these people get under your skin, they will rob you of your dreams. I don't go to a chiropractor for a toothache. I don't go to an uncreative person for the solution to a difficult problem. And I surely don't listen to an uncreative Realtor telling me that I can't buy real estate for nothing down. That's like asking Tip O'Neill what he thinks of Reagan as President of the United States. He will answer from his pre-determined bias. I have had people who have been in the real estate business for 25 years tell me that I could not do what I proceeded to do before their very eyes ... namely, turn through the multiple listing book, locate and buy a property for nothing down. Expect to be called crazy. All great people in this world started out by challenging a preconceived erroneous public opinion ... and changing it. Let comments about your sanity bounce off you like water from a duck's back. Smile inwardly. You know better. If you get discouraged, drop me a line or consult with some of the local graduates. You might be saying the wrong things. That leads us to the next suggestion.

2. Learn how to say the right things.

Let's start out with what *not* to say. You walk into a Realtor's office cold. You are carrying your *Nothing Down* manual under your arm. The "Nothing Down" on the cover is showing. You ask to see a Realtor. You introduce yourself and proceed to tell him or her that you have just taken this course entitled "Nothing Down: How to Buy Real Estate With Little or No Money Down." You tell the Realtor that you spent all of your money for the course and don't have any money left for a down payment. You also don't have any credit, job, or property to use as collateral. In short, you're flat broke and you would like to buy something.

What would you do if you were the Realtor? You bet, you would probably mutter something about "That confounded Robert Allen" and send the investor on his way with a piece of your mind. Any Realtor worth his salt knows that you only deal with "qualified" customers. Anyone who is not qualified is *a waste of time.* If you don't want to be treated like just a waste of time, learn to say the right things.

First of all, act like you know what you are doing. Study your manual, know the lingo, be prepared. You wouldn't do any less for your banker would you? In the first meeting with the Realtor, ask the following question: "May I look at a multiple listing book,
probably reply, "Certainly. What are you looking for?" "Actually, I have a goal to buy one investment home every year. I'd just like to see if there are any new listings in the book that would fit into my criteria." That should set a pretty good stage for you. The Realtor will probably ask what your criteria are. You can launch into a discussion about price or terms, and that you are interested in finding flexible sellers. Don't call them "don't wanters." You like to find sellers who will discount their price at least twenty percent for all cash (thus giving the impression that you do have lots of cash at your disposal... which, as a Nothing Down student, you do... as much cash as you care to find partners for.) By the same token, you will also deal with sellers who are willing to carry paper for full price and very flexible terms. Don't say "nothing down." That means "flake" to an uncreative Realtor. You are not a flake. You have every intention of fulfilling your obligations and helping to structure a win/win transaction for all parties ... but the Realtor doesn't understand this at first. Let him see you in action. Tell the Realtor that you know that there are not very many of these "flexible" sellers but that you are patient and willing to wait and look. After all, you do have a whole year to search.

While he is getting the MLS book, you might ask if he is familiar with any office listings of extremely motivated sellers who might fit into this category. (It is better to buy an office's own listings because they can afford to be more flexible with the commission if it is all going to stay in the office and not be shared with another office). Your whole purpose in going into the office in the first place is *to look for clues of* don't wanters. You look in the MLS book for people with low mortgage balances who indicate that they are willing to carry part of their equity in paper (using technique #32, "The Second Mortgage Crank"). You look for highly-motivated situations: transfers, behind in payments, owners of two homes, one of which is vacant, etc.

Don't expect the Realtor to know how to spot don't wanters. You have to do most of the digging. Open up the book, read the remarks section under each listing in your price range. Sometimes I even like to ask if i could have time to study the book alone. I can then sit there in private and think up creative offers to various listings. I look for the highest-probability candidates.

I copy down information. Telephone numbers of potential don't wanters . . . if that information is listed in the book. I don't need addresses. I just want to call and see how flexible the sellers are. I might call the listing agent whose number is in the listing form. The question I am trying to get an answer to is: "Just how flexible are your clients? Tell me about their problem . . . their situation. What kinds of offers do you think your client would be willing to accept?" Probe for flexibility. You can do all of this right in the Realtor's office, sitting at his desks and using his phones. Of course, you don't try to cut him out of the commission. If you find something to buy, you have your Realtor friend write up the offer for you and present it. But the point is, you take charge. You do the looking, calling, and preliminary negotiations. Try to find motivated sellers right from the Realtor's office before you ever go out to inspect the property. If it isn't going to be little or no money down (if that is your goal), then there is no use wasting gasoline.

3. It is just as difficult to find a creative Realtor as it is to find a don't wanter or a creative banker—but that doesn't mean you stop looking.

Once you find your creative Realtor, use him or her exclusively. It will be the best thing you ever did. One creative Realtor is worth a king's ransom . . . that is why they can make a fantastic living. No one else is doing it!

There are three major sources of creative Realtors.

1. *Who's Who in Creative Real Estate.*
2. *Creative Real Estate Magazine.*
3. Realtors who have taken the Nothing Down course and are active in local RAND groups.

Who's Who in Creative Real Estate—1982 Edition is available from the RAND Bookshelf, 145 East Center Street, Provo, Utah 84601, at a cost of $16.00. Investors and homebuyers will find this directory invaluable as a tool for locating practitioners in all parts of the country who are trained in creative finance.

The Creative Real Estate Magazine is a monthly publication designed to keep the creative professional updated on current ideas, techniques, and formulas. One of the most valuable aspects of the magazine is its nationwide directory of exchange groups, including the names and addresses of the group leaders. Write to P.O. Box 2446, Leucadia, California 92024, or call (714) 438-2446. The cost is $40.00 per year.

RAND Groups (consisting of those who are trained in the Robert Allen Nothing Down approach to investing) are organized in most cities in the United States. Many of the groups have members who are trained professional real estate agents thoroughly versed in how the Nothing Down Program works. If you are not sure how to contact the RAND Group in your area, write us a note at the Provo headquarters.

As a final word, Realtors are only one source of leads for nothing down purchases. If you don't feel comfortable dealing with Realtors, you might try your own ad in the newspaper to have don't wanters find you. I like to have my feelers out in several areas of my market place so that there is a greater probability of success.

Hope this helps . . . good luck and God bless.

Finding the Right Agent For You

William R. Broadbent

I have attended several meetings of real estate investors in my area During these sessions I became aware of some Problems and frustrations of the participants in their search for a qualified agent to represent them.

Let me illustrate the problem by reviewing how real estate brokerage functions.

You walk into the office of Joe Real Estate and express interest in purchasing investment property. What happens next?

1. Joe checks his office listings to see if there is anything remotely close to your "want" and probably shows you anything even halfway close. Why? If Joe is lucky and you happen to like the property, Joe earns a larger commission. We will assume that Joe has nothing in his listing inventory that you like. What happens next?

2. Joe opens his Multiple Listing Book and reviews it to see if other local brokers have anything listed. Perhaps he could sell you something and share a commission with another real estate firm. Under multiple listing rules Joe is a subagent of the seller (who is paying his fee) and is legally bound to help get the best price and terms for the seller. Not finding anything in other brokers' listings, what will Joe do next? Joe remembers a "FSBO" (For Sale By Owner) that should be just the right property for you. His inspection of the property confirms its suitability. He tells the owner, Susie Seller, that he has a potential buyer (you) and asks her to give him a short-term listing on her property. Susie feels that Joe is just another agent looking for a listing and refuses Joe's request. Will you ever get to see Susie's property through Joe Real Estate (remember, it was a natural)? Probably not.

Why would Joe introduce you, a willing buyer, to Susie, a willing seller, without any protection for his commission? You may not realize it, but due to the manner in which real estate is normally carried on, you and other customers are being excluded from a segment of the real estate market, i.e.; unlisted properties, and are usually shown only listed properties.

In the foregoing scenario you are a customer who has gone shopping and not found what you wanted. You can continue to shop from agency to agency leaving your name and requesting that an agent call you if he/she finds something. This approach can be tedious and may not produce the results you desire.

As a potential buyer of real estate who is willing to work through an agent, you will end up paying the commission on whatever you buy. A brokerage fee is built into the price of any property you purchase. With this thought in mind, you should consider employing a creatively trained real estate agent to represent you as a buyer's broker. In this capacity your agent negotiates "net" with the seller and receives his/her fee from you. Should you choose this alternative you are now a client rather than a customer and are entitled to the benefits of client representation.

This buyer's agency relationship opens up the *entire marketplace* to you (no exclusions). Your agent has the opportunity to come up with the best property that produces the most benefits for you, because he/she need not restrict the search only to listed properties. A buyer's agent will not sell you one of his/her company's listings because this would involve a conflict of interest. Your agent has no reason to have you buy quickly for fear that some other agent will steal you away and sell you something before he/she can.

Another benefit you will find in employing a buyer's agent is having a better negotiated transaction. Dealing directly with an owner or listing agent who represents the seller could put you at a competitive disadvantage. A "buyer's agent" becomes *your* negotiator. He/she can often negotiate a price and terms that will give you a lower price or better terms. Your agent can suggest concessions from the seller that a seller's agent should not mention to you.

A buyer's agent can submit preliminary offers on your behalf, subject to your inspection and final written approval. You can remain anonymous. Selling prices and terms tend to become very firm where the buyer is a well-known real estate investor, wealthy individual, or large corporation. You could authorize your agent to make offers as an agent for an undisclosed principal.

If you, as a buyer, want professional client representation, then you should hire a buyer's agent and pay his/her fee. Finding an agent who practices single agency (buyer representation is only one aspect), is not an easy task. This single agency practitioner represents only one party in a given real estate transaction and is paid by that party. *Who's Who In Creative Real Estate* (921 East Main Street, Suite F, Ventura, California 93001, 805-643-2337) has defined Single Agency and Professional Real Estate Pratice. In the 1984 directory, those listees who have adopted this standard of pratice are identified with an "SA" (Single Agency) identification in their listing.

Who's Who In Creative Real Estate is a professional directory of real estate agents trained in creative methods of acquiring and disposing of real estate. The directory assists creatively trained agents in locating one another, facilitates making geographical real estate transactions, and aids the public in locating agents who are educated in creative financing and marketing techniques. Their education is substantially above the industry average for real estate agents.

There are more agents in the *Who's Who Directory* who understand buyer representation and creative financing than any other source this author is aware of. *Who's Who In Creative Real Estate* acts as an identification source for single-agency practitioners. Since a few seminars are now being offered nationally to teach agents how to represent buyers, I anticipate a sustained growth in the number of buyer's agents and single-agency practitioners who can provide better representation alternatives for the public. *Who's Who* listees are not in every area. If no listee is in the city or area you need, look for the closest agent. If the closest agent cannot help you, ask for a referral to someone who can help you with your particular situation.

Ask people in related fields, i.e., real estate-oriented attorneys, accountants, title insurance people, etc., who are the most knowledgeable and experienced investment real estate agents in your community. Do they practice single agency or represent buyers? When you meet with an agent, use terms like "single agency," "buyer's broker," etc. If they do not know what you are talking about, you probably have not found the right people. An agent who says, "Work with me and I will get you a good deal," but does not ask you to employ him/her is probably not the right person either. If you, the buyer public, begin to ask for representation, it will hasten the change in the antiquated dual agency/subagency system that has prevailed in real estate for decades.

When investors follow some of the suggestions set forth in this article, they will experience a higher level of success in achieving their real estate objectives.

How Firm is Your Banking Foundation?

Clint Murdock

For many of us, approaching the bank for money is tantamount to a full scale assault, in enemy territory, without ammunition. The terror of asking for money from a bank is literally more than most people can handle. I would compare this fear to the first time you contemplated asking for your first date or requesting the keys to your dad's new car. The anticipation is overwhelming. I remember hearing a friend of mine describe his reaction when he decided to ask his true love for her hand in marriage. He relates that he set everything up just right. A special date, to a special place, in a romantic setting. However, the anticipation caused him to become so violently ill he had to cancel the date.

Developing a strong and personal banking relationship is essential if you are to succeed in any business or personal pursuit, especially real estate financing. The person who charges ahead in full battle gear without first reconnoitering the territory is driving toward certain failure. Only when one really knows the territory can he eliminate the bothersome anticipation and prepare for the onslaught. Knowing the territory involves knowing the limitations of your bank, what they will and will not do. It involves developing a trust between you and your banker and it also means having confidence in your bank.

Do You Know Your Bank?

Guess what? Not all banks are the same. It's true that they all seem to perform the same basic function but they may not all feel the same way about lending procedures and loan qualifications. One bank in your community may feel good about lending against various real estate projects while the bank down the street only feels comfortable with auto loans. How does your bank feel about real estate loans? Do you know? I have seen many people who refuse to change banks. Every week they bring in a loan request and every week they are turned down. The bank tells them the loan is risky and the bank is not interested in that type of loan. In some cases I believe these people simply enjoy being turned down.

You need to sit down with the bank manager and tell him what you are doing and ask him whether or not his bank is interested in considering the types of loans you will be presenting to him. If he is a good banker he will let you know what he needs and wants. If he hedges with comments like, "Sure, we'll consider any loan request," or "Real estate? What kind of real estate?", then you might be in trouble. Don't let him hedge. Get right down to the meat of the issue and establish the ground rules up front. If you bring in a loan request that makes sense and it is turned down without a very good reason, then you must consider shopping around. Banking is a very competitive business and there are many willing banks.

I do not advocate jumping from bank to bank since this type of banking will only lead to potential split-borrowing arrangements (loans at various banks) which is frowned on by bankers everywhere. Once you find a bank that will work effectively with you, you must be loyal. If that bank cannot grant a request then let that banker know that you are loyal to him but you need to shop this deal around rather than lose it. I guarantee that your banker will understand and appreciate your disclosure.

It is also important that you understand that banks differ in levels of bureaucracy. There are basically three levels of banking activity:

1. Huge multi-national banks.
2. Regional banks.
3. Local single-unit operations.

The large *multi-national operations* tend to be very structured and sometimes inflexible. They would much rather make a $10 million loan to a local real estate entrepreneur. But even more disturbing that an inflexible loan policy is the tendency of large banks to continually change bank managers. Just when you feel comfortable with one guy, another comes in to replace him and you start all over again. However, they do have one great advantage: they have unlimited resources. They will typically have fully developed mortgage loan departments with unlimited dollars to spend on what they consider to be worthwhile projects. Getting your hands on some of that loot may well be worth putting up with the bureaucracy.

Regional banks offer many of the same services of a large bank but tend to be more community oriented. This community orientation results from the fact that regional banks normally have branches located in a more limited area. For example, XYZ regional bank may have ten branches located in the Santa Clara Valley of California. They are usually controlled by local interests and therefore are geared to satisfy local needs. Regional banks may not have as many resources as the larger banks but they can accommodate most local needs in a very satisfactory manner. I would recommend regional banks as prime lenders.

Finally, the *small independent bank*. These banks are normally owned by several local business people who know nothing about banking. Small banks have limited resources and, therefore, are limited as to whom they can lend to. They seek out the little guy and work very hard to develop a lending relationship. You cannot count on this size of bank to make long-term real estate loans but you have a real opportunity to develop a "line of credit" relationship that will allow you to take advantage of good deals. If you haven't visited with the president of a small bank, you might be missing an excellent opportunity.

Do You Know Your Bank Manager?

In my opinion, the most important person in any bank is the bank manager. No matter what size the bank, the manager is the key. The bank manager, after all, is held responsible for everything and anything that goes on in his operation. If his unit is profitable and growing he will receive his 10% raise and a pat on the back. If, on the other hand, his unit is unprofitable or has unusual problems, he might just receive a pat on the posterior and a fond fairwell. By the time a person reaches the level of bank manager he has at least demonstrated an ability to make certain decisions or the bank is desperate for a warm body to fill a vacancy. Managers of small branch banking units are normally less experienced and less capable than those who are entrusted with the larger branch units. My advice: Concentrate on getting to know managers of larger banking units.

The loan officer who works for the bank manager is typically a nice guy who may or may not be on his way up. He is typically given a "controlled" level of authority, depending on the trust his manager has in his abilities. By "controlled" I am referring to the fact that it is typical for the bank manager to allocate only a limited amount of lending and decision-making authority to those who work for him. Bank loan officers are not typically gauged by how much business they develop or how many loans they put on the books, so what do they care if your loan is approved? Please understand also that most loan officers must obtain the branch/bank manager's approval for all loans anyway. The point is simple: Who do you think has more to gain by aggressively seeking loans? And who really has the authority to make loan decisions? Obviously the answer is the bank manager. If you are ill, you want to see the doctor, not the nurse. So it is with banking. If you need money, go to the decision maker. Build your foundation with him rather than his "second" man. It is true that developing a relationship with a bank manager is not all that easy but being patient will pay dividends. Remember, cut out the middle man.

How do you get to know your bank manager? There are a number of excellent ways, let me list a few for your consideration: (1) Marry his sister. (2) Join a local civic club such as the Chamber of Commerce, Rotary, etc. I have found that bankers tend to dominate such organizations. It's just a matter of finding out which they prefer. (3) Move next door to him. (4) Make it a point to introduce yourself when you are in the bank. Invite him to visit your business and then make certain he does. From then on make certain you speak to him whenever you are in the bank. Get his advice (even though you probably know more than he does) on interest rates, the future of real estate, and the local sports team. (5) Borrow some money from him. And, (6) Be certain to pay him back.

It is important to have a plan and then work your plan. When you approach your banker for a loan, make certain you know what you want, how you plan to use the proceeds and provide more than one source of repayment. Make the banker feel that you know what you are doing.

How Do You Feel About Your Bank?

It is only natural to feel a certain amount of anticipation about your bank. This anticipation is due basically to a lack of understanding about banking. It's one thing to cash a check and chat with the tellers but it's another thing to approach a banker with a loan request. Too many people have approached a banker for a loan only to be turned down — not because the request was bad in principle, but because the banker asked too many questions that could not be answered properly. Most people fear being questioned about their proposal. The simple solution is to be properly prepared with the right answers. If you are confident in your presentation, then you have nothing to fear.

Remember, banks are businesses, just like you. They love to make money, just like you. But they hate to lose money, just like you. They are there to make loans since most of their profit comes from lending money. The more money they can lend, the more profit they can make. Banks who fail to loan out their money are doomed to failure. On the other hand, those banks who make too many bad loans are also doomed.

When you approach a bank for a loan you need to understand that they want to do business with you. They would like to lend you money. Once you develop a positive attitude about the purpose of banks and the pressure on bankers to make loans, you will then be in a position to obtain funding for your projects.

Summary

If you want to win with banks, you have to develop a firm foundation from which to operate. Pick your bank carefully and understand what they can or cannot do for you. Gain the confidence and trust of the bank manager. And, feel good about your banking relationship. For the person of "limited capital tolerance" you must work a plan and then make it work. Money is available. Why not make your fortune by using the bank's money?

How to Communicate
With Your Banker

Don Tauscher

Communicating with bankers is an art, to say the least. Most of the difficulty lies in that the banker does not understand our business, and, by the same token, neither do we understand his. If our specialty is creative real estate, we automatically have two strikes against us. More than likely, the only real estate person your banker ever came in contact with *personally* was the "jungle fighter" who sold him his home. The banker relates to that real estate person much the same way he relates to the used-car salesman. "Respect" and "credibility" are only words in the dictionary that describe doctors, lawyers, and bankers. Let's face it — 95 percent of the real estate persons have the image of the machete-swinging, throat-slashing jungle fighter. You may have seen in your newspaper some time back the result of a nationwide poll asking public opinion of respected professions. The real estate salesperson ranked third from last, edging out used car salesmen and politicians. Is it any wonder our banking relationship begins from behind the eight ball?

To get out of the 95 percent hat of disrespect and into the five percent hat of credibility takes time and patience — together with a deliberate effort to better educate the banker and ourselves in each other's ways. If our way is creative real estate, the chore of educating the banker is that much more difficult. He simply does not understand. His educational system teaches only cash, marketable securities, and short-term *first* mortgages. It's almost impossible to understand and appreciate someone else's blisters if you haven't walked in their shoes.

One area of communication that the real estate person (the 95 percenter) fails miserably in is at the time of the loan interview. At that meeting, we are explaining what we want the money for and how we are going to repay it. It is said that in a normal business conference only ten percent of what is heard is retained. Compound that by the fact that the banker probably had about twenty similar conferences that day and you have a situation where all the loan requests are run-of-the-mill, average, and routinely handled — unless one is different (a five percenter).

I would suggest that you handle your loan request differently from the 95 percent. The following steps may help:

1. Write a cover letter explaining everything you want to convey at the interview — specifically itemizing:
    a. How much money you want to borrow.
    b. How long you want it for.
    c. What you want it for.
    d. How you will repay it.
    e. Alternate source of repayment (this one the 95 percent overlook!)
    How will you repay the loan when due — if your primary source fails?

2. Attach *readable* copies of whatever pertains to your specific request — financial statements, tax return, appraisals, etc.

3. Set your interview appointment at least one week prior to the meeting of the bank's loan committee. (The 95 percent come in the day they need the money!)

4. Ask yourself if you would make the loan if you were in the banker's shoes. Ask yourself: "What are the negatives in my request?" Have answers for all your questions!

5. Reveal any pending or upcoming situations that could affect your financial condition — such as estate settlements, divorce, suits, etc. Bankers also dread surprises.

Communication is only one important area within the cultivation of a personal banking relationship and the loan interview/application is an important part of the communication process. It is a step in the right direction, perhaps enabling you to borrow money when others cannot.

The art of communication that is most difficult however, is that of educating your banker to the ways and means of the creative real estate marketplace.

A few pointers that might assist are:

1. Submit frequent financial statements — semi-annual if possible.
2. Occasionally mail your banker articles on creative real estate, underlining key points that might relate to your current situation.
3. A monthly luncheon wherein you would update each other — your specialties and his — (sharing a creative formula at this time is most

beneficial).

4. Advise your banker of creative real estate seminars as they come into the area.

5. Invite him to a marketing session once a year.

There are only a few suggestions and while they may not have any direct benefit, you are establishing the fact that you are different from the 95 percent.

Once the banker has a basic understanding of creative real estate, give him real world examples of completed transactions — preferably yours! Over a period of time, he will become a believer in you, giving you credibility — a *rarity* for the real estate person.

When your relationship is *well* established, *and only then*, creative financing techniques and formulas for banking your know-how will be favorably considered.

Try this one *if* you have such a credible relationship: **Tauscher's Anti-Recession Formula:**

Situation: Money is tight and expensive. Buyers are scarce and normal sources of income are minimal. You've established a secured line of credit with your bank that you can rely on when *you* need it. The bank has a first mortgage lending policy as follows: 75 percent of appraised value, five-year term (balloons okay), and a current interest rate. You ask them a key question: "Suppose I already owned a first mortgage that met all your criteria, why couldn't you loan me 100 percent of face value (or current balance)?" Their answer has to be "Yes, we can!" — providing the criteria is the same as a direct loan on real estate.

Example: You find a $20,000 (current balance) first mortgage in the creative marketplace that you can buy for $15,000. It pays out in five years, the real estate securing the mortgage is worth $30,000, and the interest rate is 12 percent. Under your line of credit, you borrow the full current value of $20,000, buy the mortgage with $15,000, and pocket the spread — $5,000. Of course, if the bank rate is higher than 12 percent, you will have to adjust the spread to compensate. The mortgage you buy is hypothecated as security under your line of credit.

The bank's security is threefold:

1. They have you on a note (already acceptable and approved under your line of credit).

2. The person making the payments on the mortgage you purchased.

3. The real estate itself.

Conclusions:
1. You've made $5,000 ± in a tight real estate market.
2. The bank is amply secured and have made a good loan.
3. The worse the money market is, the more opportunity you have.
4. The worse the real estate market is, the more opportunity you have.
5. The process is worth repeating to the extent of your line of credit.

In summary, and worth repeating, is that your ability to bank creative real estate transactions is directly related to, and dependent upon, your credibility with the bank. Borrowing money when others cannot could be your key to survival — it is certainly a key to growth in creative real estate.

Questions and Answers on Dealing With the Professionals

Richard J. Allen

Question:

"How do I get the seller or Realtor to accept a promissory note as my earnest money deposit?"
R.B., Chicago, Ill.

Answer:

When using a promissory note, you have not actually paid but have just agreed to promise to pay a specified amount during a limited time. A broker-Realtor cannot reject a promissory note as it is required that he present all offers. A seller can, however, reject the note. But if he is a "hardened" don't wanter, or very flexible, he shouldn't care anyway.

In order to use a promissory note successfully, you may have to sweeten it up some way. Try offering more in a note than you would if it was cash. For example, offer a $500 note where if it was cash you would only offer $100. Another method might be to say in the offer that you will make the note negotiable upon acceptance of the offer or at closing.

If you are using the shotgun approach and writing and presenting many offers, the promissory note as an instrument for your down payment could make things much simpler for you. One other thing might help and that would be to use a typewriter when filling out a promissory note rather than doing a handwritten one. It lends to greater credibility with the seller and looks much more professional. For further reference see *How To Write a Nothing Down Offer.*

Question:

"I am negotiating on a house with a Realtor who is also the seller's agent.

Am I wise to do this or will it be difficult to get my terms accepted?"
T.F., Miami, FL

Answer:

According to current practice in the real estate industry, the agent represents the party paying the tab; i.e., the seller. Even where there are two agents involved (the listing agent and the selling agent who brings you the opportunity), they are both paid out of commissions paid by the seller.

Who represents the buyer? Actually *no one!* The agents involved have the obligation to bring to light for the buyer any aspects of an arrangement that are in violation of the law, of course; however, the agent represents primarily the interests of the seller. What can be done for the poor old buyer? *Caveat emptor!* The buyer always has the option of hiring a consultant from the real estate industry on an hourly basis or entering into a buyer's broker arrangement with an agent (where the buyer himself pays the commission).

Question

"We have been trying to put a transaction together involving an FHA repossession. It is a small apartment complex. We have worked out the details with HUD, but are having a problem with our lender. At first, everything was fine. We paid our appraisal and application fees. They said there would be no problem. Now there has been a series of un-returned calls and vague answers. What should we do?"
S.V., Oklahoma City

Answer:

Any good lender must provide quality service or they will not be in business too long, especially in this market. There is a definite possibility that you could lose the repo if you don't get the loan in a prudent time period. You should meet with the lender face-to-face as quickly as possible. If they are going to produce, the details must be worked out and finalized. If they are not, you need to find out immediately so you can find another lender. It is better to lose a few dollars on upfront fees than to lose an excellent investment.

Question:

"What do you do when the real estate agent refuses to present your creative offers?"
R.D., Nashville

Answer:

This is a crucial problem throughout the country. Unfortunately, not all real estate agents are fully informed concerning alternative financing possibilities. The term "creative finance" can come to have a negative connotation in areas where a few unscrupulous investors have managed to catch the public eye with shady con-artist deals where sellers have been left holding the bag. Not everyone realizes that "creative finance" is a problem-solving approach where all parties can win, including the agent. This is especially true of the agent who hears "nothing down" and sees his commission going out the window. He doesn't realize that "nothing down" does not imply the absence of cash, but only a different source of cash.

Therefore, the buyer who runs into an agent roadblock should consider one or more of the following strategies: If a "buyer's broker" is the problem, he should be replaced quickly. If the selling or listing broker (agent) is the problem, you have an educational challenge on your hands. Explain how your approach will be win/win for all parties concerned. Show how you can solve problems to the benefit of everyone. Explain that fully 60% of real estate transactions currently involve some aspects of creative finance. Build trust with the agents. Your goal is to meet with the seller personally (accompanied by the agents, of course) in order to explain your program.

If that does not work, remind the agent that his professional code of ethics requires him to present all offers. You might write out the following passage from the Realtor's code of ethics and show it to the agent:

The Realtor shall receive and shall transmit all offers on a specified property to the owner for his decision, whether such offers are received from a prospective purchaser or another broker.

The Realtor, acting as listing broker, shall submit all offers to the seller as quickly as possible.
(Standards of Practice, 7-1 and 7-2.)

If you feel you cannot achieve the cooperation of the agent in gentle ways, you might explain that you are certain your offer is sound and that you are now prepared to lodge a complaint with the Board of Realtors or with the State Department of Real Estate (whatever is most appropriate for your area). You have the right, of course, to approach the seller "person to person" in order to make your case known. The goal is not to circumvent the agent, but to solve problems.

If all else fails, you can always find another property, especially in a buyer's market. Look especially for properties that are free and clear or with low mortgages. Such properties often can be "cranked" in order to generate sufficient funds for commissions and other costs. Look also for properties with mortgages that have been sold to Fannie Mae—then take advantage of the FNMA refinance program to raise the necessary funds. If your area is particularly conservative, look for the For Sale By Owner (FSBO) opportunities where no Realtor is involved.

Finally, do your homework in lining up partners who have cash to invest but little time or expertise in creative acquisitions. Then tell the Realtor up front, "Your commission will be taken care of through the cash down payment." That's music to a Realtor's ears! Above all, don't give up! The creative individual will find a way to achieve his or her goals!

Question:

"Is it a good idea to use a buyer's broker in purchasing property? How does one go about setting up such an arrangement?"

S.S., Provo, Utah

Answer:

The conventional approach in the real estate industry throughout the country today is based on a system where the agent supposedly represents both buyer and seller equally. However, this approach has a built-in conflict of interest. The listing agent is hired by the seller. The selling agent working closely with the buyer is also supported out of commissions paid by the seller (even though the money is paid into the transaction by the buyer). Who, therefore, represents the buyer? The answer is "no one." Neither listing agent nor selling agent may act against the interests of the seller.

Under such an arrangement, the buyer has only two options. He may decide to proceed without representation. In such a case, all agents involved must, of course, be honest with him and disclose to him any detrimental factors involved in the deal or the property involved; however, they are under no obligation to reveal to him confidential information shared with them by the seller concerning the latter's flexibility.

The second option for the buyer under the prevailing system is to hire his own agent. He might elect to hire someone on an hourly consulting basis to review the details of a transaction. Alternately, he might elect to hire the agent on a commission basis to oversee the entire deal. In either case, the agent is acting only in behalf of the buyer. He is paid by the buyer and represents only the interests of the buyer. There is no conflict of interest. The "buyer's broker" or "buyer's agent" now has the assignment to go out and locate the appropriate properties for his client, whether or not the properties are listed. Even though this system has not yet caught on in the United States, the advantages for creative buyers are apparent: needs being precisely met, clear lines of responsibility and agency, and added efficiency in the finding and negotiating process. A creative buyer and a compatible, well-trained buyer's broker constitute a formidable team for effective investments.

PART X:

Creative Follow-Through: Now That You've Got It, What Do You Do With It?

1. BASIC TAX PLANNING

Your Best Partner: Uncle Sam

Richard J. Allen

By now most investors are familiar with the new "Accelerated Cost Recovery System" and the greater tax savings it provides for real estate investors.

Let's walk through an illustration and see how the details pencil out. Suppose you bought a five-unit building on January 1, 1984, for $100,000 with $10,000 down (value of the building alone is $80,000).

And let's say the operating situation is as follows:

Net Operating Income	$9,750
Annual Debt Service	9,060*
Cash Flow	$ 690

*(including $1,004 loan reduction)

You want to calculate your rate of return for the first year, including the tax advantages under the new IRS depreciation schedule. Here's how you do it, based on the four areas of income, depreciation, equity buildup, and appreciation:

A. Income (cash flow) —

Cash flow	$ 690
Down Payment	$10,000
	6.9% return

B. Depreciaton (tax savings)—

Under the Economic Recovery Tax Act of 1981, 15-year accelerated cost recovery is now allowed for properties placed in service beginning in 1981.

(One also has the option of using 15-, 35-, or 45-year straight-line depreciation.) This example shows how the "Accelerated Cost Recovery System" works for the first year of ownership, assuming a full-year's recovery. The IRS specifies the percentages of recovery to use for the various years of recovery, depending on the month when the property was placed in service. The following IRS chart shows the prescribed depreciation percentages (recovery) for the first four years of ownership. Your tax accountant can fill you in on all of the details. Note: for properties placed in service after March 15, 1984, use current IRS guidelines.

15-YEAR REAL PROPERTY TABLE
(Other than Low-Income Housing)

Mo. Placed in Service	1st	2nd	3rd	4th
1	12%	10%	9%	8%
2	11%	10%	9%	8%
3	10%	11%	9%	8%
4	9%	11%	9%	8%
5	8%	11%	10%	8%
6	7%	11%	10%	8%
7	6%	11%	10%	9%
8	5%	11%	10%	9%
9	4%	11%	10%	9%
10	3%	11%	10%	9%
11	2%	11%	10%	9%
12	1%	12%	10%	9%

* Table valid for properties placed in service between January 1, 1981 and March 15, 1984.

In our example,

$$\text{Cost recovery} = \text{value of building without land} \times \text{IRS recovery \%}$$
$$= \$80,000 \times 12\%$$
$$= \$9,600$$

$$\text{Tax loss} = \text{cost recovery minus cash flow and loan reduction}$$
$$= \$9,600 - \$690 - \$1,004$$
$$= \$7,906 \text{ (first year)}$$

$$\text{Tax savings} = \frac{\text{Tax loss} \times \text{Tax Rate}}{\text{Down payment}}$$

$$= \frac{\$7,906 \times 0.30*}{\$10,000}$$

$$= 23.72\% \text{ return } *(\text{assuming a 30\% tax bracket})$$

C. Equity buildup —

$$\frac{\text{Loan reduction}}{\text{Down payment}} = \frac{\$\ 1{,}004}{\$10{,}000}$$

$$= 10.04\% \text{ return}$$

D. Appreciation —

$$\frac{\text{Building cost} \times \text{Appreciation rate}}{\text{Down payment}}$$

$$= \frac{\$100{,}000}{\$\ 10{,}000} \times 10\%$$

$$= 100\% \text{ return}$$

Total Rate of Return from Investment in First Year:

I = Income (cash flow)
D = Depreciation (tax savings)
E = Equity buildup
A = Appreciation

	With Leverage	Without Leverage
I	6.90%	9.75%[1]
D	23.72%	−0.45%[2]
E	10.04%	0
A	100.00%	10.00%
Total Return	140.66%	19.30%

[1](based on NOI)

$$[2]\frac{[(9600 - 9750) \times 0.30]}{10{,}000}$$

Based on the old way of figuring depreciation (assuming a 20-year life for the building), the rate of return from tax savings would be only 6.92%. The new "Accelerated Cost Recovery System" increases this to 23.72%, making Uncle Sam a rather good partner! As noted, your total rate of return, using the new system, is 140.66% the first year. Without leverage (if you paid $100,000 cash for the same property), the return is only 19.30%.

From our perspective, the Economic Recovery Tax Act of 1981 is the greatest thing to happen for real estate in many a year. The expert in leverage acquisitions should take full advantage of it, especially during a buyer's market.

Tax Advantages of Selling on Contract

Wade B. Cook

All through my book *How to Build a Real Estate Money Machine* I mention the tax advantages of selling on contract. When I started using this approach, saving on taxes wasn't one of my major considerations, but after setting up several good contracts, I began questioning the method I was using to claim profits. I knew I would have to claim the profits, but since I wasn't receiving that whole amount at one time, how would I know what to pay?

About this time my accountant was reviewing my financial situation. "You really like this, don't you?" he said. "You get to buy a lot of properties and create these great contracts, and you get your money back and turn it over so you can do it again— not to mention these net monthy payments." My answer o his question was, "Yes," but it became an emphatic "YES!" when he said, "Wait until you see the tax advantages you'll receive for doing it this way." I wanted to shield as much as I could from the IRS, but I didn't think it was going to be this good.

The best way to explain these advantages and have it easily understood is to go through the details in question and answer form. The following are typical questions asked in my seminars, augmented by some of my own to help clarify a few points.

What is an installment sale?

The sale of real property priced over $1,000 where payments are made in two or more years.

Can I receive more than 30% of the sales price as a down payment and still qualify for these tax advantages?

Yes. The law has been changed so that now the seller can receive any amount as the down payment and still qualify.

Why is claiming my profits this way such an advantage?

Because it lets you spread the payment of your taxes out over the entire length of the contract.

But how do I know how much to claim?

On any sale that qualifies for installment sale consideration you claim only the portion of any principal payment received which represents profit.

That sounds exciting. Tell me how much I will have to claim this year on the following sale. I purchased a house for $30,000 (nothing down) and put $3,000 into fixing it up. My selling expenses came to $2,000. I sold it for $50,000 with $5,000 down. I received payments of $450 for 12 months of which the principal portion totaled $1,000 for the year.

You will pay that portion of the $6,000 ($5,000 down payment plus $1,000 monthly principal payments) which represents profit. (See the sample Form 6252.)

Form **6252**	**Computation of Installment Sale Income**	OMB No. 1545-0228
Department of the Treasury Internal Revenue Service	▶ See instructions on back. ▶ Attach to your tax return. Use a separate form for each sale or other disposition of property on the installment method.	**1982** 81

Name(s) as shown on tax return — Identifying number: 123-45-678

A Kind of property and description ▶ Single Family Residence
B Date acquired (month, day, and year) ▶ 3-12-80 C Date sold (month, day, and year) ▶ 4-5-81
D Was property sold to a related party after May 14, 1980? (See instruction C) . . . ☐ Yes ☒ No
E If the answer to D is "Yes", was the property a marketable security? . . . ☐ Yes ☐ No
If you checked "Yes" to question E, you must complete Part III.
If you checked "No" to question E, complete Part III for 2 years after the year of sale.

Part I Computation of Gross Profit and Contract Price (Complete this part for year of sale only.)

1 Selling price including mortgages and other indebtedness (Do not include interest whether stated or unstated)	1	50,000 00
2 Mortgages and other indebtedness buyer assumes or takes property subject to (see instructions)	2	36,000 00
3 Subtract line 2 from line 1	3	14,000 00
4 Cost or other basis of property sold	4	33,000 00
5 Depreciation allowed or allowable	5	-0-
6 Adjusted basis (subtract line 5 from line 4)	6	33,000 00
7 Commissions and other expenses of sale	7	2,000 00
8 Add line 6 and line 7	8	35,000 00
9 Subtract line 8 from line 1. If result is zero or less, do not complete rest of form	9	15,000 00
10 If question A is principal residence, enter the sum of Form 2119, lines 12, 15, and 19	10	-0-
11 Gross profit (subtract line 10 from line 9)	11	15,000 00
12 Subtract line 8 from line 2. If line 8 is more than line 2, enter zero	12	1,000 00
13 Contract price (add line 3 and line 12)	13	15,000 00

Part II Computation of Taxable Part of Installment Sale (Complete this part for year of sale and any year you receive a payment.)

14 Gross profit ratio (divide line 11 by line 13) (for years after the year of sale, see instructions)	14	100%
15 For year of sale only—enter amount from line 12 above; otherwise enter zero	15	1,000 00
16 Payments received during year (Do not include interest whether stated or unstated)	16	5,200 00
17 Add lines 15 and 16	17	6,200 00
18 Payments received in prior years (Do not include interest whether stated or unstated)	18	-0-
19 Taxable part of installment sale (multiply line 17 by line 14)	19	6,200 00
20 Part of line 19 that is ordinary income under recapture rules	20	-0-
21 Subtract line 20 from line 19. Enter on Schedule D or Form 4797	21	6,200 00

But won't I have to claim my entire $15,000 profit?

Yes, but over the entire course of the loan.

How do I figure that?

The easiest way to figure it is to use the IRS Form 6252. (See sample.) In this case, your profit on the house is $15,000. You divide that profit by the contract price of $50,000 and you will get the ratio to use when figuring how much to claim. $15,000 divided by $50,000 equals 0.3 or 30%. This year you will claim 30% of the $6,000 that you received. (You claim only $1,800.)

Do you mean that I was able to recover my invested money, create a $17,000 equity contract netting $170 per month (12 x $170 = $2,040 each year) and all I have to claim is $1,800?

Yes.

What about next year?

That 30% ratio will continue for the length of the loan. Let's assume that the portion of the monthly payments which is principal totals $1,200 next year. You then would claim 30% of that, or $400.

Are there ways that I could avoid claiming even these modest amounts?

Yes, even though you'll have to claim it, there are ways to shelter it. In chapter 13 of my book we go over rental units and long-term capital gains. I'll let my explanation there answer the question.

Where do I put this on my tax forms?

Come up with the figure each year on Form 6252 and transfer that amount to Schedule D.

Schedule D—isn't that the form for Capital Gains?

That's right. This transaction could also qualify for long-term capital gains, which means that if you held this property for over one year, you would have to claim only 40% of the gain. Back to your example. This year you would have to claim only 40% of the $1,800 or $720!

What happens if my buyer makes additional principal payments?

Those payments are treated just like regular payments. The portion representing profit is claimed.

I've just figured the ratio on the sale of a house and it involves a lot of numbers after the decimal point. How many of these numbers should I use?

Seven or eight. That might seem strange, but in order to get the figures on lines 21 through 24 to add up correctly, you'll need them all.

When I sold my house I maintained the underlying mortgage. A friend said my profit was the difference between my payment coming in and my payment going out. Is this true?

No. The amount of the monthly payments coming in and going out has nothing to do with the profit of this transaction. They also have nothing to do with the ratio. These amounts (profits and ratio) need to be calculated according to the simple way explained on Form 6252.

But is the interest paid out deductible? And doesn't the interest received have to be claimed?

Interest is interest and has nothing to do with capital gains. Interest income is treated as ordinary income and must be claimed. (The amount goes on the front page of your 1040.) The interest expense can be a deduction and is reported on your Schedule A.

What about the amount of principal coming off the underlying loan?

It has no tax bearing.

What can I do if I have claimed some depreciation expense already?

That amount would be subtracted from your cost basis. You won't be able to claim it twice. (See lines 5 and 6 of Form 6252.) One additional note: Take all the depreciation expense you can. Being able to reclaim it here— especially if long-term—is a great way to avoid paying taxes.

I bought a property and refinanced it. When I sold it, my cost basis was $33,000. The amount of the refinance loan was $36,000. I did this to free up some cash. then when I sold it I let my buyer assume the loan and pay me my equity on a second note. What do I claim now?

Like the previous example, you'll have to figure your profit ratio and apply it to any principal payments received. But in this case you will also have to figure in the amount by which the assumed loan is greater than your cost basis. In this instance it will be $3,000 ($36,000 assumed loan and $33,000 cost basis).

How can I avoid having to claim this?

Don't let your buyer assume it. Carry a wrap-around contract for the entire amount. (Note: Line 10 of Form 6252 takes for granted that the buyer assumes the underlying mortgage(s). If this is not the case, write in "mortgage not assumed.")

Can you give an example of a transaction where more than a 30% down payment was received?

Yes. See the second example of IRS Form 6252 on the next page.

Form **6252**	**Computation of Installment Sale Income**	OMB No. 1545-0228
Department of the Treasury Internal Revenue Service	▶ **See instructions on back.** ▶ **Attach to your tax return.** Use a separate form for each sale or other disposition of property on the installment method.	19**82** 81

Name(s) as shown on tax return	Identifying number 123-45-6789

A Kind of property and description ▶ .... Duplex
B Date acquired (month, day, and year) ▶ 3-12-80   **C** Date sold (month, day, and year) ▶ 4-5-81
D Was property sold to a related party after May 14, 1980? (See instruction C) . . . . ☐ Yes ☒ No
E If the answer to D is "Yes", was the property a marketable security? . . . . ☐ Yes ☐ No
  If you checked "Yes" to question E, you must complete Part III.
  If you checked "No" to question E, complete Part III for 2 years after the year of sale.

Part I   Computation of Gross Profit and Contract Price *(Complete this part for year of sale only.)*

1 Selling price including mortgages and other indebtedness (Do not include interest whether stated or unstated) . . .			1	50,000 00
2 Mortgages and other indebtedness buyer assumes or takes property subject to (see instructions)	2	36,000 00		
3 Subtract line 2 from line 1	3	14,000 00		
4 Cost or other basis of property sold	4	37,000 00		
5 Depreciation allowed or allowable	5	-0-		
6 Adjusted basis (subtract line 5 from line 4)	6	37,000 00		
7 Commissions and other expenses of sale	7	2,000 00		
8 Add line 6 and line 7			8	39,000 00
9 Subtract line 8 from line 1. If result is zero or less, do not complete rest of form			9	11,000 00
10 If question A is principal residence, enter the sum of Form 2119, lines 12, 15, and 19			10	-0-
11 Gross profit (subtract line 10 from line 9)			11	11,000 00
12 Subtract line 8 from line 2. If line 8 is more than line 2, enter zero			12	
13 Contract price (add line 3 and line 12)			13	14,000 00

Part II   Computation of Taxable Part of Installment Sale *(Complete this part for year of sale and any year you receive a payment.)*

14 Gross profit ratio (divide line 11 by line 13) (for years after the year of sale, see instructions) . . .			14	.785714-2
15 For year of sale only—enter amount from line 12 above; otherwise enter zero			15	-0-
16 Payments received during year (Do not include interest whether stated or unstated)			16	5,200 00
17 Add lines 15 and 16			17	5,200 00
18 Payments received in prior years (Do not include interest whether stated or unstated)	18	-0-		
19 Taxable part of installment sale (multiply line 17 by line 14)			19	4,085 71
20 Part of line 19 that is ordinary income under recapture rules			20	-0-
21 Subtract line 20 from line 19. Enter on Schedule D or Form 4797			21	4,085 71

What happens if a subsequent buyer cashes me out?

Your ratio has been established. Basically all your profits at that percentage would then be claimed.

What happens if I use my contract equity for a trade?

It is added to the cost basis of your new property no matter what ratio it is traded at. For example, your seller may give you only 70% of the contract value.

How do I claim my profit if I buy a contract? I purchased a $10,000 mortgage for $6,000.

You figure this the same way as before. You divide your profit by the contract amount. $4,000 divided by $10,000 equals 0.04 or 40%—Forty percent of all *principal* payments will be claimed as they are received.

A man owed me $5,500 and couldn't pay. I agreed to take a $10,000 real estate contract as payment in full. Do I have to claim the entire amount?

No. Your cost basis is $5,500. Just like in the last question, you figure your ratio: profit equals $4,500 divided by the contract amount of $10,000 which is 0.45 or 45%. Forty-five percent of each principal payment would be considered profit. (Note: If the $5,500 represented some sort of payment for goods or services — meaning that it wasn't a loan — then your cost basis would be zero and you would have to claim 100% of the principal payments as they are received.)

What if I sell my personal residence on installment sales?

Selling on contract is only one of the tax advantages homeowners have. There are several others. Sit down with a good tax consultant and go over all of your possibilities.

If my buyer doesn't assume my loans and the amount of equity between my receivables and my payables is growing, will I have to pay taxes on the growth?

No. You claim profits according to the computation. Your equity growth has nothing to do with this.

Do I have to use the installment sales method if I sell on contract?

No.

When would it be advisable to claim the entire amount in the year of the sale?

This is hard to answer. I want to say *never,* but I guess there could be a situation for someone, somewhere to claim it all. I've never seen anyone wanting to do it once they have understood the ramifications. Let me explain. Suppose you had a modest income one year and you decide to claim it all right then. Let's look at some things that are pertinent.

1. Let's suppose you claim all the profit that year because it doesn't affect your tax structure too much. But, what would it be like if you claimed only part of it? (In our first example you would be claiming $1,800—if short-term—instead of $15,000.) Could you get refunds (minimize the tax due in other years) with income averaging back four years and ahead two?

2. When you claim your profit five, ten, and fifteen years down the road, you'll be paying your taxes with inflated dollars. Why pay with current dollars when it can be spread out?

3. What happens if you have to foreclose on your buyer a few years from now? You've already claimed your profit so now you'll have to back up, figure the new value basis, etc., and do a nice song-and-dance routine to get your money back.

Conclusion

How can I benefit from this way of claiming my profit?

There are several answers to this, but they all center on controlling your money. This tax computation allows you to turn large quantities of property and pay very little taxes as you go. It allows you to keep your money free and clear and keep it moving. The installment sales method lets an investor be just that—an investor—and not have to feel like he is working for the IRS.

You May Not Know How Successful You've Become, But the IRS Does

Wade B. Cook

Investing is sometimes the master game—especially when it comes to taxes. Like the game "Monopoly," the goal is to control as much as possible. The easiest way to stockpile your fortune is to *preserve* as many of your assets as possible. Why? Because assets, in fact, pad your tomorrows. Asset accumulation is the reason we're out here working so hard Who, then, should control them? The answer is *you*. The IRS does not play games. On the contrary—it is all too real. The IRS plays tough and plays for keeps. The following is a list of "pointers" to help your short- and long-term tax planning. It is given as a general guideline for preserving and protecting your cash, your equities, and your growth.

Current Tax Planning

The main emphasis here is to pay as little as you can and to *pay as you go*. Keep yourself knowledgeable on the following:
1. Installment sales.
2. All forms of depreciation expense.
3. Whether you're an investor or a dealer.
4. Rental records.
5. Capital gains—time periods and amounts.
6. Proper record-keeping.
7. Anything else that will help you defer current taxes.

Intermediate Tax Planning

The main emphasis here is to build something that will do more than "maintain." The following points should be understood:
1. You should understand how one year's taxes affect others.
2. Should you incorporate and get the tax advantages of pension and profit-

sharing plans?

3. Learn how to create a large monthly income which is sheltered by tax deductions.

4. Fine tune your working knowledge of "deductions and credits."

Long-Term Tax Status

Your "chips" are yours to have and to hold. What happens when you want to slow down or when you're not around?

1. Know your state laws governing how property is held. Is it held as "tenants in common," where your portion goes to your spouse, or is it "joint tenancy," where your portion goes to your estate? Know your options in these cases and choose whatever will be most beneficial in your estate planning.

2. Is your life insurance ample to cover:

a. Your present standard of living for your family?

b. Any estate taxes that will be due?

c. Any debts that you handle in your ordinary course of business, but which would be cumbersome to your dependents?

3. Is your life insurance owned by the right person?

4. Is there any group of receivable payments that will come due (balloon notes, etc.) which might cause hardship? Conversely, are your monthly or yearly receivables spread out so your tax burden is lightened?

All time frames of investing are important. It's impossible to do something today that has no effect on tomorrow. Because of this, it is important to stay ahead by knowing where you're heading.

Asking the right questions is sometimes more advantageous than having the right answers. Surround yourself with professional people and functional reference books to ensure that the right questions are asked. Then, your time will be free to prepare your investments to gain optimum tax advantages, today and years from now.

How To Buy Nothing-Down Tax Benefits

There has been much written on the difference between benefits and features. In order to understand the goal of this article, though, I'll need to cover the basics, and then the difference between a tax liability, a tax deduction, and a tax benefit will be clear. Ultimately we're after tax benefits. Let's see how they come about.

The main difference between a feature and a benefit is that a feature remains with a product whether you buy it or not. A benefit is derived only by buying and using something. A feature is the good engine in a car. A benefit is the gas savings the good engine produces.

In taxation, a feature is a depreciation expense, for example, but a benefit is the money saved because of the ability to claim the expense—money that can actually be spent on something else.

All tax deductions are the parents of benefits. For instance, let's say that Mr. Adams has an income of $30,000, producing a tax liability of $5,281. He will be paying this money to the IRS *unless* he can find tax deduction which will adjust his $30,000 income. For the sake of the example, let's find him $5,000 in tax deductions. Now his adjusted gross income (AGI) is $25,000. His taxes now are $3,784. This $5,000 in expenses just bought him $1,497 in cash.

You might think that is not very much, but look at what happens if the deductions totaled $10,000. His AGI is $20,000 and his taxes are $2,511 or a savings of $2,770.

If we could find Mr. Adams $22,600 in deductions, he wouldn't have to pay any taxes whatsoever.

Are we saying that Mr. Adams needs to spend $22,600 so he won't have to pay taxes? Not at all. Let's go back to the $5,000 in deductions that resulted in a tax savings of $1,497.

The question that needs asking here is how much is this $5,000 tax deduction? If it costs $5,000, then we might as well consign ourselves to a life of hopelessness, send all the tax consultants home, and let the IRS have a heyday. But what if we can get this deduction for less than the actual tax savings?

The actual cost, then, of the savings (benefits) is offset by the cost of obtaining them. But wait! Is that all? Might not there be other benefits? The answer is a resounding "yes!".

● What if the property that we purchased to buy the benefits actually makes us a profit—more spendable cash?

● What if the property grows in value so that whenever we go to sell it we make more profit—to spend or buy more tax benefits?

● *And what if the same deductions that we get this year will continue for the next twenty years with no additional cash outlays?*

Just a small note to exclaim the beauties of real estate: No other form of investment covers all three of these aspects as does Real Property.

Leverage

It is plain to see that the less out-of-pocket money it takes to buy these tax benefits, the more power each of your dollars wields. I'm not going to run up to the nearest oasis and drag some Arabian sheik away from his harem to extol for us the mystery behind wealth, because we all know the importance of productivity. The more we can get each dollar to produce its maximum, the less work we will personally have to do.

With this in mind, we see another great value of investing in real estate. The more leverage we use with our money in buying tax benefits, the more leverage we use to produce the other returns we value so highly: income and equity appreciation. For example, if $1,000 buys $5,000 in tax deductions, could it possibly also buy $50 a month in *income* and $5,000 a year in *equity growth?*

A Dilemma

After talking with so many of you at the Nothing Down seminars, I have found that the following situations are unanimous:
- You want to get ahead and you realize that some sort of equity accumulation will be the only vehicle to get you there.
- You have either quit your job or plan to do so soon.
- You want all the other things in life that real estate can provide.

Now comes the dilemma. It seems that with the increase in activity that produces wealth comes an increase in activity by the IRS to take away our wealth. For those of us that are moving onward and upward, the problem is magnified in that the greater the wealth, the more tax deductions are needed—and needed at a smaller price. The answer is not as hard as it seems. As a matter of fact, our more prosperous sheiks will tell us that the answer lies in more (or greater) leverage. That's why so many of you greatly benefit from the Nothing Down concept—because it is the ultimate in leveraging.

We can look far and wide for definitions of a *tax shelter*, but the answer lies right in the words themselves. Tax shelter is just that. Something that shelters your income from tax liabilities. View it as an umbrella if you will. When you have income you create a shelter to protect it. Almost every real estate investment has a built-in umbrella. All the owner has to do is learn how to open it.

Borrowing Against Your Contracts

Many property sellers who have sold on contract for the purpose of deferring their taxes often find themselves in need of cash. One method of obtaining this cash is to discount and sell their contracts; however, this often creates the same problem that they were trying to avoid—that of receiving too much cash and then having to pay taxes on it.

Another way to get at the money without having tax liabilities is to pledge the contract (or mortgage and note or deed of trust and note) as collateral for a loan.

The only concern is to make sure that the agreement is drawn up to ensure that the contract is not being viewed as sold but merely put up as security for the loan. How do you ensure this? Make sure that the title to the contract remains in your name. One other caution: If the amount of the contract is close to the amount of the loan *and* the payments are made directly to the lending institution, the transaction will probably be deemed a sale. Usually the amounts are different so there is no problem, but even if they are close there could be a problem.

Let's set up a collateral agreement to show how Mr. Smith holds a $20,000 mortgage and note on a property he sold to Mr. Jones. He applies for a loan at his friendly neighborhood bank for $15,000 using the mortgage as security.

Step 1. The assignment (pledge) is accomplished by filling out the bank's assignment papers or security agreements. If you sign a form that will actually be recorded, make sure it states something to this affect: "This assignment is given for collateral purposes only."

Step 2. The bank may want the contract payments coming in to them. Try to set it up so the payments first go into your savings account and then are disbursed to the bank.

The more control you can maintain over the contract, the less likely such an agreement will be deemed a sale.

Dealer Versus Investor

The question often arises as to whether a person is a *dealer* or an *investor*. The answer is important because of the tax consequences.

Tax Consequences

The main tax ramifications of dealer versus investor lie in the treatment of the sale of property. The dealer's proceeds are considered ordinary income while the investor's proceeds are capital gains—thus qualifying for long-term rates. Also, an investor may use the tax advantages of tax-deferred exchange (1031) while the dealer may not. If the distinction is close, the following will help you structure your investing to gain optimum advantages from the tax laws.

Determination of Status

The main factor lies in the purpose for which property is purchased. If the property is purchased "primarily for the sale to customers in the ordinary course of his trade or business"(I.R.C. Sect. 1221(1)), then that person would be considered an investor. Of foremost consideration in determining the purpose for which property is purchased is the frequency of sales—unless the frequency is caused by circumstances beyond the control of the property owner. For example, an investor may have to liquidate several pieces of property because of serious illness. The following list gives other factors to consider.

Dealer

1. Frequent sales.
2. Purchased for resale.
3. The sale of property is the owner's primary source of income.
4. Quick reinvestment of sale proceeds.
5. The property produces no rents.
6. Sale of property after improvements.
7. Sale for receiving appreciated value.

Investor

1. Occasional sales.
2. Purchased for rental income.
3. The sale of the property is only a minor part of the owner's total income.
4. No reinvestment of sale proceeds (at least not immediately).
5. Rents received are substantial.
6. Sale of property without improvements.
7. Sale for liquidation of the investment.

Summary

It is readily apparent that the "intent" of purchasing property in addition to the frequency of "buying and selling" determines whether one will be considered an investor or a dealer. There is no set answer to the question. It is usually answered by a combination of the preceding factors. The bottom line is this: If purchased for resale, the resulting sale is ordinary income; if purchased as a rental, the resulting sale is capital gain.

We are not advocating that you structure your whole investment plan around being considered an investor. Many dealers are very successful, looking for other ways to shelter their income. They wouldn't consider trading the high volume of properties they are turning for just the "capital gain" advantage allowed to an investor. Make sure you weigh your alternatives carefully.

Questions and Answers on Tax Matters

Richard J. Allen

Question

"Our accountant told us that all depreciation taken under the new Accelerated Cost Recovery System is to be recaptured as ordinary income. What advantage is there to using the new system?"
S.T., Seattle

Answer

If you are speaking about residential property, we believe your accountant is in error. Our tax advisor, Paul DeBry of the accounting firm Squire & Co., has researched this important issue for us and provides the following response. Check this out with your tax accountant:

"You asked about the new ACRS rules for cost recovery of property which replaced the old depreciation rules. You asked about the recapture provisions under the new law. There is a difference under the new law in the recapture rules pertaining to real property whether it is "residential" or "non-residential." Gain on the disposition of "residential" property on which accelerated ACRS deductions have been taken is ordinary income to the extent that the ACRS deductions exceed the recovery that would have been allowed if the straight-line method had been used over fifteen years. Therefore, if the straight-line method is elected, all gain is capital gain. If the accelerated ACRS method is elected, then gain to the extent of the difference between the accelerated and straight-line would be ordinary income.

"On non-residential real property under the accelerated method of ACRS all gain on the disposition of such property is ordinary income to the extent of all ACRS deductions. Thus, the recapture is no longer limited on non-residential property to merely the excess of the accelerated over the straight-line depreciation. However, if the straight-line method is elected, all gain is treated as capital gain.

"It would appear, in summary, then, that if a person were to buy residential property, he would not be adversely affected by taking the accelerated method of ACRS. However, that is not the case in non-residential property. If a person buys non-residential property with the view to selling that property withing a few years, it would probably be better for him to elect the straight-line method of deducting the ACRS so that he can get capital gain on the sale. If he is going to hold that non-residential property for a long time, then he might be better off by taking the accelerated ACRS method."

Question

"Can I take a tax deduction for the cost of attending investment seminars?"
K.S., Denver

Answer

We have asked our tax accountant, Paul DeBry of the accounting firm Squire & Co., to research this issue and provide an opinion. Investors will want to confer with their own tax accountant on this issue, but here is what Paul DeBry reported to us:

"There are two possible approaches in order to deduct the expenses of a real estate course. One is an educational expense, and the other one would be as an investment expense. As an educational expense it would be possibly deductible under Section 162 IRC, and as an investment expense under Section 212 IRC. It would appear that there would be no question as to the deductibility of that fee for people who were actively involved in holding property for investment purposes. The question arises as to those who have no investment property and are taking this course in order to become investors in real estate. Under Section 162 IRC, education expenses are deductible if they are to maintain or improve skills in your present occupation, profession, trade or business. If they are preparing you for a new profession, trade or business, the expenses are not deductible. If you are meeting the minimum requirements for a new profession, they are also not deductible. The question, then, is whether you are already involved in a trade or business as an investor in real estate. If so, the expense would be deductible. If not, it would apparently not be deductible.

"The other possibility for deduction involves Section 212 IRC, which deals with investment expenses. The tax court has held that investment advisory expenses are deductible as nonbusiness expenses whether they relate to "existing" investments or to investments "to be made." (Abrams, T.C. Memo 1964-256.) The Court of Claims, however, denied a deduction for the cost of a 'credit rating service' paid for in seeking new investments. The court said that the 'nonbusiness' expense deduction was limited to those relating to 'existing' investments. Here the court relied in part on the regulations for Section 212 IRS (regulation 1.212-1(g)) which states that fees for investment counsel paid by a taxpayer in connection with investments "held" by him are deductible under Section 212 IRS. In this case the court said that the taxpayer had to have counsel relating to investments which were "held" by the taxpayer. Although this may or may not be consistent with Code Section 212, the taxpayer should be aware that this is the position of the Internal Revenue Service, and if the taxpayer does deduct these types of investment expenses, he should expect to have them disallowed by the Internal Revenue Service.

"There are several cases which deny the taxpayer investment expenses connected with investigating prospective businesses. In one case, the court denied a taxpayer a deduction for travel and other expenses incurred in connection with locating and investigating the possibility of purchasing a business. In another case, the court denied expenses incurred in preliminary activities pursuant to the organization of a bank, since the expenses were made in an attempt to obtain income by the creation of a new business. Expenses incurred for engineering and travel while investigating the advisability of purchasing a plant were disallowed because they were only expenses for a preliminary search for a potential business opportunity and were, therefore, not deductible. Travel expenses and legal fees spent in searching for a newspaper business with a view to purchasing it were not deductible as an expense of producing or collecting income because the taxpayer had no existent right or interest in income with respect to which the expenditures were incurred. There is another case where the expenses were disallowed because the taxpayer did not have an existing interest or right in potential future income. Also expenses incurred by a taxpayer in inspecting and evaluating perspective investments with a view toward diversifying his existing investment portfolio were not deductible under Section 212 IRC. Expenses incurred in investigating foreign properties for possible investment were non-deductible in another case. Expenses were not related to the existing property interest of the taxpayer.

"In summary it would appear that those who were not actively involved in real estate investments would probably have a tough time getting a deduction for these expenditures based on the foregoing."

2. PROPERTY AND CASH FLOW MANAGEMENT

I Never Met a Property I Couldn't Manage – It's the People

David A. McDougal

Several years ago I met a real estate broker from Denver who claimed to sell more income properties each year in the city of Denver than all of his competitors combined. He listed all of his competitors in a brochure and no one had challenged him for over five years. His sales office was a converted Safeway store and I had reason to believe he was telling the truth. He was a multi-millionaire in his mid-fifties and he also claimed to have owned more rental properties in the city of Denver than anyone else.

This gentleman was giving a seminar in Salt Lake City, and he had obviously practiced what he taught. He explained that after high school he got a job as a brick mason. After having worked on one project for several months, the builder got into financial difficulty and the bank was repossessing the property. Our friend realized that if he were going to get anything back for the work he'd put in, he'd have to negotiate a deal with the bank. This he did, and several weeks later he was the owner of this apartment building with a large mortgage. That introduced him to the world of real estate. He quickly ran up his fortune and today is a comfortable multi-millionaire.

He made one statement during the seminar that has always stuck with me. He said that it had been his experience that the people who were most successful in investing in real estate were those individuals who knew how to work with people, not those who concentrated on the numbers. As an example, he said that engineers and accountants generally make poor property managers. His experience had taught him that the best property managers were school teachers.

I've thought a great deal about that, and I think he is generally right. I think the number one problem of don't wanters is *management*. It is true that there are those who run into financial difficulty and quickly become don't wanters. But if they understood financing well enough to get into the deal in the first place, they can generally handle the financing later on. The real problem is management. There are many good deals, however financially sound, that people don't want simply because they can't cope with the management. We love to buy real estate, we love to sell or refinance real estate and reap the rewards, but we hate to manage. If we could solve the management problem, we would probably hold our properties much longer, have fewer headaches and be much richer in the long run.

Property managers have never been in a better situation than they are today. If you don't have good tenants, this is the time to get them. This year there will be substantially fewer than one million new housing starts. This has only happened twice in the past twenty years. The vacancy rate across the United States today is less than 6%. Rents are strong because there is such a demand for housing. Because of these market statistics, we are in a position to select our tenants carefully, write strong rental agreements, and place our property management on as close to automatic pilot as possible.

Vince Lombardi maintained that at the beginning of every football season every one of his football players had to go back to basics. Whether his football players were veterans or rookies, they all went through the same fundamentals and reviewed the same program to get back to winning football games. It's the same with whatever we do. Those who practice the basic fundamentals are the most successful. This is especially true with property management. The most important decisions you will ever make in management are your choice of tenants and the agreements that you make with them from the very beginning. After that point, if you have problems, you either didn't follow the fundamentals or you used poor judgment.

Good tenants are so important that I would gladly pick a good tenant over a positive cash flow. In the long run, good tenants will save you money. Bad tenants contribute to late rent payments or no payments at all, maintenance problems—which could be much more expensive and costly than a vacancy itself—and an attitude towards you and your property that could send you to the mental hospital.

Good tenants, on the other hand, lead to prompt payments, low vacancy factors, and better maintenance—which results in higher appreciation. I've always considered vacancy to be the monster of negative cash flow. I also believe that bad tenants can be worse than vacancy.

Bad tenants cause damage to property and contribute to expensive maintenance costs. They are oftentimes difficult to evict and almost impossible to work with. I would almost rather have an empty unit than a bad tenant. At least then your property would not deteriorate as rapidly and you have the immediate opportunity of finding someone—a good tenant—to rent it. In this kind of market, that's an excellent possibility.

If you have a vacancy and are not attracting good potential tenants in this kind of market place, I can only imagine three different problems that could exist. All are violations of the Nothing Down investment philosophy. First, your property is located in a bad neighborhood and a poor location. The rule is: We don't buy properties in those kinds of locations to begin with. Second, your property is in such poor condition that nobody wants to rent it. If that's the case and you bought a property to fix it up, you'd better fix it up if you expect to rent it. There is nothing wrong with a fix-up if you fix it up. If you leave it in bad condition, you are no better off than the don't wanters who sold it to you. The final reason for not attracting good tenants is that your rent is so high that it is above the market price. Perhaps you've increased the rents dramatically to offset negative cash flow, and now your rents are out of line. If that's the case, you'd best be prepared to handle the negative cash flow in other ways.

As I said before, the most important decision you make in good property management is selecting your tenant. The second most important consideration is your agreement with that tenant. Rental laws vary from state to state and different guidelines must be followed. But there are three basic rules I think we sometimes overlook that could really put us into the driver's seat.

Rule Number 1: It's your property and you set the rules. If vacancies were high across the nation, people would have a tendency to jump for the first renters who come along. However, in this kind of market, we can be more selective. If we turn down one potential bad tenant, we probaby won't have to wait any longer than a couple of days for a better one to come along. The rent lost on those two or three days is going to be substantially less than the cost of handling a bad tenant. In this kind of market, the tenants don't set the rules and they don't tell you what they will or will not do. You simply outline the contract, and if it's a win/win offer, you will have plenty of takers. It has been my experience that people are basically good. If given the opportunity and proper motivation, they will respond well, take good care of your property, and be grateful tenants.

Recently one of my tenants brought me the rent in person rather than sending it through the mail. She is always on time with the rent and just wanted to stop by to tell me how much she appreciated living in the home and wanted to assure me that she was taking very good care of it. Everything was in good condition, and she intended to stay there for as long as I owned the property. You would never guess the home that she lives in is a rental unit. She looks and acts like a homeowner because she takes such good care of the lawns and garden. I'm sure the people in her neighborhood think she owns that home.

Rule Number 2: You must spell out what is expected of the tenant in the terms and conditions of the contract. Don't assume anything. What you leave out or omit, tenants will simply decide for themselves. For example, if you say nothing about whether or not they can have pets, they assume it is all right to have pets because there is no specific rule against them. The best management technique you could possibly develop is to have a clear understanding on all matters with your tenants.

The first property I was ever involved in managing was in Hawaii. It was a beautiful home right on the beachfront and was rented by the week as a vacation home. When the first tenants came, the first week I was there, I (being young and inexperienced) was anxious to please them in every way. I checked with them in the morning and I checked with them in the evening to see if there was anything I could possibly do. The home was self-contained and had everything necessary for a comfortable week. But because I was so anxious to help, the people treated it as if it were a hotel. They expected my wife and I to make up the beds, do the linen and provide clean towels every day. At the time, my wife and I both had full-time jobs and were doing this as a part-time project. The rent was low for that kind of rental and the people were expected to provide for themselves during that week. They had their own washer and dryer, and enough towels to survive a month.

After meeting all of their needs and wants for a week, I thought, "There's got to be a better way." Those tenants left well-satisfied, I think, but I was totally exhausted. When the next tenants arrived, I took them into the living room and asked them to be seated. I explained all of the amenities that were on the estate and where the nearby shopping stores were. I explained that this was set up as a vacation for a week and that everything that they needed was supplied right there. If there were any problem or emergencies they were welcome to contact me, but that everything they needed was self-contained within that building.

When these tenants knew they were responsible for their peace and comfort during the week, they were much more careful not to track sand into the home. Instead of wet towels being dropped on the floor, they were carefully hung up so they could dry and be used the next day. The people treated the house as if it were their own and enjoyed themselves because they had so much piravy. I loved it because I didn't have to do anything except clean it after they left. I found it was easier to clean this time than after our previous tenants.

Rule Number 3: The third rule is to stick by your guns. It doesn't do any good to set up the rules according to your standards and to have a mutual agreement with all parties about how it will take place unless you are willing to enforce it and stick by your agreement. This is a two-way street. If you've made commitments to them as a landlord, you should certainly live up to your part of the deal. If they violate conditions of the contract, you should be firm and immediately reach a solution that will be beneficial to both of you. As you become more and more experienced, you will soon recognize those tenants with a sincere problem whom you can work with and those who are taking advantage of you and must be replaced.

Currently, in many areas of the country, property values are temporarily depressed—artificially so—because of high interest rates. The replacement cost for any kind of construction continues to remain high, and therein lies the true value of your real estate property. I continue to be impressed that even though people say real estate prices have leveled off in many areas of the country, that rents continue to grow and climb. This being the case, the simple law of supply and demand will dictate that these properties will grow in value. I think we'll have a major readjustment in the near future when new and different mortgage vehicles enter the marketplace.

If we follow these guidelines and conservative rules, we will do well with our investment portfolio. It's important we always remember the win/win philosophy. If we provide a comfortable place to live at a reasonable rent with good conditions, we ought to expect the very best in tenants. If we fall short in any of those areas, we can't expect the results from our tenants to be any better. It is true that there is a wide range of properties in the rental market. There certainly is a place for a full range of rental housing—from inexpensive to luxury. We ought to be in step with the market and know what it dictates. Even though I am aware that inexpensive, low-income housing must be provided, I am very much opposed to the philosophy of the slumlords. I think they immediately invite tenant problems, they invite government legislation and control, and they cause most of their own headaches. If we are poor property managers, we invite our own problems. If we're good managers, we eliminate our problems.

If we could become such effective property managers that our real estate went on automatic pilot, we would have the perfect vehicle for success and wealth. Don't be a don't wanter because you don't know how to manage your property. Learn how to manage your property and you are on the road to financial freedom.

Tenant Supervision: The People Approach to Management

Jack Miller

Experienced property managers will tell you that they have never been attacked by a *duplex*. At no time has a *house* called them away from supper to repair a leak. All the vacant building *lots* under their control wait their turn passively. No, the most disruptive source of the manager's pain and suffering originates with the *tenants*.

For some reason or other, this aspect of investment is largely ignored by most management courses in spite of the fact that therein lies the real key to real estate as an estate building tool. Regardless of the high yields, tax benefits, safety, etc., investors stay away from management responsibilities in droves because of the irritation potential it offers. The solution is quite simple. Instead of thinking of oneself as a property manager, one needs only to redefine the management function in terms of *supervision*.

What does a supervisor do? First, he defines the job he wants to be done (long-term care and preservation of his rental house, with prompt payment of rents indexed to inflation). Next he sets forth the qualifications of the people he wants to do the job (stable, skilled craftsmen with families who will appreciate a decent home in a good neighborhood and who will be able to earn enough to pay the rent. They will be motivated to keep the property in repair in exchange for rental credits or a long-term rental agreement, and will have the tools and skills to do the job.) Then he will seek out the personnel he wants, choosing them carefully by reviewing their past experience (Where did you live before? Who was the owner? Have you references?) as well as their potential for doing the job he wants (Would you be willing to do your own repairs if I give you a reduced rent? Will you be able to pay your rent *ahead of time* each month without my having to actually collect it from you? Would you be interested in a long-term rental?).

Once selected, the supervisor will provide the new tenant with a description of his duties in the form of a rental agreement which details everything expected. It will ideally contain both positive (discount on the rent) and negative (late charges, eviction, loss of discount) incentives. There will be a short training period which will serve to establish the implementation of the policy as it applies to the specific case (The first violation earns a verbal warning and the placing of the tenant on probation. The second incident causes double late charges to be levied and double loss of discounts, subtracted from the security deposit.) In the event it becomes apparent that the tenant is not going to be able to measure up to the requirements of the supervisor, action is taken to eliminate him, and the process is repeated.

As in any business, termination is expensive and inefficient. Good supervisors realize that, as in any building program, careful attention to a good solid foundation is the key to a sound management structure. Therefore it is foolish to sacrifice selection criteria just to fill a vacancy when the tenant might later have to be evicted. Taking the longer view, the supervisor should be willing to pay for the vacancy in the knowledge that a poor tenant is more expensive than a vacancy. Actively seeking out the right tenant can pay off in management efficiency for years to come. Rental property should be run like a business, not like a social experiment or a hobby. Owners must be able to terminate tenants without it being traumatic. Likewise, they must be impartial in their administration of the property, keeping within the requirements of all laws.

Now for the rewards. Good tenants make management a cinch. They rarely leave of their own volition. They maintain the property. They pay their rent. They don't hassle the owner. They improve their living quarters with landscaping, room additions, patios, garage conversions. In return the supervisor rewards them. We offer a "Star Tenant" program for those who have stayed with us twelve months without being late on their rent, performing their own repairs. For them we offer the free use of our waterfront condo, employment assistance for them and their children if needed, access to our wholesale connections for appliances, building materials, etc. In short, we take care of them as valued employees in much the same manner as any employer. We take an interest in their welfare, helping them with personal problems.

The combination of being a demanding supervisor, ruthlessly weeding out those who can't meet our standards, and at the same time, being genuinely interested in seeing that the needs of our valued tenants are met has produced an enviable management record. Our turnover averages about once every two years or so. Average maintenance expense per house per year is about $34. Occupancy is more than 100%. We are able to travel nine months out of the year, away from the rental property with no significant loss of rents or vacancy, and without any on-site managers. Rents are paid automatically by tenants who don't want to let us down.

What this really means to the estate builder is that, without any outside staff, a portfolio of many single-family houses can be established and maintained without the constant irritation usually associated with rental management. It all boils down to putting the management emphasis on the people rather than the property, then letting them help you to meet your objectives.

What to Do About Rent Controls

Richard J. Allen

Of the nation's 27 million rental units, an estimated 2% annually (over 500,000 units) are converted to other uses, destroyed, or abandoned. In recent years, the number of multi-family units has been actually declining each year—more are being diverted or dropped than constructed. The number of rental homes is also declining. This situation exacerbates the already tight rental market, where vacancy rates nationally are only 5% (under 1% in Los Angeles). Demand is increasing, and the supply problems are not being solved very quickly.

Adding to the dire situation is the fact that construction costs are outpacing both inflation and rents. Michael Sumichrast, senior economist for the National Association of Home Builders, estimates it will take until 1990 before rent increases could rise sufficiently to attract private construction equal to the demand.

This high demand would seem to create a climate favorable to real estate investments. By and large that is true, except for one cloud on the horizon—rent controls. Rent controls are adding to the supply shortfall by forcing some apartment owners to sell out or convert their properties to condominiums. In New York City alone, well over 30,000 apartment units are taken off the market each year. According to a study by the New York Federal Reserve Bank, during the ten-year period ending in April 1979, the rise in operating costs in rent-controlled buildings in New York City amounted to 122%, whereas the total rent increases amounted to 76%. Meanwhile, nationally, a great number of apartment units are converted into condos each year. For example, in 1979 about 145,000 apartment units were converted in this way, according to statistics compiled by the U.S. Census Bureau and the National Association of Home Builders.

Where does this situation leave the renter? Unfortunately, he is left more and more out in the cold—unless he can qualify for a loan and come up with the standard down payment for a home or condo. The best advice for the renter is to acquire creative finance skills in order to weather the storm and plan for a sound financial future!

Where do rent controls leave the landlord? A bit apprehensive and on guard! He feels secure about the enormous demand for housing, but he is concerned that rent controls are interfering with the laws of supply and demand. He knows that rent controls as a cure are worse than the disease. Writing in the *Reader's Digest* a few years ago, Senator Thomas F. Eagleton concluded: "Throughout my political career I have worked to promote decent housing for poor and elderly Americans. Opposition to rent controls is consistent with this record. *The Washington Star* put it best by comparing such controls to hard drugs: 'Starting is euphoric. Trying to stop is painful. Continuing is disaster.'"

What can a landlord or investor do? Here are several considerations:

1. If possible, concentrate your investments in locations where rent controls have not been enacted.

2. Consider including smaller units in your portfolio (duplexes, trip-lexes, single family homes). Small units stay immune to controls longer.

3. Consider tenant participation plans with single family homes. Tenants willingly pay higher monthly payments in exchange for part ownership in the property. (This also solves the management problem.)

4. Consider lease options. Once again, the higher payments are endured by the tenant of a single family home if he or she knows that part of the payment goes toward the future down payment and ownership of the home. Once again, management problems are solved because the tenant treats the house as if it were his or her own.

5. In areas that are not affected by rent controls, some investors have taken the precaution of raising rents appreciably while at the same time giving large discounts for timely payment each month. The net payment doesn't change, but the rent level is higher in case of eventual control and there is a variable discount cushion.

6. Work carefully to provide the best possible service to your tenants. That way everybody wins and the tenant remains satisfied longer. Let them know the reasons why you must, from time to time, raise the rents (increased taxes, increased utility costs, etc.).

7. Consider the possibility of converting some of your units to condo-miniums, but get the best possible advice on the process.

8. Brainstorm this issue of rent controls in your ACRE/RAND meetings. Invite speakers to come who are experts on the subject (property manage-

ment experts, informed government officials, attorneys, etc.). Use your numbers to effect change—write your city fathers, your state legislators, your senator, etc. Let your views be known.

9. Above all, stay informed and conversant with the issues so that you can represent your perspective articulately and persuasively.

The Question of Absentee Landlording

Richard J. Allen

Question

"I have recently moved from Chicago. I left a very nice home there with the intent of keeping it as an investment. I hired a real estate agent to manage it for me. It now has been vacant for three months. I want to keep the home, but this has become a frustrating situation. Could you give me some ideas? *M.A., Scranton, PA*

Answer

As a general rule it is not usually a good idea to hire a real estate agent as your property manager. They make their money by listing and selling property. They usually do not have the time and in many cases the expertise to manage property. One suggestion might be that you hire a professional management company. You could contact the Apartment Managers' Association and ask for recommendations. A reputable management company . . . if it is worth its salt . . . will take care of all matters relating to the operation of the property including renting the property, collection of rents, payment of expenses and day-to-day maintenance. The management company will take care of everything and will only call you for major decisions. A good management company is well worth the fee you pay it. It makes good business sense to stay on top of the management company and insist on regular and timely reports. You might also have someone you know in the area drop by the property on a periodic basis and give you an independent report.

Other solutions might be to use a form of tenant equity participation or long-term lease with option to buy. By using either one of these tools you would have an tenant with an interest in keeping it in excellent condition, thus safeguarding your investment.

3. HOW TO SELL YOUR REAL ESTATE CREATIVELY

What Do You Do When You Become the Don't Wanter?

Robert G. Allen

Like it or not, we all become don't wanters sooner or later! That's right. Sooner or later, if you are in the marketplace buying (as you should be) you are bound to buy a lemon... that is the nature of risk. You should see some of the property I have bought over the years! In reality, you win some (most) and you lose some (a few). You have to have the attitude, "I knew it would happen ... sooner or later I had to slip up and buy a property I had no business buying." Now, what you do when you end up with a bad situation —notice I didn't say bad property... there are no bad *properties*, just bad *ownerships*, according to A.D. Kessler—determines your success or failure. Let me give you a few principles to follow when this inevitable problem arises.

First. Do your homework before you buy. An ounce of prevention is worth a pound of cure. We are finding that the reasons that most don't wanters give for their problems are simple: *negative cash flows* and *short-term balloons.* May I counsel once again. Don't buy a property with a negative cash flow that you can't handle. And avoid short-term balloons like the plague unless you know exactly what you are doing. For the record, I rarely give a note with a balloon less than five years unless I am planning on selling the property quickly. If you just follow this one bit of advice it would eliminate much of the don't wanteritis down the road.

Second. Diversify heavily into real estate. What I mean, of course, is to buy several properties. This reduces the risk to your overall portfolio if one of your properties should have problems. This is one reason I like single-family homes. I buy several smaller properties rather than a few large ones because if one of my properties should cause me trouble it represents only a minor portion of my entire portfolio and I can "dump" it without ruining my program. On the other hand, suppose I owned a large 50-unit apartment building and the neighborhood deteriorated (or rent controls were introduced): I would be left holding a huge white elephant with not much marketability. If I own ten properties and one of them goes sour I can sell the bad apple and concentrate on the rest without losing much sleep.

Third. Cut your losses and run with your winners. This is an old stock market adage which also holds true in real estate. The tendency of the neophyte investor is to hold onto his precious real estate, troubles and all, either hoping for a miracle or burying his head into the sand of neglect. I see so much of this ... and those of you who specialize in foreclosures can agree with me that people are so emotional and irrational when it comes to unloading a problem property. I recommend, "Get rid of your bad situations!" They only drag you down emotionally. Salvage as much as you can and get out. You can't be positive and aggressive and creative when you are being eaten alive by a don't wanter property. Learn from your mistakes, determine to never make the same mistake again and get back out in the market place with renewed wisdom and confidence.

Fourth. Be creative in disposing of your bad properties. Since you are armed with an arsenal of creative techniques for acquiring property, you should not overlook the fact that the *Nothing Down System can be used in reverse in disposing of unwanted properties.* In other words, what you can buy with nothing down can be easily sold with nothing down ... and you should have learned by now that there can be win/win benefits for each party in doing it this way. When we sold our previous home and moved into our present home, we decided to use a nothing down technique to move the vacant home. We knew that it would take months to sell in the soft market at that time, so we sold it with nothing down and an 18-month balloon payment. If I had kept my property hoping for a cash sale I would have had to carry the monthly payments for as long as a year ... with all of the emotional stress that goes with selling a home. How do you go about selling a don't wanter property? You act like a don't wanter ... you dribble some blood in the water to attract as many sharks as possible. The best way to do this is to run a very flexible ad. And what do you think would be the most effective ad? Of course, *nothing down.* I have read ads in different newspapers which have headlines such as, "Nothing Down," "No Qualifying," "I'm down. Kick me."

The point which I wish to make is this: Attract as many buyers as you can. Learn what benefits they are looking for. Just because you are advertising for a nothing down deal doesn't necessarily mean that the eventual sale will be nothing down. Once you learn what your buyers are looking for, you may be able to suggest other win/win alternatives. Pick the strongest buyer for your purposes and move the property. You must, of course, expect your share of flaky callers (it may give you some empathy for the process you have to go through to find nothing down properties), but this is only normal. You are looking for the one or two really interested buyers in the market place where an advantageous deal can be made. Remember to look through the book *Nothing Down* or the seminar manual to find the three or four techniques which you could use to sell your property with nothing down. In California, the "raise the price, lower the terms" technique in conjunction with the sale of the created second trust deed and note are used frequently as a method of getting the buyer into the property without cash while at the same time generating a cash amount for the seller through the sale of the note. You may suggest that your buyers raise cash through the use of credit cards or short-term bank loans. There are thousands of alternatives if you think about them.

Another alternative for moving a don't wanter property is the use of exchangors. As explained in my book and in the seminar, exchangors are organized in marketing groups in most major cities in the United States. The best way I know of for getting rid of unwanted property is to contact a local exchangor, list your property with him or her (paying a commission, of course) and let the exchangor present your property at a local marketing meeting. These creative exchangors are well-versed in the benefits theory and have experience in moving don't wanter properties. ("Don't wanter" is right out of exchangor vocabulary). The creative real estate magazine published in Leucadia, California, prints a complete list of exchange group presidents in the country. (Write to Box 2446, Leucadia, California 92024.) Incidently, you might be interested to know that of the seven properties I bought in San Francisco with *The Los Angeles Times* challenge, four of them were from exchangors or their clients. You can see how valuable they were to me.

Remember also the "lemonadeing" technique which shows you how to add sugar (cash) to a lemon (don't wanter property) to make it palatable. Sometimes you can buy yourself out of a bad deal by trading your cash and equity for someone else's property.

If you are suffering from an unbearable negative cash flow, perhaps you can solve your don't wanter problem without selling your property at all. Maybe you should sell only half of it. This is what you call *syndicating the negative* (Wasn't there a song about this? . . . Accentuate the positive, Eliminate the negative?) Do you think that you would have any trouble selling one-half ownership in a property for *nothing down* if you require your partner to pay *all* of the negative cash flow? The answer, as you should have guessed, is *absolutely not!* There are thousands of buyers out there who would love to join with you in partnership for a share of the benefits. In essence, you make the down payment and they make the monthly payments. It's a win/win partnership.

Remember, the odds are you will be a don't wanter yourself someday. When that happens, don't despair. It's only a small barrier. Cross over it and be on your way to financial independence. There is no other way.

Seller Beware: The Negative Down Payment

Dick Lee

When I was growing up there was a phrase that I read a lot in the newspapers: *Caveat Emptor.* It means "Buyer Beware." You don't hear about it much anymore because we've got a lot of laws about full disclosure on the part of the sellers, truth in lending, truth in advertising, and so forth, so the Emptor doesn't have to Caveat as much as he used to. (Still, the prudent man will employ the blue ribbon test; namely, if it looks too good to be true, it probably is.)

There's a new thing coming down the pike which could harm sellers of real estate, what I call the negative down payment, and if some of the deals I've been seeing lately are forerunners of things to come, I say, "Seller Beware!"

I've been in real estate as an owner since the Sixties, and have been advising owners since about that same time. From that perspective, there have been three distinct phases in buying/selling real estate, and now we're adding two more:

1. Positive down, positive cash flow.
2. Positive down, zero cash flow.
3. Positive down, negative cash flow.
4. Zero down, negative cash flow.
5. Negative down, negative cash flow.

Let's consider these in turn, so we'll understand what's happening today in the context of what has happened in the recent past.

1. Positive down, positive cash flow

In the Sixties and early Seventies, inflation, building prices, expenses, and rents were all flat. They were all predictable, so when a buyer shopped for a building he took the rental income, subtracted the fixed expenses (they really were fixed in those days) and found his net income. He then offered a price and down for the building that would give him a predictable 10% cash return from the spendable on his down payment. This was triple the 3% that banks were paying as interest, but the extra return compensated him for the extra risks. On a short-term basis, the 10% was his only cash return because the building price didn't go up significantly and the mortgage certainly didn't go down much. He did get the advantage of depreciation, of course.

On a longer-term basis, his gain included equity buildup, due to some modest paydown of the principal, and perhaps a modest increase in the value of the building. Of course, neither of these were available to the buyer until he sold.

So from the buyer's viewpoint, he tied up his cash but he got a quite acceptable 10% return on it. From the seller's standpoint, he usually got all of his equity out in cash, since the buyer often paid cash to a new loan (80% and even 90% loans were common in those days). Even if the seller took a 10% second TD, he got the rest of his equity in cash.

2. Positive down, zero cash flow

In the early Seventies, many perceptive people, largely turned on by William Nickerson's book, recognized that inflation was well underway and that the value of things would increase as the value of dollars declined, so they could look for a fairly short-term (3-5 years) appreciation of the building. Sale prices were no longer flat. But mortgage rates were still flat; the banks were liberal with mortgages with 30-year fixed interest rates that were themselves under the true inflation rate. The banks were letting buyers rent 90% of the building's purchase price at a rate that permitted fast equity increases. Consider:

	Purchase	1 Year Later	2 Years Later	Notes
Price/Value	100,000	110,000	121,000	(1)
Mortgage	90,000	90,000	90,000	(2)
Down/Equity	10,000	20,000	31,000	(3)

(1) Assume growth in market value at 10% per year.

(2) Assumes virtually no paydown in first two years. Assumes 7%-8% interest rate, but would have been a buy at 10% or 12%, although most people didn't recognize it then or now.

(3) Note that even though the inflation rate is only (only!) 10%, the

leverage provided by the 90% mortgage financing allows the owner's equity to increase by 100% in one year, and 121% in two years.

Given this scenario, the perceptive buyer could afford to pay a higher price. The higher price meant a higher debt service, and for a given down payment, the buyer had to be satisfied with little or no cash flow. But what's a 10% cash on cash return, compared with a 100% or 200% growth in your equity? So the zero cash flow phenomenon was born. The sellers weren't concerned; they had a healthy down payment, and would be glad to take the building back if the buyer stubbed his toe, because they'd keep the down payment and get back a building that would be worth more (assuming the owner financed part of the price by taking back a second TD, as more and more of them did.)

3. Positive down, negative cash flow

This is only a step from the previous situation; let's now examine the mid and late Seventies; inflaction is roaring along and people are bidding up the price of buildings. This drives up the cost of debt service, so the buyer has to ante up the difference from his pocket. Meanwhile, a new element creeps in, short-term second trust deeds. In the inflation-flat Sixties, seconds were almost always for seven years, and typically amortized over this eriod. In other words, there was no lump-sum balance, no balloon to pay off. But not only was inflation increasing, the *rate of increase* of inflation was increasing, so people could see the dollar cheapening before their eyes, and seven-year second trust deeds followed the Edsel into oblivion. Sellers would now only take five-, three-, and even two-year seconds.

The point to keep in mind here is that in all these prior cases, there was a significant down payment; the buyer had a strong motivation to make the deal work, and the seller could be sure of his down payment, and maybe better.

4. Zero down, negative cash flow

Now we're getting to the point of the story. Inflation marches on and the deals get wilder and wilder. Two recent ones will be instructive. In the first, a lady was offered $500,000 for her 15-unit bread-and-butter building. The down payment was a liberal $170,000, 34%, out of which she had to pay about $35,000 commissions and fees, leaving her $135,000. She would take back an AITD for the other $330,000. Underlying the AITD would be her present first TD of about $100,000, and a second of about $12,000. Her question to me was, should she pay off the second TD from her $135,000 proceeds? Luckily she had bought the written offer.

I read it and immediately spotted the hook: the offer was contingent on the buyer getting a second, subordinate to her AITD, in escrow. The "second" would be subordinate to her AITD and would really be a fourth, junior to the $100,000 first, the $12,000 second, and her equity of $18,000 in the AITD. Nevertheless, it would be a "hard money" trust deed, secured by her own property.

In other words, the seller's total "cash" down payment would be obtained by the buyer putting an additional $170,000 of secured debt on the building! Incidentally, no bone fide hard money lender would make a loan without at least a 25% buyer's equity.

Now, if this buyer is an honest person, he'll work hard to improve the building and he'll pay the extreme negative cash flow. (He borrowed his down payment, using the building itself as security, remember?) But what if things go bad? What if there's an economic downturn, or a tenant's strike, or he loses his job, or whatever? The buyer, at least for a year or so, has little or no economic motivation to hold the building. He has no money of his own invested in it. If things go bad for whatever reason (or even if he just decides to milk the building) he can just stop paying on his AITD and the hard money fourth. It will typically take a month, probably two, before anyone forecloses, then over three months for the foreclosure period.

The seller would of course bid the building in at the value of her AITD at the sale, and she may be bailed out by the hard money fourth. This would be all right, but here's another twist. The buyer can't put the hard money fourth on the building prior to close as he doesn't yet own the building, so he prevails on the seller to co-sign with him. If this happens, the seller would end up owning her own building again, but would be responsible for the fourth as well. She would now owe the $170,000 she got as a down, but remember, she only got $135,000 net after selling costs and commissions.

5. Negative down, negative cash flow

I was recently approached with a purchase offer for a building I own in a bread-and-butter area. I think it's worth about $295,000. The "buyers" presented me with an offer of $375,000, $80,000 more than my asking price! I was to get $20,000 cash down, they would assume a $122,000 first TD, get a new hard money second TD of $50,000, and I would have a third TD for the balance, payable interest only for five years with a balloon for the total amount at the time. Even if it were an honest deal, I would have been stupid to take $20,000 to give them the benefit of five years of inflation appreciation, but the hooker was this: I was to get my $20,000 from the new hard money second, and they were to get a check for $30,000 at close of escrow! These buyers would have no economic motivation to hold the building, and at the first downturn they could milk the building for five months after which I'd get the building back. But I'd owe $50,000 more on it, due to the new hard money second, which I'd have to assume, make payments on, and pay off or have assumed when I resell the building. In either case, I'd be out $30,000, the $50,000 less the $20,000 cash at close of my original sale escrow. Here is a truly negative down payment!

This phenomenon is not new; it's been done with variations before, the usual one where the building is a residence worth $100,000, with a $40,000 first TD. The buyer puts $20,000 cash down (less, if he can, of course), assumes the old first and gives the seller a second of $40,000. Many retirees will take this deal, especially when the prior 30% limitation applied to installment sales. The buyer then, a few months after the sale, with all payments made in time, would ask the seller for permission to refinance the first, offering to up the interest rate on the seller's second and maybe giving him a bonus of $500-$1,000. The buyer then refinances the first to $70,000, pocketing the $10,000 proceeds. He is now said to have "financed out;" he has gotten his $20,000 down payment back, plus $10,000 to boot. The loser? No one, if the buyer is honest and industrious, can handle the strong negative cash flow, and hold the building until its value increases through inflation enough so that there is an equity beyond the $110,000 of mortgages against the building.

But in this case, the buyer had his own money up front and the seller could decline to subordinate. At the present time the buyers don't want to put *any* of their own cash in a deal, and even try to get some of ours! Such transactions could have happy endings, yet they sometimes lead to foreclosure.

The moral: *Seller beware.* There are unscrupulous buyers out there. Check your offer out. See if there is unnecessary exposure to risk on your part. Don't assume everything will work out well. It might, I hope it will, but what happens if things go bad? Take the time to really understand your transactions.

PART XI:

From Theory to Practice: Putting Creative Finance to Work For You

The Great San Francisco Real Estate Adventure: The Ultimate Test for "Nothing Down"

Robert G. Allen

Editor's note: The events of January 12-14, 1981, as reported by Bob Allen in a special reprint from the Real Estate Advisor *(March, April, May, 1981), constitute one of the most unique and remarkable chapters in the history of creative real estate financing. To our knowledge, this is the first time a major U.S. newspaper has challenged a major financial entrepreneur to perform on his advertising claims by engaging in a sponsored experiment open to public scrutiny.*

Since February, 1980, Bob had been saying in advertisements in every major city in the country, "Fly me to any city. Take away my wallet. Give me a $100 bill for living expenses. And I'll buy an excellent piece of real estate within 72 hours without any of my own money down." Only a person very secure about the integrity of the "Nothing Down" investment system would venture to speak words like that. But Bob Allen, who had developed this system, knew it would work. He had tested the 72-hour project successfully in a number of cities. Even Ralph Nader had backed down on a threat to challenge Bob's claims. But here were the editors of The Los Angeles Times *saying, "Show us!" In effect, they were giving Bob a national platform from which to substantiate his claims and they would report it whether or not he succeeded.*

Bob accepted their challenge, triumphed in a city of their choice, and the rest is history. (See the extensive feature article in the February 1, 1981 Business Section of The Los Angeles Times.*)*

The following article is Bob's blow-by-blow account of the "Great San Francisco Real Estate Adventure" — what it meant for him and what it means for you. We commend it to you as the most candid and instructive account available of how the nation's foremost "Nothing Down" artist goes about his task.

In November of 1980 I received a telephone call from a Mr. Martin Baron from *The Los Angeles Times.* He called to see if I would be receptive to a challenge to buy a property within 72 hours with nothing down according to my famous advertising statement. I agreed readily and requested that he send me a formal written challenge. He replied a few days later with the following letter.

Los Angeles Times

December 2, 1980

Mr. Robert Allen
3823 North Pebble Lane
Provo, Utah 84601

Dear Mr. Allen:

In advertisements promoting your new book, "Nothing Down," you state: "Send me to any city in the United States. Take away my wallet. Give me $100 for living expenses. And in 72 hours I'll buy an excellent piece of real estate using none of my own money."

The Los Angeles Times financial section challenges you to do just that. In a previous telephone conversation, you accepted the challenge. And you suggested that a 72-hour period between Jan. 10 and Jan. 15 would be most convenient for you.

Here is what we propose: You will fly to Los Angeles on Sunday, January 11 and stay overnight in a hotel. On Monday, at a predetermined time, I will meet you and accompany you to a city we have selected. Upon arrival at the city, you will have 72 hours within which to buy an "excellent piece of real estate" using none of your own money. You will buy the property for yourself, without mentioning the Los Angeles Times.

I will accompany you every step of the way. The Times intends to write a story about this challenge whether you succeed or fail.

Here is how expenses will be handled: The Los Angeles Times will pay the cost of your tourist-class flight to Los Angeles. We will pay the cost of a single hotel room for the night of Jan. 11. We will pay the cost of transportation to the city we have selected. Upon arrival in that city, you will hand me your wallet and we will hand you $100 for living expenses during the next 72 hours. We will pay your tourist-class flight home from the city we have selected.

We look forward to your earliest possible response.

Sincerely,

Martin Baron
Staff Writer

cc: John Lawrence, Assistant Managing Editor, Economic Affairs
     Paul E. Steiger, Financial Editor
     Dan Fisher, Assistant Financial Editor

TIMES MIRROR SQUARE / LOS ANGELES, CALIFORNIA 90053 / TELEPHONE (213) 972-5000

Although I had bought property many times before in short periods of time with nothing down, I had to feel just a little apprehensive in reading this letter. (Yes, even Bob has his doubts from time to time.) My neck was really going to be on the line this time. If I failed, I would have a lot of egg on my face since I had boasted to the world in over a million dollars' worth of print advertising that I could indeed buy property with nothing down. My wife also expressed her concerns. "Honey," she would question, "Are you *sure* you can do it? I have great faith in you, but..." "Sure, I can!" I replied.. but in my mind I could see some major obstacles that would have to be overcome in order to make a success of this:

• I would have to worry about room, board, and transporation... and fit them into a budget of less than $100. This would obviously slow me down... steal precious time. Most Americans have a car, a home, or an apartment and access to a telephone. I would be deprived of these basics, and would be forced to acquire these at minimal cost.

• I would have only 72 hours—three days—in which to find and sign up a don't wanter with nothing down. Although I have said that "once-in-a-lifetime deals come along about every three days," I began to wonder if I might have been just a little optimistic. Maybe my previous experiences with quick nothing down purchases (see *The Nothing Down Advisor,* May, 1980, about my Miami condo purchase) were just flukes. Maybe they really were just "once-in-a-lifetime" deals. Could I have just been lucky? Was my luck about to run out?

• I would have a companion to tag along with me. Would this reporter get in the way? Would he detract from the negotiation? How would I explain his presence? Would he make me nervous?

• I would be dealing in a totally new real estate environment. I would have to feel out the city. Where were the good neighborhoods? Where were the bad ones? This also would take precious time.

These were just a few of the major obstacles that were concerning me, let alone the other minor ones such as no cash, no credit, no job, etc. There were a few times when I would wake up at night and wonder why any grown, sane(?) man would leave his family and friends to venture out into a hostile environment with everything to lose and little or nothing to gain... except a little publicity.

These were some of the thoughts which were running through my mind as I stepped aboard the airplane to Los Angeles. I arrived in Los Angeles on Sunday evening, January 10, at about 8:30. A room at the Marriott Hotel was supposed to have been reserved for me, but when I arrive at the desk, they had never heard of me... and of course, there was no room at the inn. They sent me around the corner to a Travelodge for the night. I awoke the next morning at 4:45 for my regular morning jog and then walked to the lobby of the Marriott to meet Marty Baron at 6 a.m. sharp. I was ready to go. My mind was clear. There were no more fears or doubts. I knew I could do it (if I can get up at 4:45 in the morning to run, I can do anything). Marty introduced himself and we got into a Marriott van to take us to the Los Angeles International Airport. On the way over, the reporter told me that the city they had picked was San Francisco. This hit me like a ton of bricks ... although I smiled and calmly said, "Great!" I searched the computer in my head for information.

"San Francisco. On the negative side: Highest-priced real estate in the United States. Average-priced property well over $100,000. Notorious negative cash flows. Unusual city layout. Not like other cities with normal, average subdivisions. Rent control. Worst classified section of any major city newspaper... very few ads, even less FSBO's. High-priced living expenses; motels and hotels over $50 per night.

"On the positive side: At least it wasn't New York City, with high prices and few creative real estate people. It could have been worse. One of the best cities for creative financing because high prices have forced sellers to carry paper. Our seminars have done well here because people are open-minded, free-wheeling, risk-oriented. San Francisco is one of my favorite cities in the world. If I have to buy somewhere, why not here?"

As we boarded the plane for the short one-hour flight to San Francisco, Marty handed me a copy of the weekend issue of the San Francisco newspaper. I discarded all of the sections except the real estate and classified sections. The real estate section contained dozens of display ads showing properties being sold by developers in the Bay Area. It also contained several interesting articles about creative financing. The only reason for looking at this section is to get a feel for the market. The ads seemed to show some flexibility, but my real desire was to scour the classified section of the paper. In turning to this section I found the following:

● The homes-for-rent section contained few ads and none which indicated that the property owner would consider selling or leasing with an option to buy (an important clue).

● The condominiums-for-sale section contained only fifteen separate ads concerning properties located in the city of San Francisco. I found just two ads worth circling. I eventually bought one of these two properties (more on this later).

• The homes-for-sale-in-San Francisco section contained only nine ads total. I circled four of the ads.

There were, of course, dozens of other properties advertised outside the San Francisco area but my game plan was to buy at least one property (no matter what it would cost) within the city limits of San Francisco. Then, once I had completed the requirements of the challenge, I would attempt to buy other properties in areas where the prices and ultimate negative cash flows would not be so scary. The general lack of for-sale ads in the weekend newspaper began to make me wonder if I would be able to buy *one*, let alone several others. I began to explain my selection process to Marty when a lady across the aisle of the airplane leaned over and asked what we were doing. I explained that we were going to buy a property in San Francisco and then asked if she knew any Realtors who might be able to help us. She gave me the names of two Realtors who had offices in the city and gave me her name for a reference. I now had my first lead (although this ultimately turned out to be one of my first mistakes).

As the plane touched down in San Francisco, I began to feel the pressure build. We walked off the plane and toward the baggage-claim area, where once reclaiming our luggage, we proceeded outside. There, with some smiles and a small ceremony, Marty handed me a traveler's-check pouch filled with five $20 bills. I reluctantly handed him my wallet (which I had just bought the night before at the Marriott in Los Angeles — I couldn't let him see my old beat-up one). It was 8:30 a.m. We walked back upstairs to the Travelers' Aid desk where I hoped to be able to obtain a map of the city . . . but the aide had left. I also wanted to get a current edition of the Monday's newspaper to check the classified ads, so I stepped to the nearby newsstand to pay for the paper but couldn't find my money. I had misplaced, already, the only money to my name! Upon backtracking to the Travelers' Aid station, I found the five $20 bills sitting there untouched on the counter where I had left them abut five minutes before. I breathed a sigh of relief and Marty and I laughed about what might have happened if I started the day out with *no* money for living expenses.

I then tried to place a call to the RAND chairman, Joe Marino, from San Francisco. He wasn't in. I was hoping he could shed some light on the names of a few creative Realtors in the area. Since he wasn't in, I decided to proceed into town and do some cold calling on real estate offices. The airport limousine cost $3.25 to downtown San Francisco. During the 30-minute ride I spent most of the time scouring the new newspaper and found to my delight a much better offering of real estate ads. The condominium section contained more than twice the ads of the previous day (36) and there were ten times as many homes advertised (99). I could hardly believe the difference . . . and it made me feel a little more comfortable. Upon arriving at the bus terminal, we checked our luggage into a coin-operated luggage box, costing 50¢, which we split. Already I had spent $3.25 for transportation, 10¢ for a phone call, and 25¢ for storage; a total of $3.60. It may not seem like much to you... but it was almost all I had in the world... at least for the next 72 hours.

In the yellow pages we found the address of the real estate company recommended to us by the lady on the plane. It was about a mile walk to TRI Realty located on Van Ness Avenue. We began walking and arrived a short time later. The moment of truth had come. I would have to start to strut my stuff.

My original game plan (see the April 1980 issue of *The Nothing Down Advisor*) called for me to find a hotel or motel room first, to set up a "base of operations" with maps and an available phone. By going directly to a Realtor first, I was deviating from my game plan. I was cocky... and was going for a story instead of for the property. I assumed, wrongly, that if I could buy a property from the first real estate office we walked into, it would "sound" real great in the article eventually to appear in *The Los Angeles Times*. It just proves that even the "guru" sometimes doesn't take his own advice. Deviating from the game plan cost me two precious hours, as I will now explain.

We walked into the office and announced our intentions. "We would like to speak to one of your agents about buying a piece of property." A well-dressed woman presented herself and listened intently as I foolishly explained that I needed to buy at least one property in the next day or so. I asked if she understood creative financing, and she proudly described how she and her office were well-versed in the ins and outs of little-or-no-money-down deals. I requested a copy of an MLS book and began scouring the pages. I looked for the sections of town with the cheapest prices and looked for the following clues:

● Properties with low mortgage balances.

● Properties where the seller indicated in the remarks section of the listing form that he would be flexible, would carry a second, would carry paper, or gave other clues to flexibility, such as "present all offers," "no reasonable offer refused," "seller transferred and very anxious," etc. There were dozens, and I pointed this out to Marty.

The first target property was located at 219 Grafton (I will never forget that address), priced at $87,000 (about the cheapest property in the entire MLS book). While I was filling out our first offer, the agent was making calls to several of her big developer clients to see if they had properties which they would consider selling for nothing down. After two or three calls she had found a few 5% or 10% down deals, but nothing for absolutely no cash. She went out to talk to the other agents in the office and asked them if any of their clients had anything to sell with nothing down. One gentleman did have a client who would sell his half interest in a condo for nothing down... but that wasn't quite what I had in mind (later on, I would use this same technique to get rid of some of the properties that I eventually bought). I finished writing up my offer and presented it to the agent. It read as follows:

"Buyer to assume existing first mortgage on the property subject to the existing terms and conditions.

"Seller to obtain second mortgage of approximately $30,000 through lender of seller's choice.

"Buyer to assume payments on second mortgage loan.

"Buyer to execute a note and deed of trust in favor of seller for the balance of seller's equity with terms as follows: Interest to be 12%. Terms to be five years or less with no prepayment penalty. Monthly payments will not begin for three years at which time they will be interest only until term of loan.

"Seller to pay all closing costs.

"Seller to warrant all plumbing, electrical, heating, air conditioning, and appliances to be in safe and proper order at the close of escrow."

She blanched upon reading it (which was my first clue that her apparent knowledge of creative financing was not quite as deep as she had indicated). We retired to a table to prepare to write another dozen or so offers and she began (I assumed) to get the process of presenting the offer started. She returned in about five minutes with an entirely different attitude.

"Management feels," she started, "that your offer is not the kind of offer that we would like to present. We do not feel that we would like to represent you." Actually, I don't blame her a bit. If I had been management, I would probably have done exactly the same thing. You can imagine my surprise ... and embarrassment. If I hadn't been accompanied by a *Los Angeles Times* reporter, it might not have been so bad ... but ... I knew that under California real estate law the agent was obligated to present *every* offer no matter how ridiculous — but rather than pursue it I decided to exit graciously and get back to my original game plan. There is no use trying to educate a Realtor who is opposed to you ... and she, most definitely, was opposed to me at this point.

I requested permission to continue to look through the MLS book

. . . which she reluctantly granted and left us alone to do our research. I copied down the addresses and the agents' numbers of fourteen properties that I was particularly interested in and prepared to leave. Before saying goodbye, I requested permission to use the phone and placed a call to the chairman of the East Bay RAND Group, Dick Holzhauer (long distance).

Dick had just finished his long weekend as an air-traffic controller and had the next three days totally free. I learned that he had a real estate license and asked if he would like to help me buy some property by presenting offers on the fourteen properties I had found in the MLS book. He readily agreed to meet me at the St. Francis Hotel in downtown San Francisco in an hour and a half. That left us enough time to catch lunch and do some more calling.

As Marty and I walked toward the St. Francis, we talked and joked, but deep inside I was steaming at having lost so much time. I admit to being just a little intimidated by the high prices in the Bay Area. . .and this first bad experience didn't make me feel any more comfortable. We found a Burger King about three blocks from the hotel and I spent about $2.00 for a meal. We then walked back to the St. Francis Hotel (San Francisco's most prestigious) where I located a phone booth, some yellow pages, and began to call. One of the fourteen properties listed in the MLS book particularly interested me. It had listed in the remarks section that the seller would be very flexible. . ."Try $1,000 down." I called this number first and found that the property had sold several weeks ago. . .of course. But the agent I talked to seemed to be very receptive when I approached him about the idea of a nothing-down purchase. In fact, he gave me the addresses of two properties which would be excellent candidates — except for the fact that they were, according to him, in seedy areas. I decided to take down the addresses of the properties and have a look at them later. I really wasn't interested in properties in poor locations, but if I got desperate. . .

Calls placed to other real estate offices proved to be less than fruitful. Most people were miffed when I explained up front that I needed to buy a property with nothing down. Some gave it a try and asked me to call them back in a few hours while they chatted with their clients, but the return calls always turned out to be wild goose chases. It was getting to be about the time we were supposed to meet with Dick Holzhauer. We walked to the drive-up entrance of the St. Francis Hotel and waited for a few minutes. I pulled out the newspaper and began to search for the few good don't-wanter ads. The best ad seemed to poke out at me:

8% DOWN
Townhse w/spec. view. 2 BR, 1½ BA, 3 decks, $158,000.
No qualifying. OWC 2nd. T.D. Open Sun 1-4,
5407 Diamond Hts Blvd. 921-3394;364-5445

I asked Marty to stay outside and wait for our ride while I went back inside to make just one more call. Sometimes you can feel a nothing down deal. I could feel this one. It was full of clues . . . less than 10% down, no qualifying, OWC (Owner Will Carry). Whenever you find an ad with several good clues like this you know that the seller's motivation is not cash. And that is what you are looking for.

I called the first number and talked to a woman who seemed to be a friend of the owner. She explained that the seller had bought the property for him and his wife to live in — but that they had decided on another home and had bought it. There was some mention about the sellers' living in Washington State and commuting. The wife was an airline stewardess. I asked why the 8% down payment. She said it would be used for closing costs and to pay her a small fee for helping the seller move his property. I explained that I was trying to buy a property with nothing down and asked if she felt that this might be a possibility with this particular property. She said that the seller was very creative and would probably be able to work something out. I asked the woman how she would get her fee. . .and she replied that she would take a note. I was, of course, ecstatic. I made an appointment to meet her at the property in an hour. She was on her way out of town but would swing by the property as a special favor to me.

I walked back outside just as Dick Holzhauer drove up. I explained to him that I had just made an appointment to see a property in an hour and that it was a top priority item. Since we had an hour to kill, he suggested that we drive back to his office and pick up the phone numbers of some RAND members who were agents in the San Francisco area (Dick was a licensed agent with a real estate company in the East Bay and wasn't too familiar with San Francisco real estate). He thought that we could drive back across the bay to Alamo, pick up the numbers, and make it to our appointment in time. As it turned out, we were a little too optimistic.

After taking extra time to find the condo, we arrived at 5407 Diamond Heights Blvd. about 45 minutes late. The woman I was supposed to meet there had long since left. I was crushed. I knew that this was the property that I would buy, but time was slipping by. While we were standing there a tenant in one of the condos arrived and opened the front entry door. I walked in after him and asked him about the place. He was a renter and seemed very pleased. How much rent do you pay? $600 per month. "May I look at your unit to see what it is like? I am planning to buy a unit in this building," I asked. He obliged. It had a beautiful view. "Do you know what the unit for sale is like?"

"Oh," he said, "That is a beautiful unit. Much better than this one. It would probably rent for $800 or more a month. They just finished repainting, carpeting, and redraping the entire place."

I was so near and yet so far. We left the units and walked back to the car making small talk. I tried to act nonchalant but I'm sure that both Dick and Marty could tell I was uptight. It was getting late by now.

We stopped at a nearby shopping center to use the pay phones. I called on the fourteen properties I had copied out of the MLS book that morning. Dick Holzhauer in an adjoining booth also began calling. Not much luck! I called back the office that had listed the "Try $1,000 down" property. I figured that if you can find a creative Realtor you'd better stick with him. This time one of the agents mentioned a property that he was trying to sell personally. Yes, he would accept nothing down. He gave me the address and we jumped into the car to go look at it. It was not too good looking — I wouldn't have taken it if you had given *me* money to take it. My hopes were dashed once again.

By the time we arrived at the bus depot where we had placed our bags in the locker, it was after 5 p.m. and getting dark. I opened the yellow pages and started looking for cheap hotels. The cheapest I found after about a half-dozen calls was $34 a night with telephone calls running at 30 cents apiece. Other rates were higher but calls were only 19 cents apiece. I took down the address of the Travelodge in San Francisco's seedy Tenderloin district (porno flick heaven) but asked a shop attendant at the bus depot if he knew of a cheaper hotel close by. He called the Hilton but their special rate was $52 per night. Too high. We stopped at two other hotels on our way to the Travelodge but they were also over $50 per night. We paid cash for a double at the Travelodge. They didn't ask for I.D. — I guess they were used to folks who just paid cash. Luckily, I was able to split the cost of the room with *The Los Angeles Times* reporter.

We put our bags in the room and stepped out for a bite to eat. Down the street was a Jack-in-the-Box. The special cost $2.12 for a sandwich, fries, and shake. I would have ordered more but the fries were terrible and the sandwich didn't win any prizes. All over the restaurant the dregs of the city had also congregated for a cheap, fast meal. It was kind of depressing — to think that a portion of humanity had no better place to look to for a solid meal.

We arrived back at the hotel. Dick Holzhauer took his leave of us and we settled in for the night. I changed to my jogging suit so I would be more comfortable and began to set up shop. I opened the current issue of the paper and began to circle ads again. The don't wanters seemed pretty sparse. It didn't look too promising. Before I launched into the marathon phone calling, I placed a collect call to my wife in Utah. I didn't have too much to report. . .and she didn't hesitate to tell me that she was about as nervous as I was. About eleven of my precious 72 hours had slipped by with no concrete result and I had to admit to her that I was counting on the evening calls to redeem me. Before we hung up, I had her go down to my office and look up the names of some exchangors located in the Bay Area. She looked up the names in the monthly issue of *The Creative Real Estate Magazine* (Box 2446, Leucadia, California 92024; (714) 438-2446) which publishes a list of all of the presidents of all the exchange groups throughout the United States. As you may or may not know, these groups meet regularly to discuss marketing of properties for their clients — many of whom are don't wanters (exchangors originated the term "don't wanter"). I figured that if I was looking for don't wanters I'd better begin at the source. She gave me three names and telephone numbers out of at least fifteen to choose from.

When I hung up I immediately called the directory assistance for Burlingame to find the home number of the first of the three names on my list. The operator gave me the number of a Mr. George Simpson whom I called and found at home. I explained that I was from out-of-town, that I needed to buy at least one property for nothing down during the time I would be in the area and asked if he could think of a client he represented or knew of who might be willing to sell with nothing down. He said that he thought that he could help me but he would like me to call him in the morning when he could check his listings. I hung up with a small burden lifted off my shoulders. . .I had another lead to a potential nothing down deal. (I learned the next day that the exchange group of which George Simpson was the president met on the second and fourth Mondays of the month. If I had been on the ball, I probably could have attended their meeting that very day and bought several properties right at the meeting. Even though I wasn't a Realtor, I could have asked to go as someone's guest.)

I next began calling all of the FSBO ads in the paper. Most of the sellers were interested in a small 5 to 10% down with hard terms but were not in a position to offer nothing down terms due to their own circumstances which required some cash. And some cash I didn't have. I called the second number of the "8% Down" as which I had called earlier, and got an answering service. I left my name and an urgent message to have the person call me back immediately. Other calls to real estate offices that had run ads in the paper were fruitless because no one was in the offices at night. After about ten less-than-successful calls, I struck pay dirt again. The ad I called on read as follows:

$850 — $1,000/mo. VIEW & NEW 3 BR 2 BA w/deck & frpl. Pac. Hts So w/OPTION TO BUY. Ownr 563-2945; Agt 922-2700.

Of course, the major clue here was the option to buy. This particular ad had not appeared in the Sunday paper. I called and reached the owner who answered in a heavy French accent. She began answering my questions in broken English, so I decided to switch into French. (If you don't have cash or financial strength, you are forced to use what you have. One of my assets was a knowledge of the French language acquired as a Mormon missionary in French Polynesia—Tahiti—from 1967 to 1970. I later graduated from Brigham Young University with a B.A. in French. If you've got it, flaunt it, so they say.) She was obviously very pleased that I could converse so well with her in her native tongue and we had a nice ice-breaking conversation for several minutes. I learned that her husband was the director of a French-speaking exchange school in San Francisco. They had built three condominiums as investments and were looking to attract renters who could be converted to owners through the option technique. As it happened, the Realtor handling the sale was eating dinner at his client's home that evening so the French lady passed me to the Realtor for further information.

I was introduced to a Lou Meyer who proceeded to tell me that the units were free and clear. I explained my situation and she proposed that I refinance one of the units with an 80% new loan and that her clients might accept, as the remainder of their equity, a second mortgage for the other 20% (the Second Mortgage Crank technique). We discussed her ability to find the right bank...which is crucial in this kind of deal. Then, I tentatively set up an appointment to see the property for the next morning. I was a little hesitant due to the high price of the units involved: $175,000, $185,000, and $195,000. She was an excellent salesperson and pointed out that this was an up-and-coming area of town where prices were less than $100 per square foot. Only a few blocks away, properties were selling for two- and three-times that figure. I agreed to see her because she seemed to be so knowledgeable about financing. She even indicated that she and her husband owned a unit for which they might consider a nothing down offer for the right person.

Obviously, I had struck a gold mine with this call. *She understood the language of creative financing and it was music to my ears.* Although I had originally planned to buy the least expensive property I could find, I was beginning not to care what it cost . . . just as long as the property was a nothing down deal. I had to fulfill the terms of the challenge which didn't mention anything about negative cash flows. Lou asked me for my number and I hesitantly gave it out. (Can you imagine what she would have thought of me if she figured out which hotel I was staying at?) I mentioned to her that I could meet her at the St. Francis Hotel in the morning if she wished. (By name-dropping the St. Francis, I assumed that she would figure I was staying there and think more highly of me . . . and obviously it worked.)

About this time I received a call from the "8% Down" person who informed me that the owner was in town but could not be reached. I told him that it was imperative that I talk to him before the night ended. I knew that we could work out a deal and I needed to talk to the seller fast before someone else got to him — *"You Snooze, You Lose."*

He said that he would try to make contact with the seller. I went back to the phones but without much luck. I made another call to the "8% Down" fellow to see if he had reset with the seller yet, but still no luck.

I decided to call it a day and retire about 10 p.m. to cut my losses short and start out the next day fresh with two or three good leads. Marty lay back on his bed and watched as I sweated through the evening. I could tell that he was enjoying my predicament but there was nothing I could do about it. He was really a nice fellow and we joked about running (which we shared in common) and other common interests, like a duplex he had bought recently.

At about five after ten I turned out the lights and lay in bed staring at the ceiling thinking how lousy the first day had turned out to be. At exactly 10:12 p.m. the phone rang and a Mr. Rocky Lane was on the line, the "8% Down" owner. I explained my desire to buy a property with nothing down in the next day or so — and would he be interested? He asked, "You wouldn't happen to be the guy who wrote the book, would you?" "Yes," I confessed. He laughed. "Oh, sure. I'll sell it for nothing down." He explained that he had given my book to one of his agents for Christmas but had never read it himself because "I was sure that I knew everything that was in there." We made an appointment to meet him at his office in Menlo Park the next morning at 10:30. I hung up the phone and let out a yell of joy. I knew now that I had a good one on the line (one of seven, eventually)— and barring a lot a bad luck, I would soon have my first deal in the bag. Marty seemed a little miffed that my fortunes had turned so quickly. Needless to say, when the lights went out for good that night, my spirits were flying high as a kite.

II.

The alarm beeper of my Seiko wristwatch pierced me awake at 7 a.m. I had slept soundly and with much less anticipation after the phone call of the previous night. It looked as though I would be able to put a deal together before the deadline. The pressure wasn't completely off, however. I have learned over the years never to count my escrows before they have closed. There are always a million minor details to crop up and get in the way of a perfectly simple verbal agreement. The appointment was set for 10:30 that morning but it was at the seller's office about 30 miles south of San Francisco in Menlo Park. We would need transportation. I determined to call Dick Holzhauer, the East Bay RAND Chairman...but it was too early to bother him. And it was time for my morning run. I could think about such matters after I had shown my body who was boss (at least for another day). I slipped my jogging suit on and bounded out into the cold, crisp San Francisco air. It was still dark. I tried to descend the front staircase from our motel on the third floor but it was locked and padlocked with an iron-meshed grill. I began to wonder about the wisdom of venturing out into this district of the city without a 300-pound bodyguard.

As I proceeded to jog down the street past the Greyhound Bus Depot I began to notice the low life huddled in doorways and sleeping on benches. They had been out in the cold all night long. Their clothes were filthy. They were hollow-eyed and hopeless. One grisly figure stooped over a small charcoal fire he had lit on the sidewalk. I ran on faster through the morning air. I felt lucky to be able to run amidst such unsavory characters. I bought a paper and began to scour the morning classified ads for new don't wanters. The morning was beginning to break and throngs of commuters poured out of the subway portals and scurried off to their respective offices.

I sat and pondered on the irony of the scene. I had been challenged to come to this city to prove that I could buy the best investment in the world, real estate, with absolutely none of my own money...as if I were no better off than a beggar on the street, with nothing to my name. All around me the beggars began their daily pleas for money and here I sat on a nearby park bench with no money in my pocket but enough knowledge in my head to make me a millionaire again and again. If only those beggars knew what I knew and were willing to pay the price to put that knowledge into action...

Upon returning to the motel, I called Dick Holzhauer and left a message for him to meet us at the motel that morning at about 9:30. I communicated with Lou Meyers, the real estate agent whom I had called the previous evening, and set up an appointment for 9 a.m. Marty Baron, the reporter, was showered and dressed by the time I returned. We caught a cab to the Meyers' property (splitting the cab fare) and met Mr. Meyers there with a key to show us through. It was in a fairly good neighborhood called South Pacific Heights. The property was a new condominium consisting of three units stacked in three stories. They were all very large with three bedrooms each. Two units were rented out already, and the middle unit was vacant. The price tag was $185,000. The seller owned the property free and clear and would consider an offer where a first mortgage of 80% be placed on the property and a second mortgage of 20% could cover the difference. It was essentially a nothing down offer with a necessity for bank financing. I wasn't too thrilled about the price (since I am partial to $50,000 condos) but kept this property in mind as a back-up in case nothing else went through.

The husband then drove us to a beautiful condominium that Lou Meyers owned in a family trust. It was large, with spacious views, in Noe Valley. Price tag: $295,000, but the terms could also accommodate a nothing down offer. (When you find the right seller or agent, the job gets a thousand times easier. This woman obviously was not frightened of creative offers and even suggested them.) As the husband drove us back close to our motel, I wrote up an offer on the first property and gave it to him to give to his wife. It was the second formal offer which we had written during our stay. We told him to drop us off on Market Street because we had another appointment nearby. I surely didn't want to let him see the motel we were staying at.

We stopped in a bakery for breakfast. . .and since I was feeling a slight bit cocky I offered to buy. I think it cost about two dollars for donuts and beverages. When we returned to the motel, Dick was waiting for us and we checked out. My phone bill for the previous night came to $17.01. My money was beginning to run out.

We arrived in Menlo Park sometime after 11 a.m. I had called to say we would be a bit late. The offices of Richard (Rocky) Lane were located in an old restored mansion called the Bright Eagle. I have never before seen such an opulent job of restoration. Mahogany paneling everywhere. Plush carpets. Fine furniture. It was stunning. Rocky came to greet us and ushered us into a large conference room displaying an enormous solid wood table with encircling leather chairs. It was a scene out of a movie. . .in fact, I couldn't have scripted it better myself. Rocky was a young energetic man sporting a well-groomed reddish beard. . .open-necked shirt and dripping with gold everythings. We hit it off immediately because he could tell that I was a "taker" (a serious buyer who knew what he was doing). He did not seem to mind the presence of *The Los Angeles Times* reporter or Dick Holzhauer. He was not aware why they were present since they had been introduced as my friends. Rocky began to expound on the reason for his flexibility and what he planned to do with the notes he would obviously be taking back. It was fascinating. He wrote part of the offer and I wrote the other. He would dictate to me what he wanted and with a few minor adjustments I accepted. We were on the same wavelength. It was probably the quickest and easiest negotiation session I have ever been involved with. The deal we structured was as follows:

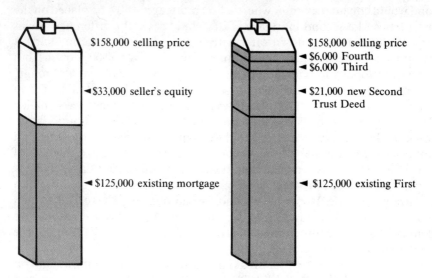

$158,000 selling price

$33,000 seller's equity

$125,000 existing mortgage

$158,000 selling price
◄ $6,000 Fourth
◄ $6,000 Third
◄ $21,000 new Second Trust Deed

◄ $125,000 existing First

The seller's equity was $33,000. He would accept a $21,000 note secured by a second T.D. plus a $6,000 third and a $6,000 fourth. He planned to sell the $21,000 note for about $15,000 in cash to a client. The $6,000 note he would give to his friend and partner who had helped him find, fix-up, and sell this unit. (He also was present in the room.) Rocky would keep the $6,000 fourth for himself. All of the notes bore an interest rate of 10% (at the seller's suggestion) and had payments of interest-only monthly for three years and then a balloon.

We ran into two small snags with respect to the $21,000 note that Rocky would be selling to his client. Obviously, he wanted to offer his client some sort of security in knowing that the person paying on the note (me) would be good for the money. Rocky first suggested that we raise the price of the unit to $173,000 and show on the deposit receipt and offer to purchase that I had made a down payment of $15,000. Then, in a separate attached addendum, I would be credited back the $15,000 as a fund for negative cash flows and improvements on the property. I went along with this but didn't feel quite right about it. At this point I just didn't want to blow the deal. Actually, it is not wise to play these kinds of games in offers and can be illegal in some states depending on how it is handled. In this case, I knew that Rocky would probably personally guarantee this note so there would be no ramifications.

The second problem came when he asked me for my financial statement. I told him that I would rather not provide it. . .since, under the terms of the challenge, I was not supposed to offer a statement. He could see that I was balking and concluded by saying that it wouldn't matter what I wrote on my financial statement. . .just that he could have something in writing. This seemed to satisfy us both and we signed the offer. I gave him $1 for earnest money deposit which we all laughed at and when it was all signed up I pulled out a copy of my book, autographed it to him "Thanks a million," and gave it to him. As it turned out, he had bought my book for his friend as a Christmas present, but he had never read it. As he put it, "I knew everything in that book so I didn't think I needed to read it."

We departed sometime after noon. As we walked toward the car I breathed a deep sigh of relief. The challenge had been fulfilled. . .*now the rest of time was just for fun!* I determined to see just how much fun we were going to have. We stopped at a restaurant for lunch and I splurged about $5. Then we drove to the office of George Simpson, the exchangor I had called the previous night. His line had been busy so we had not been able to tell him we were coming. His office was located near the San Francisco Airport in a small upstairs office shared with one other Realtor. I stated by case again. . ."Do you have a client or do you know of another exchangor who has a client who would be willing to sell a property with nothing down?" He explained that he had a client who owned a free and clear house in San Francisco worth about $80,000. He agreed to let me put a new loan on the property for $50,000 and give back his client a second mortgage for the balance of the equity. I wrote up the offer there in his office and added that the seller would have to pay all closing costs of obtaining the new loan and share $5,000 of the proceeds of the new loan with me at closing. I reasoned that I would probably need some extra cash to cover negative cash flows and closing costs on any other properties that I would buy while in San Francisco. . .so if this seller was willing to "share the wealth," I wouldn't refuse the money. He assured me that his client was a real don't wanter and would do as he suggested.

The property was located in a not-so-hot area of town, but I felt that if I could crank out $5,000 cash I would overlook its bad points. I wouldn't have trouble offering for sale with nothing down if I didn't want to keep it after the closing. George had received an offer to exchange this single-family home for a 19-unit apartment building in Stockton, California, but he felt that his client would not be willing to take on the management. I suggested that I would be willing to be the third leg in an exchange if necessary and wrote up another offer proposing that his client exchange her house for the 19 units and that I would buy the 19 units from her in a three-way exchange. George now had two offers to pursue to see which one seemed the most feasible to all parties involved. All things being equal, I would have rather had the 19 units, but the house would be just fine.

Before I left, I asked him for the names of other exchangors in the area that he felt I should call to find other nothing-down deals. He gave me the names of three men who had offices on the east side of the bay where Dick Holzhauer had his office. He gave me the name of Hy Vitcov, a fellow exchangor, who had just mentioned in their last meeting that he had a client who wanted out of a home in Sacramento and would accept paper as a down payment. I called him immediately from George's office and found out that he did indeed represent such a client. We negotiated the terms right on the phone. I wrote up an offer on the spot and since Mr. Vitcov was not available to deliver the offer to his client for a quick presentation (remember, I didn't have much time), I offered to drive over to his client's apartment and leave the offer under his door so that he would find it as soon as he came home from work.

We took our leave of George Simpson and drove to San Mateo to a luxury apartment complex to locate Mr. Vitcov's client. Dick and Marty stayed in the car while I went to leave the offer. I ran into a problem. The front door was locked with a buzzer system. No one was home at the apartment so I had no way of leaving the offer. As I stood there outside the locked door, another tenant came and opened the door with his key and I slipped in behind him unnoticed. . .feeling like a common burglar. . .but I got in to accomplish my task.

Once this was accomplished we decided to shift gears and locations. I felt that I had had enough of the high San Francisco prices and would like to see what the other side of the bay could offer. We drove to Dick's office in Alamo just south of Walnut Creek, California. On the way to the office we stopped off at the Alamo high school where Dick's young 16-year old son was playing a soccer game. Regulation time had just expired as we arrived. Mrs. Holzhauer was there to cheer her son on. We stood there on the sidelines and watched through two overtimes. The game ended in a zero/zero tie. Marty slipped into the school to find a phone. He needed to call his editor to tell him that I had been successful in buying at least one piece of property. His editor was very disappointed. Marty also arranged for us to meet an Associated Press photographer the next morning at 9:00 a.m. at the condominium for the triumph pictures.

By this time it was getting to be late afternoon. Dick Holzhauer, our congenial host and chauffeur, has a perfect work arrangement. He works as an air-traffic controller from Thursday through Sunday and has the rest of the week to spend as an investor and real estate agent. He has his license with a lively office in Alamo, California. He had told his colleagues that the "famous" Robert G. Allen, author of the "infamous" book entitled *Nothing Down* would be in their very office that afternoon and that he would use it as a home base to do some nothing down buying. When we blew into the office that evening, several of the agents were still working and a few wanted to have me autograph their copies of *Nothing Down*. I'm sure that they didn't expect me to look so young (although I was then 32, I look 25) and some didn't know what to expect. We settled in to make some calls from the multiple listing book. I chose several promising listings and had Dick start calling the listing agents to see how flexible their clients would be. I felt that my best shot would be to get in contact with the exchangors that George Simpson had referred me to that afternoon. I called Phil Lamarche, located in nearby Walnut Creek, to see what kind of nothing-down properties he had available. Luckily, I caught him home and found him very receptive to a creative offer. He indicated that he owned two Sacramento houses that he held in a family trust which he would be willing to sell with nothing down. We made an appointment for the following day for lunch. Another exchangor was equally as amenable to a creative offer. I had really struck a vein of gold with George Simpson. Of the three people he had referred me to, all three had properties which would fit perfectly into my plan.

About this time we received a call from Lou Meyers of San Francisco who indicated that the offer that I had left with her husband that morning would be acceptable to her clients with some minor changes. She suggested that I meet with her at her office to discuss the changes...and to talk about some other properties that she had for sale. Things were looking up. However our luck with calling agents cold out of the MLS book was not as good. We made a verbal offer on a property to an agent in a nearby town who then relayed our verbal offer to her client on the phone. We were attracted to this particular listing in the MLS book because the agent had indicated that her client would be *extremely* flexible...present all offers, etc. This agent called back in a few minutes, after having discussed our offer with her clients, to tell us that her clients weren't *that* flexible. So we struck out on that one and a few others. Sometimes the magic works and sometimes it doesn't! One of the women agents in Dick's office was watching this with interest and happened to casually mention that she knew that one of the agents in another office of this same chain had mentioned to her that he would be *very* flexible in selling his condo in

Walnut Creek. She knew him to be one of the best creative agents in the company and indicated that he might be willing to work something out with us. We got his number and called. He was very flexible and obviously a don't wanter. I wanted to go and look at the property at once but he declined. . .a bachelor had some company over for the evening and I understood. We set a time for 3 p.m. the following afternoon.

By this time I was beginning to feel a bit tired. I had one solid deal in my hip pocket and several others biting on the line. The third day was shaping up to be a big one. Dick suggested that we catch a bite to eat at the nearby soup-and-salad restaurant. We happily called it a day and all went to eat. The soup and salad were great (and cheap). Afterwards we drove across the street to the Alamo Gardens Motel (the cheapest and perhaps only motel in town). A double ran us $26.65 but there was no phone. I didn't care about the phone...I didn't want to go near a phone. I counted how much money I had left...I was down to $24.03. No matter...it was time to relax. I lay on the bed and Marty Brown quizzed me on each of the deals so that he could understand them enough to write about them. Then we talked about my philosophy of life. It was after eleven before we turned the lights out. I was exhausted and my head hadn't hit the sheets before I was sound asleep. The events of the next day promised to be spectacular and I would need all the sleep I could get.

III.

I began the third and final day of the challenge with my usual early morning run. The day was still dark as I pounded down the pavement against the flow of oncoming headlights, wondering what this day would have in store for me. By the time I returned to the motel room, Marty was dressed and ready to go again. Dick Holzhauer came over about 8 a.m. and we prepared for the trip across the Bay into San Francisco. There was a bit of good news. Dick had received a message overnight in his realty office that the Hy Vitcov offer on the $35,000 home in Sacramento had been accepted as written. That meant that we now had two firm accepted offers on nothing down properties.

The trip to the Diamond Heights condo, the first accepted offer, took about 45 minutes. We used the keys which the owner had given us to let ourselves in. The Associated Press photographer had not arrived yet. I was a little apprehensive as I turned the key in the door and walked into the unit for the first time... in essence, I had bought the unit sight unseen (which, of course, I do not recommend). I wondered if the unit would measure up to the "excellent" rating for properties I had told the *Times* reporter I would buy. To my surprise and relief, the unit was immaculate... newly draped, painted, and carpeted. The view from the balcony was stunning. There were two bedrooms and two bathrooms. When the photographer arrived, we set about to shoot me from every angle using every imaginable lens. He joked as he took my picture about how he and his girlfriend couldn't afford a property this nice... you know, not enough down payment and probably couldn't qualify for the loan, etc., etc. It always amazes me how many people don't seem to grasp the ease of buying property with nothing down. The average person has so much difficulty overcoming his programming to conventional ways of doing things that he can't comprehend a new way of doing things... even when you show them graphically, as I had done with this condo.

After the condo pictures we drove to our next appointment. Lou Meyer, the agent on the $185,000 three-bedroom condo, was waiting for us in her office on Vallejo Street... actually, her office was in her multi-million dollar home. Here was an obvious expert in real estate investing... and I could tell from the conversations that we had had on the phone that she was no stranger to creative financing. It is such a pleasure to deal with an equal—a peer. We hit it off well. She mentioned other projects she was working on and for which there might be a possibility for some creative financing, although not for nothing down. We finally got around to the offer. She wanted me to make some minor adjustments in the offer... so minor they have since slipped my mind. I agreed and signed the counter offer and she said that she would get her clients to initial the changes and we would have a deal. As we sat in her spacious office/den and looked out over the Golden Gate Bridge and the Bay I couldn't help smiling. *The Los Angeles Times* reporter, beside me, taking in this whole scene, had to be impressed. It was going to be a great story.

Upon leaving Lou's office, we drove to a pay phone to call the escrow company which was handling the closing on the Diamond Heights property. There was a hang-up concerning the closing costs and I knew then that the closing, which was scheduled for that afternoon, would not take place. Just as well. This would give us more time to buy some more property. We drove, then, to George Simpson's office (since his line was busy) to see if the offer on the $80,500 single-family home had been accepted. He had no news for us, so we stopped for lunch... my last expenditure, as it turned out. Then we drove to Walnut Creek, across the Bay again, to visit with another potential nothing down seller. Mr. Phil LaMarche, the broker of Energetic Equities in Walnut Creek, had been recommended to us by George Simpson as a creative exchangor and Realtor. As it turned out, Phil owned personally, in a family trust, two single-family homes in Sacramento which he had taken in a trade and would be willing to sell for nothing down. He showed me pictures of the properties and they seemed acceptable. Both properties were rented.

I was impressed with Phil's thoroughness. He was concerned with the reasons for my investment goals, i.e., nothing down . . . and exhibited the admirable traits shown by knowledgeable, professional real estate counselors who take the time to understand the motivations of the clients they deal with. We started out by explaining our mutual goals. I, of course, wanted to get in with nothing down. He wanted to sell his properties and would be creative in the terms if we could structure the deals so that he could get some cash out of the sale. He suggested the "raise the price, lower the terms" idea . . . coupled with the use of discounted mortgages. For example, he suggested that we raise the price of one of the houses by about $4,000 from around $39,000 to approxmately $43,000. He would take back a second and a third mortgage and would sell the second mortgage on the open market for cash. This was essentially the same technique used to buy the Diamond Heights property, except, in the first example, the seller had not required me to give him a higher price than he was asking. I was willing to pay a higher price for the property, but only on my terms—nothing down. Phil diagrammed the deals on a blackboard in his office. He had obviously done this many times. He asked me what he thought would be fair (the first person to mention a number loses). He suggested that we arrive at a rate 1% less than the going rate on conventional owner-occupied mortgages with a standard 20% down payment. I agreed. He immediately got on the phone and called a mortgage company to get a quote on their rates. It came in at 14.75%. We thus agreed that the rate on our notes would be pegged at 13.75%. There was a three-year balloon. This would also generate about a $250 per month negative cash flow on each house, but I figured that I could sell one-half interest in each house to the present tenant or other renter to cover the negative cash flow.

Phil wanted to raise the price a little higher on both houses and I asked him if the properties were listed for sale with commissions built in for participating brokers. He said that he had set it up that way. Then, in order to lower the price slightly, I told him that it would only be fair to reduce the price of the houses by the three percent that he would have been willing to give to a participating broker. This saved me about $2,500 on both properties.

I was beginning to feel the weight of the challenge about this time in the afternoon. It was getting close to 3 p.m., and as Phil's secretary typed up the final contracts and I signed them, I started to get claustrophobia. We were all jammed into Phil's small office; Marty Baron on my left and Dick

Holzhauer on my right. Every word that came out of my mouth I knew was being recorded for the eventual story. I felt enormous pressure to perform . . . to live up to the legend. I knew that at least twenty people in our seminar operations and everyone at Simon and Schuster were counting on me to pull through. I have never felt such an enormous weight before . . . and I hope never to feel it again.

As soon as Phil had signed the copies of the contracts I began to feel a little lighter. We left his office with four solid contracts signed . . . the challenge was being met in a big way. The last stop on our schedule was the condominium owned by Bob Laurence in Walnut Creek. We drove through the neighborhood around this last property and I immediately knew that this was one of the best areas, if not the best area, of town. The units were immaculate. The unit itself was priced at $174,000 and had four bedrooms. It was probably the best buy of the eventual seven properties bought. Bob had just listed the property for sale the day before and I was making the first offer. He was a don't wanter. He had some bills to pay and needed out as soon as possible. I knew that I would not be up to another drawn-out negotiation like that with Phil LaMarche. I was beat. I asked Dick Holzhauer to handle it for me and as long as it was nothing down I would agree.

I sat in the living room, totally drained and mindlessly watching the Merv Griffin Show. Every once in a while, Dick would ask me a question and I would respond. The basic offer was that I would assume the payments on the first mortgage of $93,000 and that the seller would obtain a second mortgage of about $60,000 for which I would also assume the payments. The rest of the seller's equity would be taken back in the form of a third mortgage. The Realtor's fee, in this case, Dick Holzhauer's, would be in the form of a fourth mortgage. Another nothing down deal . . . but once again, the payments of about $1,800 per month would be staggering. I would be taking a gamble that I could find a buyer or a co-partner to take this one off my hands in time for the first mortgage payment. I mulled over the problems in my mind before I signed the offer. I rationalized that I never would buy a property with such negatives as a normal investor . . . but I finally said, "What the heck?" and signed it anyway. What would another $174,000 worth of debt do?

With this last property under our belts, we got back into the car and got on the freeway heading toward Dick Holzhauer's office. I knew that I didn't want to follow through on any more of the good leads that we had been able to generate during our three-day odyssey. I was exhausted. It was time to quit. My clock showed about a quarter past five on the third day of the challenge. There were still another fourteen-plus hours left before the

72-hour limit ran out. Nevertheless, I reached into my pocket to see how much cash I had remaining from the $100 which had been given me only 57 hours earlier. I had one remaining $20 bill. In a slight display of ceremony I autographed the bill and presented it to Dick Holzhauer as a small token to our unselfish chauffeur. I was now flat broke. Marty, sitting in the back seat, handed my wallet back. The challenge was over . . .

When we arrived at Dick's office we received a telephone call from Lou Meyer. She was calling from San Francisco to tell me that her clients had signed and accepted the offer on the $185,000 condominium in San Francisco. That meant that we now had six firm accepted nothing down offers as follows:

Rocky Lane	Condominium	San Francisco	$158,000
Hy Vitcov	Single-family home	Sacramento	35,000
Phil LaMarche	Single-family home	Sacramento	43,715
Phil LaMarche	Single-family home	Sacramento	46,500
Bob Laurence	Condominium	Walnut Creek	174,000
Lou Meyer	Condominium	San Francisco	185,000
			642,215
Offer pending:			
George Simpson	Single-family home	San Francisco	80,500
			$722,715

There was still one pending offer with a good probability of being accepted. George Simpson had still not presented the offer to his client on the $80,500 house in San Francisco (and I was not to learn that the offer had been accepted until about a week later). If this offer would be accepted, it would bring our total purchases to a grand total of $722,715 . . . not bad for 57 hours. We left the office and drove back across the Bay to a hotel near the airport. I was more tired than I have felt in years. There was some talk of sitting down after dinner and going over the details of each deal for *The Los Angeles Times* reporter . . . but I knew that I would not be up to it. As soon as we checked in (in separate rooms, thank heaven) I took off all my clothes and soaked for about an hour in a hot tub. Shortly thereafter, room service arrived with a huge meal of seafood and three different kinds of ice cream . . . I savored each bite slowly. It felt good to be rich again. And then I slipped off into sleep. Bone weary. I had taken on *The Los Angeles Times* and won. Miracles never cease.

How to Overcome the Ten Biggest Roadblocks to Your Investment Success

Robert G. Allen

Recently my brother Richard sent out a questionnaire asking our graduates to tell us of the major barriers which are impeding their success in the Nothing Down Program. He entitled it "Barrier Analysis." We have received a great response and have tabulated the answers. You might be interested in knowing what the top ten barriers are. Here they are in order of greatest concern:

1. Negative cash flows and balloons
2. Lack of capital resources
3. Tax and estate aspects
4. Lack of time
5. Getting partners
6. Lack of equity resources
7. Setting specific goals
8. Finding don't wanters
9. Negotiation
10. Creative acquisition techniques

Since there seems to be such concern about how to overcome these barriers, I would like to take you through an analysis of each of them and show you how I solve these problems.

But before I do, let me tell you my attitude toward barrier analysis. Those of you who are inordinately concerned with the barriers confronting you are not thinking creatively. In a real sense, almost all of these top ten barriers are merely figments of our imagination... they are simply excuses that we create to give us an out for not doing what we know we have to do. I hope that my *Los Angeles Times* $100 challenge has taught us all (even myself) something about barriers. As far as I am concerned, there are no barriers. None. In my mind, there are no barriers that stand in the way of my buying real estate. I have no excuses. When I look at myself in the mirror every morning I can truly say to myself that the only person standing in the way of my ultimate success is myself. That might sound harsh, but it is true. Now, with that in mind . . . let's talk about some solutions.

Barrier Number One

The first barrier mentioned is *negative cash flows and balloons.* Interestingly enough, the major reasons people give when they become don't wanters, according to our analysis, are just these two . . . negative cash flows and balloons. In other words, the greatest barriers to getting into real estate and the greatest reasons for getting out of real estate are the same. So what do you do about it? First of all, be very careful when you buy. Don't buy without doing analysis first . . . be able to afford your negatives if you are buying a property with reverse cash flow. Elsewhere in this volume you can read about my system for analyzing every property before I buy it. The property must score at least a 12 out of a total score of 15 to be acceptable to me . . . although there are reasons for buying properties with lower scores. I have also set in my mind that I won't buy a property with a balloon less than five years away. I just won't buy it. Now, during my *Los Angeles Times* challenge I did buy one property with a two-year balloon but I did so knowing beforehand that I would be disposing of it immediately. If you plan on keeping a property for the long run you want to avoid balloons.

Unfortunately, there is a dilemma we all face in buying property. In order to avoid negative cash flows (or to buy creatively), we sometimes need to create balloon mortgages. There are tradeoffs that each of us needs to analyze when buying. Would I rather have a negative cash flow and avoid balloons? Or would I rather have no negative cash flows and negotiate for a seller carry-back notes or mortgages with short-term balloons? This is a decision that you must make for yourself. Personally, I don't like either and therefore increase my search to find the four situations where they are not a factor.

For those of you who can't afford negative cash flows and who also want to avoid balloon mortgages, there is another solution. Sell half interest in your properties either to an investor-partner or to the tenant who plans on living long term in the property. A partner is easy to find to cover the negatives if a nothing down deal is offered. In one of the recent seminars I taught, a student stood up and offered to assume up to a $450 monthly negative in exchange for half of the ownership of the property. Advertise in the paper. Your headline would read: "Nothing Down . . . Need partner to pay $250 per month negative cash flow on my property in exchange for half ownership and no management hassles." It is better to own half of something than all of nothing. So my three solutions to negatives are as follows:

1. Don't buy without analysis.
2. Negotiate for no payment notes carried back by the seller.
3. Sell half interest in the property to a partner for covering the negative.

Three solutions for balloons are:

1. Don't accept less than a five-year balloon unless the deal is too good to pass up or you plan on moving the property immediately.

2. Always negotiate for a 12-month extension beyond the due date of any balloon. You may have to pay for the privilege. I offer to pay $500 to $1,000 for an extension . . . but it makes me feel comfortable to know that if the money market is bad—like it is this year—I will at least have some breathing room if I pay for it.

3. Use a partner's cash to buy down to older low-interest-rate long-term mortgages. Cash the seller's equity out and negotiate for extremely low prices.

Barrier Number Two

The second major problem facing our surveyed graduates is *lack of capital resources.* I teach in the seminar that the motto of all creative investors should be *"If I don't have it, somebody else does."* This is the essence of leverage. Using other people's strengths. But you have to use the win/win philosophy to be able to use other people's assets. You have to combine one person's strength with another's weakness to make a winning team. If you don't have the capital assets to get your ball rolling, you must look for those who do have the assets but who don't have the time or the expertise to use them. I am reminded of a story from the seminar manual. One of our very successful graduates works with a wealthy attorney in buying properties. In the beginning this student had no money or assets. He approached an attorney who had money but no time to invest in looking for property. They worked together marvelously because one could not live without the other. So the major solution to the problem of capital assets is to borrow some . . . either from your friendly banker or from a partner. Remember, if you don't have what you need, someone else does. And you can probably convince that person in a win/win way to lend you what you need in exchange for some of the benefits of real estate.

Barrier Number Three

The third problem most frequently mentioned as a barrier to our students is entitled *tax and estate aspects*. This is beyond the realm of the course we teach so I can only suggest that you do as I do...you hire a competent accountant and tax planner. It is not cheap, but they save you thousands in the long run. If you are worried about paying too much in taxes the simple answer is buy as much property to depreciate as you can.

Barrier Number Four

The fourth barrier is *lack of time*. I can just hear you saying, "I'm so busy at my job I don't have time to look for property." As far as I'm concerned, you have to do a priority time study to see where your time is being spent. Anyone should be able to budget two to five hours a week for property acquisition. It should be a regular time. Involve your family ... whether your spouse or children. A few years ago I hired my brother-in-law and he looked for properties full time for me in exchange for a salary and a part ownership in the properties we bought. We ran newspaper ads to attract don't wanters to minimize the time we spent looking for flexible sellers. Instead, they called us, and it made our job a hundred times easier.

And, of course, an excellent alternative is to use Realtors. There are many Realtors in your RAND groups who would be happy to find property for you and handle many of the details which take so much of your time. Use them. The commission is well earned. To recap then,

1. Budget your time better.
2. Involve your family.
3. Place an ad in the paper to attract don't wanters to you.
4. Use Realtors, especially the creative ones in your RAND Groups.

Barrier Number Five

The fifth barrier is *partners*. How do you find partners? The chapter in my book on partners discusses several sources: Relatives, friends, business associates. Even the seller himself. I feel that the problem that many of you are having is not in finding potential partners but in getting up the courage to ask a partner to join with you in investing in the best investment in the world. What has always worked for me was to work backwards. Find the deal first. Locate the property that has enormous benefits... that you know you will have no trouble discussing with a partner. Once you have found the great deal, your desire to own it will force you to find a partner to help you accomplish your goal. I have often asked seminar graduates the following question: "If I could find you a great property that could be bought with nothing down, no negative cash flow, and no management hassles, would you let me use your credit to obtain a new loan and give me 50% of the deal?" I always have no problem finding a taker. The answer, then, is not to wait to find a partner (if this is what is stopping you) but to get out there in the market place and find a property that any partner would be happy to own with you.

Barrier Number Six

The sixth barrier is *lack of equity resources.* I think this falls under the category of partners. Once again the motto is: If you don't have it, . . . somebody else does . . . and they may be sitting next to you at this very moment. Have you asked?

Barrier Number Seven

The seventh barrier is *goal setting.* I'm not quite sure why this would be a barrier. It seems so straightforward to me. If you want to be a millionaire in seven years or less, you have to get a million dollars in debt as quickly as possible. For every dollar of debt you acquire today you can expect to reap a dollar's worth of equity in seven to ten years from the day you acquire it... provided you don't sell. Or at the very least, get in the habit of buying at least one property each and every year for the next ten years. If you want to be a millionaire in ten years you will have to buy at least two excellent, below market properties a year. Set your goals! Put them in writing! Display them in a prominent place in your home and read them daily! And then let your subconscious mind work out the best way for your goals to become a reality.

Barrier Number Eight

The eighth barrier is *finding don't wanters.* This can be a sticky problem but there are easy solutions. One fellow wrote recently that he had called 37 people without any positive results . . . and he was a bit discouraged. Remember that we all have feasts and famines . . . and you may be in a famine for a while. I have them all of the time. Thank heaven, I didn't have a famine when I was with the *Los Angeles Times* reporter in San Francisco a few years ago. I think that the best ways of finding don't wanters are in the following order:

1. Place your own ad in the paper. Be creative! Have you thought about a billboard? Maybe ten of you should go together and rent a space and share the leads. It's a thought.

2. You need to let people know that you are in the market. Have you

visited ten real estate offices lately and told them that you are in the market?
Until you have, you can't gripe about a dearth of don't wanters. It takes
time.

3. Deal with people who understand don't wanters . . . like exchangors
around the country. Is there a local exchange group that meets regularly?
Let the exchangors know that you are a "taker" for property.

4. Use the multiple listing book. I have said that if you and your Realtor
turn to any two pages of an MLS book you should be able to buy at least
one property from those two pages with nothing down. Use technique #32,
"The Second Mortgage Crank" in conjunction, for example, with Fannie
Mae existing loans for non-owner-occupied situations.

Barrier Number Nine

The ninth barrier is *negotiation* . . . and the only way to get good at it is
practice . . . and to remember always the win/win philosophy: Always look
for the seller's benefits. How can he win by this offer? Practice, practice,
practice.

Barrier Number Ten

The tenth barrier is *creative acquisition techniques* . . . and there are more
than enough in your seminar manual or my book. You don't need to learn
more techniques, you need to study what you have and learn how to put
them into action. It has been said that there is no difference between a
person who can't read and a person who won't read. Don't get caught up in
the paralysis of analysis. when in doubt, don't read something, DO
something.

I hope that these ten barriers are not stopping you from doing what you
know that you must do. They haven't stopped me. They surely haven't
stopped the winners of the Million Dollar RAND Table each year. And
they haven't stopped our graduates from buying over billions of dollars
worth of real estate each and every week. Good luck. The ball is in your
court!

"Successful People Often Have More Failures Than Failures Do, But They Keep Going"

—Herb True

Robert G. Allen

I have put off writing this article for longer than any other because I knew that it would cause me the most pain to write. It has to do with my failures as an investor... and I knew that to do this article justice I would have to reach back in my memory and dredge up all of the gory details, analyze them and extract from them pearls of wisdom that might help you from making the same mistakes I have been prone to make.

Over the years I have bought millions of dollars worth of real estate with great success. If you want to read about some of the successful transactions you can turn to my book *Nothing Down* or review the seminar manual. On balance, I am happy to say that I have come out way on top. But there have been some bleak moments. And that is what I want to write about in this article. Our competitors tell only the rosy side. But I want you, as my intimate associates and colleagues, to know of the downs as well as the ups so that you can avoid the mistakes I have made.

If I were more interested in my "image" of how you perceive me (as perhaps a "master" investor) I would not dare write as I do. But I am more interested in teaching you that this business of investing is not easy... and you will have your moments of wanting to throw in the towel (or the amortization book) and go back to the stock market. I know I did. I have taken comfort from the above quote which I have used to title this piece. Read it again now. It may be your only friend when times get rough and your spouse and your whole family put pressure on you to abandon your "crazy" notions.

The system of investing that we teach in our basic "Nothing Down" seminar cost me about a quarter of a million dollars to perfect. The bulk of this money was spent on bad investments I entered into as I was floundering around trying to discover the secret of making a fortune in real estate. And all of this was without the help of any specific program or RAND group to fall back on. As I look back on these experiences, I have isolated five major *Don'ts* that I urge you to consider carefully:

1. Don't deviate from the "Nothing Down" program.
2. Don't place too much trust in others.
3. When in trouble, don't act like a don't wanter.
4. Don't get carried away with short-term balloons.
5. Don't get so busy buying that you forget to pay attention to the details.

1. Don't deviate from the "Nothing Down" program.

It has been said that if you don't learn from history, you are bound to repeat it. I have learned my lessons from history and I never intend to repeat them. If you think education is expensive, try ignorance! My ignorance cost me $250,000. Now I make sure never to deviate from my program. Several years ago I was a speaker at the Investment Exposition in San Francisco. The keynote speaker was Elliot Janeway, the noted economist and investment advisor. He stated in his address that there is always one safe, smart place to be and that, rather than diversifying into many areas, it is wiser to concentrate all of one's efforts in that one safe, smart investment. He recommended South African gold stocks. Of course, I recommend residential real estate at least for the next decade. To prove my point, I asked the attendees at the Expo to help me with a survey. I asked for a show of hands of all those who knew a millionaire personally. Then I asked them to indicate how their friend had made his million. I went through a list of all of the investments represented at the Expo and here are the results from a group of about 100:

Gold and silver—2	Securities—1
Antique collections—1	Overseas investments—0
Stamps—0	Precious gems—1
Coins—1	Options—1
Rare artwork—0	Franchises—0
Diamonds—1	"Off shore banking"—0
Commodities—1	Treasury bills and savings accounts—0
Investing clubs—0	Real estate—30

Did you get my point? Stick to the program of investing in real estate! It produces more wealth than all of the other so-called investments combined. Don't let anyone lure you away from your program. The program is buying existing, well-selected, income-producing homes and apartment buildings in stable neighborhoods and hanging on to them for the long run. There is a pyramid scheme flourishing right now in California. Don't be fooled! There is only one long term safe place to have your money or your lack of money: *real estate.* This does not mean office space, recreational property, commercial space, shopping centers, or any other form of real estate. Just single family homes and apartment buildings (in non-rent control areas). I deviated once from this basic truth by thinking I could handle a subdivision of 43 homes. This was totally out of my area— development. I was in over my head and luckily was able to extract myself after a loss of only $100,000. Whenever I have been tempted to wander from what works best, I get burned. If someone approaches me about the greatest money maker in the world, I just smile and tell them I don't have any money to waste at the moment. They get the message. Do you get the message?

2. Don't place too much trust in others.

As a beginning investor I assumed that all real estate was good. I located an ad in the newspaper for a three-acre parcel of land selling for only $12,000 with only $5,000 down and 8.25% on the balance. I called and made an appointment to look at the property and the smooth-talking owner convinced me that the property was a real "sleeper." Its dimensions were 100' x 1326'. It looked like a needle on the county plat maps. He conned me into thinking that it would be perfect for an airline pilot to build his home on and a landing strip in the back. I swallowed hook line and sinker. The only "sleeper" was me. I was forced to trade the property eventually for a 2.5 acre parcel of land in San Luis Obisbo, California, which I have not seen to this day... and which I suspect is in the middle of nowhere. Bye-bye $5,000 cash. I trusted the seller too much without resorting to common sense. But to make matters worse, about a year later the same gentleman approached me again with another deal on the home and three-acre parcel right next to the property he had sold me before. (He knew a sucker when he saw one.) This time I was convinced to put down $3,000 to buy a house with a $7,900 balloon due in about 8 months. I made the payments on the home while trying to sell it and when the balloon came due without a buyer in sight I was forced to accept the fact that I had been conned again. The property was in the wrong location at the wrong price with the wrong owner—me. I simply gave the property back to the previous owner and walked away from about another $6,000 cash. Once again my emotions got in the way of a sound investment. The facts did not add up but I was swayed by the excitement of making a deal. I guess what I am leading up to is simply to follow the advice of the Master: Be as harmless as a dove but as cunning as a serpent.

I had to learn my lesson one more time the hard way. My largest loss of all came again because I refused to listen to reason and let emotion get in the way. I remember the story of a man who was asked by a rather unsavory individual to lend him $100. He responded that he wouldn't think of lending him as much as 10¢ because the odds were that he would never see his money again. Then the crook upped the ante. He offered the man 200% on his money if he would lend him the $100 bill. This time the man relented and lent him the money. He was caught up by the greed of getting 200% on his money without recognizing that the facts were still the same: *the odds were still that he would never see his money again!* I was faced with exactly the same decision when a partner and I were approached with an opportunity to invest in a condominium conversion project. A total of $35,000 was needed and a projected profit of several hundred thousand dollars was at stake. I borrowed my half of the money from another partner by offering a high return on his money. To make a long story short, the controlling partner left town suddenly in the middle of the project and left my other partner and me holding the bag. We tried to pick up the pieces only to find that things had been bungled so badly there was no hope of salvaging it. Bye-bye $100,000. I listened to emotion instead of reason... and it cost me a lot of sleepless nights, a strained family situation for about a year, and a lot of cash. I was able to pull myself out of the mire by repeating aloud, "Successful people often have more failures than failures do. But they keep going." I knew that I was not a failure. I knew I would make it over the hump some day if I could just keep going. And I tried to learn the lesson: *Trust everyone, but always cut the cards.*

3. When in trouble, don't act like a don't wanter!

If you have never been a don't wanter you should have the privilege someday. It is frightening and totally disorienting. It makes you think irrationally... and that is the opposite of how an investor must act. I have described in my book the following experience:

The first multiple unit I purchased was a seven-unit building located in a fairly decent part of town on a busy street. The building was a converted home and had seven furnished apartments. Since the original structure was at least fifty years old, the plumbing was just beginning to cause weekly problems.

It took only a couple of months for me to realize that the good terms I'd received when I bought the building was the only good thing about the property. One morning at about 1:30 I was awakened by a telephone call from an upset tenant. She whispered, "Mr. Allen, I think you'd better get over here right away. The tenants in number seven are having an orgy." I rushed over immediately to find a drunken party in full progress. Since this was the third time this had happened, I called the police and went home.

All that summer I received similar complaints once or twice a week. "Mr. Allen, Ben in number three is running a heroin operation. He's smoking marijuana right now. I think that you should do something before he harms one of us."

"Mr. Allen, the unwed mother in number seven is having a brawl with her friends on the lawn."

"Mr. Allen, someone broke into our apartment last night and stole our television set." (As it turned out, Ben in number three, my resident manager, who *was* running a heroin operation, was arrested two days later with the television set in his possession. He was stealing from the tenants to help buy heroin.)

"Mr. Allen, I'm moving out of here unless you ask the people in number seven to leave immediately."

The last straw was when I cosigned with my trustworthy Ben of number three on a $200 loan to help him buy a pickup truck. Of course, I had no idea that he had been stealing things from other tenants. When the police caught him with the stolen TV set, they gave him two alternatives: either he leave town before the sun set, or go to jail. And so, he left town that night. In my truck! Every month when I made out that $22 check to pay for the small loan I had cosigned on, I remembered the seven-unit building and I swore that I would never get involved in another situation like that. I was a don't wanter.

Early that fall I put the building on the market for exactly the same price I had paid for it eighteen months earlier. I was suffering from a severely advanced case of *don't wanteritis.* I wanted to get rid of my property at all costs. Luckily I found someone to buy the building and cash out my equity.

But this decision was irrational. Rather than selling, I should have solved the real problem which was the management of the property. I did not know how to manage. I would have been much better off to keep the property and turn the management over to a professional management company. This same property which I so hastily sold for $69,000 three years ago sold again one year after I sold it for $85,000. It then sold again for $106,000. And now, it is on the market again. What's the new asking price? $129,500! And someone will come along and pay it. A don't wanter is very often short-sighted and concentrates only on his immediate problem. If I had realized my problem and solved it without selling, I would have made $60,000!

If you are in over your head, don't act like a don't wanter. Relax. Think about your most logical move. Go to your RAND group for advice. The worst thing you could do is to lose your cool. As a last alternative you could still come out smelling like a rose by advertising to sell your property for nothing down in the newspaper at a higher price. Someone may come along and take the property off your hands at a profit. If I had been smart in the above example I would have raised my price by $10,000 and sold for nothing down. It would have made me a $10,000 profit which I could have used as a down payment on my next piece of property.

4. Don't get carried away with short term balloons.

I have mixed feelings about this next piece of advice. Every year since I began my quest for financial freedom I have had to cope with large balloon payments. This causes a lot of pressure, but on the other hand it forces me to save money! I doubt if I would have ever been able to acquire as much property as I now control if I had not forced myself to find the money for another balloon payment. But I have made myself a promise that there will be no more balloons coming due within less than 5 years if I can help it. In fact, *no* balloons is the ideal situation. I often talk to graduates of the seminar and hear their stories of "short fuse" notes coming due in 12-18 months. It makes me cringe because too much of this leads inevitably to financial ruin. Please review your investment program. If you have been relying too much on the balloon down technique, perhaps you had better take a breather... after all, if you are buying too much property, you have not been negotiating effectively. Maybe you need to be a little tougher... and wait for a better deal to come along.

5. Don't get so busy buying that you forget to pay attention to the details.

I have often said that real estate investing is much like fishing. It's fun to get out in the fresh air in the mountains. It's fun to plan for the big fishing trip, to get away from the rat race for a while. It's fun to fish for the "big one" and to ultimately hook one. It's exciting when you finally haul it in. And for me, that's where the excitement ends. Because then I have to kill the poor thing... and worst of all, clean it. That's work. And I hate work. It almost takes the fun out of eating it.

Real estate is the same way. It's fun to find a don't wanter and to put together a perfect win/win deal, especially when it's nothing down. But that's where the fun stops and the work begins. Because then comes the management, the tenant hassles, the plumbing problems. If I weren't sure that this would be the only way for me to reach financial independence, I might be tempted to throw in the towel at the sign of the first late rent payment. I have said time and time again on the radio and TV talk shows recently: *"I hate real estate."* Real estate is not sacred to me. Financial independence is! I know that I will have to sacrifice in order to win the prize and so I grit my teeth and bear it.

But even all of this knowledge still is not enough to tend to the details sometimes. A few years ago I made the mistake of letting a local management company take over the day-to-day operations of my properties. I had decided that I wanted no more to do with them. But then I also let them assume control of the vital details . . . and I delegated control to them without following through to check up on them. One day from out of the blue I received a $10,000 bill from my company. It seems they had not done a proper job . . . and upon closer examination many of my single family homes were vacant or occupied with undesirable tenants, one of which owed $1,300 in back rent which I have only recently been able to collect. Once again, I had to learn my lesson the hard way. You cannot delegate the responsibility of your property to someone else unless you have the courage to follow up on the little details to make sure that they are being taken care of. I have always had a hard time when it comes to execution . . . although I am great in coming up with the ideas and understanding the big picture. If you are prone to be this way also, I can offer this piece of advice. The money is made in attending to the details. This life is full of great starters but only the great finishers get what they want. As Robert Frost once said, "Life is a ton of Discipline." I am still learning this lesson—and I'm sure that I'm not through paying for my ignorance.

I hope that you haven't been discouraged by all of this. In fact, I have attempted to encourage you by all of this. As I look at it, if I can make it after all of the money that I have wasted in my mistakes, then anybody who follows my program point by point cannot fail! You don't have to make the same mistakes I did. And if you do, don't give up hope. Real estate is the most forgiving of all investments. Successful people often go through more failures than failures do. But they keep trying.

The Boston "Ruff Company" Challenge

Robert G. Allen

On June 23, 1982 I appeared on Howard Ruff's new television show, "The Ruff Company," which is taped in Boston. In the course of the interview, I found occasion to repeat my famous statement, "Send me to any city in the United States. Take away my wallet. Give me $100 for living expenses. And in 72 hours I'll buy an excellent piece of real estate using none of my own money."

Howard said, "I know that you can do that. But can someone here in my audience do it? And can they do it here in Boston?"

I said, "Of course!"

And he said, "Prove it".

And that is how the challenge came about.

"The Ruff Company" people notified me on July 15, as I recall, that the challenge date would be Thursday and Friday, July 22 and 23. As soon as I had definite dates I began to go into action. What I am about to describe to you now is how I go about finding property for no money down, what principles guide my action, what specific steps I take . . . and, hopefully, how you can do the same with some study and practice.

The most important thing to remember when buying property for nothing down is that 90% of the sellers, Realtors, attorneys and bankers you talk to will tell you that what you are trying to do is impossible. That shouldn't get you discouraged. I guarantee you that there are plenty of nothing down properties in your city. Don't listen to the skeptics. The graduates of my nationwide seminar are located in every major city in the United States and buy collectively Billions of dollars worth of real estate every year . . . with little or no money down. It can be done. And you can do it.

People are generally skeptical because they don't understand what

"Nothing Down" means. They assume that there is absolutely no cash in the transaction . . . the seller gets no cash, the Realtor gets no cash commissions and the buyer doesn't come up with cash out of his own pocket. Not so. There are at least 50 ways of buying property with nothing down . . . and many of these techniques involve cash. But the goal of a nothing down investor is not to use any of his own cash.

The real secret is to learn how to find "don't wanters." What is a don't wanter? This is a motivated seller. . . a flexible seller. And how many don't wanters are there? Our research shows that as many as 20% of all the sellers who advertise their properties for sale in the classified section of the local newspaper are willing to be creative in the sale of their properties. As many as 2% of the sellers in a marketplace are highly motivated . . . some even desperate. I'll prove this to you in a minute.

What are some of the causes of such distress? There are dozens of reasons, but the prevalent ones are divorce, transfer, management headaches, having bought a new home without selling the first home (two mortgage payments), retirement, and profit taking. You must learn how to find highly motivated sellers who have problems that they need solving.

Just because you are dealing with problems doesn't mean that you have to feel that you are taking advantage of anyone. In our seminars, we teach what we call the "win/win" philosophy. We try to teach our graduates how to find sellers who have problems that need solving. You would be surprised at the change in the tone of your negotiations when, instead of being an adversary, you become a problem solver.

The first step in finding a don't wanter is to know where to find them. There are four major sources. I'll list them in their order of importance.

1. The Newspaper. The newspaper is the cheapest and most productive source of leads to flexible sellers. My first request of "The Ruff Company" staff was that they immediately send me a copy of the local classified ads. When I read these ads I look for clues to flexibility. I look for *blatant* clues . . . like "nothing down" or "low down". And I look for *subtle* clues . . . like "owner will carry some financing." I go through the entire paper searching for every ad which indicates clues to serious flexibility. From the Boston paper of Sunday, July 11, 1982, I circled thirty-five ads which interested me. As it turned out, one of these thirty-five ads belonged to the seller who eventually sold us a property with nothing down. I can almost guarantee that there are a half-dozen or more nothing down properties among the thirty-five I circled . . . if the right techniques are used in negotiation.

Below you will find the ads I circled.

You will notice the real blatant ones right off. Look at the first few. Then there are lots of ads which indicate that the seller is willing to sell or to lease with an option to buy. This is a dead giveaway. If a person is willing to lease with an option to buy later, he is really trying to give you a subtle hint that he doesn't need cash! What he probably needs is someone to come in and make his monthly payments on his vacant home that he can't sell.

The ad for the property we eventually bought indicates some very flexible and creative sellers. They will sell with a small down payment, zero interest, or a lease option. What they are saying... although they never say "nothing down"... is that they want to have a problem solved and they are willing to entertain any solutions.

It has never failed me in the many times I have been challenged to buy property in various cities... Miami, San Diego, San Francisco, etc.... that I buy at least one property from a simple clue that I read in the newspaper. These clues are available for anyone to read. But most people read the ads backwards. What I mean by this, is most people look for what they want in a property... its size, location, amenities. Then they set up an appointment to see the property. And if they then like it they make an offer. This is far too much work for me. I am not interested in what a property looks like until I know about the financing. If I can't buy it with a nothing down technique I'm not interested. So I can do almost all of the work on the phone. I don't waste time and money looking at properties until I know I can buy with nothing down. Much more efficient.

As soon as I had done my ad-circling, I called Joe Donofrio, the person that the "Ruff Company" had selected out of the studio audience to complete the challenge with me. I read to him over the phone the ads I had found which showed the most promise. I had him call the sellers to see if there was a possibility for a nothing down sale.

In the three or four days which Mr. Donofrio spent in calling on these ads he located at least three serious don't wanter situations which would eventually lead to nothing down transactions. One property was owned by an out-of-state owner who had to move and leave the unit vacant. The payments were heavy and the seller had indicated extreme flexibility in solving the problem. One other unit was owned by a developer who had only a few units left in a condominium project. When Joe first approached him about a nothing down offer, the seller declined. But Joe left his number with the developer who called back a few days later and agreed to accept the offer.

I can't emphasize enough that this is a numbers game. Only one out of ten sellers will be agreeable to such flexible terms. The nine are very vocal. They will almost be offended by your audacity. But when you find a real don't wanter, you will be welcomed. You just have to have the persistence to keep up your search until you are successful.

2. Creative Realtors. The second source of flexible don't wanter sellers is through creative realtors. And there aren't very many of them. So when you find one, he or she is worth his or her weight in gold. My best luck of finding creative realtors is looking for "exchangors." An exchangor is a creative Realtor. Exchangors usually band together in Exchange Groups nationwide. They are trained in creative problem solving. They understand flexibility. They are not afraid of the nothing down offer so long as it can be structured in a way to solve the seller's problem and give him adequate security. I subscribe to a national magazine which lists the names and addresses of all exchange presidents in the United States. The *Creative Real Estate Magazine* is published monthly, costs less than three dollars an issue, and is full of practical ideas on creative real estate. You can call (714) 438-2446 in Leucadia, California for more information. I looked in a back issue of this magazine to find the name of the president of the Boston Exchange Group. It was listed under New England Real Estate Exchangors and gave the name of May Hashem of Hashem Realty in North Redding. I called and found out that she was no longer the president of the group but found that her son, Jack, was an active exchangor. I asked him if he had any properties which would be suitable nothing down purchases. In the next day, he had found at least one excellent property . . . a duplex. And he had referred me to two or three other creative individuals who also located properties for me.

It is important when dealing with Realtors to deal with professionals who understand the creative process. Most Realtors are not schooled in creative financing and serve as roadblocks rather than as the facilitators they should be. Don't waste time with uncreative Realtors. Finding a good Realtor to work with is every bit as important as finding the right flexible seller. Most people don't like to take the necessary time to search for the right people. But once you find the right people, the whole process becomes very easy. That is why I am never afraid to accept a challenge to buy property with nothing down. When you understand the right concepts, techniques and strategies, it is almost impossible *not* to find a nothing down property.

Using these two sources of finding don't wanters was all that was necessary for Joe and me to find an excellent property for sale with nothing down. We had found, even before I arrived in Boston to film the purchase, at least seven excellent properties which we could have purchased. The hard part was putting everyone's schedule together so that we could film the actual negotiation at the property. I arrived in Boston at 10 p.m. Thursday evening. Joe and I narrowed our selection down to one property and by the next morning before noon the entire purchase had been filmed. And that evening we appeared on "The Ruff Company" to tell about it.

The property was a two-bedroom, two-bath condominium priced at $80,000 with an assumable 12.75% first mortgage of $57,000. The seller agreed to accept a $23,000 second mortgage for the entire balance of his equity. The interest rate in the first year was 12% with a monthly payment of $50. This was scheduled to increase in later years. The seller's motivation to be so flexible was the fact that he had bought four condominiums out of foreclosure from a savings and loan. He was willing to be flexible in the way he took his profit.

3. The Multiple Listing Book. If I had exhausted the supply of don't wanters both in the newspaper and through creative Realtors, I would have then gone to the next best source of don't wanters . . . the local multiple listing book. Realtors have a central listing of all properties for sale in the Boston area. The book has pictures of almost every listed property complete with all pertinent sale information. A novice investor doesn't really realize how many clues there are in this information. Even most Realtors don't understand how many nothing down techniques could be used to sell their own listings . . . all with win/win solutions to the seller's problems.

In our seminars, I have someone bring a multiple listing book and I have student call out a random number in the book . . . we turn to that page and find a property to buy with nothing down. Once you understand the techniques it is that easy. If you want to study one of the techniques which is very powerful, turn to page 148 in my book, *Nothing Down*. Here I describe the Second Mortgage Crank technique. If you don't have a copy of my book, I am told that you can check it out of your public library . . . although there is a waiting line to read it.

4. Hard-Money Lenders. One last source of don't wanters is banks, savings and loan associations, and finance companies. Most lending institutions have been forced lately to repossess many properties on which they have lent money. The tough economic times are the cause. But most people don't realize that these financial institutions which put on such a hard facade when you approach them to solve your problems . . . are as flexible as can be when you approach them to solve one of their problems. And the problem that they are most concerned with is how to get rid of all of these foreclosed properties. They don't want them! And they are very generous in their terms to help you take these properties off their hands. You may not find many nothing down deals but you can negotiate excellent below-market financing with excellent below-market prices on these bank properties.

Well, this has been a rough sketch of "The Boston Challenge." I have tried to teach you the basics, but there is much more to learn if you want to be an accomplished investor. Even if you only want to buy your own home, I would recommend that you buy or borrow a copy of my book and read it from cover to cover to get the overall picture.

If you want to use real estate as a vehicle to take you to financial independence, I would recommend my newsletter. The cost is $96 for a yearly subscription. But the best part of the package is our toll-free hotline which you can use as often as you like. If you have a question, a problem, or an opportunity you can call the hotline and have one of my assistants talk you through exactly what you should do to put your deal together. Some have even called right from the negotiating table to ask for specific advice.

Our guarantee is the most confident of any newsletter in the United States
... if you haven't bought at least one property with our help during the first
six months of your subscription we don't deserve to get paid. We'll refund
your money... and you can keep your copy of *Nothing Down* which all first-
time subscribers receive as a bonus. We want you to be successful.

Good luck and happy buying.

Making It Big
On Little Deals

John Schaub

For nearly fourteen years I have been buying, selling, and investing in various kinds of real estate. Looking back over those years, a casual observer may draw the incorrect conclusion that I was consciously trying to make all the mistakes I could. I have a knack for getting into deals that cost me not only time, but also my hard-earned money. These mistakes were the result of a hyperactive buyer in a market in which I perceived I could get rich quickly.

Over the years I have developed a philosophy of investing which I call "Making It Big on Little Deals." Some of you may have heard of the three-day seminar by the same title I teach in buying and managing single-family homes. Many of the mistakes I have made have been related to "big deals." I have owned several larger properties ranging from apartments and motels, to operating businesses, to land. Each of these properties have caused aggravation and shaved years off of my life expectancy with no compensating large profits to make me feel better.

I have therefore concluded that I can make bigger profits and enjoy my life more by buying and managing "little deals," specifically good houses in good neighborhoods. I now use a simple strategy of buying only from those people who really want to sell and are willing to give me a real bargain. Then I keep the house and rent it to good people, until someone who really wants to buy it offers me more than it is really worth.

At this point in life, I can look back over several hundred transactions in which I was the buyer or seller, and institute a little self-analysis. It becomes apparent that at certain points in this adventure I was compulsive about using certain financing techniques to acquire property which later proved very expensive in terms of long-term profit.

An excellent example of one technique which I became very proficient at using is that of the balloon note. I found that almost anyone would sell a property to me in the event I would promise to pay them the total amount that I owed them in a short period of time, say three to five years. In one year I acquired quite a large number of houses using this technique, only to discover five years later that the only way I could pay off all of these balloons was to sell the properties, or to refinance them to raise the cash for the balloons.

You could guess that the year my balloons came in, the interest rates were at an all-time high, and therefore the real estate market was depressed. Even though I had projected that these houses would go up enough in value in five years to easily pay off these balloons, I found myself unable to quaify for enough loans to pay them all off. When I attempted to sell them on relatively short notice, for enough cash to pay off the balloons, there were very few buyers.

To shorten a sad tale, I sold several good properties which had no balloons at prices far less than what I thought they were worth in order to pay off balloons on properties which were less desirable. I also changed my buying strategy to include the following "Never Sign A Balloon Note." I find that now with my new balloon note policy there are many sellers I cannot deal with because they insist on being paid off in full in a short time. I leave those houses for the people who want a thrilling experience.

Today some buyers are signing notes to sellers when they purchase, promising to pay them an amount which will increase each year because the monthly payments will not cover the interest due. For example, in the event I would buy a house from you and agree to pay you sixty thousand dollars at fourteen percent, the payments of interest-only; would be $8,400 per year or $700 per month. Now if our note read that I had to pay you only $500 per month with the balance of the unpaid interest to accrue and compound with the balance ballooning in seven years, when the note came due I would owe you $87,450.

If the house did not appreciate more than $27,450, your only profit would be in the net rent you had collected, and any tax advantages you would realize. Of course, at the end of the seven years if you sold the property or gave it back to the original owner instead of paying the balloon, you would have to repay that tax savings.

To protect myself from falling into that trap, I adopted another policy "Buy Only Properties With Amortizing Loans." That eliminates interest-only loans, and less-than-interest-only loans as described above.

A major benefit of borrowing only from sellers and avoiding all types of institutional financing is that as a buyer you always have a choice as to what kind of loans you will sign. When you borrow from a bank, there are rigid policies about the type of terms and the paperwork that you will be required to sign. Banks also want personal guarantees and a peek at my financial statement, and I will not cooperate with either "request." "Never Borrow From Any Institution" is a policy which will keep you from paying retail interest rates and dramatically increase your chances of surviving in the jungle of real estate investing.

On several occasions I have been able to renegotiate some of the terms on a note with a private lender, years after the deal has closed. Often it is possible to extend the term of the loan in exchange for raising the payments, not the interest rate. A bank would want a new appraisal, new loan fees, and a higher rate to renegotiate the payment schedule.

Sometimes you can negotiate a discount for early payments. For example, if I owed you $10,000 payable at $100 per month at ten percent interest, and found that I had an extra five thousand dollars, I would offer to pay you five thousand dollars today instead of $100 for the next seventeen years. Many people could put $5,000 to good use that would just blow $100 per month.

By paying early at a discount, I increase my profit in the house and reduce my debt and overall risk. Obviously my cash flow will now be $100 per month more, which in itself is not a bad return on a $5,000 investment. There are tax consequences of prepaying debt at a discount, and you should consult your accountant before filing your return. However, the profit you realize will outshadow the tax effect in most cases.

Buying good houses with good financing is only half the battle. Next you have to collect rent for a length of time to either pay off the debt or until you can sell the house at an acceptable profit. Most buy properties with the idea of reselling them at a large profit in the not-too-distant future. It is interesting, though, as you continue to raise the rents, how much fun it is to just keep those houses and spend the cash flow.

I still own houses that I purchased ten years ago, and I have no intention of selling those properties now, as they make money each month. The strong positive cash flows that these properties produce allow me to purchase other houses with marginal cash flow, but with large tax advantages and long-term profit potential.

I dislike management as much as any other landlord. Fortunately my average tenant stays over four years, and this lack of turnover makes my job as a manager of dozens of tenants easier. The key to attracting good long-term tenants is buying the right property in the beginning. Slum properties will never attract good tenants no matter how cheap you make the rent. Ask yourself if you would move your family into a substandard house just because it was cheap.

None of the duplexes, apartments, or condominiums I have owned and managed have attracted tenants that stayed as long, payed as well, or maintained the property as well as the tenants in my houses. Today I will "Buy Only Above Average Houses In Good Areas," and strongly suggest you do the same. It is unfair to treat the subject of management so lightly, as I spend nearly a solid day in the three-day seminar explaining my system in detail. But no matter what system you use to manage, the key is the type of property you buy.

Large equities tempt you to refinance old loans to pull out some of your equity. This strategy can be disasterous. Your properties with the larger equities are the safest in your portfolio, and have the best cash flows. Should you refinance to buy more property, your good cash flows will disappear, and you may find yourself buying more houses which themselves have no cash flow.

In addition, many of your older loans are at lower interest rates and are fully-assumable by another owner at the same interest rate. The new loans available typically are at much higher rates, require personal guarantees, and often have interest rates which will vary with the market, or increase upon the transfer of the property to another owner. These factors reduce your long term profit and risk, so please, "Don't Refinance Good Loans."

In conclusion I'll confess that I have broken all of the above policies, and each time I have it has cost me plenty. It always seems easier at the time to say *yes* to a balloon payment, or to go to the bank to borrow the down payment, and the temptation to refinance and grab that cash is always there. But you take such actions at the risk of all of your potential profits down the road.

The road to wealth, even in a conservative investment like houses, is lined with pitfalls. In the event that you are to be one of the few that *makes it big,* you will have to establish your own policies and stick with the ones that work for you.

John Schaub has experience in all phases of real estate. For six years he was an active Broker in Florida specializing in investment properties. In 1976 he had accumulated enough properties of his own that he retired from the general brokerage to spend full time buying and managing for his own account. That same year he teamed up with Jack Miller and together they began teaching the now famous, Making It Big On Little Deals Seminar. This three-day, intensive class, which is still taught by the authors, is constantly rated as the number-one seminar in the country on buying and managing single-family houses investments. The class is conducted only six times a year and you can receive a schedule of classes by writing to John Schaub, 1938 Ringling Blvd., Sarasota, FL 33577, or call (813) 366-9024.

Myths and Magic in Creative Finance

Richard J. Allen

There is a lot of value to the practice of sharing ideas and experiences. No one in our business has a monopoly on creativity. New approaches are constantly being tried out and perfected by active investors throughout the Nothing Down network of many thousands of graduates. Valuable new insights into the world of real estate investments are being developed at every turn.

Just how to pull together all the new ideas from such a far-flung group of people is a challenge. However, a recent study of the Nothing Down graduates completed by a faculty-supervised research team from Brigham Young University Graduate School of Business in Provo, Utah, sheds some light on the subject. The team carried out an extensive telephone survey based on the latest scientific techniques of data gathering and statistical analysis.

Among other things, they learned that around 25% of the graduates in the system have purchased at least one property since taking the seminar. As it turns out, that amounts to a level of buying in excess of $1 billion worth of real estate per year. A lot of property! Looking back, 94% of those surveyed who had purchased property expressed their approval of the nothing down methods. The figure was 88% in the case of those who had not purchased property—still a very high level of endorsement. The system works!

Here is a listing of the eight major insights uncovered by the BYU research project:

To begin with, the report shoots down three sacred cows or investment myths that tend to creep into the minds of some investors if they are not careful.

1. **The Myth of the Supersalesman.** One of the questions asked by the

survey was this: "Is salesmanship important when using nothing down methods?" Among those who had bought property since the seminar (we'll call them "buyers."), only 10% felt strongly that salesmanship is important. However, among those who had bought no property (we'll call them "criers."), fully 30% agreed strongly that salesmanship is an important aspect. Since both buyers and criers were about even in their response to questions designed to measure self-image in being successful barterers or salesmen, the implication is clear. Those who are successful don't feel it is all that important to be supersalesmen. Those who have not yet bought property tend to feel much more strongly that they need to be supersalesmen to succeed. The moral: Don't wait to buy real estate out of a concern about putting your salesmanship to work. With a good working knowledge of creative finance and an ability to generate trust in sellers, you just plain don't need to be supersalesmen—that is a myth.

2. **The Spare Time Myth.** The university study found no significant difference in the success of nothing down graduates as a function of how much spare time they have. Ouch! That hurts! Here we have been depending on this excuse for all our procrastination. Another sacred cow shot down. The implication is this: Those who succeed at the nothing down system are evidently capable of getting the job done in spite of a busy schedule. If they don't have the time, they either find the time or find someone else who has the time and can do the job for them (partners, family members, associates, professionals, etc.).

3. **The Silver Spoon Myth.** The study could not uncover any rational evidence why personal wealth, as such, should be essential to success in the nothing down system. That puts us all in the same boat. ("You always run out of money before you run out of good deals!") Likewise, age, marital status, or general education level are not significant factors.

Besides shooting down these three myths, the BYU study uncovered five major principles that apply to nothing down investing. When applied correctly, they work magic in creative real estate investing. I have set aside the technical jargon of the report and provided my own terms, drawing on the statistics for support. Here are the principles to look for:

1. **The Elbow Grease Principle.** We have already alluded to the level of activity among buyers in the Nothing Down network—around $20 million per week or over $1 billion per year. Among the buyers, the average investment was 2.6 properties each ($220,000 worth of real estate), the median property value being around $60,000.

One in four persons surveyed had bought at least one property. Among those who had not purchased a property, fully two-thirds—and here is the lesson to be learned—had not even tried; they had neither invested significant effort in finding properties nor made any offers. Therefore, we can restate the Elbow Grease Principle as follows:

"If you don't try, you don't buy." Or, putting it more positively: "If you try, you buy." It's an age-old bit of wisdom, that anything worthwhile has to be worked at. Even the best of systems is lame without effort.

2. **The Hot Coal Principle.** The BYU study substantiated one of our suspicions: The sooner a graduate acts on the nothing down approach, the better are the chances for success. The longer one puts it off, the harder it is going to be. The survey called for a response from the graduates to the statement: "Anyone can succeed using nothing down principles." Two-thirds agreed strongly with this statement during the time frame of six months after the seminar. Only one-half agreed with the statement if it had been between six and twelve months since they took the seminar. After twelve months, only one-third agreed with the statement. The longer away from the fire, the colder the coals become. It is an important action principle that we must act quickly to follow through on our convictions.

3. **The Battery Charger Principle.** Those in-the-know stay informed. It is a fact of life. Fully 94% of the persons surveyed agreed that it is very important to keep learning about investment principles. You just cannot let the battery go dead. These figures tell the whole story:

	Buyers	**Criers**
Have attended more than one seminar (besides Nothing Down):	50%	25%
Active in the ACRE/RAND group:	80%	60%
Attend ACRE/RAND group each month:	50%	25%
Study materials regularly:	90%	68%

It is vital to keep those batteries charged up fully. Sometimes we get to feeling so sophisticated that we forget to be teachable and willing to keep learning. Keeping up-to-date will often change a crier into a buyer.

4. **The Cliff Principle.** The survey asked for a response to the statement: "I like my investments to be very secure, with no chance of losing everything." Among the buyers, one-fourth agreed strongly with the statement, as compared with one-half among the criers (non-buyers). Evidently non-buyers are concerned about risk-taking to the extent that it interferes with action. It is a fact of life that important ventures sometimes require us to take risks. We have to choose between comfort and active involvement. There comes a point when we have to jump off the cliff.

5. The Bullseye Principle. According to the BYU study, if you have written goals, your chances of succeeding with the nothing down program are far better than if you leave your goals to chance. Among the criers, only 30% had developed written goals. Among the buyers, the figure was 50%. The implication is that even the buyers could have been more successful in hitting their bullseye if they had developed a written game plan. Let all take note. Our success depends upon it!

The final two lessons to be learned from the nothing down graduates came to light while I was completing work on the book *How to Write a Nothing Down Offer.* This volume of fifty case studies selected from among the hundreds submitted by graduates over the past few years details the purchase of over $10,000,000 worth of real estate. The case studies cover a total of 61 transactions in 35 different cities—in all, 543 rental units in 256 different properties ranging from $3,000 to $3,000,000 per transaction (the average price being $166,411, with a median price of $72,000).

The first thing that struck me about this great cross-section of nothing down buying was the ingenuity of graduates in combining creative finance techniques in a given purchase. Each transaction involved anywhere from one to nine of the fifty nothing down techniques, the average number being *four.*

By determining the details of the situation at hand, especially the needs of the seller, the investor was able to perceive which combination of techniques would lead to the best win/win outcomes. Here is a listing of the most frequently used techniques (showing the incidence of a given technique expressed as a percentage of the total number of times any technique showed up in the tally).

Title	Technique No.	Percentage Frequency
Contract/Wrap-around Mortgage/Carry Back	4	19.3%
Balloon Mortgage	6	13.4%
Second Mortgage Crank	32	6.4%
Borrowing Realtor's Commission	19	5.0%
Partner's Cash/Your Expertise	45	5.0%
Renter's Deposits	21	4.5%
Ultimate Paper Out	1	3.5%
Rents	20	3.5%
Moving the Mortgage	36	3.5%
Borrowing Against Life Insurance	13	2.5%
Creation of Paper	15	2.5%
Small Amounts from Different Banks	24	2.5%
Borrow Partner's Money (as investment)	42	2.5%

The second thing that struck me as I wrote the book was the pattern of risk-reduction strategies cultivated by the buyers. The most frequently used technique of all was the contract purchase, especially in combination with the balloon mortgage. However, the buyers were careful to structure their transactions to avoid negative cash flows and short-fuse balloons. In most cases, the balloons were not due for five years or longer. Some deals involved seven- or even ten-year notes. Many cases involved fully amortized owner carry-back notes of as long as thirty years! The point is that the graduates were careful to avoid situations they could not handle. Good advice any day of the week!

The other dimension of risk-reduction showed up in the documentation. Seasoned investors develop an inventory of clauses and phrases that they always write into their offers. In some cases the sellers will balk at the contingencies, but an experienced investor will always try anyway. The book *How to Write A Nothing Down Offer* gives full details on this aspect of real estate investing. A summary of the main points is provided elsewhere in this volume under the title " 'I Agree/You Agree:' How to Write Risk-Free Offers." However, here are a number of the more obvious examples to point you in the right direction:

Balloon Extention Contingency — "Buyer shall have the right to extend the balloon payment, at his option, for an additional twelve months, provided a principal payment of $_____ is made to the Seller on the original due date of the balloon."

Substitution of Collateral — "Buyer has the right to substitute collateral of equal or greater value on the second mortgage (second trust deed, etc.) at any time, with the Seller having the right to approve."

First Right of Refusal on Carry Back Note — "This arrangement is contingent upon Buyer having first right of refusal on the second note and deed of trust (etc.) if Seller should decide to sell the note."

Limitation of Damages — "In the event the Buyer fails to complete the purchase as herein provided, the earnest money deposit shall be retained by the Seller as total and entire liquidated damages."

Eliminating Personal Liability — "The liability of this contract shall be limited to the property itself and shall not extend beyond this."

There are dozens of additional risk-reduction clauses that are frequently used by seasoned investors. Consult *How to Write A Nothing Down Offer*, then work closely with professional Realtors, title company officers, tax accountants and attorneys to achieve the results you want.

In summary, here are the ten greatest lessons to be learned from the nothing down graduates out in the field:

1. You don't have to be a supersalesman to succeed.

2. You don't need a great deal of spare time to make the program work.

3. Your own personal wealth, age, marital status, or general education level need not be significant factors in your success.

4. "If you don't try, you don't buy."

5. The longer you wait to act, the harder it gets.

6. You have to stay informed through seminars, newsletters, and frequent review of the techniques.

7. You have to be willing to take risks.

8. The chances of success are far better if you have written goals.

9. You need to know which techniques to use in meeting the seller's (and your) needs in a given situation.

10. Learn the strategies the pros use to reduce risk as much as possible.

From our perspective, these ten lessons have great merit. Adapt them for use in your own program and let us know how things work out for you. Happy investing.

Questions and Answers About Putting Creative Finance to Work for You

Richard J. Allen

Question

"I'm in a situation where I could be transferred but don't know where or how soon. I took the Nothing Down Seminar recently and am excited to get started. Should I wait until my transfer comes and begin my program in my new location, or should I start here while my excitement is high?"
D.E., Chicago

Answer

By all means get started immediately. Our research shows that success in buying real estate is a function of how quickly one takes hold after the seminar experience is over. You are twice as likely to maintain a success attitude towards nothing down buying if you make your first purchase within the first six months as compared with waiting for a year. (The average time lapse between the time of the seminar and the first purchase is 3.68 months.)

The question is what strategy to use if you feel your transfer might be imminent. There is no problem if you concentrate on transactions that turn properties over rather quickly to generate cash. The problem comes in managing properties you buy to hold. If you buy to hold, make sure there is sufficient cash flow built in to afford competent property management. Some investors have had good success with professional property management companies, especially if you check up on them frequently and have local backup to assess their performance. Other investors use payrolled on-site management (with multi-units) or turn to equity participation or lease options for single-family homes. With equity participation in particular there is a built-in maintenance incentive for the occupant, who treats the property as if it were his or her own (which of course in part it is). The upshot: Don't wait to buy real estate, but make sure proper arrangements are made for the management before your move. Absentee landlording is one of the primary causes for don't wanteritis. The cure is sound management.

Question

"I am very excited about my investment program. I took your seminar and then jumped in and started investing—with some success. Meanwhile, I have become bored with my job and feel like I should resign and start investing full time. Should I?"
D.P., Los Angeles

Answer

There are great advantages to becoming a full-time independent investor—what Bob Allen calls "creative self-unemployment." It frees you up to put all your time and talent into building your own empire instead of someone else's. You control your own financial destiny. You can use your knowledge of real estate and creative acquisition techniques to become financially independent. The rewards can be significant if you prepare for such an important move in a businesslike manner.

However, there are cautions to observe. Becoming a full-time investor should be a rational decision, not an emotional one. You should not quit your job until you have adequate financial reserves, perhaps enough to cover six to twelve months of living expenses, or an adequate outside monthly cash flow. If you are not financially prepared for the move, you will spend too much time worrying about money and scrambling for daily funds.

Moreover, as soon as you quit your job and cut off your steady income, you also relinquish your credit. One graduate told us that he had quit his job to invest full time. He had considerable reserves in the bank, and his wife was working. However, he went to a bank to get a second-mortgage loan and found that he could not gualify. The Nothing Down System provides strategies for acquiring property without the Big Four: cash, credit, income, and financial statement. However, to make a full-time effort of it, you should be prepared for any eventualities, especially in tight-money times like these. Reread Chapter 21 on "Creative Self-Unemployment" in Robert Allen's book *Nothing Down.* You might have the courage and know-how to make the move, but look before you leap!

How to Speak Creative Finance: Mastering the Language and Terminology of Creative Real Estate Investing

Richard J. Allen

Welcome to the circle of those practicing creative finance approaches to real estate investing. We thought you would enjoy reading the following dialogue as preparation or review for your investment activities. With a little practice, you'll find that creative finance terminology will become second nature to you—perhaps it already is! At the end of the dialogue you will find an alphabetized listing of the numbered entries printed in bold type in the text. Have fun! We look forward to having you as a participant in the ACRE/RAND Investment Program.

Meet Doug:

Doug is a professional—bright, progressive, competent at his job. But he is new to real estate and a bit frightened by the welter of new vocabulary items used in buying and selling property. He needs a little coaching.

Meet Mark:

Mark is an investor who knows from experience how to transact deals using creative financing. The vocabulary is second-nature to him by now. Still, he hasn't forgotten how tricky it was, at the beginning, to distinguish between puzzling things like: wrap-around mortgage, a second deed of trust, and a quit-claim deed. Let's listen to their conversation. Whether your name is Doug, or Jim, or Judy, perhaps this dialogue will help demystify real estate for you.

Doug: This real estate world is a bit baffling to me, Mark. I wonder if I am capable of learning the "script."

Mark: Like every other human activity, Doug, the world of real estate investments has its own rules and setting. It's a dramatic setting—a stage with many roles and actors. There are really only two villains: fear and ignorance. The hero is the creative person who invests judiciously and progresses towards financial independence. The play is a tragedy if the main player lacks initiative and gets eaten alive by inflation. The play is a romantic farce if the main character wastes his time eating pie in the sky and dreaming of lost treasures that he'll never see. The only script that makes sense is the one where the hero takes charge of his affairs, plans carefully, sets specific goals, masters the "Nothing Down" creative financing system, and puts it into effect. He doesn't wait to buy real estate; he buys real estate and waits.

Doug: There seems to be a huge supporting cast to this production. How am I going to sort them all out?

Mark: (laughs) It's not as complex as you might think. Basically we're talking about a *buyer* and a *seller.* Of course, legal documents tend to use stuffy terms. Even so, all you have to do is keep your "—ees" and your "—ors" straight. The *vendor*[1] is a person selling something to the *vendee*[2] (or buyer). Sometimes they talk about the *grantor,*[3] the person who transfers interest in a piece of property to the *grantee*[4] (or recipient). There are other parallels. In the rental market, for example, the *lessor*[5] (landlord) gives to the *lessee*[6] (tenant) the right to occupy a rental space. You see, the "—ors" have something to *o*ffer (remember the "o" in "offer" and relate it to "—or"). The "—ees" have something to g*e*t (remember the "e" in "get" and relate it to "—ee").

Doug: That reminds me. I could never keep mortgagor and mortgagee straight.

Mark: It's easy. The *mortgagor*[7] (borrower) has something to offer—he offers a mortgage or trust deed (i.e., a secured I.O.U.) to the bank in order to obtain a loan. The *mortgagee*[8] (bank) has something to get—that's the mortgage or trust deed setting forth the provisions according to which the loan is to be repaid.

Doug: What's all this about a don't wanter?

Mark: The don't wanter is one of the main characters in the play! A *don't wanter*[9] is a person who is willing to sell his or her property flexibly— i.e., by giving you either *your* price or *your* terms (sometimes even both). The *terms*[10] refer, of course, to the amount of down payment, the size and frequency of the repayment amounts, interest rate, and so on. A true don't wanter is anxious to help you acquire his property. Perhaps only 5% of the sellers are true don't wanters. So we have to know how to locate them. That's an important part of the Nothing Down seminar.

Doug: How about the other professionals out there?

Mark: People involved in the sale of real estate have various titles. The *real estate agent*[11] (or *broker*[12]) is licensed in the state to negotiate a real estate transaction for another party for compensation. The *Realtor*[13] (a title, capitalized) is an agent or broker who is an active member of a local real estate organization affiliated with the National Association of Realtors, a professional association holding to a prescribed code of professional ethics. A *real estate salesman (salesperson)*[14] is licensed to transact real estate business but not by himself; he or she has to work under the direction of a broker. The broker, under the law, is the one who has the agent relationship with the person who seeks professional services.

Doug: Who is going to help me with all the documentation of real estate transactions?

Mark: That is the *title company officer,*[15] one of the most important professionals available to you. He serves as a neutral third party drawing up all the legal paperwork needed to transact business in real estate. The title company is equipped to carry out thorough examinations of the public records concerning a property and confirm its ownership, find out whether there are any encumbrances or liens against it, and any other facts that might affect its sale. The title company issues a *policy of title insurance*[16] guaranteeing compensation to the holder of the policy if any defects or problems with the title should show up later. The title company officer also frequently serves as the *escrow agent*[17] who holds and disposes of documents or funds according to the instruction agreed upon by the buyer and seller.

Other important professionals include the *appraiser,*[18] who is trained to give an estimate or opinion about the value of the property in question. If the appraiser has the title *Member, Appraisal Institute (MAI),*[19] he or she holds the highest title or designation given by the American Institute of Real Estate Appraisers. Besides the appraiser, you may often need the services of a competent *real estate attorney*[20] to advise you on legal aspects of real estate, as well as a competent *accountant*[21] to handle the financial records, advise you on taxes, etc. In some areas, for example, it is customary for attorneys to perform many of the functions of the title company officer outlined above. You might also be using a professional *property manager*[22] to help you with the management of your portfolio.

Doug: It's a relief to know that I'll have a team to work with in putting all of this together. Could you give me some help with the world of real estate finance and ownership?

Mark: Sure. Basically you'll be dealing with "hard money lenders" and "soft money lenders." The former are the people whose business it is to lend money under very strict conditions of qualifying and repayment. Here we are referring to the *commercial savings banks*[23] (usually specializing in short-term loans) and the *savings and loan associations*[24] (up until recently almost exclusively long-term mortgage loans for residential real estate). There are also the *finance companies*[25] who mainly deal in second mortgage loans (usually at a very high rate of interest and for shorter repayment periods of 5 to 10 years or less). The "soft money lenders" are the people who lend without such strict requirements of qualifying and with more flexible repayment terms. Here we are thinking of the seller himself, who will frequently finance the sale of his property on a contract. *Partners*[26] you might be dealing with also belong to the soft money camp.

Doug: How about the specific terms having to do with ownership and borrowing money.

Mark: The most basic term of ownership is the word *deed*,[27] which is the written document that is signed and acknowledged by the maker and serves to transfer ownership (i.e., the *title*[28]) of property from one person to another. There are refinements to that, of course. A *warranty deed*[29] is one in which the seller or grantor guarantees (warrants) that good title is being conveyed, whereas a *quitclaim deed*[30] simply transfers whatever title or right the seller has in the property at that moment and contains no warranty about the general quality of the title being conveyed. You'll see how the quitclaim deed can be used to protect you when *you* sell a property: you'll have the buyer execute one in your name and leave it with the escrow agent (title company officer) who will be instructed by buyer and seller to give it to you in the event the buyer defaults. That way you have security and protection.

Doug: How about the vocabulary of financing? I know what a mortgage does, but I would be hard pressed to define it.

Mark: The word *mortgage*[31] comes from the French and means essentially a "pledge until death." That is a rather solemn kind of I.O.U., isn't it? In reality, the documentation is not complicated. Basically you have two papers: one is the promissory note (I.O.U.) setting forth the terms of repayment of the loan. A second paper serves as the security document and says in essence that if you fail to perform according to your promise, the lender has the right to take over the *collateral*,[32] in this case the property you have pledged as security for the debt. Usually the collateral is the specific property that is being purchased with the funds being borrowed. That's what happens when you buy your own home, for example. You go to the bank or S&L and say: "If you'll give me the money to buy this home with, I'll turn around and pledge it as collateral to secure the debt I have incurred in order to buy it in the first place."

Doug: What is the difference between a mortgage and a deed of trust? Don't they serve the same purpose?

Mark: You are correct, Doug. Keep this in mind as I explain the difference—for loans secured by real property, there are always two basic documents involved: a note (I.O.U.) covering the borrowed funds, plus a security document pledging the real property as a back-up to the loan. In some states the security arrangement is based on a *mortgage*[33]; in other states it is based on a *deed of trust*.[34] Here's how they differ. The mortgage arrangement involves two parties (borrower and lender), while the trust deed involves three: the borrower *(trustor)*[35] and lender *(beneficiary)*,[36] plus a third party called a *trustee*.[37] Title of the collateral property is conveyed in trust to the trustee with the condition that the trustee is to reconvey the title to the borrower upon satisfaction of the note (in this case called a *trust note*[38]).

Doug: What happens if the borrower defaults on the loan?

Mark: In the case of the mortgage, the lender will take legal action by proceeding with the *foreclosure*[39] process and the sale of the collateral property to satisfy the debt. In the case of the trust deed, the trustee already has statutory power (by state statute) to take steps to sell the collateral property to satisfy the debt. Since the foreclosure process for a mortgage is a judicial process—that is, it has to go before the courts, with court cases, court dates, and the like—it takes longer than a trust deed foreclosure. In some states a mortgage foreclosure takes as long as 13 months, while a trust deed foreclosure takes only 3-4 months.

Doug: What if there is no bank or savings and loan association involved, and the owner himself or herself serves as the lender?

Mark: That happens frequently, particularly in times of tight money. There are two basic approaches to seller financing. One involves what is called a *contract of sale*[40] or sometimes a *contract for deed*[41] or a *land contract*.[42] I think you understand what I mean by contract: a written agreement between buyer and seller containing the price and terms, a valid legal description of the property, and all other stipulations agreed to. In the case of such a contract (contract of sale, contract for deed, or land contract), the deed (hence title) does not actually pass to the buyer until the conditions of the contract are satisfied.

Doug: It sounds like what happens with an auto loan. You don't get title until the last payment is made.

Mark: Exactly. It works the same way when you buy real estate on a contract of sale. Meanwhile, the buyer gets all the benefits of property ownership, including appreciation, tax advantages, etc. Even though he doesn't have title until the conditions of the contract are met, he still has what is called *equitable title*.[43] Equitable title means that he benefits from (owns) any increase in his equity even if he doesn't yet have the deed.

Doug: What documents are involved in a contract arrangement?

Mark: There are three to keep in mind: the *contract*[44] itself, a *warranty deed*[45] which the seller executes in favor of the buyer, and a *quitclaim deed*[46] which the buyer executes in favor of the seller. The two deeds are held in escrow by the title company or other escrow agent involved. The buyer gets the warranty deed after he has satisfied the conditions of the contract. If the buyer defaults, the escrow agent is instructed to release the quitclaim deed to the seller, who then recovers his property with a minimum of difficulty. Do you get how it works?

Doug: It's getting clearer to me. I am certainly glad that the title company officer can see to it that all the documents are prepared correctly. What is the second approach to seller financing?

Mark: The other approach is referred to as a *wrap-around mortgage*[47] or in some areas as an *all-inclusive trust deed (AITD)*.[48] Let's suppose the property has a loan against it. The owner's *equity*,[49] then, is the difference between the *fair market value*[50] of the property and the amount of this indebtedness.

Doug: Just a minute. What do you mean by "fair market value?"

Mark: *Fair market value*[51] is the sales price a willing buyer and a willing seller agree upon when both are reasonably informed as to all the pertinent facts and neither is under any compulsion in the transaction. Of course, when the owner is a don't wanter, he might be willing to *discount*[52] his equity and the actual sales price will be below fair market value.

Doug: Clear enough. Go on.

Mark: Well, as I was saying, suppose there is already a loan against the property you want to buy. If you negotiate a wrap-around mortgage or an all inclusive trust deed with the seller, you agree to sign a note that covers not only the balance of the seller's equity (after the down payment—if any) but also the amount of the existing loan against the property.

Doug: Why would the seller agree to do that?

Mark: Well, suppose the existing mortgage or deed of trust was costing the owner 9% interest, and you agree to an 11% figure for the "wrap" or AITD. On the amount of the existing mortgage or deed of trust (sometimes called the *underlying mortgage*[53] or *underlying deed of trust*[54]), the owner then picks up a 2% spread on money that isn't even his. Of course, he gets the full 11% on his equity above the original loan.

Doug: Not bad! Does title actually transfer in such an arrangement?

Mark: Yes, the buyer actually receives a deed and title transfers. And that is what has stirred up a bit of controversy the last few years. If the underlying mortgage or deed of trust was set up fairly recently, let's say within the last seven or eight years, it probably contains a *due-on-sale clause*,[55] sometimes referred to as an *alienation clause*[56] or a *non-assumption clause*.[57] Such a clause states that the lender has the option of calling the entire balance of the loan due should the property be sold and title transfer to another owner. Thus it is possible, especially in the case of a wrap-around mortgage or an AITD, that the lender could call the existing loan all due and payable upon sale of the property.

Doug: What are the implications?

Mark: It would mean that the bank would want to have the new buyer *assume*[58] the existing loan; that is, take over the primary responsibility for repaying it, go through the normal process of qualifying, and probably pay an *assumption fee*[59] and a higher interest rate. The controversy arises when you come back to the issue of whether the bank actually has the right to exercise the due-on-sale clause, especially in cases where its interest is not jeopardized by the sale and transfer of the title. This issue has been widely litigated in the courts across the country. The most famous of such cases is the *Wellingkamp Decision*[60] in California (1978) which stated that state-chartered savings and loan associations do *not* have the right to accelerate the loans in such instances. Naturally the federally chartered S&L's felt they were exempt, so the controversy continued to rage. Recently the United States Supreme Court ruled that lenders *do* have the right to enforce the due-on-sale clause.

Doug: Wouldn't it be safer to assume the existing mortgage or deed of trust in the first place and make arrangements to pay off the seller's equity in a mutually agreeable way?

Mark: It depends on how you stand on the issue, whether you are willing to pay the assumption fee and higher interest rate and what the legal patterns are in your area. Always seek competent legal advice in such matters. Of course, if the existing mortgage or deed of trust is one that is insured (guaranteed) by the *Federal Housing Administration (FHA)*[61] or the *Veterans Administration (VA)*,[62] it is always assumable as is. There is never any problem assuming an FHA or VA loan—no qualifying at all, and you have to pay only a small fee, around $50. The orginal borrower, of course, had to qualify for such a loan, but the person *assuming*[63] the loan does not have to qualify. It is the *conventional loan*[64] (i.e., non-FHA or non-VA) with a non-assumption clause that is at the center of controversy. It is only this latter type that causes concerns in the case of the wrap-around mortgage or AITD.

Doug: But doesn't the contract of sale method also involve properties that might have existing loans against them?

Mark: Yes, but you will remember that in the contract approach, title does not actually pass until the conditions of the contract are satisfied. For this reason, some buyers turn to the contract method where necessary, rather than the wrap-around mortgage or AITD (where title is actually transferred). They are acting on the theory that the contract approach does not violate the provisions of a non-assumption clause in the underlying mortgage or deed of trust. The precedent for this line of reasoning is the *Lassen-Tucker Decision*[65] in California (1976), which seems to have become the basis for legal opinion in such cases in a number of other states. Of course, competent legal advice in your own area is essential. The implications of the recent Supreme Court decision are still being sorted out.

Doug: I suppose that things can get fairly complicated if the same piece of property serves as collateral for different loans at the same time.

Mark: Well, it's really less complex than it sounds. That's where the *Office of the County Recorder*[66] comes in. While this office might have slightly different names in different locations, the function is the same—to "*record*"[67] mortgages, deeds, liens, and other important documents affecting a title of real property. The process of recording makes real estate transactions a part of the general public record, thus protecting the persons involved. When you set about to buy a piece of property, you will arrange for a title company to conduct a *title search*[68] of the public records to make sure you have all the facts concerning the property in question.

Doug: Is that where the designation first, second, third mortgage, etc., comes in?

Mark: Right. This designation refers to the order in which mortgages or deeds of trust are recorded in the Office of the County Recorder. A *second mortgage*[69] or *second deed of trust*[70] is one that happens to be recorded later in time than the *first mortgage*[71] or *first deed of trust.*[72] In a foreclosure procedure, the proceeds from the sale will go to pay off the loans in the order in which they were recorded.

Doug: Is there any limit to the number of *liens*[73] that can be placed on a property?

Mark: There is no magic in the number of such liens. The critical factor is the *security*[74] involved. Let's say a property has a fair market value of $100,000, with a first mortgage of $60,000. The remaining equity of $40,000 is theoretically available as security for additional loans. There might be a second for $20,000, a third for $5,000, and so on, until the property is totally encumbered (100% financed).

Doug: You say "theoretically available."

Mark: Banks usually loan only up to 80% of the value of the property. Sellers, on the other hand, or private individuals, might be induced to accept notes covering the entire value of a piece of property. That's why it is frequently more advantageous to work with private parties.

Doug: What if the property in question serves as security for loans totalling *more* than its fair market value?

Mark: We say then that the property is *over financed.*[75] One must be cautious in such cases not to cross the threshold of legal propriety. One must be cautious to avoid offering real property in a fraudulent way as collateral for a loan. Always seek legal advice in such matters.

Doug: Could you sketch out the general contours of the acquistions process?

Mark: Certainly. After you have located a flexible seller (don't wanter) and conducted one or more fact-finding sessions, you will want to complete your analysis of the property. Your major concerns will be location, condition, and financing. For properties larger than four units, the APOD is useful in financial analysis.

Doug: APOD?

Mark: Yes, the *Annual Property Operating Data*[76] form. It's a standard form that summarizes the expenses and facilitates calculating the *net operating income*[77] of a property (gross scheduled income less all of your operating expenses). Using the net operating income and the value of the property, you can calculate the *capitalization rate*[78] for the property.

Doug: Sounds a bit far out to me.

Mark: Not really. The cap rate, as a percentage, is simply the net operating income divided by the value x 100. For example, if the N.O.I. for a given 5-unit property is $8,000, and the value is $100,000, then the cap rate is

$$\frac{8,000}{100,000} \times 100 = 8\%$$

It's easy.

Doug: Now that I've got it, what do I do with it?

Mark: It's a comparison index. If properties in your area are showing cap rates of 7, 8, or 9%, then this 8% property might look pretty good to you. It's in the financial "ballpark." On the other hand, if the cap rate for a property is 4% in the same area, you might not be too thrilled with it. Either the seller is asking too much for the property, or there is a serious problem with the expenses, forcing the N.O.I. to be too small. In any case it is a red flag for you and almost certainly indicates a *negative cash flow*[79] situation when you go to make the payments on the loan.

Doug: That's what you refer to as an *"alligator."*[80]

Mark: Right. Anytime you have to *add* money from your own pocket to take care of a property, you've got an alligator. Of course, there are small alligators and large alligators. The bigger they are the more likely they are to eat *you.* Sometimes a careless investor will wake up and find that he's got a whole hungry zoo!

Doug: How do you avoid alligators and zoos?

Mark: That's where *creative financing*[81] comes in. After you have decided that a seller is flexible and his property is desirable, it's up to you to find the combination of creative (alternative) financing techniques that will enable you both to win. You solve his problem, and he solves yours. That's what we call *the win/win philosophy.*[82] The idea is to find a mutually agreeable way to buy the property for little or no money down out of your own pocket, with the arrangement structured so that you avoid negative cash flows and also balloon payments that are too oppressive.

Doug: By *balloon payment*[83] you mean a repayment schedule where a large sum comes due sometime down the line.

Mark: Exactly. You might make regular monthly payments for a period of time, say five years, and have the balance due in one balloon sum at the end of that period. In some cases, this might be a good way to go, but one can get carried away with it, particularly if the balloon payment is short term. One thing is for sure, such short-term balloon payments make the time slip by quickly!

Doug: What are some of the creative finance techniques you would recommend?

Mark: That's the subject of a whole session in itself. There are dozens of such techniques that might be applied in a given situation. That's the core of the *Robert Allen Nothing Down Program.* It's the most comprehensive creative finance program available.

Doug: Let's talk about the actual buying process. What is the first document that I will have to know about to buy property?

Mark: Because almost all transactions start with an agreement or offer to buy, the first document is an *earnest money agreement*[84] or *offer to purchase.*[85] This agreement states that a person is ready, willing, and able to buy. There are blank spaces provided for the terms of the transaction—provisions for price, interest rates, monthly payments, and any other conditions the buyer wishes to include. The seller then has the right to accept the offer "as is," reject it, or modify the terms. If he accepts the offer, he signs it, and the paperwork moves on to closing. If he rejects the offer, the deal is off. The buyer may submit another offer. If the seller modifies the agreement, he makes the changes or adds an addendum and sends it back to the buyer. In effect he is now making an offer to the buyer. This type of offer/counteroffer could continue through several changes. Once they both agree, the agreement is signed and then moves on to closing.

Also, most people now use standard (pre-printed) forms which cover the whole range of possible terms. These forms are designed for filling in the blanks. If the wording is not exactly what you want, feel free to adjust it with the help of a competent professional. This wording will have to stand the test of time because it lays the foundation for the terms that will be on subsequent documents. It's important to make sure that it's just what you want.

Doug: Is an *addendum*[86] something that is added to the earnest money?

Mark: Yes, usually on a separate sheet of paper. Reference needs to be made to the original document that it will be added to and more specifically to the paragraph or term on the original document that it will affect.

Doug: You mentioned *closing*.[87] Isn't the deal finished when both the buyer and seller agree to the terms?

Mark: Even though the earnest money dictates what will now take place, the deal is not closed. Closing means that the proper papers are drawn up, signed, and recorded. If you are asked by an *escrow company*[88] to come in for a closing, it means everything is ready. Once completed, title to the property transfers or an interest shows against the title as in the case of a real estate contract.

Doug: Is that all that an escrow company does?

Mark: Drawing up the papers is just part of it. As I said earlier, the escrow company also orders a *title report*[89] and later a *title policy (policy of title insurance)*.[90] This lets you see whether or not the property is free and clear or whether it is encumbered by other liens. It states whether the seller has the right to transfer title. It would be a good idea to request copies of the actual documents that stand against the title to the property, especially if you're assuming those loans.

The escrow company also balances the books. They get the exact figures on the balances of the loans. They figure out the taxes and insurance, etc., and prorate it to the day of the closing (or other agreed date) so you'll only pay exactly what you owe.

Escrow companies also hold documents or money while waiting for other stipulated conditions to be met. It's advisable to get a good escrow officer on your team of experts.

Doug: What is the difference between a *title report*[91] and a *policy of title insurance*[92]?

Mark: A title report is a current reading of the title status of a property. It shows all liens and encumbrances against a property and even any judgments or restrictions against the people or corporations who have an interest in the property. It will also show the current status of the property taxes. This report is also called an *abstract of title*.[93]

One step up from a report is a *policy of title insurance*.[94] A Title Insurance company researches the chain of title and everything else concerning the property (including verifying the legal description and any easements), and once they're certain everything is in good standing, they will issue a title insurance policy to the buyer insuring him against problems which might arise in the future for reasons not then apparent. This is also called a *certificate of title.*[95]

Doug: So once I know that the seller has good title, the deal can proceed to closing.

Mark: That's right. If all is okay, the seller has a *marketable title,*[96] meaning that he can sell or transfer his interest in the property.

Doug: It seems that the legal description appears on every document. Why can't we just use the street address?

Mark: Street addresses are not specific enough in that they don't refer to the actual size or boundaries of the property. Originally a plot map was drawn, and the legal description referred to that actual map. The legal description will be a *lot and block number*[97] (then city, county, and state), be computed by *metes and bounds*[98] (technical measurements) or by *government survey.*[99] The reason these are used is to avoid confusion and problems. If continually used in every transaction concerning a property (and used without changes), a good standard is set, and boundary and easement problems will be lessened.

Doug: It seems like the *chain of title*[100] is really important.

Mark: It is. The chain of title shows the different owners (or lien holders) of a property. It shows what instruments (deeds, mortgages, etc.) were used to transfer title through the property's history. We've previously talked about the different deeds and documents; now it's fun to see how a property has gotten where it is.

Doug: You mentioned that the escrow company figures out the *closing costs.*[101] What are they, and who pays them?

Mark: Every state has a different set of closing costs. The common ones are the fees required to buy title insurance and pay for the escrow company's services. The buyer's charges for insurance, taxes, etc., are not actually closing costs, but they are figured on the same paper. Some states charge a tax (excise) on every property each time it's sold. There could also be revenue stamps to purchase. All of these fees are usually a small portion of the selling price, and most of them are divided between the buyer and seller. Your escrow company can give you a good estimation of what they will be.

Doug: You said that the earnest money was a down payment. Can you explain further?

Mark: Accompanying the agreement is usually an amount of money or at least a promise to pay. This may be called a *deposit,*[102] but whatever it's called, its purpose is to show the buyer's earnestness. If the deal goes through, this amount becomes part of the down payment or purchase price. If the deal is terminated, this money is retained or returned to the party not at fault.

Doug: Is there always a *down payment*[103]?

Mark: Most properties today are purchased with some sort of financing (either by the seller, a bank, or someone else). The down payment is the amount of money (or whatever satisfies the seller) between the sales price and the amount being financed. Down payment is frequently shortened to "down."

Now that we've covered all the basic terminology of creative financing, you should be ready for the Nothing Down Program.

Doug: I'm on my way! There's no stopping me now!

INDEX TO HOW TO SPEAK CREATIVE FINANCE
(Numbers refer to superscripts in the text.)

About the Authors

ROBERT G. ALLEN

Robert G. Allen is an investor, author, and lecturer. His first book, *Nothing Down*, was a colossal national best seller, remaining on the prestigious *New York Times* best seller list for 46 weeks in 1980 and 1981, then returned to the list in 1983 and 1984. His two-day seminar has been taught to over 100,000 graduates, who buy billions of dollars' worth of real estate per year on their way to financial freedom. He is chairman of the board of The Allen Group, Inc., which, among other things, publishes a monthly newsletter entitled *The Real Estate Advisor*. Because of his many financial achievements as well as his community and church service, he was voted one of the Outstanding Young Men of America in 1982. He lives in Provo, Utah, with his wife, Daryl, and their three children, Aimee, Aaron, and Hunter. His second book, *Creating Wealth,* also spent many months on all major best seller lists in 1983 and 1984.

RICHARD J. ALLEN

Richard J. Allen is a writer, communicator, and consultant in the areas of investing, personal and organizational management, adult learning, and applied behavioral science. He holds the Ph.D. from the Johns Hopkins University in Baltimore, Maryland, where he served nine years on the faculty, including five years (from 1974 to 1979) as Director of the evening College Division of Arts and Sciences.

He entered the consulting field in 1979 as President of Educational Design Consultants, Inc., which he and his wife, Carol, founded. For the past three years, he has been applying his organizational and management skills to the task of making the Robert Allen Nothing Down Seminar America's most popular and effective creative finance program.

In 1981 he became president of The Allen Group, Inc., a corporation whose mission it is to foster the use of wise investment principles featuring alternative financing techniques. He is the author of the popular real estate investment casebook *How To Write A Nothing Down Offer So That Everyone Wins.*

He lives with his wife and their four children in Provo, Utah.

DON BERMAN

Don Berman has taught "Creative Real Estate Acquisition" and "Small Property Management" to over 20,000 students from coast to coast. A former investment banker and owner of a securities firm licensed by both the Securities and Exchange Commission and the National Association of Securities Dealers, Don is also past president of the Nevada Real Estate Securities and Syndication Institute. Presently a partner in his own real estate firm, specializing in investment real estate and creative problem solving, Don also currently owns and controls a diversified real estate portfolio including motels and single-family units. Don is the author of *The Owners' System — Simplified Small Property Management and Control* plus numerous articles for real estate publications. An active real estate investor and exchangor, Don is listed in *Who's Who in Creative Real Estate* and resides in Reno, Nevada.

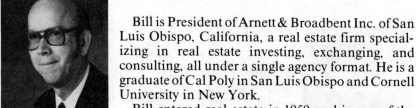

WILLIAM R. BROADBENT

Bill is President of Arnett & Broadbent Inc. of San Luis Obispo, California, a real estate firm specializing in real estate investing, exchanging, and consulting, all under a single agency format. He is a graduate of Cal Poly in San Luis Obispo and Cornell University in New York.

Bill entered real estate in 1959 and is one of the early pioneers in the evolution of creative real estate. He is an active broker, investor, author, and instructor.

In the mid 70s he founded Who's Who in Creative Real Estate, a professional directory of real estate agents trained in the creative acquisition and disposition of real estate. The objectives of the directory are to help creatively educated agents find one another at a national level to facilitate geographical transactions, and to raise public awareness of the real estate professional.

ROBERT J. BRUSS, J.D.

Robert J. Bruss writes the nationally syndicated "Real Estate Mailbag" question and answer newspaper column, the "Real Estate Notebook" newspaper feature about real estate trends, "Real Estate Law and You" explanations of recent court decisions affecting real estate, and the "Real Estate Book Review" features. The Chicago Tribune-New York News Syndicate distributes these features to several hundred newspapers nationwide.

Originally from Minneapolis, Bruss graduated from Northwestern University's School of Business Administration. He received his J.D. law degree from the University of California's Hastings College of the Law in San Francisco. Bruss is a California attorney and real estate broker.

Since 1968, Bruss has been involved in ownership of investment properties, primarily houses, apartments, and commercial properties. He gained much of his practical how-to-do-it real estate sales and management insight as Investment Manager in San Francisco with Grubb & Ellis Company, Realtors, one of California's largest statewide brokerages.

In addition to his real estate writing and investing, Bruss teaches Real Estate Law and Real Estate Practice at the College of San Mateo. He has also taught continuing education classes for the University of Southern California's statewide real estate program. His book, *The Smart Investor's Guide to Real Estate,* published by Crown Publishers, Inc., New York, is now in its third edition.

WADE B. COOK

Wade Cook started his investing career in the mid 1970s by borrowing $500.00. With Wade's innovative ideas and gutsy follow-through, this small amount resulted in the purchases of well over several million dollars worth of real estate.

In 1979, when traditional sources of money dried up, Wade developed a system for investing that works in any kind of economy. The result of this "Money Machine" system is instant cash flow by both selling and buying real estate right.

Wade is the author of the popular book, *How to Build a Real Estate Money Machine,* plus 13 other real estate books, tapes, and aides. He is a featured speaker at seminars and conventions across the country and a frequent guest on popular radio and TV shows.

Today Wade, in addition to his speaking activities, serves as Chairman of the Board of Investment and Tax Publications, and serves as a member of the board of directors for several investment groups across the country.

Wade, along with his wife, Laura, and their three daughters currently reside in Provo, Utah.

SAM F. HALL

At the age of thirty, Sam F. Hall had already accumulated a portfolio of income producing properties valued at over one million dollars. He has since spent several years as an investment counselor and has traveled around the U.S. teaching hundreds of novice and seasoned investors various techniques he uses in purchasing income properties for little or nothing down plus avoiding the monthly negative cash flow potential nothing down purchases often create.

Mr. Hall has written two timely real estate investing books, *Positive Solutions to Negative Cash Flows* and *How to Find Real Estate Bargains.* He has also written numerous articles appearing in such newsletters as *The Real Estate Advisor, The Financial Freedom Report,* and *Inside Real Estate.*

DICK LEE

Dick is that rarity, a real estate income tax counselor who actually owns real estate! Now owner and operator of hundreds of units, Dick's first building was 100% vacant at close of escrow — but cash flowing in six weeks! That was sixteen years ago and he hasn't looked back since.

Earlier a top corporation executive and holder of bachelors and masters degrees in both physics and business administration, Dick has for over two decades concentrated on income tax counseling and real estate, and has a wealth of hard experience and knowledge, both as a tax consultant and as owner/operator of residential income property.

Listed in *Who's Who in the West* and a member of Lloyds of London, Dick is a nationally recognized speaker and lecturer and has been featured on a number of radio and TV talk shows. His books include *Tax Tips for Apartment Owners* and *How to Pay Zero Income Tax — Legally,* and he has just finished a four-cassette album on real estate. Dick was co-producer of an Annual Tax Minimization Seminar, and has been associated for many years with millionaire Mark W. Haroldsen, and is a featured speaker at his major seminars.

Dick practices what he preaches: since 1979, with an annual income of over $100,000, Dick has paid zero income tax.

JACK MILLER

Jack Miller is the Pro's Pro. A Nationally recognized Exchangor, Manager, and Enterpreneur and Investor, his uniquely original techniques, developed over 30 years in real estate, have become industry standards among sophisticated and fledgling investors and entrepreneurs. Since the early 70s, Jack's seminars on Buying, Managing, Financing, Exchanging, and Optioning single family houses have sent thousands on their way to success. Indeed he numbers some of real estate's most successful investors among his graduates. For the better part of a decade, Jack has expanded his audience throughout all 50 states, Asia, Europe, and the Carribean basin through his investment letter, *The Common Wealth Letters*. In it he continues to give his graduates up to the minute advice in the building and sustaining of their personal portfolios. A sought after speaker, he is a founding member of The International Newsletter Association, having conducted seminars in many parts of the world. Jack is one of only 18 members of the Exchangor's Hall of Fame. He was named Creative Real Estate's Educator of the Year in 1980 and Exchangor of the Year in 1977 but he prefers to be thought of as a successful landlord and entrepreneur. For further information concerning his publications and seminar schedules, write to him at P.O. Box 24837, Tampa, FL 33623.

DAVID A. McDOUGAL

David A. McDougal is the executive vice president of The Allen Group and president of his own marketing and financial management company. The McDougal Corporation. His real estate background includes sales, property management, building, and development, ranging in size from single family homes to multi-units, commercial property, and is currently involved in a major year-round theme park.

He served a full-time mission for The Church of Jesus Christ of Latter-day Saints from 1970-1972 in England. David graduated from Brigham Young University with a degree in Political Science in 1975. Upon graduation, he was appointed Director of Development at Brigham Young University — Hawaii campus where he spent four years before going into real estate full time.

Mr. McDougal is married to the former Karrie Fitzgerald and they have one son, David Jr.

CLINTON L. MURDOCK

Mr. Murdock is the author of a new book entitled *The Bucks Start Here,* a behind the scenes look at banking policies and credit analysis. As vice president, manager and member of the board of directors of a bank, Mr. Murdock knows bank operations inside out, including how loans are reviewed and approved or disapproved and what kind of credit you need in order to get loans quickly.

Now serving as a member of the board of directors and as vice president at a major corporation, Mr. Murdock works his skills in financial arrangements, loan approvals and accounting. Mr. Murdock graduated from Brigham Young University and is a credentialed university instructor.

WILLIAM NICKERSON

William Nickerson is the internationally known author of the pioneer million-copy bestseller, *How I Turned $1,000 Into a Million in Real Estate — In My Spare Time.*

He has written several books, including his latest sequel, *How I Turned $1,000 Into Five Million.*

Although keeping real estate a spare-time investment, he has continued to upgrade property, and his net worth has now passed $7 million.

Bill devotes most of his time to writing and lecturing, encouraging a growing multitude to reap the fruits of free enterprise. He estimates that the profits of his disciples total several billions, as many thousands of his millions of readers have proudly reported that they have passed the million mark.

HOLLIS NORTON

Hollis Norton is a living example of the fact that the "Nothing Down" system works. He's an electronics engineer who spent many years in the aerospace industry until the famous "crash of '69."

In 1974 Hollis lived in a $200 per month apartment and had little to show for his years of labor in the work-a-day world. Then he discovered real estate investing and began his "five year plan." Today he owns millions of dollars worth of real estate in, five states and has a net worth of over two million dollars. He now resides in a beautiful home overlooking Lake Tahoe.

Hollis Norton is typical of many persons who have learned the secrets of real estate investing and have persistently followed their plans. Now he can do what he wants to do . . . and since he cares for people, he spends several months each year telling crowds all over the United States how they can become financially independent.

In the past six years he has lectured to over 200,000 persons. In keeping with his desire to share the latest, most up-to-date, most workable and unstandable real estate investing system available, Hollis has joined with Robert and Richard Allen to explain the "Nothing Down" system if investing.

RICHARD PHILLIPS

Richard Phillips was born and raised in Baltimore, Maryland, and like his brother, Wayne, decided to make a career of music. He studied classical music at the Peabody Conservatory in Baltimore, and was the first guitarist in the United States to receive a degree in that instrument. After successfully concertizing around the world for several years, Richard decided to "supplement" his musical income with real estate investments.

After successive and profitable real estate ventures in California, Richard and Wayne decided to try their success formula right in their own hometown of Baltimore. They formed the now famous "Phillips Brothers" partnership in 1978 and, through the many government loan programs they earned to master so well, the rest is now history. Richard became a licensed broker in 1979. His particular specialty is management of investment property, and structuring partnerships and joint ventures for the purpose of acquiring and controlling real estate.

RICHARD C. POWELSON, Ph.D.

Richard C. Powelson, Ph.D. is nationally known and recognized as one of the top creative financing experts in the U.S. and has been called upon to speak at various real estate conventions and meetings throughout the country. He has been featured in several real estate publications and interviewed on both radio and TV regarding real estate and financing of real estate.

Richard is a Past President of the Illinois Association of Realtors and a Past Director of the National Association of Realtors. He has owned and operated several real estate companies specializing in all phases of real estate, has lectured for several colleges and universities, and has helped write and research other financing books and seminars. Richard has also counseled and negotiated several million dollars worth of real estate acquisitions and sales for various clients, as well as himself.

For the past several years he has traveled extensively throughout the U.S. and Canada giving seminars on real estate and real estate financing on an individual basis, and also for William Nickerson, author of *How I Turned $1,000 into 5 Million — in my Spare Time,* and more recently for Robert Allen, author of the books *Nothing Down* and *Creating Wealth.*

This vast background and experience alone make him very much in demand across the country. He brings great enthusiasm, motivation and expertise to his lectures, yet teaches in a way that's very easy to understand. His several thousand graduates attest to this by the very fact that they are buying millions of dollars worth of real estate each and every year.

Richard has his Ph.D. in Business and Real Estate.

DAVID A. READ

Dave Read is a native of Nevada, where he has been involved in real estate and creative financing since 1969. A Realtor and Broker, David is past president of the Nevada Chapter of the Real Estate Securities and Syndication Institute (RESSI), and is Vice President of the Reno Board of Realtors. He holds the professional designation of G.R.I. (Graduate Realtors Institute).

Mr. Read is a successful practitioner of creative real estate investments, owning some 163 units of rental property of all kinds (single-family homes, apartments, condos, rooming facilities, and motels).

David spends about half of his life practicing what he preaches, and the other half of it teaching others creative ways to become financially independent. He is past chairman of the Nevada Association of Realtors Education Committee, and teaches creative financing techniques in advanced classes and also on the college level.

JOHN SCHAUB

John Schaub is a real estate investor from Sarasota, Florida, who has specialized in single family homes. During the past thirteen years, John has acquired well over a hundred properties, and currently manages his portfolio of over fifty properties in six states. He continues to acquire properties, and still favors a well located single family house as the best investment available for the small investor.

In 1976 John started teaching others the techniques that he uses to acquire and manage properties in a seminar titled *Making it Big on Little Deals.* Over ten thousand investors have heard John speak and are now using his ideas to buy and manage their own portfolio of single family houses across the country.

Schaub is a graduate of the University of Florida with a degree in business administration. He has been a featured speaker at numerous national financial conventions, including Howard Ruff's, The National Committee for Monetary Reform, Robert Allen's ACRE Convention, and the Florida Association of Realtors. He was an active Realtor for ten years and has served as president of the Florida Real Estate Exchangors, an organization of over eight hundred Realtors specializing in tax deferred exchanges and investment properties. He authors a quarterly newsletter and has authored and co-authored several books on the subject of real estate investments.

John's seminar has been ranked the number one seminar in the country for those interested in buying and managing houses. Due to the fact that John teaches each class personally, only seven of these intensive three-day classes will be offered in 1984.

DON W. TAUSCHER

Don Tauscher left the comfortable world of banking to seek the more interesting and creative life as a real estate developer, exchangor, and investor. In his teaching, he shares his unusual history and perspective as both a banker and a borrower. From being president of a $70,000,000 commercial bank, he became one of the top producers in sales of commercial real estate in the early 1960s. When severe recession hit his town of Orlando, Flordia, Don's fortunes plummeted and he faced bankruptcy. He credits his creative real estate education with saving his banking relationship, thereby making it possible to pay back considerable debt, and making a believer of his banker.

Don believes in making things happen. He is a Certified Commercial Investment Member (CCIM) of the Realtors National Marketing Institute, Past Chairman of the Orlando Exchangors, Past President of the Flordia Real Estate Exchangors, Trustee of the Academy Network, Academy Certified Exchangor (ACE), and 1981 "Exchangor of the Year" for Florida. After earning a degree in business administration at Rollins college, Don was graduated from the University of Wisconsin Graduate School of Banking. His education in real estate is equally extensive.

More recently, Don has made famous his unique application of a paper formula, *The Paper Caper*, whereby bank and borrower profit from the spread in discounted paper. He freely shares this creative use of borrowed funds, giving his students unheard-of opportunities to make profit. Don is widely recognized as the authority on successful borrowing from commercial banks. The emphasis in his teaching is how to borrow when others cannot—using your God-given talents to think creatively, perhaps differently. As one of the most sought-after speakers in the nation, he divides his lecturing time between conventions and his popular seminar, *Borrowing Money Successfully*, which is periodically scheduled in major cities.

Index

Bibliography

The following titles will provide supplementary information on real estate investing in all its dimensions. Most can be obtained conveniently by mail through The ACRE Bookstore; see the address below.

Allen, Richard J.
—*How to Write a Nothing Down Offer So That Everyone Wins.* A casebook based on Robert G. Allen's Nothing Down System of creative real estate investing. Features 50 actual case studies.

Allen, Robert G.
—*Nothing Down: How to Buy Real Estate With Little or No Money Down.* The classic handbook for nothing-down buyers.
—*Creating Wealth.* Shows exactly how to create a wealth-building program tailored to suit individual situations.
—*Robert G. Allen's Real Estate Advisor: The Action Newsletter of Creative Real Estate Investing.* Richard J. Allen, Editor. Monthly 12-page newsletter; one-year subscription.
—*Creating Wealth With Little or Nothing Down.* Eight hours of instruction. Six tapes and workbook.
—*Real Estate Cookie Cutters.* Twelve unique real estate investing techniques. Six tapes.
—*Tape-of-the-Month Subscription.* Monthly update and instructions from Mr. Allen and other leading real estate authorities. One year.
—*Special Reports.* A set of three special reports by Mr. Allen: *Launching Yourself Into Financial Self-Reliance, Recession Tactics,* and *The Great San Francisco Real Estate Adventure.*

The Allen Group
—*Robert G. Allen's Creating Wealth Conference.* Full proceedings. Twelve tapes and workbook.
—*Robert G. Allen's Annual Nothing Down Conference:* "Mastering the Creative Approach to Real Estate Investing." Full proceedings. Sixteen tapes.

Beck, John
—*Forced Sale Workbook and Tape Package.* Learn how to buy distressed real estate at bargain

prices. Eight tapes and workbook.

—*Partnership Package.* Two tapes and 20-page pamphlet with 60 pages of forms.

—*Options Package.* Two tapes and 24-page pamphlet with contract forms.

—*How to Get Rich Giving Away Real Estate.* Book and tape.

Behle, John

—*The Paper Game: How to Profit Through Buying, Selling, Trading, Creating, and Improving Real Estate Paper.* Instruction manual plus glossary of terms used in the acquisition of discounted mortgages.

—*The Paper Game Tape Package.* Eight tapes which enlarge upon the material in the book.

Berman, Donald M.

—*The Owners' System: Small Property Management and Control.* Self-guiding, self-contained management system for small properties.

—*Cash Flow . . . Make It Positive!* One-day seminar home-study course. Six tapes and 65-page workbook.

—*Ten Commandments of Small Property Management.* Four tapes and workbook.

—*Rental Unit Resident Application Forms.* Package of 50.

—*Residential Occupancy Agreement Forms.* Package of 25.

Bruss, Robert

—*The Smart Investor's Guide to Real Estate: Big Profits from Small Investments.* Basic real estate investing.

—*How to Avoid the Due-on-Sale Clause.* Twenty-three-page report.

Childers, John

—*The Lazy Way to Buy Real Estate: Steps to Building Wealth.* Six tapes plus *Creative Amortization Schedule Handbook.*

—*The ABZs of Buying Property.* Six tapes and *As You Begin* manual.

Cohen, Herb

—*You Can Negotiate Anything: How to Get What You Want.*

Cook, Wade B.

—*How to Build a Real Estate Money Machine.* How to buy and sell real estate on contract.

—*How to Build a Real Estate Money Machine Tape Package.* Two tapes.

—*Pay No Taxes With Real Estate.* Use recent real estate tax changes to maximize your tax benefits.

—*Things Your CPA Never Told You.* Companion to *Pay No Taxes.* Two tapes.

—*How to Pick Up Foreclosures.* Step-by-step procedures for acquiring property from distressed sellers.

—*Cook's Book on Creative Real Estate.* A casebook of creative real estate transactions.

—*Owner Financing.* Pamphlet.

—*Real Estate: The Best Game in Town.*

—*The Three Entity Approach to Investing in Real Estate.* Pension, profit-sharing, and trusts as investment vehicles.

—*Legal Forms.* Sample contracts, forms, and agreements.

—*Record Keeping System.*

—*Big Bucks by Selling Your Property.* The art of making money by selling property.

—*The First National Bank of Real Estate Clauses.*

—*Wade Cook's Real Estate Newsletter.* Monthly; one-year subscription.

—*Money Making Seminar.* Eight tapes.

—*The Complete Foreclosure System.* Four tapes, workbook, and forms.

—*Good Deals.* Taped seminar. Eight tapes.

Curran, Wes

—*Paper.* Six tapes and 80-page workbook.

—*Foreclosure.* Six tapes and 180-page workbook.

—*Creative Success Formula.* Eighteen tapes and 300-page workbook.

—*Purchase Offers.*

Dawson, Roger

—*Time Management: Taking the Pressure Out of Life.* One tape.

—*Your First No-Money-Down Purchase.* One tape.

—*Yes! Yes! Yes! Getting Them to Say "Yes!" with Negotiating Tactics.* Six tapes.

—*Yes! Yes! Yes! Workbook.* Two-hundred page companion to tapes.

—*29 Closes for Real Estate Investors.* Four tapes.

—*How to Start: Buying Foreclosures.* Six tapes and workbook.

—*Winning at the Table.* Six tapes and workbook.

—*Let Me Take You By the Hand.* Six tapes.

Drummond, Phil

—*Control Without Ownership.* Lease options. Four tapes and workbook.

—*How to Make the Ultimate Purchase Offer.* Clauses and techniques. Six tapes and workbook.

—*How to Get Start-Up Funds.* Tape and workbook.

—*How to Write a Firm But Fair Lease/Rental Agreement.* Tape and workbook.

—*Complete Real Estate Investor's Training Portfolio.* Includes all of the above items by Mr. Drummond, plus *How to Get Started in Real Estate Investing* (five tapes and workbook), and a one-year subscription to *Phil Drummond's Investor Alert* newsletter, packaged in an attractive attaché case.

Dykes, James M.

—*Real Estate Bargains.* Includes *How to Find Real Estate Bargains,* six tapes; *How to Create Real Estate Bargains,* twelve tapes; and *Computer Analysis.*

Fox, Claire R.

—*Syndicating Single-Family Homes: How to Form Group Investment Partnerships Using Other People's Money.*

Gibson, Don

—*Cash at the Close: Real Estate Tools and Techniques.* Eight tapes, workbook, and contract and forms package.

—*Starting Over Again in Real Estate.* Four tapes.

—*Fortunes in Foreclosures.* Four tapes.

Glubetich, David
— *How to Grow a Money Tree: Earn 20 to 30 Percent and More by Investing in Safe, Hi-Yield Second Mortgages and Trust Deeds.*
— *Double Your Money in Real Estate Every Two Years.* How to turn inflation to your advantage.
— *The Monopoly Game: The "How-To" Book of Making Big Money with Rental Homes.* Buying and managing the single-family rental home.

Hall, Sam F.
— *Positive Solutions to Negative Cash Flows.* Dealing with balloon notes, lease options, shared appreciation, discounted mortgages, refinancing, seasonal demand properties, and others.
— *Positive Solutions to Negative Cash Flows Tape Package.* Companion to the book.

Koon, Nick
— *How to Become a Millionaire Buying Single-Family Homes.*
— *How to Get Started.* Six tapes and workbook.
— *Structuring Cash Flow.* Six tapes and workbook.
— *Hard-Nose Management.* Six tapes and workbook.
— *Getting Started—My Story.* One tape.
— *Will You Make It in Real Estate?* One tape.
— *Rules for Screening Tenants.* One tape.
— *Beginner's Barter Kit.* Eight tapes.
— *Building a Zero Tax Bracket.*

Land, Joe
— *Paper: The Ultimate Tool for the Real Estate Investor.* Purchasing real estate using discounted mortgages, trust deeds, corporate bonds, etc. Eight tapes and workbook.
— *Tax Strategies for the Real Estate Investor.* Eight tapes and workbook.
— *Real Estate Tax Update.* Monthly newsletter; one-year subscription.

Milin, Mike and Irene
— *Landlording Made Easy.* Sixteen tapes and workbook.
— *Cash Flow, Cash Flow, Cash Flow.* Eight tapes and 213-page workbook.
— *Money-Making Clauses That Get Results.* Two tapes and workbook.
— *Pennies on the Dollar.*
— *Real Estate Investor Analysis.* Newsletter; one-year subscription and hotline.

Morris, Hal
— *Crisis Real Estate Investing.* Low-risk guide for protecting assets and avoiding disaster.
— *How to Stop Foreclosure.* How to save your home and property.
— *Foreclosure Systems.* Eight tapes, workbook, and bank/savings and loan computer printout.
— *Equity Sharing: An Answer for the '80s.* Six tapes and five contracts.

Murdock, Clint
— *The Bucks Start Here: How to Win With Your Banker.*
— *A Comprehensive Guide to Financing Options for Real Estate.* Expandable loose-leaf format.

Learn about loan sources for financing single and multiple residences, etc.

—*Bank Lines of Credit: How to Get Them, How to Use Them, and How to Grow with Them.* Includes two complete sample loan request packages.

Napier, Jimmy
—*Invest in Debt.* Investing in discounted mortgages.

—*Combination Offer.* Includes *Invest in Debt* described above, plus *Money Maker: 2-Day Home Study Course* (eight tapes), *Money Maker Report* newsletter (18-month subscription), and *Live at Caesar's Palace: Guest Appearance with Jack Miller* (eight tapes).

Nickerson, William
—*How I Turned $1,000 Into Five Million in Real Estate.* Fixing-up investment property to build equity.

Phillips, Wayne
—*How to Get Government Loans.* Finding and using low-interest loans for qualified investment properties.

Prigal, Ken
—*The Winning Offer.* Six tapes and comprehensive manual.

—*Profits with Partners.* Book and four tapes.

Robinson, Leigh
—*Landlording.* One of the best books available on property management.

Santucci, Danny
—*Successful Estate Planning: It's Your Money —How to Keep It Now That You Made It.* Eight tapes and workbook.

—*Real Estate and the IRS: How to Keep the IRS Out of Your Pocket.* Eight tapes and workbook.

—*Concepts and Mechanics of Exchanges.* Six tapes and book.

—*Tactics for Tough Times.* Eight tapes and workbook.

—*Estate Planning Combination Offer.* Includes all of the above, plus *Investment Vehicles for Real Estate Investors* (manual), *Tax Shelter Planning and Analysis* (manual), and *Wills and Trusts* (manual).

Smith, Dave
—*The Time Value of Money.* Understanding the principles involved in financial transactions; using the HP 12-C Calculator. Eight tapes and workbook.

—*HP-12C Calculator.* Available only with the above package by Mr. Smith.

Smith, Hyrum
—*The "Focus" Time Management Seminar.* Eight tapes. Eight-hour course including instructions on time management, effective goal-setting, and full utilization of the *Franklin Day Planner System.*

—*Franklin Day Planner System* with Executive Vinyl Binder. One year plus storage binder.

—*Franklin Day Planner System* with Leather Binder. One year plus storage binder.

Southard, Jim
—*Real Estate Wealth-Seeker's Guide.* Eight tapes and workbook.

Steele, Robert

— *Creative Real Estate: Problem-Solving Formulas.*

— *Creative Real Estate Tapes.* Ten tapes.

— *Fifteen Ways to Buy, Sell, and Exchange Real Estate Without Using Cash.*

— *Fifty Ways to Acquire Real Estate.*

— *An Extra House as an Investment.*

— *The Real Estate Exchange Market and How It Operates.*

— *Mortgage Investments: Principles and Methods.*

Tauscher, Don

— *Borrowing Money Successfully.* Developing banking relationships — how to bank when others cannot. Twelve tapes and workbook.

— *Paper Magic.* The creative use of paper formulas to acquire investment real estate. Four tapes and booklet.

Wayner, Stephen

— *Money-Making Tools.* Creative methods to buy real estate, including wraparounds, equity participation, trusts, etc. Six tapes and workbook.

— *I'm on Your Side.* Over 150 items (includes checklist) that belong in a real estate contract, plus Real Estate Analysis Sheet. Six tapes and workbook.

— *Wayner's Legal Forms.*

Zick, Barney

— *How to Make Your Real Estate Fortune.* Six tapes and workbook.

— *The Midas Touch.* Six tapes and workbook.

— *How to Buy Right.* Six tapes and workbook.

— *How to Become a Paper Millionaire.* Six tapes and workbook.

— *How to Win with Equity Sharing and Small Syndications.* Six tapes and workbook.

— *Equity Sharing and Small Partnership Agreements.* Fourteen actual documents.

The ACRE Bookstore
The American Congress on Real Estate
A Membership Organization of The Allen Group, Inc.
•145 East Center Street • P.O. Box 9000 • Provo, Utah 84603-9000
(801) 373-8000

Write to the above address for a current price list. Credit card holders may call toll-free (800) 453-1364 to obtain prices and order at the same time.